THE OXFORD
HISTORY OF
MODERN WAR

THE EDITOR

CHARLES TOWNSHEND is Professor of International History, Keele University.

THE OXFORD
HISTORY OF
MODERN
WAR

EDITED BY
CHARLES TOWNSHEND

NEW UPDATED EDITION

OXFORD
UNIVERSITY PRESS

OXFORD
UNIVERSITY PRESS

Great Clarendon Street, Oxford OX2 6DP

Oxford University Press is a department of the University of Oxford.
It furthers the University's objective of excellence in research, scholarship,
and education by publishing worldwide in

Oxford New York

Athens Auckland Bangkok Bogotá Buenos Aires Calcutta
Cape Town Chennai Dar es Salaam Delhi Florence Hong Kong Istanbul
Karachi Kuala Lumpur Madrid Melbourne Mexico City Mumbai
Nairobi Paris São Paulo Singapore Taipei Tokyo Toronto Warsaw

with associated companies in Berlin Ibadan

Oxford is a registered trade mark of Oxford University Press
in the UK and in certain other countries

Published in the United States
by Oxford University Press Inc., New York

© Oxford University Press 2005

The moral rights of the author have been asserted
Database right Oxford University Press (makers)

The text of this volume first published 1997 in *The Oxford Illustrated History of Modern War*
First issued as *The Oxford History of Modern War* 2000

British Library Cataloguing in Publication Data

Data available

Library of Congress Cataloging in Publication Data

Data available

ISBN-13: 978-0-19-280645-1
ISBN-10: 0-19-280645-9

3

Typeset by
Cambrian Typesetters, Frimley, Surrey
Printed in Great Britain by
Clays Ltd, St Ives plc

PREFACE

This book aims to place the development of war in modern times in a wide cultural framework. Though it is rooted in military history, it is more than a history of warfare. Violent conflict is as old as humanity, but modern war is generically different. It stems from an epochal change in the structure of European states that took place between the sixteenth and eighteenth centuries, and transformed their military power. This 'military revolution' had two consequences of global scale. First, it ended for ever Europe's vulnerability to invasion and conquest from the East: a liberation symbolized by the defeat of the Ottoman besiegers of Vienna in 1683. Second, it launched Western Europe on a course of global dominance. The imbalance of military power between modernizing and traditional states grew until, in the nineteenth century, only a handful of the latter could resist European control. A complex process of economic, social, and political modernization generated the phenomena of the 'nation in arms', and ultimately, in the twentieth century, of 'total war.'

Modern war was created by more than simply military techniques, or military technology. It came to enlist every aspect of life. Historians of war work on a correspondingly large canvas. Traditional military history, concerned primarily with strategy and tactics, has evolved into a broader and deeper study of the relationship between war and society. The contributors to this book have aimed to draw together a range of interpretations to clarify this complex relationship, providing both a historical account of the development of war, and a thematic analysis of its key elements. The impact of technology and the experience of combat are treated alongside the social impact of modern war and the evolution of efforts to limit its destructiveness by international law and organizations.

Since the first edition of this book some of the tendencies charted in it have become more dramatically evident. The attempt to find effective ways in which the international community can use military force to counter genocide and other catastrophic forms of political breakdown has raised the question whether there can be such a thing as 'humanitarian war'. The breakdown of some states has been accompanied by a 'privatization' of military forces, raising the question whether modern war itself has not become obsolete. The attempt to find a military response to the growth of terrorism, most spectacularly signalled in the 9/11 attacks, has underlined the huge implications of this. Although the grim aftermath of the rapid American military conquest of Iraq in 2003 may have called into question the confidence of some military thinkers in the effectiveness of technology, it is consistent with earlier experiences of thwarted military triumph—such as that of the German invaders during the 'people's war' in France in 1870–1. It is precisely the social complexity of modern war that has rendered its impact so far-reaching. An understanding of the limits of military power is vital to our future, and it can only be reached by careful historical analysis. That is what this book sets out to provide.

C.T.
November 2004

CONTENTS

LIST OF PLATES

LIST OF CONTRIBUTORS

Jeremy Black is Professor of History at the University of Exeter. His 60 books include *Warfare in the Eighteenth Century* (1999), *War—Past, Present and Future* (2000), *Western Warfare 1775–1882* (2001), *Warfare in the Western World 1882–1975* (2002), *World War II: A Military* History (2003), *Rethinking Military History* (2004).

John Bourne is Director of the Centre for First World War Studies at the University of Birmingham. He is the author of *Britain and the Great War* (1989, 2nd edition 1991), *Who's Who in the First World War* (2001); and editor (with Peter Liddle and Ian Whitehead) of *The Great World War 1914–1945* (2001), and (with Gary Sheffield) of *Douglas Haig: War Diaries and Letters 1914–1918* (2005).

John Childs is Professor of Military History at the University of Leeds. His books include *The Army of Charles II* (1976), *Armies and Warfare in Europe 1648–1789* (1982), *The Nine Years War and the British Army 1688-1697: The Operations in the Low Countries* (1991), *The Military Use of Land: A History of the Defence Estate* (1998), and *Warfare in the Seventeenth Century* (2004).

Jean Bethke Elshtain is Laura Spelman Rockefeller Professor of Social and Political Ethics at the University of Chicago. She has written or edited twenty books, including *Public Man, Private Woman: Women in Social and Political Thought* (1981, 2nd edition 1992), *Women and War* (1987), *Just War Theory* (1990), *Democracy on Trial* (1995), and *Just War Against Terror: the Burden of American Power in a Violent World* (2003).

Alan Forrest is Professor of Modern History at the University of York. His publications include *Conscripts and Deserters: The Army and French Society during the Revolution and Empire* (1989), *Soldiers of the French Revolution* (1990), *Napoleon's Men* (2002), and (with Jean-Paul Bertaud and Annie Jourdan), *Napoleon, le Monde et les Anglais* (2004).

David French is Professor of History at University College London. He is the author of *British Economic and Strategic Planning, 1905–1915* (1982), *British Strategy and War Aims, 1914–1916* (1986), *The British Way in Warfare 1688-2000* (1990), *Raising Churchill's Army: The British Army and the*

War Against Germany, 1919–1945 (2000), and *Military Identities: The British Army, the British People and the Regimental System, 1870–2000* (2005).

John B. Hattendorf is Ernest J. King Professor of Maritime History at the US Naval War College, Rhode Island. He is the author of *England in the War of the Spanish Succession: A Study of the English View and Conduct of Grand Strategy, 1702–1712* (1987), *Naval History and Maritime History: Collected Essays* (2000), *The Evolution of the US Navy's Maritime Strategy, 1978–1986* (2004), and editor of *War at Sea in the Middle Ages and the Renaissance* (2002).

Richard Holmes is Professor of Military and Security Studies as Cranfield University. His many books include *Firing Line* (1985), *Redcoat: The British Soldier in the Age of Horse and Musket* (2002), and *Tommy: The British Soldier on the Western Front* (2004). He was general editor of the *Oxford Companion to Military History* (2001). He has presented seven series of BBC historical documentaries, from *War Walks* (1996) to *In the Footsteps of Churchill* (2005), and was a territorial infantry officer for thirty-six years.

Richard Overy is Professor of History at the University of Exeter. His books on twentieth-century history include *The Air War 1939–1945* (1980), *Why the Allies Won* (1995), *Russia's War* (1998), *The Battle of Britain* (2000), *Interrogations: The Nazi Elite in Allied Hands* (2001), and *The Dictators: Hitler's Germany and Stalin's Russia* (2004). He is the general editor of *The Times History of the World*.

Douglas Porch is Professor of National Security Affairs at the US Naval Postgraduate School, Monterey. He has written *Army and Revolution: France 1815–1848* (1974), *The Conquest of the Sahara* (1984), *The French Foreign Legion* (1991), *The French Secret Services: From the Dreyfus Affair to Desert Storm* (1995), *Wars of Empire* (2000), and *Hitler's Mediterranean Gamble* (2004) (published in the USA as *The Path to Victory: The Mediterranean Theater in World War II*).

Adam Roberts is Montague Burton Professor of International Relations at Oxford University. He is the author of *Nations in Arms: The Theory and Practice of Territorial Defence* (2nd edition 1986), *Hugo Grotius and International Relations* (1990), *United Nations, Divided World* (2nd edition 1993), and editor of *The Strategy of Civilian Defence* (1967) and (with Richard Guelff) *Documents on the Laws of War* (3rd edition 2000).

Mark Roseman is Pat M. Glazer Chair for Jewish History at Indiana University, Bloomington. He is the author of *Recasting the Ruhr: Manpower, Economic Recovery and Labour Relations* (1992), *The Past in Hiding* (2000), *The Villa, the Lake, the Meeting: Wannsee and the Final Solution* (2002), and editor of *Generations in Conflict: Youth Rebellion and Generation Formation in Germany 1770–1968* (1995) and (with Carl Levy) *Three Post-war Eras in Comparison: Western Europe 1945–1989* (2002).

Philip Towle is Reader in International Relations at the Centre of International Studies in Cambridge. His most recent publications include *Enforced Disarmament form the Napoleonic Campaigns to the Gulf War* (1997), *Democracy and Peacemaking: Negotiations and Debates 1815–1973* (2000), and as editor (with Margaret Kosuge and Yoichi Kibata), *Japanese Prisoners of War* (2000).

Charles Townshend is Professor of International History at Keele University. His books include *Political Violence in Ireland: Government and Resistance since 1848* (1983), *Britain's Civil Wars: Counterinsurgency in the Twentieth Century* (1986), *Making the Peace: Public Order and Public Security in Modern Britain* (1993), *Ireland: The Twentieth Century* (1999), and *Terrorism. A Very Short Introduction* (2002).

Martin van Creveld is Professor of History at The Hebrew University of Jerusalem. He has written seventeen books, including *Hitler's Strategy 1940–1941: The Balkan Clue* (1973), *Supplying War: Logistics from Wallenstein to Patton* (1977), *Fighting Power* (1982), *Command in War* (1985), *Technology and War* (1989), *The Transformation of War* (1991), and *The Rise and Decline of the State* (1999).

Part I

The Evolution of Modern War

I

Introduction

The Shape of Modern War

CHARLES TOWNSHEND

'The musket made the infantryman and the infantryman made the democrat.' It would be hard to find a pithier expression than this one, in General J. F. C. Fuller's book *The Conduct of War*, of the idea that modern war and modern society are symbiotically linked. The triumph of standardized, economical foot-soldiers over individual, extravagant horsemen—in a word, the triumph of the ordinary people over the aristocracy—represented the decisive juncture of modernization. 'Boney' Fuller, like many military officers of his generation, was hardly an admirer of modernity as a whole, and especially not of democracy. In the same way, the mass armies that accompanied it were an object of suspicion if not of contempt for those who hankered after the traditional virtues of military elites. Yet their sense of the profound change that had come about was accurate enough.

Modern war is the product of three distinct kinds of change: administrative, technical, and ideological. These changes cannot all be seen in any unambiguous way as 'progress', though they seem to be irreversible. Nor have they developed at the same pace. Military technology, for instance, has produced the most striking and indeed terrifying symbols of modern war: the machine-gun, the rocket, the atomic bomb. The increase in power and sophistication of weapon systems has been exponential. Between the first general adoption of efficient firearms in the seventeenth century

and the production of breech-loading guns and smokeless pro-
pellants in the middle of the nineteenth, the pace of change was
slow. Improvements in technique (professionalism, training, and
tactics), rather than in technology, brought the most substantial
results. Later the balance altered.

Technological change may look like an independent process,
governed only by the extent of scientific knowledge and the limits of science and manufacturing. But military institutions have
tended to be more conservative than other social groups. Soldiers have seldom led the way in technological development, and
have often been reluctant to welcome new weapons. Tradition
has always been important in fostering the *esprit de corps* of
fighting units, and can lead to fossilization. So can the tendency—actually strengthened by professionalization, which removed young princes and nobles from high command—for
senior officers to be substantially older than their juniors. There
are many striking examples of failure to embrace new technology, none perhaps more disastrous than that of the imperial Chinese navy, which could have had the world's most advanced
naval artillery in the early sixteenth century, but rejected it in
favour of traditional ramming and boarding tactics.

The reason for this lay not simply in mental conservatism, but
in the functions the Chinese navy had to perform. Its actual opponents were not battle fleets similar to itself, but Japanese pirate
bands. Plainly, technology is the creature as well as the creator
of social and political conditions. In Europe, during the slow
phase of weapon development, other profound changes were
happening. The process often labelled 'the rise of the modern
state' was a cocktail of administrative, economic, and social developments. Some of these, such as the growth of standing armies
and of military professionalism, were not without precedent (as
John Childs points out in Chapter 2). Their novelty in the sixteenth century was in contrast to the protean military institutions
of the Middle Ages, which had taken their flexible shapes from
the irregular pattern of military obligations amongst sovereigns
and subjects. In England the shift from the unpredictable results
of the negotiations between Charles I and his parliaments to the
regular structure of the New Model Army exemplifies the

change; after that even England, which was permitted the luxury of an anti-military attitude, never lacked a standing army.

In Europe, moreover, several states were emerging simultaneously as rival powers. Their competition provided a powerful impetus to military innovation, and their frequent wars tested and honed these experiments. The result was the 'military revolution', though this concept did not appear until the 1950s, when Michael Roberts carried out his pioneering research on the Sweden of Gustavus Adolphus. Roberts argued that a set of interlinked developments between the mid-sixteenth and the mid-seventeenth centuries had transformed the nature of war, and the states which waged it. The overthrow of feudal cavalry by infantry led to a dramatic enlargement of armies, and a parallel growth in the administrative and financial structures needed to maintain them. In the process, the apparatus of the state became for the first time distinctively modern: personal fealty was replaced by public service.

In the forty years since it was proposed, the military revolution hypothesis has been first extended and then challenged, mainly on the grounds that the pace of change was not fast enough to make the concept of 'revolution' meaningful. Certainly some central strands of the process, such as the growth in the size of armies, may not have followed the pattern suggested by the original hypothesis. It is probably impossible to identify a point at which a critical mass of the elements of modern war had been brought together: was it when the matchlock was replaced by the flintlock musket, or perhaps when the socket bayonet (replacing the primitive plug variety) at last integrated firearms with the ancient steel *arme blanche*? In the longer view, though, the scale of change was decisive. By the late eighteenth century the 'sinews of power', as one historian has described the fiscal-military institutions of Britain, had been permanently transformed.

The final transformation of war (as Fuller argued) was propelled by the French Revolution. The transformation was at least as much a perceptual as an operational shift. Jeremy Black holds that the contrast between eighteenth-century and revolutionary warfare has often been exaggerated. Karl von Clausewitz, above

all, whose writings provided the most influential military interpretation of the Napoleonic epoch, always harped on that contrast. For him its essence was not technical, or even
organizational, but psychological. The Revolution changed the
minds of men and women. After the Legislative Assembly decree
la patrie en danger (1792) there were no limits to their commitment to defend it. The decree of the *levée en masse* in August
1793 projected an image of mass mobilization that has never
lost its force:

From this moment until the enemy is driven from the territory of the
Republic, all the French people are permanently requisitioned for the
armies. The young men will go to the front, married men will forge
arms and carry supplies, women will make tents and clothing, children
will divide old linen into bandages, old men will be carried into the
squares to rouse the courage of the soldiers, to teach hatred of kings
and the unity of the republic.

Revolutionary rhetoric was seldom matched by reality, but, as
Peter Paret holds, the fact that this rhetoric was employed at all,
something unthinkable a decade earlier, marked a change with
tremendous practical significance. Revolutionary soldiers had a
wholly new kind of self-respect, and were treated accordingly.
The conduct of war became more urgent and ambitious. Lazare
Carnot, the organizer of the new republican armies, called for
unlimited war, *guerre à outrance*, prosecuted 'to the bitter end'—
the extermination of the Revolution's enemies. In the words of
the Jacobin Saint-Just, 'the republic consists in the extermination
of everything that opposes it.'

To Clausewitz, the artificiality of eighteenth-century states
had been the root cause of their caution in war. Battle had not
necessarily been avoided, but had often not been sought; superior strategy might do without it. Occupation of provinces and
capture of fortresses were the real objects of operations. In place
of this the Revolution, releasing the volcanic natural force of patriotic citizenship, restored the clash of armies to its proper place
at the centre of strategy. In the eighteenth century, no battle had
led to the destruction of a defeated army. The rapid pursuit required would have been too risky to the victorious side: logisti-

cal chaos and wholesale desertion would have wrecked it. The French revolutionary armies, by contrast, sought battle with frightening determination. The battles themselves did not change dramatically in scale, at least until Wagram in 1809. (There Napoleon brought some 160,000 troops into action, as compared with a scant 16,000 at Rivoli or Marengo, and around 70,000 at Austerlitz.) What changed was their frequency.

The mass mobilization launched by the 1793 decree did not itself alter the nature of military organization or methods. In so far as the revolutionary armies employed new tactics—such as the large-scale use of skirmishers and sharpshooters (*tirailleurs*), and the substitution of column for line formations—these had been prefigured by older commanders and theorists. Neither was there a revolutionary change in the logistics of military operations. Although the French armies were able (and indeed forced by shortage of cash) to 'live off the country' more flexibly than their predecessors, because their easier discipline allowed troops to forage more freely, there were still fairly strict limits to this flexibility. Above all, the supply of munitions imposed firm restrictions on movement. But the surge of recruitment allowed French armies to continue advancing even after sustaining serious losses: this put tremendous pressure on their opponents. And ultimately the increase in strength made it possible to ignore fortresses and abandon the old obsession with siege warfare. Napoleon noted that an army of 250,000 could easily detach a fifth of its strength and still be able to overrun an entire country. At a stroke the logistical straitjacket of the past was thrown off.

Here was the explanation of what appears at first sight, as Martin van Creveld has said, incomprehensible: with technological means no more advanced than those of his predecessors—indeed he was quite conservative in this sphere—'Napoleon was able to propel enormous forces right across Europe, establish an empire stretching from Hamburg to Sicily, and irreparably shatter an entire world.' The impact of this astounding adventure can hardly be exaggerated. It was the dynamism of Napoleonic strategy coupled with the scale of his objectives—the overthrow not just of armies but of entire states—which revealed to Clausewitz the elemental truth of what he called 'absolute war', war without restraints or limits, following the logic of force alone. 'If one side uses force without compunction', he wrote at the beginning of his great work *On War*, 'while the other side refrains, the first will gain the upper hand. It will force the other to follow suit; they will drive each other towards extremes.'

It is not uncommon, especially in the English-speaking world, to suggest that Clausewitz's reputation has been over-inflated, and that his perceptions have little contemporary relevance. But, amongst analysts of war, Clausewitz is in a category of his own. It is not that all his ideas are universally true—certainly as far as tactics and strategy are concerned—but that his writing is uniquely sensitive to the human dimension of modern war. In fact he rejected the pretensions of 'scientific' laws of war to universal validity, and emphasized the power of genius to transcend boundaries. His writing exudes a sense of what the leading philosopher of his time, Immanuel Kant, called 'the crooked timber of humanity'.

No sooner had Clausewitz sketched out his radical vision of absolute war than he retreated a little from it. His famous insistence that war can only be sensibly understood as an instrument of policy, 'a continuation of political activity by other means'— the means were different but the ends must make political sense—was a way of saying that not all wars would thenceforth necessarily display the extremism of the French revolutionary model. Limited political objectives would still produce limited wars. The extremism of absolute war was also held back by a much more elementary force, what Clausewitz labelled 'friction'. Everything in war looks simple, he noted disarmingly: 'the knowledge required does not look remarkable, the strategic options are so obvious that by comparison the simplest problem of higher mathematics has an impressive scientific dignity.' Yet while 'everything in war is simple, the simplest thing is difficult. The difficulties accumulate, and end by producing a kind of friction that is inconceivable unless one has experienced war.'

Underneath all this, though, the essence of modern war remained. 'Once barriers—which in a sense consist only in man's ignorance of the possible—are torn down, they are not easily set up again.' Every future war would tend to demonstrate the same basic characteristics: mass mobilization, ideological motivation, ruthless prosecution. War would increasingly be seen as the acid test, not merely of military and economic strength, but more fundamentally of the viability of states, and the strength of nations. In the words of a member of the Frankfurt Parliament during the German revolutions of 1848, 'mere existence does not entitle a nation [*volk*] to political independence: only the force to assert itself as a state amongst others.' The ideological foundation of states after the French Revolution was nationalism, and the wars of the nineteenth century were primarily national conflicts. In fact, the nineteenth century saw a remarkable reduction in the frequency and duration of major (and even minor) wars. But the stakes were high and the outcomes transformed the political structure of Europe.

In the nineteenth century, too, there was a true technological revolution in war. The advent of the breech-loading rifle fundamentally altered the traditional face of battle. Rifling itself dramatically lengthened the effective range of firearms, but early muzzle-loading rifles like the Minié actually required greater skill to maximize their effect. The Prussian Dreyse rifle was less accurate, and the design of its breech and thin firing pin (which led to its famous sobriquet 'needle gun') were vulnerable to wear and tear. But the fact that the Dreyse could be fired by a novice at twice the rate of an expertly handled Minié—some seven rounds a minute—was decisive, as the war of 1866 demonstrated. Within twenty years or so the development of such bolt-action magazine rifles as the Mauser and the Lebel, using smaller-bore bullets propelled by smokeless powder, brought infantry weapons to a level of firepower which would remain fairly constant until after the Second World War. In the same period the machine-gun was transformed from the unwieldy multiple-barrelled Gatling gun and the French mitrailleuse through Hiram Maxim's manufacture, in the mid-1880s, of a mechanism driven by the weapon's own recoil.

The final impact of all these changes did not become fully clear in Europe itself in the nineteenth century. The most striking military successes, the victories of Prussia over Austria and

France in the wars of German unification, were widely misinterpreted. Though nobody could miss the demonstration of the power of new weapons—as in the massacre of the Prussian 1st Guards Division's advance against French troops armed with the Chassepot rifle at Saint-Privat on 18 August 1870—the wars seemed to confirm that decisive victories were still possible for armies with sophisticated organization and command structures. Indeed, the Prussian Guards made what Michael Howard called 'a small landmark in military history' a few weeks later, by replacing their close-order tactics with a looser deployment in their successful assault on Le Bourget. Helmuth von Moltke was far from being a commander in the Napoleonic mould, but by developing the Prussian general staff into the vital nervous system of the army he transformed the potential of the short-service conscript force. Until then, even radical military commentators like Friedrich Engels continued to subscribe to the persistent belief that professional or long-service troops would remain superior. Modern weapons eliminated that traditional superiority, and modern staff work ensured that decisive numerical weight could be efficiently deployed. For the first time it could be said that mobilization planning was an integral part of strategy.

The sheer military effectiveness of Moltke's armies, exaggerated by the command weaknesses of their opponents, disguised the looming problems of mass warfare. Moltke himself, chastened by the frustrations of the 'people's war' in France in the winter of 1870–1, was perhaps less sanguine than his admirers and imitators. 'The days of cabinet wars are past; now we have only the people's war', he declared in 1887. 'There is not one [great power] that can be so completely overcome in one or even in two campaigns that it will be forced to conclude an onerous peace; not one that will be unable to rise again, after a year, to renew the struggle.' He foresaw a new age of Seven Years Wars or even Thirty Years Wars. The Russo–Turkish War of 1877–8 had indicated the shape of things to come: the combination of earthworks and modern weapons in the Turks' defence of Plevna held up the Russian advance for five months. This power of resistance in a state which hardly ranked as one of Moltke's 'great powers' showed what might be expected in full-scale war.

Had Europeans been able to recognize it, a still more sobering vision of the future had been provided by the American Civil War. Moltke himself dismissed the American armies—nearly half a million men on the Confederate side, over twice that number raised by the Union—as mere mobs chasing each other about the countryside. Certainly they were quite unlike European armies, more mercurial in temper and unreliable in discipline. But the failure to meet Abraham Lincoln's unambiguous demand to 'destroy the rebel army' was not simply due to lack of military efficiency. Admittedly, Union generals before Ulysses S. Grant often lacked his confidence and energy. His epigrammatic assertion that 'the art of war is simple enough; find out where your enemy is, get at him as soon as you can, strike at him as hard as you can, and keep moving on' was suitably Clausewitzian; but even he could not easily overwhelm entrenchments of the kind dug by the Confederate defenders of Petersburg in 1864. The fruitless pursuit of decisive military victories was eventually replaced by a policy of devastation, targeting the civilian roots of Confederate strength. General Philip Sheridan's systematic devastation of the Shenandoah Valley in the autumn of 1864 was paralleled by William T. Sherman's frankly terrorist six-month 'march to the sea' across the heartland of the Confederacy.

The American Civil War was a war of attrition, won by the slow mobilization of the industrial and technical superiority of the Northern states. But it was not primarily a technological struggle. The Confederacy could only succeed by making the cost of the war too great: ultimately, the war was a psychological test. On the Union side, the challenge produced a response which was, in Clausewitzian terms, absolute. But while the Confederate President Jefferson Davis declared 'we are fighting for existence', the South proved ultimately unable to draw on the resources of modern national solidarity. The war thus confirmed the European model: national will was the basis of military force.

Late nineteenth-century military thinkers faced the future with a mixture of fear and elation. Colmar von der Goltz, then a major in the German army, provided the definitive view of the modern 'nation in arms' in his book of that title (*Das Volk in Waffen*). First published in 1883, this became a best-seller both in Germany—where it ran to five editions in fifteen years—and abroad. Its key conclusion was that 'the advent of a future war is regarded with anxious expectation. Everyone seems to feel that it will be waged with a destructive force such as has hitherto never been displayed. All moral energy will be gathered for a life and death struggle, the whole sum of the intelligence residing in nations will be employed for their mutual destruction.' For him as for many of his generation, war was 'the fate of mankind, the inevitable destiny of nations'. He saw this as a matter not of ideology but of biology: the unavoidable struggle for survival. He recognized the awesome power of modern firearms—noting in one curt paragraph of his introduction, 'Even the assailant is strongly urged to carry the spade'—but held that they did not alter the underlying moral constants. 'Fighting to the last man' was never a fact, but rather a figure of speech expressing the psychological determination which would break the enemy's will. So von der Goltz could produce the paradoxical argument that 'the more startling and intense the effects of the weapons, the sooner do they produce a deterrent effect, and thus it comes to pass that battles generally are less bloody in proportion as the engines of destruction have attained greater perfection'.

A similar desperate optimism inspired the French *jeune école* to believe that fighting spirit could overcome even the numerical superiority that Germany would enjoy in a future war. They buttressed their hopes with a selective reading of the researches of Colonel Ardant du Picq in the 1860s. Du Picq's pioneering survey of behaviour in combat led him to a remarkable view of the difference between ancient and modern war. 'Man does not enter battle to fight but for victory,' he said. 'He does everything he can to avoid the first and obtain the second.' Because man is dominated by the instinct of self-preservation, primitive peoples hardly ever fight face-to-face battles. Only civilized societies produce long battles, by imposing collective duty and cohesive organization. But there were always limits to this. Modern firearms impelled men to comply with their own instincts and to avoid hand-to-hand combat. Against the terrifying sweep of gunfire, only a supreme *esprit de corps* would avail. Du Picq frankly recognized the strength of the defensive in these conditions, but his younger successors concluded that France must compensate for its overall weakness by cultivating *élan*, the offensive spirit. As one of them wrote in 1906, 'The belief that numbers are all-powerful is demoralizing; it has always been wrong, and is more so now than ever. Individual training, military education, and above all morale, are the dominant factors in the fight.'

What was not grasped was that a certain mixture of technologies might totally overwhelm the human spirit. In the Great War the 'defensive trinity', as Fuller called the bullet, the spade, and the wire, paralysed all conventional ideas of movement. Not until the aircraft and the tracked motor vehicle arrived could this technology gap be bridged. Instead there was a strange and monstrous growth of artillery. Once dominated by the new infantry weapons, and ineffective against entrenchments, artillery was revolutionized by the emergence of quick-firing high-velocity field guns, of which the French 75 mm. was the most potent, and the less glamorous but more crushing development of heavy howitzers. The inadvertent pioneers of this were the Japanese, whose victory over Russia in the war of 1904–5 delivered a shock to the whole of Europe. After suffering heavy losses in attempts to take the second-rate Russian fortifications at Port Arthur by direct assault, they used their 28cm. coast-defence howitzers, originally intended to bombard the Russian ships in the port, to smash the concrete emplacements. The process was carefully studied by the Germans, whose European war plan required the rapid seizure of the formidable modern fortress of Liege, and by 1914 Krupp had produced the artillery which was once again to render fortresses obsolete and to dominate the entire field of battle.

In 1914 this fateful combination of technologies turned the whole battlefront in western Europe into a colossal fortification. The first few weeks of campaigning, culminating in the massive 'battles' of the Marne and the Aisne, revealed that the German war plan devised by Graf von Schlieffen had been an academic fantasy. Its obsession with annihilating the enemy by encirclement on a huge scale, the *Vernichtungsstrategie*, was rooted in Clause-witzian ideas, but was carried to an extreme that Clausewitz might well have condemned. In a sense the Schlieffen Plan can be seen as a classic example of the imbalance between military and political logic, the ascendancy of 'purely military' thinking that Clausewitz dismissed as absurd. (As he put it, war has its own grammar, but not its own logic.) Yet the plan was undoubtedly political in the sense that it expressed a widely held belief amongst the German ruling class that destiny required a military show-down: 'Weltmacht oder Niedergang' ('world power or downfall').

It was this readiness to see war in existential terms that made the Great War an absolute war from the start, even before its technical demands forced the belligerent states to organize their economic and social resources to an unprecedented degree. Pro-paganda, mostly a spontaneous surge of hostility amongst the patriotic middle class rather than deliberate governmental ac-tion, instantly branded the enemy as the enemy of civilization. Working-class views were less extreme, and certainly less fre-quently published. But in general the outbreak of war in 1914 produced a sense of national unity that would have seemed al-most impossible a few years earlier. The belief in a common des-tiny moved from the fringes to the mainstream. The 'war effort' came to embrace all kinds of normal day-to-day activities. This banal dimension, as much as anything else, gave the war its per-vasive character, turning it into the first 'total war'.

Total war in the twentieth century was different from French revolutionary war in size rather than in spirit. What changed was not the state's will to mobilize its entire people, but its or-ganizational ability to do so. In some ways, even those states—Germany above all—often regarded as 'militarist' were surprisingly unready for war on this scale. It was not only the traditionally unprepared states like Britain that had to make big adjustments and try new expedients to provide both the man-power (a distinctively modern concept) and the material for the war of attrition. Britain, however, with its strong tradition of minimal government—the 'night-watchman state'—vividly il-lustrated the speed of the shift from normalcy to drastic and all-embracing wartime powers like those contained in the Defence of the Realm Act. The emergencies of the twentieth century produced a kind of 'constitutional dictatorship' which severely tested the tradition of liberal politics.

The extremism that shaped the Schlieffen Plan, and thus the geopolitics of the whole war, was repeated throughout its course. Compromise peace was universally rejected. The entire war-making capacity of societies became a legitimate military target. Hence the British imposed a naval blockade on Germany—a traditional British mode of operation, but now more crushing than ever in the past through a mixture of geographical accident and technical development. Within a year Germany was visibly beginning to starve to death, and in the last winter of the war nearly three-quarters of a million Germans were to die of hunger. Germany's response was catastrophic. Possessing a wholly new technology in the form of the submarine, Germany could not exploit it without breaking international law (a law which, as John Hattendorf shows, had been substantially defined by Britain). The decision to declare unrestricted submarine warfare, which brought the USA into the war, was not taken without long deliberation. In rational terms, it was probably an impossible decision to make, because the statistical calculations on which it had to be based were more or less hypothetical. But, in the end, the prevailing argument was visceral rather than rational. Germany gambled not just to avoid defeat, but to win a decisive victory which would enable it to dictate the terms of peace.

'Total war', the twentieth-century refinement of Clausewitz's absolute war, was produced by the familiar combination of administrative, technical, and ideological forces. In the First World War, the paralysis of strategy by the technological stalemate was answered by the vast expansion of national organization to find ever more manpower and war material. A compromise peace was ruled out by the tremendous fears and ambitions generated by nationalism. In the Second World War, still more destructive technology was put at the service of a still more ambitious nationalism. To begin with, technology seemed to offer a way round the impasse of 1914–18. The development of tanks and aircraft made possible rapid movement which might dislocate defensive forces and prevent the establishment of fixed front lines. Such was the argument of the British military writer Basil Liddell Hart in the 1920s, and such became the basis of German strategy in the 1930s. Nazism committed Germany to a stupendous programme of expansion and colonization in the east, the *Drang nach Osten* ('drive to the east') to destroy the Germans' historical enemies and guarantee their security forever. Such colossal objectives could not be achieved without war, yet another war like that of 1914 would be suicidal. Blitzkrieg was the answer. Resolution and speed of movement would outweigh material weakness.

The defeat of France in 1940, a stunning reversal of First World War experience, was not due to technical imbalances as such. As has often been noted, the impact of blitzkrieg was not so much a matter of having more, or necessarily better, tanks and aircraft, as of using them in greater concentration. The disorienting velocity of the German advance was an act of faith, which tested the nerve of the German generals almost to breaking point. Only in Russia in 1941 did the technical limits of mechanization become significant. Finally, on the Eastern Front, trench warfare as grim as that of 1914–18 returned to swamp all but the strongest concentrations of armoured units. Without command of the air, ground forces could scarcely move.

The war in the east, however, was marked above all by its ideological extremism. The German army was committed to far more than a military task. As one of its commanders, von Reichenau (6th Army), announced to his troops in October 1941, 'the essential goal of the campaign against the Jewish–Bolshevik system is the complete destruction of its power instruments, and the eradication of the Asiatic influence on the European cultural sphere'. Therefore 'the troops have tasks which go beyond the conventional nature of soldierly duty'. Hitler's notorious 'Commissar Order', requiring that all Communist Party officials should be killed without trial, was only the beginning of a vast programme of destruction and enslavement, consuming Jews in particular, and Slavs in general. The keynote of this campaign to establish the 'new order' was ruthlessness: the words 'ruthless' and 'harsh' recur throughout German operational orders in the east. The result was a hardening of civilian hostility towards the invaders, and the intensification of partisan resistance which steadily consumed German military strength.

The erosion of the distinction between combatants and non-combatants, on which so much of the slow progress towards an international law of war has been based, is one of the twentieth century's unhappiest achievements. In the Second World War, technology and ideology conspired to accelerate this process. More effective submarines made possible a more formidable blockade of food supplies; the development of long-range aircraft made possible the area bombing of cities in an attempt to undermine civilian morale as well as to destroy productive capacity. Bombloads and bomb sizes increased steadily until the devastating leap into nuclear weaponry in August 1945 dwarfed even the greatest mass attacks of the war. These attacks were, of course, carried out by the liberal democratic states of the West rather than their militaristic opponents. In this sense, technology seemed able to subvert as well as to support ideology. In his official report on the Nuremberg tribunal, Telford Taylor pointed out that 'the ruins of German and Japanese cities were the results not of reprisal but of deliberate policy, and bore witness that the aerial bombardment of cities and factories has become a recognized part of modern warfare as carried on by all nations'.

Perversely, the ferocity of modern war has been exacerbated at crucial times by the international law of war. The shock waves generated by German reprisals in Belgium in the first weeks of the 1914 campaign instantly transformed the war into a clash of good and evil. Many atrocity stories were exaggerated or even fabricated, but they rested on a bedrock of fact: the German army's deliberate policy of overawing civilians, to prevent any recurrence of the 'people's war' fought by French *francs-tireurs* against the German invaders in 1870. As in the Second World War, harshness was the order of the day. The Chief of the German General Staff, Moltke, explained in August 1914 that it was 'in the nature of such things' that military countermeasures in response to guerrilla resistance 'will be extraordinarily harsh, and even, in some circumstances, affect the innocent'.

The alternative, in the military view, was anarchy and the destruction of all restraints. The price of order was the deliberate execution of at least 5,500 Belgian civilians, and the burning of dozens of towns and villages.

The fear of partisan attack, which haunted the German conscripts in alien territory, was to become ever more familiar to armies in the twentieth century. 'People's war' had always been implicit in modern war: now it became dominant. The twentieth century witnessed a transformation in the shape of war. In 1945, as Martin van Creveld writes, 'modern war abolished itself'; that is, all-out war using all available technologies became too dangerous for great powers to wage. Military establishments reluctantly came to recognize the limits of high technology, and the enduring strength of ideological motivation. The failure of the US intervention in Vietnam was a turning-point, which coincided with the re-emergence of powerful ethnic and religious forces.

As long as the Cold War transfixed the attention of the major powers, this transformation was subordinated to traditional international concerns. But the Vietnam War had been preceded by guerrilla struggles in Ireland, Palestine, and China; a great wave of conflict in Asia, Africa, and Latin America accompanied it. Even before the final unravelling of the 'Communist bloc' in the 1980s, the encroachment of political violence within the stable western liberal democracies showed that there would be no simple triumph of liberalism. The ferocious potential of what may be called 'total people's wars' fought by paramilitary militias, rather than regular armies or guerrilla bands, began to be revealed in Lebanon and Afghanistan in the late 1970s and the 1980s. In 1992 the disintegration of Yugoslavia precipitated a war in which the last vestiges of legal protection for non-combatants were swept away by the desire for national homogeneity. 'Ethnic cleansing' in Bosnia demonstrated the full murderous potential of the high-minded liberal doctrine of national self-determination.

So 'high-intensity' war gave way to 'low-intensity conflict' (LIC). This was not so much a shift from unlimited to limited war, as a recasting of what Clausewitz called the 'grammar' of war. High-intensity war rested on classically Clausewitzian elements: concentration of force, the culminating point, decisive battle. LIC exploits their opposites: fluid positions, diffusion, and protracted struggle for the 'hearts and minds' of the people. Such conflicts dissolve the traditional distinction between war and peace, and at the turn of the twenty-first century were tending to dissolve the state itself. The dangers of 'failed states,' in which (as in Somalia) military forces become private armies, should not be exaggerated: there have always been weaker and stronger state structures. But the possible implications—especially for the growth of terrorist groups and nuclear proliferation – are sobering. LIC can involve an almost limitless spectrum of violence, from street protest to open battle, so no purely military response can be effective. Least of all, perhaps, the high-technology techniques of the so-called 'revolution in military affairs' (RMA), espoused by many in the US military who hoped to make war more tolerable by achieving the truly empty battlefield. Yet a fundamental redefinition of military forces to cope with the fluidity of LIC is an uncomfortable, if not an intolerable, prospect for societies such as those of western Europe, where the distinction between civil and military spheres has been strictly maintained, and whose political culture largely rests upon it. It may become increasingly difficult to preserve the carefully-constructed tradition of military professionalism which was so central to the shaping of modern war. If there is to be a 'war on terror'; it could become more total than any war in the past.

2

The Military Revolution I

The Transition to Modern Warfare

JOHN CHILDS

Advances in technology during the later Middle Ages resulted in new weapons which gradually modified all aspects of war between 1450 and 1700. The concomitant increase in the size of armed forces ultimately caused profound changes to the nature and government of the state. Michael Roberts has argued that these developments occurred principally between 1550 and 1650, a period which he dubbed the 'Military Revolution'. Geoffrey Parker has extended Roberts's thesis to encompass the three centuries between 1500 and 1800, stressing the contribution of the new military methods to the European acquisition of overseas empire. The concept, however, is losing its force: a steady process spread across three centuries hardly justifies the title 'revolution'. The equivalent period from the 1690s to the 1990s—the flintlock musket to the hydrogen bomb—has yet to acquire the accolade of 'Second Military Revolution'.

In resorting to war, the princes of early modern Europe could only achieve the modest results which their forces were able to deliver. Armies were usually incapable of destroying an opponent, moved slowly because of poor communications and supply, and were hugely expensive to recruit, making commanders reluctant to risk them in battle. War was fought to seize or defend land. As vulnerable areas were normally protected by castles and fortified towns, the dominant technique was the siege, a lengthy operation which often consumed an entire campaigning season: the siege of Ostend lasted from 1601 to 1604, whilst La Rochelle resisted for nearly two years (1627–8). The capture, through siege, of specific territories offered better returns on investment than the gamble of engagement. As in the Middle Ages, battles often emanated directly from attempts to relieve besieged fortresses. Accordingly, wars were decided by the depth of the purse; in other words, attrition. Economic disputes could also lead to conflict, notably the Anglo-Dutch Wars of 1652–4, 1665–7, and 1672–4, but the concern for prestige and the domination of territory, in this case the waters of the North Sea, were just as important as the friction over fishing and trade. From the mid-sixteenth century states began to squabble over colonial territories and their associated spheres of economic interest. England and Spain went to war in 1585, partly because of the former's attempts to challenge Spanish hegemony in Central America. The Dutch captured the Portuguese Empire during the first half of the seventeenth century as a means of striking at Spanish power in Europe. Towards the end of the seventeenth century, England and France clashed in North America (1688–97) whilst the Dutch came to blows with the French at Pondicherry in India (1693).

The dynastic and territorial ambitions of rulers were the principal reasons for war in early modern Europe, their lands providing the necessary resources. Nationalism was sometimes detectable, notably in France during the Hundred Years War with England (1337–1453), but it was usually exacerbated by war rather than a cause. Constrained by ritual and custom, wars generally involved a level of violence commensurate with political objectives. Change occurred during the early sixteenth century. Religious war had long been waged between Christians and Muslims in southern and eastern Europe, but the Reformation shattered the unity of Roman Christendom, bringing confessional strife into western Europe. Struggles to dominate conscience involved entire populations, leading to greatly increased levels of violence as states strove to reconvert or exterminate lost souls. Religious differences were expressed in terms of territory, a principle formalized in the Religious Peace of Augsburg (1555), and Protestant and Catholic embarked on a long century of warfare.

Spain set the pattern for confessional warfare during the sixteenth and early seventeenth centuries. Until 1541 it endeavoured to control the spread of Protestant-inspired rebellion in its European territories before launching campaigns of reconquest (War against the Schmalkaldic League, 1546–7). Against the second generation of rebels, notably the Netherlands, Spain relied upon the siege and the garrison to reconquer, subdue, and occupy, a strategy quickly copied by its opponents. The wars of sieges were long and expensive: the Franco-Italian Wars stretched from 1494 to 1559, the French Wars of Religion lasted from 1562 to 1598, the Dutch Revolt against Spain covered eighty years (1567–1648), the Thirty Years War (1618–48) was eponymous, and the episodic wars of Louis XIV started in 1667 and ended in 1714. Only the larger states—Spain, Austria, and France—or the exceptionally wealthy—the Netherlands and, ultimately, England—could compete. So costly did war become that Henry VIII's ruinously extravagant expeditions to France in 1544–6, funded from the despoliation of the English Church, determined England for fifty years to avoid Continental entanglements; its eventual war with Spain (1585–1604) was conducted by more economical methods. Rising costs were partially offset by improvements in administration and tax collection, especially in Protestant states where nationalization of the wealth of the Church greatly enhanced the fiscal power of the secular ruler.

Military economics dictated strategy. Between 1618 and 1721, Sweden expanded into Poland and the Baltic littoral. The burden of maintaining its armies was thus transferred from the homeland to the occupied territories. Making 'war pay for war' was institutionalized in the 'contribution system' which diverted the economic resources of captured territories to the support of the occupying troops. An alternative strategy was to mount a rapid and decisive campaign aimed at achieving political results without becoming involved in a long attritional war. Such thinking probably lay behind the intervention of Gustavus Adolphus of Sweden in Germany in 1630, as well as the French attacks on the Dutch Republic in 1672 and Philippsburg in 1688. These 'blitzes' nearly always failed— William of Orange's assault on England in 1688 was about the only successful example—condemning to a long war the belligerent who could not secure a speedy peace. There was then little option but to resort to the strategy of exporting military costs. A factor in Spain's fiscal embarrassments between 1557 and 1607 was its inability to transfer military expenditure to a foreign state; nearly all its campaigns were directed at regaining lost territories. Wars frequently became self-perpetuating; Sweden continued to campaign in Germany in order to dominate sufficiently large areas from which to maintain its army. French retention of the southern parts of the Spanish Netherlands during the Nine Years War (1688–97) was vital in order to extract 'contributions' to support its troops. The problem of how to demobilize soldiers who were thus maintained lengthened the Thirty Years War and occupied much of the energies of the plenipotentiaries in Münster and Osnabrück. The issue was not finally resolved until the Conference at Nuremberg (1648–50) found the money and devised a timetable by which the armies could be paid off and disbanded. A further problem was the dependence of the majority of states upon mercenaries hired from 'military enterprisers', such as Albrecht von Wallenstein, who provided the bulk of the imperial armies, or Peter Ernst, Graf von Mansfeld, a recruiter for the Protestant cause. War had grown into an international industry with its own momentum, rationale, and institutions. Governments needed to regain control.

The solution was the widespread adoption between 1650 and 1700 of the standing army, already pioneered by France in 1445 and by Spain and the Dutch Republic during the sixteenth century. Standing armies enabled states to defend their territories against the institutionalized marauding of the contribution system, to deter aggression, and to avoid over-reliance upon mercenaries. Even tiny states—Weimar, Würzburg, Mainz—sprouted standing armies. However, it remained difficult for small states to compete independently in long wars against the rich and powerful, principally France under Louis XIV between 1667 and 1714, unless they spread the financial load by joining coalitions of the like-minded or sought subsidies from, or rented their troops to, larger states fighting in the same cause.

Gunpowder originated in China in the seventh or eighth century AD and arrived in western Europe towards the end of the thirteenth century. The first cannon appeared in Flanders around 1314, England in 1321, and France in 1326, but artillery did not play an important role in battle until Castillon in 1453. Around 1460 in France, cast bronze barrels replaced the old welded and bound iron guns—by 1543, iron cannon were cast in England. Charles VIII of France took 266 cannon to Italy in 1494, and at Marignano (1515) Francis I assembled 140 cannon, a ratio of five guns per 1,000 men. Learning from the lessons of the battles of Marignano, La Bicocca (1522), and Pavia (1525), monarchs generally improved their artillery. The army raised in 1544 by King Ferdinand of Hungary and Bohemia to fight the Turks included 60 siege cannon, 80 field guns, 200,000 cannon-balls, and 500 tons of gunpowder, transported by 1,000 horses. During the second half of the sixteenth century, a ratio of at least one cannon per 1,000 men was considered essential. Prince Maurice of Orange-Nassau reduced the Dutch artillery to four calibres (6-, 12-, 24-, and 48-pounders) which could be mounted interchangeably on standardized carriages. This provoked little imitation until the Thirty Years War; Spain continued to fight the Dutch with fifty models divided amongst twenty calibres. Gustavus Adolphus further improved the manufacture and application of artillery. His Swedish army possessed one gun per 400 men, whereas its imperial opponents in Germany had one per 2,000. He also reduced the length and weight of barrels to enhance mobility. The infantry guns, some of which were the famous 'leather guns', cast copper barrels reinforced with leather and rope, were extremely light (625 pounds). After his death at Lützen (1632), however, many of Gustavus's artillery reforms lapsed and were not extensively imitated until the 1690s.

Hand-guns developed in tandem with cannon, the first manuscript reference dating from 1365. The early arquebus was little better than the longbow but the matchlock musket, developed between 1510 and 1520, was a more powerful weapon which could fire a one-ounce bullet over 300 metres. The hand-gun was a great social leveller, 'the devil's invention to make us murder one another', according to the Frenchman Blaise de Monluc.

Would to heaven that this cursed engine had never been invented . . . so many valiant men [have] been slain for the most part by the most pitiful fellows and the greatest cowards; poltroons that had not dared to look those men in the face at close hand, which at distance they laid dead with their confounded bullets.

Some Italian *condottieri* put out the eyes and cut off the hands of captured arquebusiers. The new weapons hastened the already-changing social basis of warfare; anyone could learn to fire a hand-gun and lower the mighty from their saddles. By 1550, the longbow and the crossbow, both requiring years of intensive training for effective operation, had been replaced by the musket and the field gun, which were relatively cheap to produce and could be operated after a week's instruction. This was the essence of military change: a numerous infantry armed with cheap, crude, gunpowder weapons replaced exclusive and expensive cavalry: cantonal recruitment, conscription, and the age of mass armies beckoned. Between 1550 and 1700, battles were largely decided by missile fire seeking to disorder the enemy prior to the decisive advance.

However, this shift from warfare dominated by cavalry, the social élite, to warfare dominated by infantry, the masses, was already well under way before the advent of gunpowder weapons. At the Battle of Gisors in 1188, Henry II of England's infantry defeated the French heavy cavalry. By 1300, heavy cavalry could often make little headway against pikemen and archers unless they dismounted and fought on foot. During the fourteenth century, infantry further increased its effectiveness. Before the Battle of Courtrai (1302), Robert d'Artois declared that 'a hundred mounted men-at-arms are worth a thousand foot soldiers', yet his charging cavalry was pushed into the Scheldt by the worthless Flemish infantry. The pike square of Robert the Bruce overwhelmed English heavy cavalry at Bannockburn in 1314. Although the bow had always been an essential weapon, it was its massed deployment that contributed to the destruction of the French heavy cavalry at Crécy (1346), Poitiers (1356), and Agincourt (1415). Just as the English were demonstrating that cavalry could be defeated by a combination of concentrated missile fire and dismounted men-at-arms, in Switzerland the pike square was further developed. At Laupen in 1339, a Swiss pike square defeated the Burgundian cavalry. In 1386, 1,300 Swiss routed 3,000 cavalry from Lorraine; in 1444, 2,000 Swiss fought a heroic action against 14,000 men from the Dauphin's army; and in 1476, they defeated Charles the Bold of Burgundy at Grandson and Murten.

The spread of hand-guns accelerated the foot-soldiers' domination of the battlefield but tactical formations were required which maximized the strengths and minimized the weaknesses of firearms. The *De re militari* of Vegetius (AD 383) had been a basic military textbook since the twelfth century and the Renaissance soldier likewise searched for inspiration from ancient Greece and Rome. Niccolò Machiavelli, in the *Art of War*, slavishly imitated Roman tactical organization, but the majority of theorists and practitioners employed the ancients as models for adaptation. Swiss formations, already based on the Greek phalanx and the spaced maniples of the Roman legion, added handguns to their integrated array of weaponry—pike, halberd, axe, 'Lucerne hammer', 'morning star', and crossbow. Like his Roman predecessor, the Swiss infantryman was thoroughly trained. Between 1479 and 1483, in the aftermath of the Hundred Years War, Louis XI reorganized the French infantry along Swiss lines. Each 'Picardy Band', supplemented by the 'Piedmont Bands' in 1504, contained 200 crossbowmen, soon to be superseded by musketeers, and 800 pikemen. The Spaniards also imitated the Swiss. A professional and semi-permanent infantry had evolved during the slow and methodical conquest of the Kingdom of Granada (completed in 1492) and was reorganized by Gonsalvo de Córdoba at the beginning of the sixteenth century. In 1536 Charles V restructured the Spanish standing army, at that time garrisoned throughout northern Italy, into a number of *tercios* (3,000 men), modelled on the Roman legion, armed with a mixture of blade weapons and firearms. This prototype travelled rapidly across Europe, Duke François de Guise rearranging the French infantry into regiments similar to the *tercio* in 1560. Infantry became the predominant arm because it was cheaper and more versatile than cavalry—it could fight in battle, garrison a fortress, and conduct a siege whereas horsemen were of limited utility during the two latter operations. When Charles VIII of France attacked Italy in 1498, half of his 18,000 men were cavalry; only 20 per cent of Francis I's invading army of 30,000 in 1525 were mounted. The horse fell into relative decline as firearms and artillery blunted its shock action and, up to 1700, most armies consisted of three-quarters infantry and only one-quarter cavalry. However, if well handled, mounted troops could still decide a battle, as at Rocroi in 1643 or Marston Moor in the following year.

In order to adapt Dutch infantry organization to the geographical conditions in the northern Netherlands during the central stages (1590–1600) of the Eighty Years War against Spain, Maurice of Nassau returned to the study of Rome's well-articulated legions. Just as the legion had been subdivided during the later Empire, so Maurice broke up the *tercios* into battalions of 580 men which fought in ten ranks, the pikes in the centre and the muskets on the flanks. Theoretically, the musketeers could maintain a continuous fire as each rank successively discharged its weapons before countermarching to the rear to reload. The pikemen protected the musketeers from attack by cavalry. Unfortunately, the new battalions were relatively shallow and thus vulnerable to their flanks and rear; this was countered at army level by a chequer-board battle formation, the spaces between battalions of the first line covered by echeloned battalions in the second line. The army's flanks were anchored on natural obstacles, easy enough to find in the Netherlands, or were protected by cavalry. Dutch methods required a high level of drill, discipline, and training, factors which strongly influenced the move towards permanent, standing forces manned by long-service troops.

Gustavus Adolphus refined the Dutch system. Battalions fought in six ranks which increased the frontage and, supported by their rapid-firing infantry guns, developed formidable firepower. Gustavus also introduced 'volley firing' by advancing the rear ranks of musketeers into the intervals between the front ranks. Volley firing became the basis for European infantry tactics; the inaccurate matchlocks and flintlocks were most effective when a number were discharged simultaneously. The flintlock, with a higher rate of fire and greater reliability, had virtually replaced the matchlock by 1700. Simultaneously, the bayonet ousted the pike. The plug bayonet appeared in France in 1647 to be superseded by the socket version in 1689. The latter was adopted by Brandenburg-Prussia in the same year and by Denmark in 1690. As efficiency and the rate of fire increased, the number of ranks of musketeers was gradually reduced to create a longer battalion frontage. This resulted in a battalion with so little depth that it could not adequately defend its own flanks and rear. Accordingly, each battalion butted on to its neighbours forming a continuous, though thin, line of battle. By the end of the War of the Spanish Succession in 1714, European infantry fought in linear battalions, three or four ranks deep, armed with a flintlock musket tipped with a socket bayonet. Nevertheless, battle, never a popular option and subject to the veto of Vegetius, surrendered its few remaining attractions to firearms. The heavy losses at La Bicocca in 1522 and Pavia in 1525 demonstrated that offensive action in the face of powerful cannon and muskets was highly dangerous. Although guns were the dominant weapon in sieges, it was a form of warfare in which risks could be calculated and the level of casualties thus controlled.

Gunpowder had transformed the science of fortification and sieges. Cannon firing iron ammunition rapidly demolished medieval stone walls. In 1453, Sultan Mehmet II's sixty-two heavy guns broke down the triple walls of Constantinople within six weeks. The initial response was to bank earthen revetments before and behind the wall—'ramparting'—and lower its height to present a smaller target to attacking gunners. At Nettuno (1501–2), Antonio da Sangallo the Elder transformed the medieval tower, which had protruded from the wall to give the defending artillery an all-round field of fire, into a triangular bastion with retired flanks. Such projections from the wall both forced the hostile cannon to fire from longer range and enabled the defenders to enfilade attackers. Gradually, during the sixteenth and seventeenth centuries, the geometric design of the bastion trace, the *trace italienne*, was developed. Antonio da Sangallo the Younger, Michele San Michele, Jean Errard de Barle-Duc, the comte de Pagan, Sebastien le Prestre de Vauban, and his Dutch contemporary Menno van Coehoorn brought the *trace italienne* to maturity. Huge, complex fortifications, manned by garrisons which were much smaller than the armies needed to attack them, could withstand prolonged sieges. Yet, no matter how sophisticated the fortifications, a successful defence depended upon the willingness of the civilian population to undergo the rigours of a siege. When they were not, as at Mons in 1691, the costly earthworks were useless.

The new fortifications were expensive and often beyond the means of cities and small states yet, without them, they fell victim to greedy neighbours and predatory princes. Each of Amsterdam's twenty-two bastions cost half a million florins. Vauban took six years and 5 million livres to fortify the town of Ath whilst the construction of the brand-new fortress of Neuf Breisach extracted 4 million livres from Louis XIV's treasury. The cost of fortification was a prime factor in the extension of monarchical power. Siena's existence as an independent city state was fatally compromised during the mid-sixteenth century by the huge cost of building artillery fortifications. Even Rome had to abandon its scheme of fortification half-finished because of the enormous expense. Between 1682 and 1691, Louis XIV spent 8.5 million livres per annum on fortification although this was insignificant compared with the cost of besieging a fortress. The siege of the Huguenot stronghold of La Rochelle (1627–8) by the army of Louis XIII cost a reputed 40 million livres. If fortifications represented the biggest and most expensive civil engineering works of the age then sieges were its greatest test of large-scale organization and finance.

Between 1445 and 1624, the French establishment (i.e. the total number of soldiers employed by the state) in peacetime averaged between 10,000 and 20,000 men; the troops guarded the person of the monarch and garrisoned the frontier fortresses. During wartime, this cadre was expanded to a maximum of 55,000, the level reached under Henry IV during the final stages of the French Wars of Religion. The size of individual field armies rarely rose above 20,000 men. During the middle and later decades of the seventeenth century, the military establishment of France was significantly increased. In 1629 French peacetime standing forces probably remained as low as 12,000 men but by 1665 this figure had risen to 72,000, by 1669 to 131,000, and it averaged around 150,000 during the 1680s. In wartime, the increases were even more marked. The wartime establishment of Louis XIII was over 200,000 troops in 1636 and averaged 150,000 throughout the period of French involvement in the Thirty Years War (1635–48). However, these were 'paper' figures and a reduction of perhaps 50 per cent is necessary in order to reach a realistic estimate of the number who actually served. During the War of Devolution (1667–8) France placed 134,000 men under arms, over 279,000 men served annually towards the end of the Franco-Dutch War (1672–8), whilst during the Nine Years War and the War of the Spanish Succession (1702–14) the French establishment reached a peak of over 400,000 men. Field armies also expanded until in 1695, at the height of the Nine Years War, the French army in the Low Countries numbered 115,000 men. This represented an unsustainable summit. The burden of these huge field armies overbalanced national economies and, for the remainder of the eighteenth century, field armies reverted to a mean of about 50,000 men.

This pattern was repeated across most of Europe. The size of both field armies and national establishments, in those few states with permanent military institutions, remained fairly static during the sixteenth and the first part of the seventeenth centuries but then grew enormously during the second two-thirds of the seventeenth century as the standing army was widely adopted. There were several reasons. First, wars grew more protracted, requiring additional men over longer periods. Secondly, as the artillery fortifications spread throughout the main theatres of war in the Low Countries, eastern France, northern Italy, and the Rhine Valley, so armies had to find both garrisons and besieging forces. Fortresses were troop-hungry and, although a certain amount could be achieved by urban militias and *ad hoc* organizations, the main burden fell on the professional armed forces. The demand was partially met by replacing expensive cavalry with cheaper infantry. Thirdly, as states became more unified, centralized, and geographically identified during the seventeenth century, a process which both underlay and resulted from the religious flux of the 1500s, so the need for national defence became more urgent. This was particularly the case in Germany where numerous quasi-independent states had emerged as a result of the Protestant Reformation. Through repeated invasion and depredation, the Thirty Years War had demonstrated that territorial security could only be achieved by devoting resources to defend the state with the *trace italienne* and permanent troops. By clause cxviii of the Treaty of Westphalia (1648), every prince in the Holy Roman Empire was allowed to 'keep up as many men in his own dominion as he shall judge necessary for his own security'. Finally, military changes hastened developments in state administration which had been initiated during the early sixteenth century. The struggle of European rulers to centralize and unify their states was assisted by the spiralling costs of warfare which meant that individual nobles and entrepreneurs could no longer challenge the monarch on the field of battle—the French Wars of Religion, the Frondes, and the English Civil Wars were the last serious aristocratic spasms—and the 'monopoly of violence' passed to the Crown. France, Denmark, Sweden, Russia, and the Italian and German states all witnessed, during the middle and later decades of the seventeenth century, the rise of supercharged personal monarchies governing states in which local privileges and franchises were steadily reduced in the face of growing centralized power and bureaucracy. One of the key steps in this process was the emergence of the standing army.

The standing army—that which exists in both peace and war—was scarcely a novel concept. The Roman army had been the most notable of many predecessors: the Saxon *housecarls*, the Norman *familia regis*, and the Venetian forces founded in 1404–6. There were two stages in the development of the long-service standing army: the first occurred during the sixteenth century and the second after the Peace of Westphalia brought the Thirty Years War to a close in 1648. Charles VII of France had founded a national army during the final stages of the Hundred Years War but it was under Francis I that the *compagnies d'ordonnance* evolved into a permanent army. They were composed of professional volunteers recruited through a state agency. The sixteenth-century standing armies of France and Spain were intended to fight in wartime, and garrison fortresses and citadels in occupied territories during time of peace. Thus the Spanish *tercios* garrisoned bases in northern Italy, fought the rebellious Dutch in the Netherlands and Protestants in Germany, and countered the Turks in North Africa. The second period of growth, after 1648, was based on different priorities. It was also more widespread, involving small states as well as large. The practice of hiring mercenaries grew increasingly unattractive and expensive as wars became longer and more frequent. With fortifications to garrison and states to defend, it made more sense for rulers to raise and pay their own troops directly from amongst their own populations. Mercenaries were still employed but the entrepreneur, the middle man, was circumvented and individuals contracted directly with the state.

In 1664 Elector Ferdinand Maria of Bavaria possessed the nucleus of a standing army of 1,750 men; in 1675 this had expanded to 8,000. The troops of Hesse-Kassel were paid off at the end of the Thirty Years War but, by 1688, the new standing army numbered over 10,000 men. There was no army in the Duchy of Jülich-Berg in 1652; by 1684 it had 5,000 troops. Although a standing army was unknown in England until 1642, the Civil War spawned the New Model Army of 20,000 in 1645: during the Restoration (1660–88) the English standing army rose from 3,000 to over 20,000 men. Brandenburg-Prussia began building an army during the 1650s which had exceeded 40,000 by 1713. After the Conference at Nuremberg in 1650, Emperor Ferdinand III of Austria retained 25,000 foot and 8,000 horse to form the nucleus of the Austrian standing army. States which had possessed standing armies before 1648 — France, Spain, and the Dutch Republic — further augmented their peacetime establishments. Although most of these armies were recruited by voluntary enlistment or the press-gang, between 1620 and 1682 Sweden introduced and refined a system of partial conscription based on the division of the country into cantons or military districts, the 'Indelningsverket'.

Military and security factors only partially explain the second phase of the emergence of the standing army. As states centralized and unified, so their rulers were able to extract higher proportions of the national wealth through taxation. Whether the new armies preceded the rise in taxation thereby creating the need for additional revenue, or whether the higher taxation preceded and thus permitted the maintenance of peacetime standing armies, remains somewhat uncertain. Whatever the sequence, the higher state revenues were spent almost exclusively on the military: armies, navies, and fortifications. The huge costs of war reduced the Spanish Crown to declarations of technical bankruptcy in 1607, 1627, and 1647, whilst its principal army in the Low Countries was often emasculated as its troops mutinied for want of pay on over fifty occasions between 1570 and 1607. The lesson was clear: if states were to maintain large standing armies, they needed to squeeze higher revenues from their subjects and make better and more efficient use of that money. Between 1679 and 1725 the proportion of the total state revenues of Russia devoured by the army and the navy ranged between 60 per cent in peacetime and 95 per cent in wartime. During the Nine Years War and the War of the Spanish Succession, 75 per cent of English government expenditure was poured into the army (40 per cent) and the navy (35 per cent). France spent 65 per cent of its total revenues on the army and 9 per cent on the navy during the Nine Years War. Some states were increasingly able to afford these spiralling commitments. From colonies in the Americas, India, and the West and East Indies, great wealth entered England and the Dutch Republic and was taxed by increasingly efficient administrations. Public finance and banking became so organized in these countries that the state could regularly borrow huge sums of money through institutionalized national debts.

The new armies were needed as much to secure the state from within as to defend its borders from attack. The imposition of higher taxation and the broadening of the tax base within society provoked insurrections which could only be suppressed with the aid of the army that had initially created the need for more revenue: France suffered revolts in the Boulonnais in 1662, Guyenne in 1664, and Brittany in 1675. Additionally, the threats to an ordered and deferential society which had emerged both during and after the Thirty Years War further demonstrated that absolute monarchs required their new armies to act as robust domestic police forces to control dissent. Whereas the sixteenth-century standing armies of France and Spain had generally been employed to guard frontiers and occupy conquered territories, their seventeenth-century successors were also intended to garrison the homeland to suppress rebellion and maintain law and order.

As armies became more home-based, lodged amongst their own population rather than serving as occupation forces, better discipline and improved control of officers over their men were required in order to reduce friction with civilians. Indiscipline, which was acceptable or even desirable whilst collecting contributions in a subject territory, was unacceptable in the new surroundings. Troops at home had to be housed, fed, and regularly paid. Whilst on campaign, the armies of the sixteenth century and the Thirty Years War had tended to pillage or gather contributions: the better-organized and -disciplined national forces of the later seventeenth century usually paid for some of their supplies. In addition, the state hired civilian contractors to provide basic foodstuffs and transport in wartime.

Imitation and fashion were again important. After 1648 France was the dominant political, military, and cultural force in Europe. Petty German princes built Lilliputian Versailles in their capital towns and even Charles II of England decided to build a Versailles near Winchester, close to the fortress, garrison, and naval base at Portsmouth. As Louis XIV of France maintained his absolute power partly through the medium of a standing army so most rulers in Europe felt obliged to follow suit. Whatever were the objectives of the foreign policy of Louis XIV—personal glory, hatred of the Dutch, rivalry with the Habsburgs—by the Dutch Republic, the Spanish, and the princes in the Rhineland he was perceived as an enemy who wished to overturn the Peace of Westphalia and seize territory. As France attacked with ever-larger armies in 1667–8, 1672–8, and 1688–97, so it was opposed by states who felt reciprocally obliged to augment their forces. The smaller German states, which themselves could raise only limited numbers of troops, sheltered within anti-French coalitions, but the pillars of those confederations—England, the Dutch Republic, and Austria—had to recruit, or hire, enormous numbers of troops in order to combat the French military establishments, which climbed above 400,000 men during the 1690s.

Governments were little more than war machines. The administrative and bureaucratic methods which helped to centralize and modernize the state were primarily initiated in Spain during the sixteenth century, independently developed in Sweden in the 1620s and 1630s, and then refined in France by Michel Le Tellier and the marquis de Louvois. As the state assumed the running of its own armed forces from the mercenary captains and military entrepreneurs, administrators were concerned principally with organization and the acquisition of sufficient revenue. By the mid-1660s, there was a War Ministry in Paris dealing with recruitment, supply, pay, discipline, fortifications, and soldiers' health. Sweden created a College of War in 1634, England established an embryonic War Office in 1683, a War Ministry existed in Piedmont-Savoy by 1692, whilst Russia under Peter the Great endlessly experimented with administrative institutions.

Engorged state armies demanded armaments and equipment, factors which boosted the textile and metallurgical industries. Starting from a minuscule manufacturing base in 1700, within twenty-five years Russia was self-sufficient in armaments following the creation of forty new installations. At Liège, the traditional centre for weapons manufacture in western Europe, the local economy expanded substantially during the wars of Louis XIV. In 1689 English musket production extended beyond London to Birmingham. The Danish cloth industry was largely supported by the needs of 20,000 soldiers. During wartime, agriculture enjoyed boom conditions as both naval and military victualling contractors scoured Europe for the cheapest and most abundant sources of supply. Agricultural regions in the Low Countries, Germany, France, northern Italy, and England made considerable profits from war, profits which far outweighed incidental damage and destruction. The huge demand for horses promoted the breeding industry both to meet requirements and to produce more effective and efficient animals. In 1712 Peter I of Russia set up stud farms to ensure an improved supply of cavalry mounts.

Permanence led to professionalism. The chivalric traditions and *esprit de corps* of the aristocracy constituted ideal officer material. In turn, the nobility was eager to support royal institutions whilst long-service standing armies presented officers with regular pay and a career structure. The New Model Army, founded in 1645, formalized a rank structure in the English army which has endured to the present day. Officers gradually exchanged their status as contracted mercenaries for that of state employees, although this evolution was far from complete by 1700; in England, officers did not become fully absorbed in the state until the reforms of the Duke of Cumberland in the mid-eighteenth century. Early modern governments lacked the resources and the infrastructure to complete the process and officers were partly state employees but also private businessmen entrusted with the running of the national army in return for pay and institutionalized perquisites. Most regiments were technically the property of their colonel, who enjoyed the right to sell commissions as well as benefit from clothing his men and a host of other 'allowances'. Regiments remained sources of considerable profit for their officers.

Officers began to be educated for their new tasks. The duc de Bouillon established a Military Training Academy at Sedan in 1606, John II of Nassau founded the Kriegs und Ritterschule in Siegen in 1617, and in 1618 Maurice of Hesse founded the military college at Kassel. Wallenstein initiated military schools at Friedland and Gilschin. In France, Richelieu opened a college in the Temple district of Paris whilst Mazarin planned to provide military education at the College of the Four Nations. The Great Elector of Brandenburg-Prussia assembled the officer cadets into a single company attached to the Knight's College at Kolberg (1653). Colleges, however, cost money; it was cheaper to train future officers in the ranks as cadets. In 1682 Louvois established nine cadet companies for officer training. The cavalry regiments of the royal household served as officer-training formations for the French, Swedish, Russian, and British armies.

Along with the institutional training of officers went a growth in technical publications. The first modern drill book, which used illustrations instead of words, was Jacob de Gheyn's engraving of John of Nassau's sketches of drill movements, *Wapenhandlingen van roers, musquetten ende spiessen* [*Arms Drill with Arquebus, Musket and Pike*] (Amsterdam, 1607).

There was a marked contrast between Europe and Asia-in-Europe. The Ottoman Turks possessed artillery by 1389 and the janizaries were equipped with firearms by 1500. However, the Ottoman method of fighting—the Turkish Crescent—reflected the racial and geographical divisions within the Empire rather than the requirements of modern war. Although effective during the fifteenth century, by the time of the siege of Vienna in 1683 the Turkish method of war-making was outmoded: they had failed to master the art of fortification, their cannon were of poor quality and too massive for flexible deployment on the battlefield, whilst their military organization, which rested on slavery and feudalism, could not compete with the professionalism of western Europe. Partial reform occurred after 1699, whilst during the eighteenth century a series of European advisers attempted to modernize the artillery and military education. Finally, under Selim III (1789–1807) ties with the decaying military institutions were cut and a new army was created on European lines.

Military modernization coincided with the expansion of Europe into Africa, Asia, and America. In many of these regions, the shape, purpose, level of violence, and length of indigenous warfare were controlled by ritual. One of the principal purposes was often the acquisition of slaves. Firearms and cannon—weapons of indiscriminate violence—were inappropriate to a style of warfare which customarily devolved into a series of individual combats in order to effect capture. Killing was not the main purpose. European warfare was concerned with capturing territory not people; enemy soldiers were simply pawns in the greater game, not ends in themselves. During the sixteenth and seventeenth centuries the rituals governing the conduct of war in Europe diminished. Attempts were made to resurrect ritual, especially in relation to the siege, after 1648 in order to control the excesses of violence which had characterized the Century of Religious War (as in the sack of Magdeburg, 1631). The 'Jurists'—Hugo de Groot or Grotius, Richard Zouche, Samuel Pufendorf, Cornelius van Bynkershoek, and Emerich de Vattel—tried to regulate the conduct of war through the medium of international law but their success was, at best, partial. Beyond Europe even such feeble codes of conduct had no application. Colonists, armed with weapons and attitudes of destruction, swept aside Asian and South American armies before they had time to adjust. Superior weapons were an important factor but the European approach to war was decisive.

European energy encountered methods of making war which were largely stagnant. In the Americas, Europeans came to conquer, exploit, and settle. Hernán Cortés and 500 Spaniards seized the Aztec Empire in Mexico (1519–21) and Francisco Pizarro with 168 Europeans crushed the Incas of Peru (1531–3); the Stone Age rapidly succumbed to European technology. However, in North America the English settled in Virginia after 1607 and Massachusetts from 1620, and France founded Quebec in 1607—native Amerindians quickly acquired the gunpowder weapons. During King Philip's War (1675–8), both the Amerindians and the colonists of New England realized the futility of fighting pitched battles and switched to guerrilla tactics. By these effective methods the Amerindians were able to slow the westward movement of the English settlers. North America was eventually conquered by the fort, disease, railways, and weight of numbers.

Whereas conquest and economic exploitation lay behind the European colonization of the American continent, the control of the lucrative spice trade was the principal motive for expansion into Asia and India. Expeditions burst upon the Asian seaboards with great violence: Portugal took Goa in 1510 and Spain seized the Philippines in 1560. Once European colonists secured toeholds in these territories, they introduced the proven strategy of occupation by fortification and garrison. The trading posts were defended by artillery fortifications according to the *trace italienne*: Malacca was fortified after 1511 and Manila from 1585. Few peoples outside Europe and the Near and Middle East developed fixed fortifications; only in India were strongly defended towns common. Not only did the bastioned trace ease European occupation but it also made it extremely difficult for the Indians or the Indonesians to expel the colonists as they lacked the techniques and experience with which to attack the new fortifications springing up in their midst. However, in India, European expansion into the inland regions was slowed by the Mughal Empire (1526–1857), which possessed firearms, cannon, and plentiful manpower. The Portuguese, French, Dutch, and English colonists were not able to make much headway in India until the sepoy system was introduced by France in the 1740s.

Gradually, the European model of warfare—violence, killing, firearms, professional organization, and bastioned fortification—spread across the world. Countries which lay beyond the main trade routes and wind belts—Japan, Korea, and China—managed to shut out foreign influences and remain introverted. However, by 1700, the foundations, methods, and attitudes which enabled Europe to conquer much of the world during the eighteenth and nineteenth centuries had been established.

3

The Military Revolution II

Eighteenth-Century War

JEREMY BLACK

At sea eighteenth-century warfare was dominated by the European powers, but on land they were but one group among a number of important military states. In technological and organizational terms there was little change in warfare, on land or sea. In terms of social context the most far-reaching development was the War of American Independence (1775–83), a successful popular struggle that led to the creation of a potentially major new state. The leading global powers were Britain at sea and China and Russia on land. In a series of conflicts, of which the Seven Years War (1756–63) was the most significant, Britain defeated France and its ally Spain and became the most dynamic maritime and colonial power in the world. These conflicts were a reflection of the political importance of trade in Britain and of the extent to which growing trade increased both the British mercantile marine, creating a large pool of sailors that could be used in wartime, and customs revenue, thus helping to finance a massive programme of naval construction.

A strong navy protected Britain from French invasion, most significantly in 1692, 1708, 1745–6, and 1759, and served as the basis for imperial expansion. In the War of the Spanish Succession (1701–14) Britain conquered Gibraltar and Minorca from Spain and Nova Scotia from France. The British fleet under Admiral Vernon on the unsuccessful expedition to Cartagena in modern Colombia in 1741 — twenty-nine ships of fifty to eighty guns—was larger than any European force yet seen outside European waters. In the Seven Years War the British gained Canada, Dominica, Grenada, St Vincent, Tobago and Senegal from France and Florida from Spain. In that war Britain had displayed the global potential of its amphibious power by seizing Guadeloupe and Martinique from France, and, in just one year (1762), Havana and Manila from Spain. After the defeat of France and its allies in India in the 1750s and early 1760s, culminating with the capture of the leading French base, Pondicherry, in 1761, Britain was the major European power in the subcontinent. It was therefore best placed to make gains at the expense of native rulers and thus strengthen its position for future conflicts with other European powers. In 1764–5 the British East India Company gained Bengal and Bihar, making it the major territorial power in the lower Ganges valley: victory at Buxar (1764) was particularly important. The defeat of Tipu Sultan of Mysore in the Third Mysore War of 1790–2 led to modest gains in southern India; victory in another conflict in 1799 was followed by the acquisition of most of the region.

The American War of Independence led to a number of important British losses, including the Thirteen Colonies, Florida, Louisiana east of the Mississippi, Tobago, Minorca, and Senegal, but Britain retained Canada and its Indian and Caribbean possessions. Furthermore, it emerged from the conflict as still the leading European, and thus world, naval power, and this strength was emphasized in the post-war years as the Pitt ministry spent much on the navy, the alliance of the United Provinces (Dutch) was gained in 1787, and France became steadily weaker. Naval strength was complemented by overseas gains. Settlements were founded in Australia (1788) and Sierra Leone (1787) and the British presence in the Pacific increased. The way was thus prepared before the outbreak of the French Revolutionary War for the widespread acquisition of the colonies of other European powers that was to be such a marked feature of the period 1793–1815, a period in which Britain's gains included Ceylon, Mauritius, the Seychelles, Cape Colony, Trinidad, Tobago, St Lucia, and Guyana.

By 1789 Britain had recovered from its set-backs during the

American War and was clearly the strongest of the European maritime and colonial powers. Only thus was it able to resist Napoleonic France. In the long term, it was this feature of Britain's international history that was most distinctive and important. Aside from the myriad consequences for British society, economy, and public culture of this colonial and maritime success, the impact of empire as a proof of providential favour and a pointer to mission and purpose, themes that can readily be sketched out throughout the following century, there are also the consequences for the Continent. What has been recently termed the Napoleonic integration of Europe failed in large part due to British opposition. Thanks to its naval power, Britain was the leading commercial power and thus best placed to finance opposition to France. The political, cultural, and social consequences were crucial: the distinctive feature of European society was its division among a number of competing states, and this was to remain the case as industrialization, urbanization, mass literacy, and mass politics spread.

If British naval strength was a crucial feature of eighteenth-century warfare, and the most obvious expression of European technological and organizational attainment, it would be mistaken to see non-European peoples simply as responding to European imperialism. Indeed, in much of Asia the Europeans were still peripheral to power politics. This was particularly true of east Asia, continental south-east Asia, Persia, and much of central Asia.

The leading military power in Asia was China. Chinese military strength was based on a buoyant economy, a population that rose from 100 million in 1650 to 300 million in 1800, and a well-organized government presided over by able emperors. Under the K'ang-hsi Emperor (1662–1722) the Chinese conquered Taiwan (1683) and, after some hard fighting, Mongolia (1690–7). There was fresh fighting, with the Ili of western Mongolia, in the 1730s, leading to Ili submission in 1735. Military intervention in Tibet in 1718–20 led to the establishment of Chinese suzerainty. This was challenged by a rising in 1750, but that was suppressed and a protectorate was established. An Ili rising in the 1750s was also suppressed, and the imposition of Chinese control as far as Lake Balkhash was helped by the outbreak of smallpox among the native tribes. In 1758 the Chinese occupied Kashgar, and the conquests in eastern Turkestan were organized into the province of Sinkiang. Expeditions sent against Burma in 1766–9 were less successful, but in 1792 the Chinese advanced to Katmandu and the Gurkhas of Nepal were forced to recognize imperial authority.

A common military theme underlay many of the Chinese campaigns along with many of the other wars of the period: the struggle between the forces of relatively organized settled agrarian societies and nomadic or semi-nomadic peoples. The agriculture of the former supported larger populations and thus the resources for substantial armed forces and, thanks to taxation, for developed governmental structures. Nomadic and semi-nomadic peoples generally relied on pastoral agriculture and were less populous and their governmental structures less developed. They did not therefore tend to develop comparable military specialization, especially in fortification and siegecraft. Whereas the agricultural surplus and taxation base of settled agrarian societies permitted the development of logistical mechanisms to support permanent specialized military units, nomadic peoples generally lacked such units and had a far less organized logistical system: in war they often relied on raiding their opponents.

This organizational divide, which owed much to factors of terrain and climate, was linked to one in methods of warfare. Nomadic and semi-nomadic peoples exploited mobility and generally relied on cavalry, while their opponents put more of a stress on numbers, infantry, and fortifications. In certain areas, such as Amazonia, Australasia, California, the Pacific, and north-eastern Siberia, there was also a divide over the use of firearms, with the native peoples not employing gunpowder weaponry. Across much of Asia, however, and increasingly also in North America, the diffusion of firearms was such that both sides were thus armed. The Amerindians proved formidable foes. In combat they chose an opponent and aimed specifically at that individual. The Amerindian was more likely to be well practised in the aimed firing of his weapon than European regulars or colonists. He had probably spent years snap-shooting at moving animals, and could fire his gun from many different positions. In general, however, only the forces of the more developed societies deployed artillery, the production of which required what was for the period a sophisticated industrial base and the specialized use of labour.

The clash outlined above was widespread. It can be seen in the Russian attempt to subjugate Kamchatka and north-east Siberia, in the inroads of Nadir Shah of Persia and later the Afghans into northern India, in the struggles between the Turks and the Bedouin Arabs, and between the Russians and both the Cossacks and the Crimean Tartars, and in the maritime raids of the Bugis in the East Indies. In his *The Decline and Fall of the Roman Empire* (1776–88), Edward Gibbon claimed that 'Cannon and fortifications now form an impregnable barrier against the Tartar horse.' He indeed saw them as leading to a shift in global military power that had broken the cyclical process by which Europe was exposed to devastating invasions by 'barbarian' peoples from central Asia. Gunpowder had given infantry the advantage over cavalry and this was not simply a military shift, but also one that reflected, sustained, and developed a broader alteration in political and economic power. Although gunpowder weaponry had been effective on the battlefield from 1450 to 1520 on, in the eighteenth century this became increasingly apparent in Asia. British victories over Indian forces at Plassey (1757) and Buxar established their power in Bengal: skilful use of such weaponry compensated for the marked numerical inferiority of the British. Indian rulers, especially the Marathas and the rulers of Mysore, hastened to adopt tactics and weapons used by the European-officered forces.

Similarly, within Europe, the victory of armies using the concentrated firepower of disciplined infantry and their supporting artillery over more mobile forces that relied on the use of shock-power in attack can be seen in the British government's defeat of the Jacobite Scottish Highlanders at Culloden (1746): the Jacobite reliance on the 'Highland Charge' led to heavy casualties. The British artillery and infantry, under George II's second son the Duke of Cumberland, so thinned the numbers of the already-outnumbered advancing Highlanders that few reached the

British lines and those who did were driven back at the point of the bayonet. The general rate of fire was increased by the absence of any disruptive fire from the Jacobites, while the flanking position of the royal units forward from the left of the front line made Culloden even more of a killing field. Lieutenant-Colonel George Stanhope reported to his brother that the Highlanders 'attacked sword in hand most furiously', but were given 'the most infernal flanking fire that ever was given … I never saw such dreadful slaughter.' The battle was decisive in both a military and a political sense. The Jacobites were crushed as a military force, and the British War of Succession, which had begun with William of Orange's invasion of England in 1688, was brought to a close.

Yet, it would be misleading so to stress the role of firepower as to neglect the autonomous nature of much land warfare. Rather than think simply in terms of a scale of achievement based on standing armies and firepower tactics, it is more fruitful to explore different contexts, pressures, and opportunities. The role of environmental adaptation is crucial: European forces had only a limited impact in Africa and, more generally, the tropics, and the British were successful in India in large part because their army there was mainly composed of native soldiers: over 100,000 in 1782. Similarly, on Java, the Dutch used local troops, although their ability to operate successfully away from coastal areas was limited, as was shown clearly in the Third Javanese War of Succession in 1746–57, and in operations against Bantĕn in late 1750.

The position at sea was different. There the Europeans enjoyed an effective monopoly of long-distance naval strength. There were other naval powers, especially Oman in the Arabian Sea and off the coast of East Africa, but none matched the Europeans. Despite its enormous resources, the strength of its governmental structure, and its local naval capability, China did not continue the long-range naval activity it had displayed in the early fifteenth century. Similarly, neither Japan nor Korea repeated earlier episodes of naval activity. Turkish naval power was important in the Black Sea and the Mediterranean, but the Turks were defeated by the Russians in the Aegean at the battles of Chios and Chesmé in 1770 with the loss of twenty-three war-ships, and in the Black Sea at the battles of the Dnieper (1788) and Tendra (1790): the Turks lost twelve warships in the latter two engagements, the Russians only one. The naval forces of the North African powers, Morocco, Algiers, and Tunis, were essentially privateering forces, appropriate for commerce raiding but not fleet engagements.

Within Europe, with the important exception of the Turks who relied on cavalry rather than disciplined infantry firepower and linear formations, the crucial element in land warfare was the essential similarity in weapons systems and tactics between the powers. There were of course differences and these could bring success, most obviously the attack in oblique order developed by Frederick the Great of Prussia in 1745 in order to concentrate overwhelming strength against a portion of the linear formation of the opposing army. Frederick devised a series of methods for strengthening one end of his line and attacking with it, while minimizing the exposure of the weaker end. This tactic depended on the speedy execution of complex manœuvres for which well-drilled and well-disciplined troops were essential. It was used to great effect in defeating the Austrians at Leuthen (1757): Frederick, benefiting from the cover of a ridge, turned the Austrian left flank while a feint attack led the Austrians to send their reserves to bolster their right. The Austrian left crumbled under the oblique attack.

Nevertheless, there was nothing to match the differences in weaponry and tactics that existed on the global scale. This did not make a sweeping victory impossible, as the Russians demonstrated in 1710 when they overran the eastern Baltic territories of Sweden after Peter the Great's crushing defeat of Charles XII at Poltava the previous year: the Swedes suffered terrible casualties as their attack on a well-defended Russian position exposed them to the more numerous Russian infantry and artillery. However, such triumphs were generally due, not to distinctive tactics and weaponry, but rather to numbers of troops, more experienced and motivated soldiers, better generalship, especially in terms of the availability and employment of reserves, terrain, and the chance factors of battle. New weapons were developed:

the bayonet and the flintlock musket in the late seventeenth century, the elevating screw for cannon in the eighteenth; they
spread rapidly. The quick introduction of successful inventions
or modifications in most European armies suggests that the importance of a technological lead over potential opponents was
well recognized. The same can be said about tactical innovation.
Any advantage was temporary.

Frederick the Great's army is generally seen as representing the
pinnacle of warfare in the period 1660–1792, but this is misleading, not least because it has led to a neglect of such contemporary forces as the Austrians under Daun, the French under
Saxe, and the Russians under Rumyantsev. In addition, Frederician tactics were most suited to the particular environment of
east-central Europe, in particular the unenclosed tracts of Bohemia and Silesia. Their limitations were to be revealed in the
French Revolutionary War from 1792, in the face of troops
fighting in open order in the enclosed and wooded country of the
Austrian Netherlands and eastern France.

Prior to that conflict, the tactics of European armies had focused on the deployment of infantry in close-packed thin linear
formations. This was designed to maximize firepower. 'After a
terrible firing of near half an hour', the French front line retreated before the British at Dettingen (1743). Soldiers used
flintlock muskets equipped with bayonets and fired by volley,
rather than employing individually aimed shot. Despite the bayonets, hand-to-hand fighting on the battlefield was relatively uncommon and most casualties were caused by shot. The accuracy
of muskets was limited and training, therefore, stressed rapidity
of fire, and thus drill and discipline. Musket fire was commonly
delivered at close range.

The infantry was flanked by cavalry units, but the proportion
of cavalry declined during the century, as a result of the heavier
emphasis on firepower and the greater expense of cavalry. Cavalry was principally used on the battlefield to fight cavalry; advances against unbroken infantry were uncommon, although
infantry was vulnerable in flank and rear. At Dettingen French
cavalry attacked British infantry only to be cut to pieces by their
firepower: 'They rode up to us with a pistol in each hand, and

their broad swords slung on their wrists. As soon as they had fired their pistols they flung them at our heads, clapped spurs and rode upon us sword in hand. The fury of their onset we could not withstand so they broke our ranks and got through; but our men immediately closed [ranks] and turned about, and with the assistance of a regiment ... who were in our rear, the French horse being between both, we killed them in heaps.' Cavalry played a crucial role in some battles, such as the British victory over the French at Blenheim (1704) and the Prussian victory over the French at Rossbach (1757), but it was less important than in the past.

Unbroken infantry was more vulnerable to artillery, particularly because of the close-packed and static formations that were adopted. The battlefield use of artillery increased considerably during the century, and by the end of the Seven Years War Frederick, who had not, initially, favoured the large-scale use of artillery, was employing massed batteries of guns. Cannon became more mobile and standardized: the Austrians in the 1750s and the French under Gribeauval from the 1760s were the leaders in this field. Other technological developments lagged. Although the first use of a submarine occurred in 1776, when the American David Bushnell tried unsuccessfully to sink HMS *Eagle* in New York harbour, it was not followed up, and experiments with the use of balloons and rockets had to wait until the 1790s.

Nevertheless, it is important to note the economic strength underlying European military power. The main Russian state arsenal at Tula produced an annual average of nearly 14,000 muskets between 1737 and 1778. In the 1760s the French produced 23,000 annually at Charleville and Saint-Étienne. The construction of warships drew on an entire trading system of naval stores, and naval dockyards such as Portsmouth, Brest, Cadiz, and St Petersburg were among the leading economic units of the period. The ability to mobilize such resources reflected the nature of society: the combination of a cash economy, underemployment, and governments that enjoyed great authority over the bulk of the population, though not the social élite, created the context that allowed a major mobilization of manpower for war. This took a variety of forms, from the systems of general (though socially unequal) conscription in eastern Europe to the wartime raising of men by methods such as the press-ganging (forcible enlistment) of sailors in Britain, but the common element was the assumption that the bulk of the population would serve if required and on terms that they did not influence, and that their views on the purposes or methods of warfare would not be consulted. Mutinies were rare, and when they occurred, as in the Württemberg army in 1758, they were the product of a very serious collapse of trust. Desertion was far more common: a dangerous protest against often desperate conditions.

The lack of interest in the views of soldiers and sailors did not mean that rulers, generals, and admirals were oblivious to the condition of their troops and to casualties. They were well aware that poor food and accommodation could lead to debilitating diseases, and they knew that experienced troops could be difficult to replace. This could encourage caution in risking battle, although it is important not to exaggerate this. Field Marshal Wade, the commander of the British forces trying to stop the French advance in the Low Countries in 1744, reported, 'If we could have an opportunity of engaging them with an equal front, I think, we ought not to decline the combat. But to attack them at disadvantage, would be rash, since the loss of a battle would be attended with the loss of the country.' The dangers of defeat were indeed considerable, but that did not prevent the generals of the period from seeking victory. Thus, in the Low Countries there were major battles in 1745, 1746, and 1747: Fontenoy, Raucoux, Lauffeld, all three victories for the vigorous generalship of Marshal Saxe, the eldest illegitimate son of Augustus II of Saxony-Poland.

Nor was naval warfare necessarily inconclusive. At sea linear tactics were also adapted to maximize firepower: warships could not fire ahead and were thus deployed to fire broadsides against a parallel line of opposing vessels. The essential resilience of wooden ships ensured that they were difficult to sink by gunfire (although they would sink if shot detonated the magazine), but cannon firing at short range could devastate rigging and masts and effectively incapacitate the ships. Battles in which no ships were sunk could, nevertheless, be both hard-fought and decisive in their impact. For example, the Battle of Rügen (1715) between the Danish and Swedish fleets left the Danes able to cut the supply lines to Stralsund, the last Swedish base in Germany. The French inability to repair damage ensured that the action off Porto Novo in 1759 left the British in command of Indian waters.

There was certainly nothing inherently cautious about generalship at this time. The ethos of the period placed a great premium on bravery, boldness, and aggressive spirit in command on both land and sea. Although administrative aspects of command were known to be of great consequence, they did not determine the culture of warfare; just as the character of the domestic rule of kings was not decided by the financial issues that they knew to be important. There is a widely held but largely misleading view that pre-French revolutionary warfare was largely inconsequential in its results and limited in its methods. This is contrasted with the supposed nature of revolutionary warfare. But it is difficult to see how the conquest of the eastern Baltic by Russia or of Canada by the British in 1758–60 can be seen as inconsequential. Decisiveness is difficult to assess; a decisive outcome of one battle does not automatically stand for decisiveness with regard to the war itself. In the latter case, decisiveness today means weakening or destroying the armed forces of the enemy to such an extent that organized military resistance is no longer feasible. It can only be achieved if one side loses a battle to which it has committed the bulk of its military organization, and if the winning side has the available resources to take full advantage of the enemy's (often temporary) weakness. In the eighteenth century situations like this did take place, but they were exceptional. Exhaustion, political changes, or a gradual deterioration of the strategic balance were much more common reasons why wars came to an end, and that was certainly true of the Wars of the Spanish, Austrian, and Polish Successions and of the Seven Years War in Europe.

Yet decisive wars did occur, for example the Anglo-Bourbon sphere of the Seven Years War; while victories in battle might be crucial in giving rise to political circumstances leading to a negotiated peace: they were decisive in framing the parameters of peace. The warfare was far from limited. Casualty rates could be very high: at Blenheim (1704) there were over 30,000, besides prisoners, out of the 108,000 combatants; and at Malplaquet (1709) a quarter of the Anglo-Dutch-German force. The exchange of fire between nearby (50–80 yards) lines of closely packed troops, the battlefield use of artillery, firing for example case-shot, against such formations, and cavalry engagements relying on cold steel all produced high casualties. Cornet Philip Brown wrote of Dettingen, 'the balls flew about like hail', and of Fontenoy, 'I admire and adore that kind Providence who hath been my great protector and preserver of my life and limbs during such a cannonading of nine hours as could not possibly be exceeded ... there were batteries [of cannon] continually playing upon our front and both flanks.' Soldiers were often brutal in their treatment of each other and of civilians, although, in general, the treatment of prisoners improved. Nevertheless, the storming of fortifications was sometimes followed by the slaughter of the defenders, as when the French stormed the Dutch fortress of Bergen-op-Zoom in 1747. In general, warfare was more savage both when regular forces fought irregulars and in eastern Europe, where religious and ethnic differences increased hatred.

War also had considerable impact on the civilian population. Aside from conflicts involving guerrilla warfare, for example in Spain, Hungary, and the Tyrol in the 1700s, the burden of military demands, particularly for men and money, pressed hard on the people of Europe. These demands did not, however, challenge the social system. The expanded armed forces of the period developed in a fashion that did not challenge the social reality of societies organized around the principles of inegalitarianism and inheritance. Larger armies brought more opportunities to nobles, who benefited both from the assumption that they were naturally suited for positions of command and from the fact that this was usually the case. Thus, armies were not forces 'outside' society, but rather reflections of patterns of social control and influence and the beliefs that gave cohesion to them. In their complex balance of discipline and the maintenance of military cohesion by less coercive methods, armed forces also mirrored society. The restriction of recruitment to men reflected normal social values.

Another important aspect of pre-revolutionary warfare was its variety. The standard images can be misleading. Alongside the classic Frederician battles, in the decades before the outbreak of the Revolutionary Wars, there was not only Russian and Austrian warfare with the Turks, but also the experience of conflict against irregulars in Europe — the French conquest of Corsica in 1768–9 which influenced Napoleon — as well as warfare outside Europe. The War of American Independence involved operations by British, French, and Spanish land and naval forces.

The American war was the first example of a transoceanic conflict fought between a European colonial power and subjects of European descent, and the first example of a major revolutionary war, an independence struggle in which the notion of the citizenry under arms played a crucial role. The creation of a new state was accompanied by that of a new army. Although many of its commanders were from the wealthier section of society, the social range of American leadership was far greater than that in European armies.

However, it would be misleading to exaggerate the novelty of the war. It was essentially fought on terms that would have been familiar to those who had been engaged in the Seven Years War. The American response to battle was to adopt the lines of musketeers of European warfare: this was the course advocated by George Washington, the commander of the Continental Army. The alternative strategy advocated by Major-General Charles Lee, which would have centred on irregular warfare, particularly the avoidance of battle, was not adopted by Washington. However, American tactics could pose major problems for the British. At the Battle of Long Island (1776) Captain William Congreve of the British artillery recorded,

I found the enemy numerous and supported by the 6-pounders [cannon]. However, by plying them smartly with grapeshot their guns were soon drawn off but the riflemen being covered by trees and large stones had very much the advantage of us, who were upon the open ground … had not the light infantry of the Guards … come up in time I believe we should all have been cut off.

In positional warfare the Americans could be defeated, their troops outflanked, as at Long Island and Brandywine (1777), or their strongholds captured, as with Fort Washington (1776) and Charleston (1780). However, more mobile American units could operate with deadly effect. At Bemis Heights in September 1777 the riflemen under Daniel Morgan concentrated on picking off British officers. The British commander, General John Burgoyne, wrote subsequently,

The enemy had with their army great numbers of marksmen, armed with rifle-barrel pieces: these, during an engagement, hovered upon the flanks in small detachments, and were very expert in securing themselves and in shifting their ground. In this action, many placed themselves in high trees in the rear of their own line, and there was seldom a minute's interval of smoke in any part of our line without officers being taken off by single shot.

The diversity of warfare prior to 1789 poses a question mark against any attempt to offer a simplistic account of the warfare of this period in order to suggest a contrast with its revolutionary and Napoleonic successors. Consideration of pre-revolutionary warfare also indicates the military consequences of governmental resources. In the case of the conquest of Corsica, France could mount the logistical effort required to deploy a considerable force, 24,000 men in early 1769, on an island where provisions were in short supply. It could also sustain defeat and yet return to the attack, proceeding systematically to obtain a planned military outcome. The construction of roads was symptomatic of the entire process. The French army had the engineering skill and manpower to create roads that could serve direct military purposes—the movement of men and, more crucially, artillery and wagon-borne supplies—as well as extending the range of routine authority. The growing role of the state in warfare, gradually replacing the semi-independent military entrepreneurs of earlier days, was readily apparent. Recruitment in Prussia and Sweden offers examples of early forms of compulsory service that affected society as a whole. This was particularly necessary for poor states; their wealthier counterparts could concentrate on raising the funds to purchase military service.

Centrally directed resources and power applied at long range. Neither was new, but the increasing scale of both, demonstrated clearly in the Seven Years War and the American War of Independence, explains why it is unhelpful to think in terms of military revolutions in 1560–1660 and 1792–1815 with an intervening period of stagnation, indecisiveness, and conservatism. It may be more helpful to think neither of revolution nor of revolutions, certainly between the deployment of gunpowder weaponry in long-range warships and on the battlefield in the early sixteenth century, and the sweeping organizational and technological changes of the nineteenth century. But that does not mean that warfare in the mean while was static. As far as the pre-revolutionary eighteenth century was concerned, the armies and fleets of the period were capable of competing for major goals. The fate of North America was settled, French hegemony in western Europe was resisted, the Turks were pushed back from much of Europe, and the Chinese greatly extended their power over non-Chinese peoples. Elsewhere, war led to the rise of powers, such as Afghanistan under the Durranis, Burma under Alaungpaya, and Gurkha Nepal, and the decline of others, such as Mughal India. War was central to the history of the period and to the experience of its peoples and it was far from inconsequential.

4

The Nation in Arms I

The French Wars

ALAN FORREST

A revolution which in 1789 held out the promise of a new civic order based on ideas of liberty and equality had by 1792 launched France into over twenty years of foreign war, broken by only one substantial truce, signed at Amiens in 1802. It was the French who took the initiative in declaring hostilities against the Emperor—'the King of Bohemia and Hungary'—on 20 April 1792, though it might be argued that the lengthy political manœuvrings of the early 1790s made conflict inevitable. In July Austria was joined by Prussia, eager to take advantage of what was perceived as French weakness, and on 11 July the *patrie* was formally declared to be *en danger*. By the spring of 1793 France was also ranged against Spain on land and Great Britain at sea. The First Coalition was formed at a moment when France also faced serious internal divisions and was rent by counter-revolutionary movements in the Vendée and Brittany. National survival had become the Revolution's foremost priority.

The early campaigns in the north and east went very badly for the French, leading to invasion scares in Paris and other cities, as French fortress towns along the Belgian frontier, like Longwy and Verdun, fell in rapid succession to the Austrians and Prussians. Soon, however, the French revolutionary armies recovered their morale, crossing the middle Rhine to capture Mainz and Frankfurt; thwarting the Prussians at Valmy when their army was threatening to overrun northern France and attack Paris;

and—far more significant in military terms—defeating the Austrians in open battle at Jemappes, near Mons. The year 1793 again opened badly. Abroad French arms suffered an embarrassing series of defeats, and confidence was dealt a severe blow when Dumouriez, the hero of Valmy and Jemappes and a former minister, crossed into Allied lines and denounced the revolutionary cause. At home, too, the armies faced a new threat with the rising of the Vendée in March, which deflected men and materials from the frontiers at a particularly sensitive moment in the war. But these were to prove temporary setbacks. By the summer of 1794 the Republic's armies had once again freed French territory from invading forces, turning the war around both on the Spanish frontier and in the north. In the Vendée, following the horrors of Turreau's *colonnes infernales*, the Convention pursued a more conciliatory line of pacification, leading to a truce in February 1795 between Hoche and Charette at La Jaunaye. After a famous victory over the Austrians at Fleurus the French were once again in a position to advance into Belgium, and in the spring of 1795 the Allies made peace. By the terms of the Treaty of Basle the Prussians withdrew from the war, ending the Coalition and leaving the French free to impose their terms on the Dutch and to annex Belgium.

With the defeat of the First Coalition the first phase of the war was effectively over, even if the peace treaty provided no more than a short respite from fighting. Once again it was the French who opened hostilities, taking advantage of their rivals' exhaustion and internal divisions. This time Prussia was neutralized, leaving only Britain and Austria as major players. But the real distinction between this and the earlier phase of the war was that the French were now on the offensive, aiming to build on their acquisitions and to gain further footholds in Germany and Italy. The *patrie* was in no sense in danger, despite the ill-fated British attempt to land an army on the Quiberon Peninsula and support the royalist insurgency in Brittany in June 1795. The campaign quickly developed into a war of conquest against France's traditional enemies, a war whose main objectives were the annexation of territory and the seizure of supplies, food, and booty. The Directory showed scant interest in the original revolutionary

rhetoric, preferring to defend its military gains by further conquests and by creating a series of defensive buffer states to the
east. As for the generals, they enjoyed more and more independent power as French armies moved further away from the
metropole. In Italy, especially, Napoleon Bonaparte relished this
new authority, taking advantage of the Directory's unpopularity
at home and imposing the Treaty of Campo Formio on the Austrians in October 1797 with only the minimum of consultation
with Paris. By February of the following year French troops were
in Rome; in May Bonaparte left for Egypt, capturing Malta on
the way. And though the Egyptian campaign might seem to have
halted his success—he was forced to leave a large part of his
army behind in North Africa—Bonaparte could point to his victory at the Battle of the Pyramids and to his substantial cultural
and scientific achievements in Egypt. French imperial aspirations
seemed to know no bounds.

After 18 Brumaire—the military coup (1799) by which Bonaparte overturned the Directory and came to power—war continued unabated, with France ranged against yet another
European alliance, this time of Britain, Russia, and Turkey. The
renewal of hostilities with Austria was not long delayed, leading
rapidly to a great French victory at Marengo. Indeed, the whole
economy was increasingly dependent on the efficient workings
of the war machine. Those who longed for peace—and there
were many in the French armies who dreamed of returning to
their families and ending the cycle of war to which they were exposed—were increasingly frustrated. And when a peace was finally signed in March 1802, it lasted only fourteen months,
during which France was already gearing itself for the next campaign. In 1804 Napoleon became hereditary Emperor; in May
1805 he had a second coronation, as King of Italy in Milan; in
November he entered Vienna, and by the following year he was
in Berlin. The years from 1805 to 1807, indeed, represent the
height of his military glory. Napoleon inflicted defeats on the
Austrians at Ulm, on the Russians and Austrians at Austerlitz,
both in 1805; in 1806 he dissolved the Holy Roman Empire before continuing his subjection of the Prussians at Jena and Auer-
stadt; in 1807 his defeat of the Russians at Friedland led to a

Franco-Russian alliance at Tilsit. By 1807 the revolutionary 'Grande Nation' had been transformed into an instrument of French hegemony covering half of Europe. France itself consisted of 130 departments; and the various sister-republics of the 1790s had become fully fledged kingdoms and principalities, often ruled by Napoleon's younger brothers and subject to the overall control of the Emperor. It had been done at little cost to the French exchequer: the armies lived off the land and plundered freely, so that the campaigns in Prussia and Poland actually made money for the government. Only Britain, whose naval victory at Trafalgar had destroyed the French fleet, remained unbeaten.

But after 1807 the tide began to turn. Napoleon's Continental System did not prove the effective weapon he had hoped against British trade. Increasingly his armies got bogged down in the Peninsula, where they faced implacable guerrilla attacks as well as field warfare. A major Austrian offensive in 1809 led to embarrassment for Napoleon at Essling, and, though his improvisation on the battlefield produced a victory at Wagram, it was gained at a terrible price. The year 1810 brought the breakdown of the Franco-Russian alliance on which so much of Napoleonic foreign policy was based. In June 1812 he launched his ill-fated Moscow campaign, sending a vast army of over 600,000 men into the field without first securing his Spanish frontier. It was an unmitigated disaster. The Russians drew the French further and further into Russia, without ever offering the opportunity of battle, and by the time they reached Smolensk, 400 miles across the frontier, the *Grande Armée* had been crippled by cold, fever, and exhaustion. The rump of the army got to Moscow, but fires and the fear of being cut off persuaded them to retreat. The Russians did not need to fight. Cossack cavalry cut down stragglers and harassed the French forces, while the snow and ice did the rest. Only some 60,000 weary troops crossed the Beresina, where the *Grande Armée* was effectively destroyed. Seeing their opportunity, the Coalition reformed, first Prussia, then Austria joining forces with Russia to ensure Napoleon's defeat. In response Napoleon had to raise a new army, much of it recruited in France itself. At

Leipzig on 16–19 October 1813 he faced overwhelming odds: an allied army of 320,000 men outnumbered him by two to one, and in the battle which followed the French were routed. Murat started to negotiate for peace: the long years of European warfare were finally at an end.

But was this in any sense a 'revolutionary war', the product of a specifically revolutionary context? Among contemporaries there were many who argued that war was a natural development, since a Europe of kings and emperors could not coexist with a revolutionary, and by 1792 a republican, nation-state. France's nearest neighbours had made little secret of their dislike of the Revolution: the Emperor of Austria, in particular, offered shelter to noble and royalist *émigrés* from France, who held court in Turin, Koblenz, and in the various principalities along the Rhine waiting for the day when they could invade France and restore the King's and their own authority. The Declaration of Pillnitz and the Brunswick Manifesto made no secret of the dreams harboured by monarchical Europe, while rumours circulated of treaties and secret deals struck between foreign rulers and the French royal family. Panic spread fast, reaching even the Assembly, where Brissot argued passionately that the Revolution must either be expansionist or be destroyed. At a popular level, too, fear of invasion and of a noble backlash contributed to the anger felt by the Parisian crowd and helped to radicalize opinion in the capital. On 18 January 1792 the Girondin deputy Vergniaud pronounced war to be inevitable. 'Our Revolution', he declared, 'has spread the most acute alarm to all the crowned heads of Europe; it has shown how the despotism which supports them can be destroyed. The despots hate our Constitution because it makes men free and because they want to reign over slaves.' And though Robespierre himself was among those who warned against premature militarism, many historians of the period have followed Vergniaud in seeing the war in ideological terms. The *patrie* was in danger; the French people had to fight if they were to survive, and the entire political order depended upon their efforts. In that sense the Revolutionary Wars were different in kind from traditional eighteenth-century conflicts between monarch and monarch, since in the event of victory one side would now seek to destroy the institutions of its enemy, the French imposing a liberal constitution on the Austrians or Prussians, and they in turn restoring the Bourbons to the throne of France. And it was the whole French people who were at war, the nation in arms defending its liberties and values when they were under attack. In the process the Revolution itself became more narrowly nationalistic, shedding its universal claim to represent free men wherever they might live and claiming that liberty was the prerogative of the French. This was the view of revolutionary leaders like Dubois-Crancé, who argued that every citizen was now a soldier and every soldier a citizen. It was brilliantly propounded by Clausewitz in the nineteenth century, when he wrote that 'war had again become an affair of the people, and that of a people numbering thirty millions, every one of whom regarded himself as a citizen of the state'.

Others, however, have come to question this highly partisan view of revolutionary warfare. The language of revolutionary politics was, after all, intensely rhetorical. It praised individual sacrifice and made heroes out of boy victims like Bara and Viala, who died in battle so that France might be free. It insisted that the war was a war of liberation, a crusade against the forces of monarchical darkness. And the revolutionaries were always tempted to believe their own propaganda. But there was no reason for their opponents to believe it. Conservative and counter-revolutionary writers poured scorn on the republicans' claims, while the Emperor and other crowned heads of Europe had their own political agenda. If they fought the French, they certainly did not do so for new and radical reasons; they regarded war as eighteenth-century rulers consistently had regarded it, as an extension of diplomacy to be used at moments when it appeared likely that they could win and press home their advantage. And France's own motives for declaring war were not very different. In 1792 each side saw the other as seriously weakened—the French looking to the moral strength provided by their cause, the Austrians to the sorry state of France's armies and their depleted officer corps. They went to war for very much more conventional reasons than has often been supposed.

If the origins of the Revolutionary Wars were tactical rather than ideological, what of the manner in which they were fought? It is undoubtedly true that the revolutionary armies brought strengths of enthusiasm and commitment unparalleled in the regiments of the *ancien régime*; and that these armies were spurred on by political speeches and republican slogans. During the Jacobin Republic, in particular, they wore overtly republican uniforms, sang political anthems, and rallied to anti-royalist battle-cries. Jacobin deputies from the Convention were sent on mission to the armies, adding political commitment to their military ambition. As Minister of War, Bouchotte encouraged the troops to read the most radical political opinions of the day, distributing newspapers to the armies at public expense. Even the newspapers of Marat and Hébert were sent out to the garrisons in the north and the east; in all, some 1,800,000 copies of Hébert's *Père Duchesne* were purchased by the War Ministry for the education of the troops. Soldiers were encouraged to attend political clubs in nearby towns, and some units formed their own, specifically military clubs inside the army. They were citizens of the French Republic, and were entitled to have access to the public sphere. Indeed, the fact that they were willing to sacrifice themselves for the common good, and to accept restrictions on their freedoms in order to secure the freedoms of others, should make them privileged citizens, quite unlike the cannon-fodder who, the revolutionaries held, made up the armies of tyrants.

This vision was not entirely propagandist. There was a period of the 1790s when ideology did count for a great deal, when officers were chosen as much for their ideological commitment as for their technical expertise, and when the men were fighting to save the *patrie en danger*. At the height of the Jacobin Republic, the suspicion of the officer class remained intense, and those appointed to senior ranks were subject to political scrutiny from Paris. The government had good reason to be suspicious. In the *ancien régime* only the sons of nobles had been eligible for officer rank in the army, with the result that the officer corps had often seemed hermetically cut off from the men it commanded. Loyal to the King rather than to the Revolution, over one-third of French officers had resigned their commissions or passed into emigration by 1791; and some of the best-known generals, among them Lafayette and Dumouriez, had defected to the enemy. The revolutionaries were entitled to believe that they needed officers they could trust, whose commitment was to the Revolution and the nation rather than to the person of the king. With the army plunged into war from 1792, they also needed substantial numbers of officers quickly; they chose them, as they were bound to do, from among the non-commissioned officers of the line regiments, the only men they had who had some knowledge of tactics or had had some degree of battle experience. The NCOs themselves were made answerable in a different way, to the men in their units for whose lives they were responsible; in 1794 sergeants and corporals were elected by the men in the ranks, who, the Jacobins believed, would choose leaders in whose skills and character they had confidence. The Revolution would have an army that was compatible with its political ideals.

But these considerations were soon overtaken by the desire for technical excellence and the thirst for victory. The period of democratic reforms in the army corresponded to the years when domestic politics were still fuelled by a certain optimism. Under the Terror these ideals became tempered by fear and the need to conform. Military justice was swift and exemplary. Officers were subject to political surveillance and poor military judgement might easily be mistaken for treason; in 1794 the *Armée du Nord* alone lost three of its commanders to the guillotine. In the ranks, such offences as looting, profiteering, and desertion to the enemy were severely punished, and special military tribunals handed down revolutionary justice in the camps. With the fall of Robespierre in 1794, much of the ideological intensity of the Revolution was lost. The Thermidorians were fearful of agitation and crowd violence; Paris in particular was tightly policed. The Directory, with its more limited constitution, concentrated on securing political order and repressing opposition from both the left and the right of the spectrum. Politicians became more concerned with routine administration and the creation of a more professional civil service. In the armies this aim was reflected in a more single-minded professionalism, whereby competence and military skill were rewarded and political views counted for less. The Directory was interested in success rather than ideology, to the point where former Jacobins retired from domestic agitation to make a new career for themselves in the military, where they could continue to serve France without the risk of persecution. Increasingly, too, the generals demanded that they be left to exercise their own strategic judgement, free from political interference. By 1796 the political *commissaires* with the armies were being withdrawn.

Virtue, in other words, had given way to pragmatism long before the overthrow of the Directory by Napoleon's coup of 18 Brumaire, which can best be seen as the continuation of that process. Napoleon's military dreams were certainly not dictated by ideology, but rather by a thirst for glory and a desire to impose his empire across the entire continent. Yet at no time did he renounce the meritocratic principles that had marked the revolutionary years. His own career had been made possible by the Revolution, his rapid promotion aided by the patronage of the Director Barras. Like Hoche, Augereau, and others, he had been given command while he was still young and enthusiastic, without regard to seniority. As the son of an obscure Corsican noble family, he could never have aspired to such elevation under the *ancien régime*; it was to the Revolution, and to the haemorrhaging of the officer ranks by death and emigration, that he owed his career, and he never sought to deny it. Both as First Consul and, after 1804, as Emperor he continued to encourage talent and service to the state. He did this both through decorations like the Legion of Honour and through the offer of political power. Both were primarily reserved for the military. Of 38,000 men promoted to the Legion of Honour between 1802 and 1814, all but around 4,000 were soldiers. Similarly, it was from the ranks of the military that were drawn the Marshals of France, who stood at the very apex of the Napoleonic élite. They were chosen on merit, drawn, as Louis Bergeron has shown, from all social backgrounds: some were nobles, some sons of administrators, while a few genuinely sprang from the popular classes of society (Ney was the son of a barrel-maker, Murat of an innkeeper, Augereau of a domestic servant, and Lefebvre of a non-commissioned officer in the army). The presence of such men among the new imperial élite communicated an important political message. It emphasized that it was state service, and especially army service, that unlocked the door to social pre-eminence, thus allowing Napoleon to perpetuate the myth that every soldier carried a marshal's baton in his kitbag. It also completed the transformation, in John Lynn's phrase, from an army of republican virtue to an army of honour.

This raises, of course, a very central question. How far was the revolutionary army ever an army of virtue, with a motivation that was distinct from other armies of the time? The revolutionaries insisted that their soldiers fought out of conviction, and that, unlike those who had been bribed and press-ganged into service under the Bourbons, their troops had volunteered for combat. This was true up to a point. The volunteers raised in 1791 did respond with enthusiasm to the call to arms, some departments even asking permission to form extra battalions rather than turn away men anxious to serve their country. But in 1792, when the Assembly issued a second appeal, the response was much less reassuring, with many rural areas failing to meet their quotas and villages offering signing-on bounties to encourage the faint-hearted. In 1792 the levy took place at the height of the agricultural year, when peasant boys were needed on the land; war was looming, and the reality of soldiering more imminent; above all, the majority of those whose patriotism drove them to volunteer had already done so a year earlier. Thereafter, though the Revolution maintained the pretence that its men were volunteers, most were in name only. The great levies of 1793, the *levée des 300,000* in the spring and the *levée en masse* in the autumn, were achieved by applying local quotas which communities had to meet; they increasingly used ballots to decide who would serve, and those who were designated, those who drew a 'mauvais numéro', were often reluctant soldiers. By 1799, the year of the next large-scale recruitment, the government had taken a further step away from voluntarism by introducing annual conscription. Under the terms of the Loi Jourdan, all young men of military age had to present themselves for medical examination, and be ready, should the army need them, to serve. It was by the use of conscription, lighter or heavier in accordance with the needs of the military, that men were found for Napoleon's campaigns.

The numbers involved were vast by the standards of the day. In 1794 the revolutionaries sought to create an army three-quarters of a million strong, and, though the generals could never say with certainty how many men were under their command, they numbered, for a brief period at least, some 700,000. This compared with a royal army under Louis XVI which consisted of 182,000 regular and household troops, augmented in time of war by around 72,000 militiamen. During the Directory, when the armies were almost constantly in the field, the War Ministry worked to targets set by the decrees of 11 and 31 October 1795 — 323,000 infantry of the line, some 97,000 light infantry, 59,000 cavalry, 29,000 artillery, and 20,000 engineers. It was to restore these norms that conscription was deemed necessary, since by 1799 numbers had fallen to around 230,000 and desertion was widespread. Napoleon, of course, made still greater demands: between 1800 and 1814 he called up over 2 million Frenchmen, or around 7 per cent of the total population. This was a massive exercise in mobilization, involving a huge investment in policing and repression to drive reluctant conscripts to the draft and to prevent rural communities from harbouring deserters. That it was largely successful, that Bonaparte could muster his *Grande Armée* for Moscow in 1812, is a reflection more of the success of the imperial administrative system than of the popularity of the army. In many rural areas, in particular, where there was no tradition of soldiering, and where the labour of the able-bodied was sorely needed on the farm, young men of military age were assured of food and work in their communities. In such regions—most notably in the southern Massif Central and the Pyrenean foothills—recruitment was widely regarded as an unwelcome intrusion by the state. Visits by gendarmes, routine punishments for mayors, and the billeting of troops on recalcitrant parents were all essential parts of the recruitment process.

The creation of a new kind of army was not achieved without a substantial restructuring of the line army inherited from the *ancien régime.* The case for radical reform was widely accepted. The line regiments, noble-led and raised in the old provinces of France, might be expertly trained in tactics and the use of weapons, but they were poorly motivated and had little commitment to the national cause. Some troops followed their officers into emigration; others deserted in 1789 to join the cause of the Paris crowd; and 1790 was marked by serious mutinies over pay and discipline. The most damaging of these, at Nancy in August, saw three regiments, including one of Swiss mercenaries, in armed revolt against their noble officers, and the suppression of the mutiny brought the army close to civil war. With the raising of new volunteer units, the situation became intolerable, since the line troops and the volunteers had different values, were paid at different rates, and held each other in open contempt. It was clear by early 1793 that a political solution was required, and quickly, since the army was already involved in combat, and confusion threatened. That adopted by Dubois-Crancé, and supported by Robespierre, was for a form of *embrigadement*, whereby the old regiments would be dismantled and new units created, bringing the young volunteers and the veterans of the line under the same officers and the same discipline. Regiments were to be abandoned: the new units, or *demi-brigades*, combined two battalions of volunteers with one of regulars, and promised a high degree of manœuvrability.

The result, at least on paper, was an army of 196 *demi-brigades* of infantry, each with a company of artillery attached, plus units of light artillery, engineers, and cavalry. This, the revolutionaries insisted, was a new kind of army, one that could draw on its reserves and use the strength of numbers—of the *masse*—in battle. The army of the 1790s, on which Napoleon would build during the Empire, was particularly strong in infantry and artillery, and it emphasized the benefits of speed and flexibility. The role of the infantry was crucial, deployed in lines and columns that could take the enemy by surprise; and the infantry would assume the main burden of combat throughout the 1790s. The cavalry, in contrast, was assigned a lesser role than it had played during the eighteenth century, largely because horsemen were expensive to train and the exodus of noble officers had affected the cavalry regiments more than others. But the Revolution did not neglect its cavalry. If its performance remained generally mediocre in the early Revolution, by 1796 both Bonaparte in Italy and Hoche in the Sambre-et-Meuse were making use of horse for skirmishing. More important, however, was the artillery, an arm which was regarded as less feudal and more committed to the new order. The numbers of artillery doubled during the 1790s, and horse artillery was used for the first time. Another innovation was the establishment of separate sapper battalions: in the *ancien régime* the only engineers had been officers, whereas now the army had its own units of sappers and miners. These were changes which gave the armies greater freedom of manœuvre, though they were less revolutionary than has often been suggested. The armies were limited by the logistical restrictions of the day. In particular, the cannon used by the artillery still had a very limited range, and supply was in the hands of independent army contractors whose efficiency was limited by the carts, horses, and mules that assured much of the provisioning in the field.

A mass army composed of young and often raw recruits demanded a rather different deployment from that of the smaller and more seasoned eighteenth-century armies, though again the extent of this change can be exaggerated. Despite the increased pool of soldiers on which the army could draw, there was no dramatic increase in the size of armies in the field, and the tactics deployed in many of the early campaigns were drawn straight from eighteenth-century military manuals. During the 1790s the combined totals of combatant troops in each engagement were actually smaller than during the Seven Years War, though the fact of having so many soldiers in reserve meant that fresh manpower was always available to replace those who died in battle. And since troops were less highly trained than in the *ancien régime*, it followed that they were more dispensable and that pitched battles could be entered into more frequently, and with less concern for loss of life. But it was Napoleon, not the revolutionary generals, who made real use of the *armée de masse*. The average number of French troops engaged in any single battle rose substantially from around 50,000 in 1793 and

1794 to over 80,000 at the height of the Empire, which, of course, forced France's enemies to follow suit to avoid being overwhelmed. The result, during the Napoleonic Wars, was a period of mass battles and heavy casualties, with armies launching rapid attacks with the aim of destroying their opponents. Generals would deliberately seek to engage with the enemy, whereas previously they had been more concerned to manœuvre and conserve their resources.

In tactical and strategic matters the Revolution built on the achievements of the eighteenth century, most notably by Guibert in infantry tactics and Gribeauval in the deployment of artillery. This was unavoidable since during the Revolution itself there were few major technological advances which could have transformed the art of war. Indeed, one of the most serious problems for the French was to find enough weapons to allow their soldiers to defend themselves. In particular, there were too few firearms to go round, and many of those were in poor condition. The emphasis on the bayonet and even, in moments of crisis, on the pike—the *arme blanche* of republican mythology—was more the result of necessity than of strategic planning. Where the revolutionaries did leave a more permanent legacy was in the field of military organization. They recognized that, with such large numbers under arms, better co-ordination and staff work were essential to efficiency. The staff officer was now a highly trained professional soldier, able to take decisions in the field, and most armies were provided with a permanent general staff. And it was recognized that individual battalions could not achieve the degree of integration that was required if armies were to regroup and disperse effectively. Hence the revolutionaries grouped their battalions in larger units—brigades, divisions, and corps—which brought together the different military skills, infantry and cavalry, artillery and engineers. By this means they sought both to draw supplies from a wide area and to achieve optimal flexibility in the field. As a consequence they were able to change tactics quickly, using infantrymen as skirmishers to engage the enemy and regrouping in dense mobile columns to press home an attack. In both the Revolution and Empire most battles started as engagements between two forces of infantry, usually advancing and defending in line formation. But the French learned to break quickly, reforming in columns so as to concentrate large numbers of troops in a single area of the battlefield. Throughout the Napoleonic period the quick interchange of line and column remained a central aspect of French soldiering, with columns used to intimidate and bludgeon the enemy's forces or to provide surprise assaults from the flanks.

Much of the success of the *Grande Armée* was due to Napoleon himself, a commander of genius who understood the benefits of swift, decisive attack and who was capable of bold improvisation on the field of battle. He knew how to talk to soldiers and how to motivate them; his presence in a battle, Wellington once remarked, made the difference of 40,000 men. Napoleon was, of course, head of state as well as commander-in-chief: the French armies never experienced the problems of a divided command which at times undermined their opponents. In the *Grande Armée* of 1805–7 he commanded in person, and his mastery of the detail of each campaign was impressive. In essence, Napoleon was not a tactical innovator; his success was due to speed of execution and excellent co-ordination. When his forces were outnumbered by the enemy, he would seize the initiative and strike a blow to the heart of the opposing army, so as to divide that army into smaller units when he could then attack on the wings. When he did enjoy numerical superiority, he preferred to employ his *manœuvre sur les derrières*. His front lines would try to distract the enemy while the rest would be directed on a circuitous route until they could block the enemy's lines of communication and attack from the rear. Variations of this tactic were used nearly thirty times by Napoleon, most notably at Ulm, Jena, and Marengo. Critics have suggested that perhaps he was too intuitive, too impulsive to have a clear plan of any campaign, that, in Owen Connelly's phrase, he only 'blundered to glory'. But that is to underestimate his ability to turn a battle by inspirational leadership, abruptly changing his plans to take advantage of others' mistakes. More serious is the charge that, by concentrating all the decision-making in his own hands, he failed to share authority or to encourage initiative in his closest commanders. In the words of Marshal Berthier, 'the Emperor needs neither advice nor plans of campaign', merely a precise execution of his orders. When he himself was not present—and he stayed with the *Grande Armée* throughout most of the war, leaving other campaigns, most notably in the Peninsula, to others—the quality of leadership was often mediocre, a fact which helped to turn the war in the Allies' favour.

But there are other explanations. With time the other European powers began to respond to the military innovations made by the French. For even if neither the revolutionary nor the Napoleonic armies quite conformed to the Clausewitzian model of absolute war, it was clear to France's opponents that the French enjoyed substantial advantages. Their youthful mass armies responded to revolutionary propaganda and to the ideal of the *Grande Nation*, and they showed more enthusiasm for their cause than did the soldiers of Russia or of the Austrian Empire. They were also fighting as free men, the beneficiaries of the social and political reforms of the Revolution, and this fact was not lost on the rest of Europe. Their enthusiasm even survived the professionalization of the French army after 1795 and the increased use of foreign troops under the Empire, and it was not matched in the other European armies of the day. The Austrian army, for instance, was expensive and highly bureaucratic, commanded by ageing generals whose tactics were quickly overtaken by the French, and until 1807 it was operating according to the stilted and over-cautious *General-Reglement* of 1769. Its Prussian counterpart seemed ossified around the regulations imposed by Frederick II. Combat doctrine and tactics were largely Frederician, and as the new King Frederick William II had little interest in the military, there was no pressure from above to change. Senior commanders were opposed to reform, looking back to the glory days under Frederick the Great, and they increasingly came to form a military gerontocracy: by 1806 of 142 generals in the Prussian army, 60 were over 60 years of age, 13 over 70, and 4 in excess of 80. As for the common soldiers, over half of them—some 200,000 in the 1790s—were foreign mercenaries who had no patriotic commitment to the state they served. In the Russian army, too, there was an unbridgeable gulf between officers and men. Officers were drawn both from the provincial gentry and from foreigners, with many of the Russian officers untrained young aristocrats who had been appointed because they were part of the Tsar's entourage. The soldiers were conscripted serfs, selected by local authorities to meet their recruitment quotas. They were robust, often brave, but they had little commitment to their cause: obedience and discipline were ensured by frequent and savage beatings.

Faced with the revolutionary and Napoleonic armies, and awakened by the reality of military disasters against them, reformers began to gain ground in the royal courts of Europe. Increasingly they realized that meaningful military reforms could only result from wider reforms to the social and political fabric. The example of Britain showed how much the military machine could benefit from economic investment and industrial growth, and French organizational and tactical changes demonstrated the need for greater social fluidity in their own societies. In Austria the Archduke Charles launched a series of reforms between 1805 and 1809 to improve the combat performance of his army, restructuring the general staff, dismissing inadequate officers, concentrating the artillery, and using the cavalry in a strike role. These reforms helped the Austrians to recover; but the Austrian army remained what it had traditionally been, an instrument of dynastic ambition rather than a mass army on the French model. Prussia also tried piecemeal reforms—notably the institution of divisions—in a bid to meet the French on even terms, but after the crushing defeats of 1806 it was clear that only major social and organizational changes would suffice. Inspired by Scharnhorst and the Military Reorganization Commission, the Prussian army was restructured, with authority vested in the state rather than company commanders, old officers dismissed or forcibly retired, and administrative decisions passed to a new centralized War Ministry. Careers were thrown open to talent, and promotion no longer granted on the basis of seniority. And from 1813 general staff officers were assigned to every general, forming the basis of a new Prussian command structure. The benefits would be clear at Leipzig. As for the Russians, they, too, were shaken out of their complacency by defeats at Austerlitz, Eylau, and Friedland, and after 1808 undertook wide-ranging reforms of both their infantry and their artillery, reforms which, combined with Kutuzov's charismatic leadership and the vagaries of the weather, contributed in 1812 to the destruction of the *Grande Armée* in Russia.

In Spain Napoleon ran into opposition of another kind: the draining, deadly attacks of the guerrilla fighter, a form of warfare which the French armies and administrators were ill-equipped to overcome. That was not, of course, all: the French were also faced with the British and with regular Spanish troops, but it was the guerrilla fighting, the determined resistance of ordinary Spaniards, that created the 'Spanish ulcer' from which Napoleon's imperial ambitions never fully recovered. It is true that he was not blessed with the most astute subordinates in Spain, and that the counter-insurgency measures adopted by his marshals were both too brutal and too indiscriminate to maintain the allegiance of local people. Only in Aragon did Suchet achieve some temporary success, but it was a success based on force, and the Aragonese soon renewed their resistance. It is true, too, that in the winter of 1808-9, when Bonaparte briefly took personal charge of operations in Spain, he subdued the Spaniards and drove out the British expeditionary force under Sir John Moore. But again this proved to be a brief respite in a long and sapping conflict, in which the guerrillas came to assume the mantle of Spanish national spirit against an unwelcome foreign invader. To win such a war Napoleon's armies would have to crush national resistance and impose foreign rule on a hostile population. The guerrillas enjoyed popular support, and they demoralized the French, picking off stragglers—as many as a hundred men a day—as well as disrupting supplies and thus contributing to the high sickness rate of the French forces in Spain. In the end it was the combined efforts of the guerrilla fighters and British and Spanish regulars which secured victory, Wellington's triumph at Vitoria in 1813 eliminating French rule in Spain and leaving Napoleon's Spanish army in tatters. The cost of the Peninsular War to France was high: some 3,000 million francs and as many as 300,000 lives. It was the cost of a serious miscalculation on Napoleon's part. His vaulting ambition and his determination to secure a final victory over Great Britain had led him to exaggerate his military capabilities. He was well able to fight on one front, particularly when he himself could be present to take charge of the campaign. But to open up two fronts—Moscow and the Peninsula—was a cardinal error, one which left his army exhausted and led directly to his fall after the defeat at Leipzig.

5
The Nation in Arms II

The Nineteenth Century

DAVID FRENCH

Before the French Revolution military service had been the hard lot of a minority of Frenchmen. After 1794 it became, at least in theory, an obligation placed upon all physically fit male citizens. The Revolution established a clear link between each citizen's civic rights and his military responsibilities. In return for the political rights and freedoms which the state now guaranteed each of its citizens, every citizen incurred the obligation to fight, and if necessary die, in defence of his nation. But if it was now the duty of every citizen to serve, each now had the same opportunity to rise from the humble rank of private to the lofty eminence of general. The officer corps, which had hitherto been largely the preserve of the nobility and gentry, were thrown open to commoners of competence and courage. The outcome was the astonishing series of victories which France's armies won between 1794 and 1812.

In the course of the Napoleonic Wars France's enemies discovered that they had perforce to follow the French example if they were to save themselves, but they did so with the utmost reluctance. The 'nation in arms' required monarchs to transform their subjects into citizens, and that was a revolutionary doctrine which was not in the least palatable to kings whose thrones had been rocked by the excesses of French radicalism. It was therefore hardly surprising that after Waterloo the ruling princes of continental Europe shared two common concerns, to place the

French Revolution and the Napoleonic Wars behind them and to re-establish a political and social order based upon wealth, status, and birth. They tried to shun adventurous foreign policies for fear that they might upset the peace of Europe and bankrupt their treasuries. They believed that if military effectiveness on the scale of the French Revolution demanded a radical transformation of their societies, the price was simply not worth paying. This meant that after 1815 most European armies quickly returned to an eighteenth-century pattern. They consisted of officers drawn from the aristocracy and gentry. The rank and file were long-service professional soldiers. They were kept apart from the wider community lest too close an association with civilians might lead to them becoming tainted with the dangerous doctrines of liberty and equality. In the eyes of Europe's princely rulers, political loyalty was more important than military effectiveness.

In continental Europe conscription remained the bedrock of the armies of the major powers. Although there was no uniform period of service across the Continent, most governments agreed that service for only a couple of years would not suffice. It did not give the army time to inculcate sufficient military discipline into the troops to make them impervious to dangerous political notions. Thus in Russia peasants were initially conscripted for twenty-five years, although this was later reduced to fifteen. In France soldiers were required to serve six years with the colours followed by another six years with the reserve. But in 1824 the government abolished the reserve and increased the period of regular service to eight years. In the polyglot Austrian Empire the length of service varied between the different regions of the Empire until it was standardized in 1845 at eight years. And to safeguard their political reliability, great care was taken to ensure that troops of one nationality were sent to garrisons in a different part of the Empire. Throughout Europe the well-to-do could avoid serving in person by the simple expedient of buying a substitute. Shortage of money meant that it was unusual for the state to call upon all of its eligible citizens to serve.

Thus after 1815 monarchs tried to create armies which would be obedient to their will and which would act as a counterweight to the corrosive force of liberalism. As the events of 1848–9 showed, they succeeded. The Prussian army followed its King's example; briefly it acquiesced in the revolution in Berlin but when it received new orders it marched back into Berlin to crush the revolution, and was hailed by the middle class as the bringer of order and discipline. In the following year it operated as the spearhead of the counter-revolution in Saxony and Baden. The Austrian army, with the exception of some Hungarian, Italian, and Viennese units, also remained loyal to its Emperor and acted as an effective tool of the counter-revolution. In the deeply confused political situation in France between 1848 and 1852 the army supported what it saw as established authority.

It was no accident that the most respected military thinker of the early nineteenth century was the Swiss soldier Antoine de Jomini. Jomini was popular because in his *Précis de l'art de la guerre*, first published in 1837–8, he was able to reassure nervous readers of a conservative inclination that in reality the art of war as practised by Napoleon had differed little from that practised by Frederick the Great. Both men had owed their success to their own genius. Both had been concerned to outmanœuvre their enemies by threatening their lines of communication, flanks, and rear. Both had won their wars by delivering superior numbers of their troops at the decisive point. Napoleon had won his victories because he recognized these timeless and 'scientific' military principles more clearly than any of his contemporaries, and not because he mobilized the dangerous forces liberated in French society by the Revolution. Jomini thus tried to abstract the art of war as practised by the French between 1794 and 1815 from its revolutionary political roots. He gave comfort to the autocratic monarchies of Europe by implying that warfare was a gigantic game of chess, played by princes and armies, and divorced from any disturbing political and social implications.

Jomini remained a popular and influential interpreter of Napoleonic warfare down to 1914. His emphasis on the need for states to use overwhelming force aggressively to achieve decisive victory underlay the war plans of every great power on the eve of the First World War. But by the 1870s a second theorist who was to wield almost as much influence had emerged, the Prussian solider-philosopher Karl von Clausewitz. After their crushing defeat at the hands of Napoleon in 1806, the Prussians had gone further than any other European power in aping French forms of military organization. But soon after the end of the war the Prussian nobility began to re-establish its dominance over the officer corps. By 1819 the independent *Landwehr*, designed to mobilize the military potential of the population, was subordinated to the regular army and its revolutionary potential was thus undermined. The reformers who had championed it were left to rot in obscurity, few men were conscripted, and the organization itself was allowed to fall into decrepitude. Even so, it remained one of the cornerstones of bourgeois liberal hopes and a bulwark against the influence of the professional officer corps in Prussian society. The gulf between the two organizations widened in the generation after 1815 as the regular officer corps came increasingly to be dominated by the Prussian nobility. The liberalism of the former sat uneasily with the reactionary attitudes of the latter.

Alone amongst the European powers after 1815, Prussia retained short service in the regular army. Every conscript was required to serve for two years with the colours before passing into the reserve. From 1859 the Prussian King, Wilhelm I, assisted by his Minister-President Otto von Bismarck and his Minister of War Albrecht von Roon, carried out a series of military reforms which ignited a major constitutional crisis in Prussia but which ensured that the Prussian army, unlike its opponents, could balance the needs of military efficiency with those of political reliability. The result was that, when the two powers went to war against each other in 1866, although Prussia had a population only half that of Austria, the Prussian army could mobilize 245,000 men compared to Austria's 320,000. Furthermore, although the Austrians began to mobilize first, the Prussians could mobilize faster. The secret of their success lay in the fact that the Prussian army was divided in peacetime into corps and divisions. Each was organized on a territorial basis and each was self-sufficient in all arms and support services. Even so, the mobilization of the Prussian forces and their concentration on the battlefield was attended by a good deal of confusion. Prussia's victory at the decisive battle of Königgrätz (Sadowa) on 3 July 1866 owed at least as much to the superiority of their infantry, armed with breech-loading 'needle guns' with which they could out-shoot the muzzle-loaders of the Austrian army, as it did to superior Prussian organization.

After 1866 all of the states which composed the newly established North German Confederation adopted the Prussian military system. Every German was liable to serve—with no possibility of a substitute—for three years with the colours (reduced to two years in 1893 to increase the turn-around of trained soldiers) followed by four years in the reserve and five years in the *Landwehr*. The latter was no longer a middle-class militia. It became a home defence force and reserve for the regular army. The liberal opposition in the Prussian Parliament had fought against these reforms in the 1860s, but their resistance collapsed when the new army gave them what they most wanted, a unified Germany. The army of the new German Empire combined short-service conscripts, supported by a large reserve of men who had passed through the regular army, transported to war by railways. The whole was organized by an élite of general staff officers, who, because they had received a common training in a common doctrine, could usually be relied upon to react in a predictable manner in whatever crisis they found themselves.

Even after the rapid defeat of Austria's long-service professional army at Königgrätz by Prussia's short-service conscripts, many defenders of the military *status quo* were not convinced of the superiority of the Prussian system. France's collapse in 1870 left no further room for dispute. In 1870, contrary to the arguments of the defenders of professional armies, the Prussian conscripts proved able to out-march, out-shoot, and out-fight their professional opponents. Just as they had in 1866, the Prussians won in 1870 because they mobilized more rapidly. The French professional army was outnumbered three to two in the opening clash of the war. After a series of costly battles on the Franco-German frontier in which both sides suffered heavy casualties, the French were forced to retreat. Following the Battle of Gravelotte on 18 August, an entire French army under Marshal Bazaine withdrew into the fortress of Metz. Napoleon III, with an army of 100,000 men, marched to their rescue, but the Prussians trapped him between the Belgian frontier and the River Meuse. At the Battle of Sedan on 1 September 1870 the French Emperor was forced into a humiliating surrender. This disaster precipitated a revolution in Paris and the establishment of the Third Republic. The Republican Government of National Defence promptly raised some half a million poorly trained and ill-equipped new troops, but their patriotic ardour proved to be no match for the well-trained Prussians. In May 1871 the new Republic had no option other than to agree to the humiliating terms of the Treaty of Frankfurt.

The Franco-Prussian War marked the end of small, long-service professional armies on the continent of Europe. After 1871 the Prussian system, an active army of short-service conscripts supported by a large trained reserve and controlled by a highly trained élite of general staff officers, became the model for every major continental European army. Henceforth the concern of every one of Europe's great powers was to develop a military system which would enable them to mobilize the largest possible army as quickly as possible on the outbreak of war. Each power believed that its security ultimately rested upon the size of its armed forces and the speed with which they could be placed in the field.

But each of the European powers was careful to adopt the Prussian model in a way which suited its own local conditions. Military reforms had begun in Russia in the 1860s in the wake of the Crimean War. The Franco-Prussian War gave them an extra impetus, but in Russia, the most autocratic of all of the European autocracies, the ideal of the nation in arms could not be pushed very far for fear of encouraging political unrest. In 1874, under the guidance of the War Minister Dimitrii Miliutin, the existing system of long service with the colours was replaced by six years with the colours and nine years with the reserve. In theory men of all social classes could be conscripted but the rich and well educated were allowed to provide a substitute or to serve for shorter periods. It was only after the Russo-Turkish War of

1877–8 that the Tsarist government established army corps and reserve units to hasten the process of mobilization. Some small steps were taken towards making service in the army resemble a patriotic duty rather than the penal servitude it had so often resembled in the past. But right down to 1914 the Russian state denied so many civic rights to so many of its citizens that, in reality, Russia was a nation in arms only in numerical terms.

In Austria-Hungary, the new Dual Monarchy, which was itself the product of the defeat of 1866, decided to divide each annual cohort of recruits into two contingents. They did so partly because of a lack of money and partly because they were afraid of encouraging nationalist opposition, One contingent served for three years with the colours, seven in the reserve, and two in the *Landwehr*, but the second group avoided regular service completely, serving for twelve years in the *Landwehr*. Furthermore, as a concession to national particularism, the Austrian and Hungarian halves of the monarchy each controlled its own *Landwehr*. It was only after the war for Bosnia-Hercegovina (1876–8) had demonstrated that existing mobilization plans worked too slowly that the army took the momentous decision to place the needs of military efficiency before those of political reliability. Henceforth it stationed the bulk of its regiments in the districts from which they drew their recruits.

The French had resisted universal military service when Napoleon III tried to foist it upon them shortly before the Franco-Prussian War. In 1868 the legislature had agreed that each annual contingent of recruits would be divided into two groups; the first would serve five years with the regular army, but the second were to serve for only five months. But they had acted too late and it was not until after the national humiliation of 1870 that the Third Republic adopted a variant of the Prussian system. The French followed the Prussian example by dividing their army into regionally based army corps to enable it to mobilize rapidly. But what they could not agree upon was the length of service with the colours each conscript should perform. The left favoured a short period of service with the regular army. The socialist politician and writer Jean Jaurès, alarmed that a long-service professional army might pose a danger to the democratic foundations of the Third Republic, drew inspiration from the *levée en masse* of 1793. He argued that a similar force would serve to unify army and nation, rather than set them at odds. In peacetime France should maintain a small army which was little more than a training cadre. Conscripts should swiftly pass through it and take their place in the reserve, ready to be mobilized when a grave national crisis arose. In peace such a force would pose no serious threat to France's neighbours, but in wartime it would be a formidable bulwark to defend the nation. If men served in the regular army for too long, the Jaurians argued, the result would be to militarize civilian society. But the right held that if the period of regular service was too short, conservative professional soldiers and the parties of the right retorted, the conscript would not have absorbed sufficient military training to make him an effective soldier. The development of modern weapons, particularly long-range rifles, machine-guns, and rifled artillery, would create a wide fire-swept zone on the battlefield. Poorly trained citizen-soldiers were only capable of fighting behind defences. Only troops who had undergone a long period of training would be capable of fighting in the dispersed formations made necessary if they were to survive. The argument was not finally settled until 1913, when the National Assembly decreed that all conscripts should serve for three years before passing into the reserve.

Italy's military reforms were dominated by three considerations: shortage of money, the unwillingness of the government of the newly unified Italian state to encourage the revolutionary aspects of a nation in arms, and its inability to decide just what was the secret of Prussia's success. The left ascribed it to the effectiveness of universal service; soldiers pointed to the effectiveness of the general staff; and conservatives highlighted the importance of obedience to the state. The outcome was that, while paying lip-service to the ideal of the nation in arms, Italian military organization fell far short of the reality. In the early 1870s three categories of conscripts were introduced, the first serving for three years with the colours before passing into the reserve, the second serving with the reserve but for nine years, and the third receiving only some elementary training. In order to help dissolve Italy's intense regionalism, the Italian army was divided into a dozen corps. However, unlike their Prussian counterparts, they were not each based on a single region but drew their recruits from every part of Italy, a policy hardly calculated to assist speedy mobilization in wartime.

Of all of the European great powers, only Britain failed to adopt military conscription after 1871. Its reluctance to do so was based partly upon political scruples and partly upon military necessity. Until 1916 the strength of liberalism remained too great to permit any British government to force its citizens to don uniform. But of equal importance was the fact that the British army existed not to fight neighbouring armies in Europe, but to garrison a world-wide empire. That made short service on the Prussian model impractical. Newly trained conscripts would hardly have time to become acclimatized to service in a distant imperial outpost before the time had come for them to take their discharge. But even the British saw that there were some lessons to be learned from Prussia. Between 1868 and 1874 Edward Cardwell, Gladstone's Secretary of State for War, transformed the regular and reserve forces. He reduced the length of service for the regulars, created a reserve for the regular army, and established localized recruiting areas by associating regular army units with reserve units of the militia and volunteers.

The mass conscript armies which emerged in Europe in the final quarter of the nineteenth century had an overt function, to preserve their states against external aggression, but they also served a secondary purpose. They were one of the vehicles through which, in the forty years before 1914, much of European society was impregnated by a mixture of militarism and bellicose nationalism. A brief analysis of the size and growth of defence spending gives some evidence of the growing importance which states placed on their armed forces. Between 1874 and 1896 defence spending in Germany increased by 79 per cent, in Russia by 75 per cent, in Britain by 47 per cent, and in France by 43 per cent. On ceremonial state occasions monarchs everywhere abandoned their sober civilian frock coats and paraded themselves in public in the gorgeous dress uniform of their favourite Guards regiment. Members of royal families received a military education and royal princes occupied senior posts in the army and navy. But, with some notable exceptions, such as the Duke of Cambridge in Britain or the Grand Duke Nicholas in Russia, royalty used its association with the armed forces to justify its own existence, not to promote the professional efficiency of the services.

It was symptomatic of the high regard in which the German army was held that in 1891 the Kaiser could insist that 'The soldier and the army, not parliamentary majorities and decisions have welded the Empire together. I put my trust in the Army.' The Franco-Prussian War brought the German army a social cachet amongst middle-class liberals which it had never before enjoyed. Henceforth the army possessed more prestige than any other German institution. Militarism—in the sense of an exaggerated veneration for the army—permeated the German middle classes to an extent unknown elsewhere. Possession of a reserve officer's commission became a badge of social acceptability in Wilhelmian Germany. The readiness with which many Germans were willing to accept orders from anyone in a military uniform was shown all too clearly in 1906 in the small town of Köpenick. An ex-convict was able to commandeer a group of soldiers, arrest the town's Treasurer and Burgomaster, and abscond with a sum of cash from the town hall, and all because he was dressed in the uniform of an officer in the prestigious 1st Foot Guards.

Late nineteenth-century militarism had its worrying as well as its comic aspects. The most portentous of these was the manner in which war came to be seen as a vital feature of the intercourse of nations. Writers like Colmar von der Goltz insisted that war was the way in which nations transacted business. The best-selling author General Friedrich von Bernhardi argued that it was a Christian virtue. Helmuth von Moltke, the Chief of the General Staff who masterminded Prussia's strategy during the Wars of Unification, denounced the idea of perpetual peace as a silly dream and insisted that war developed nobility of spirit, self-denial, courage, and the spirit of self-sacrifice. And lest these notions be thought to be purely German phenomena, it is worth remembering that it was a respected British periodical, the *Nineteenth Century*, which shortly before 1914 asserted that 'the only court in which nations' issues can and will be tried is the court of God, which is war'.

Conscript armies were not universally successful in carrying out their function of acting as a 'school for the nation'. Indeed, far from acting as unifying national totems, some armies served to reflect and widen existing social and political divisions. Throughout Europe armies continued to recruit most of their junior officers, and nearly all of their senior officers, from a narrow social spectrum of landed gentry and aristocracy at a time when the numbers and self-confidence of the bourgeois were growing and when socialists were forming trade unions and mass political parties. Most Frenchmen saw their army as a tool for national retribution against Germany abroad and an instrument of moral regeneration at home. But they could not agree upon the moral and political values they wanted the army to inculcate into each generation of conscripts. Left-wing republicans were deeply suspicious of the largely Catholic, conservative officer corps of the Third Republic. By contrast, conservative regular officers believed that they were the disinterested guardians of France's national interests. The trust which many ordinary Frenchmen reposed in their army was shattered in the 1890s by two scandals. In 1891 a politically ambitious young general, Georges Boulanger, shot himself after he had been found guilty *in absentia* of plotting against the government. Three years later a guilty verdict, based on the flimsiest of evidence, was passed by a court martial on a Jewish officer, Alfred Dreyfus, for allegedly spying on behalf of Germany. 'L'Affaire Dreyfus' became the most divisive *cause célèbre* of the Third Republic. It pitted socialists and radicals who believed that the army's treatment of Dreyfus violated the most sacred tenet of French nationalism, the rights of man, against anti-Semites, monarchists, Catholics, and senior army officers who insisted that no civilians had the right to question the inner workings of the army, the very institution upon which France depended for its national independence. After 1900 it was not France's national independence which was called into question, but the independence of the army, as a new War Minister, General André,

tried to republicanize the officer corps by the judicious use of secret files on officers and the relegation of those whose political
views or religious persuasion suggested they were out of sympathy with the Republic.

Even in Germany the prestige which the army enjoyed did not
prevent a series of squabbles between the government and the
Reichstag over the military budget. However, by 1888 the army
had all but freed itself from what little control Parliament had
once exercised over it, and an increasingly wide gap began to
open up between nation and army. As Germany became increasingly industrialized, and as the Reichstag came to include a
growing number of Social Democrat deputies, the constitutional
position of the army became the cornerstone of the struggle
against the Emperor and his conservative supporters and the left.
The War Minister had little authority over the army and control
over it fell into the hands of the Kaiser, his own military cabinet,
and the general staff. The growing divorce between army and
civilian society was further accelerated by the army's reluctance
to look outside the ranks of the *Junker* class for its officers. Jews,
peasants, and socialists were barred from obtaining commissions. This social exclusivity ran counter to Germany's growing
need for a larger army to face the threat from the Dual Alliance,
formed by the combination of France and Russia in 1894. The
division between army and nation was also widened by the
army's strong preference for recruits from rural areas on the
grounds that they were less likely to be infected by socialism. Indeed, the army was so apprehensive of socialist infection that
after the 1905 Russian Revolution it began to develop an urban
counter-insurgency doctrine.

As in France, the Italian state also attempted to portray the
army as the embodiment of patriotic virtue, the defender of domestic order, and the schoolmaster of the nation. But Italy was a
poor country, officers disliked acting as schoolmasters, and the
impact of such a policy was vitiated by a continuing lack of
funds. That meant that the Italian state could only afford to call
up a fraction of the men who were eligible for military service
each year. By 1880 each of the major continental states had one
army corps for every 2 million inhabitants. On that basis Italy

should have had sixteen corps; in fact it had only ten. Regional distinctions remained, and by 1907 the King could only lament that the Italian people still had 'to be educated, to be taught habits of discipline, obedience and orderliness' and patriotism.

Paradoxically, given the nature of the Tsarist regime, the Russian officer corps was perhaps the most democratic, in terms of its social composition, of that of any of the major European armies. In the decade before the First World War nearly 40 per cent of officers below the rank of colonel were drawn from the ranks of the peasantry or lower middle class. But a conflict developed within the officer corps between non-aristocratic 'modernizers', concentrated disproportionately in the infantry, and nobles, who continued to dominate the higher ranks of the field army. Their rivalry was considerably to hamper the Russian army's performance in the opening campaigns of the First World War.

It is debatable whether even in numerical terms late nineteenth-century European armies really did constitute 'nations in arms'. No government could afford to conscript all of its eligible manpower. France was unusual in that, following the passage of a new military service law in 1913, it began to conscript nearly 80 per cent of men of military age. But few generals wanted to implement universal service in its literal sense. They were afraid that if they did so they would only succeed in creating a semi-trained and poorly equipped horde incapable of withstanding the rigours of real war. In Russia the army could hardly stress the idea that conscripted peasants had civic responsibilities when they and their families were denied many civic rights. Conscription did little to break down the national and linguistic barriers in the polyglot Austro-Hungarian army. There is some truth in the suggestion that conscript armies assisted the process of industrialization. Each year they took a new cohort of young peasants and factory workers and the period which they spent with the colours accustomed conscripts to three facets of the capitalist system: regimentation, obedience, and low wages. But this was never their overt purpose, and many conservative generals, in Germany and France in particular, objected that time spent on civic education intended to wean the rank and file from socialism could be better spent on military training proper.

The German Wars of Unification left other legacies to Europe. When Moltke confessed that Clausewitz's posthumous master-piece, *On War*, had done more to shape his military outlook than almost any other book, he ensured the widespread dissemination of some of its author's ideas. Clausewitz was no bookish pedant. He had fought throughout the wars against the French Revolution and Napoleon and his book was a distillation of his own experiences. He examined not only the fundamental nature of war, but the relationships between war and politics, between soldiers and their civilian leaders, the function of strategy, and the nature of battle. Above all, he emphasized that war was a rational instrument of national state policy. But Moltke's generation read Clausewitz through the distorting prism of Jomini's ideas and thought they found in *On War* a close echo of those ideas. Strategy was the use of battles to achieve the purpose of war, and the best strategy was to be strong everywhere and above all at the decisive point. Victory in war came not through the occupation of a slice of the enemy's territory, but through the destruction of his army. What Moltke and many of his contemporaries ignored was Clausewitz's insistence that war was an instrument of policy and had to be kept subordinate to political ends. For them, war was merely the inevitable fate of mankind, and it was their job to wage it as efficiently as possible.

And after 1870 military efficiency was equated with rapidity of movement. The speed of Prussia's victory was attributed to the use the Prussian army made of the German railway system. The Wars of German Unification seemed to indicate that victory in the next major war would go to the powers that could mobilize their troops fastest and equip them with the very latest in military technology. The industrial revolution revolutionized military logistics and it was fitting that Britain, where industrialism began, should also have been the first country (in 1830) to experiment with using railways to transport troops; however, others quickly followed its example. In 1835 the Prussian army examined the feasibility of moving troops by rail and four years later it carried out its first experiment, transporting 8,000 men from Potsdam to Berlin. The Austro-Prussian and Franco-Prussian wars vividly demonstrated the advantages which the

Prussians had reaped by their ability to get their troops to the battlefield first. But although railways revolutionized strategic mobility, tactical mobility was not similarly revolutionized until the widespread introduction of the internal combustion engine during the Second World War. Beyond its railheads the Prussian army subsisted in much the same way that its forefathers had done when they fought Napoleon I; it lived off the land. It was a lesson which the German army was to relearn all too painfully during its opening campaign in France and Belgium in 1914.

But European general staffs learned precisely the wrong lessons from the German wars when they concluded that they indicated that the next European war would be over quickly. That was something which anyone with the perception to look across the Atlantic at the example of the American Civil War might have recognized. The North won the war which began in 1861 because it was better able to sustain the cost of a prolonged war of attrition. It had more men, and so it could pay the human cost of a series of ferocious battles which took place in northern Virginia, as each side threatened its opponent's capital. It had a larger industrial economy, so it could provide the logistical paraphernalia which its burgeoning army required and create a fleet which blockaded and slowly strangled the economy of the Confederate states. And finally, in 1863–4 President Lincoln found two generals, Ulysses S. Grant and William. T. Sherman, who were capable of employing this superiority effectively. In July 1863 Federal forces defeated what might have been a decisive Confederate offensive at Gettysburg in Pennsylvania. In the mean time in the west Grant captured the key fortress of Vicksburg and split the Confederacy in half. In 1864–5 Grant commanded the Federal troops attacking the Confederate capital, Richmond, and occupied the bulk of the Confederate armies. Sherman was thus enabled to march from Chattanooga to Atlanta and thence to the sea, before turning north in a sweeping manœuvre during which his troops deliberately devastated the Confederacy. The last Confederate army surrendered in April 1865. The war should have provided plenty of lessons about how belligerents would be compelled to mobilize all of their national resources if they were unwilling to accept the outcome of the first battles as final. In the same way, Sherman's march through the Confederacy pointed to the full awfulness of total war for soldier and civilian alike. But many European commentators followed Moltke and dismissed the war as having little relevance to their situation. They believed that it had become prolonged because of the unpreparedness of the belligerents and the professional incompetence of their soldiers.

Only a handful of observers foresaw that the next great war would be a test of national will and resources rather than a conflict between armies. In 1898 a Polish banker and railway magnate, Jan Bloch, produced a five-volume study, *The Future of War in its Technical, Economic and Political Aspects*, suggesting that such a war would ultimately end when one of the belligerents collapsed because of famine and revolution at home. One of the few soldiers of note to agree with him was the British imperial proconsul Lord Kitchener. Far from being merely a great poster, as Lloyd George was later to claim, Kitchener was a prescient strategist who recognized in 1914 that a conflict between the European great powers, far from being a brief affair, would degenerate into a long war of attrition.

An effective army needed more than properly trained soldiers led by competent officers; it also needed the most modern weapons and the most modern transport system. The arms races of the kind which Europe experienced in the Edwardian era were not autonomous phenomena. They reflected the fact that European society on the eve of the First World War was becoming increasingly bellicose. The fact that the Franco-Prussian War had been decided by the outcome of the battles on the frontier remained one of the cardinal lessons of that war which every general staff took to heart. Consequently each of them strove hard to persuade their political masters, and through them the public at large, of the overriding need to prepare in peace for war. They were assisted by right-wing pressure groups like the German *Kriegerbund* and *Wehrverein* and the French *Ligue pour la service des trois ans*. Their ideas were disseminated by a combination of the cheap jingoistic press and the popularization of the ideas of writers like Darwin and Nietzsche. Together they helped to promote the notion that war was part of the natural order of the world.

For almost the whole of the period from 1871 to 1914 the French and Germans vied with each other to ensure that they had a superior standing army and greater numbers of reservists than their rival. Even in liberal England the 'yellow press' pioneered by Lord Northcliffe promoted the policies of the Navy League and the National Service League. They argued in lurid terms that if Britain did not spend more money on its navy and adopt conscription for home defence its days as a great power were numbered. Each of these organizations claimed to be above politics and to place the national interest above mere party politics. In reality they abhorred parliamentary democracy, they tried to militarize the youth of their nation, and they directed their appeal towards the working class by highlighting the catastrophe which would overcome them if their country was defeated. Only patriotic self-sacrifice and discipline, they insisted, could save their country from moral and political decay. In 1912 a retired general, Friedrich von Bernhardi, published a bestselling book, *Germany and the Next War*, in which he argued that the German people must be roused and made ready for the coming war. In France, after the Agadir Crisis of 1911, a rising tide of chauvinism emerged, fed by books, newspapers, and right-wing politicians, a tide of ideas which became even more noticeable during the parliamentary debates on the introduction of the Three-Year Service Law in 1913.

Arms races did not inevitably lead to war. For two decades after 1884 Britain, France, and Russia engaged in a naval arms race, but they never came to blows, and the competition was ended peacefully by the Anglo-French Entente of 1904 and the Anglo-Russian agreement of 1907. Nor were all late nineteenth-century wars caused by arms races. The Russo-Turkish War of 1877, the Sino-Japanese War of 1894, the Spanish–American War of 1898, and the two Anglo-Boer Wars of 1881 and 1899–1902 were caused by combinations of territorial ambitions, dislike of the other state's ideology, and political disagreements, not fear that the other side was arming too quickly.

But it would be equally mistaken to suggest that the Edwardian arms race played no part in heightening international tension in the decade before 1914. It did contribute towards the belief that war was inevitable. The pace was set by Germany, in an attempt to shift the world balance of power in its own favour. German naval expansion provoked a response in Britain, and after 1906 the two powers competed to see which of them could produce the larger fleet of dreadnought battleships. But in 1912 the Russians, rapidly recuperating from their defeat at the hands of the Japanese in Manchuria in 1904–5, threatened to create an army which would dwarf that of Germany. This provoked the Germans into increasing spending on their own army in a bid to keep pace, and that in turn prompted the French Three-Year Service Law.

There were countervailing voices, and armies were not universally popular. Following the humiliating defeat at the hand of the Abyssinian Emperor Menelik at the Battle of Adowa in 1896, Italy was beset by a wave of anti-militarism, peasant risings, socialism, and republicanism which shook the prestige of both the Italian Parliament and the monarchy. Conscripts did not always join the colours willingly. Many young Italians and Russians emigrated to the USA rather than undergo compulsory military training. The growing cost of defence was one reason why most European states witnessed the growth of a vociferous peace movement in the decades before 1914. In Britain and America some liberals argued optimistically that international arbitration and the growth of free trade would one day make war redundant. Socialists were amongst the most vociferous critics of armies and militarism. In Germany the Social Democratic Party attracted a growing number of votes and by 1912 it had become the largest party in the Reichstag.

But nowhere was the conviction that the next great international crisis could only be resolved by fighting held with more determination than amongst the senior officers of the Habsburg army. In 1907 Conrad von Hotzendorf, chief of staff since 1906, wanted to take advantage of the Messina earthquake to attack Italy. On that occasion he was dissuaded. But seven years later, following the assassination of the heir to the imperial throne by Serbian terrorists, tragically, no one could dissuade him. Convinced that Austria-Hungary was essential to the fulfilment of their own ambitions in the Near East, Germany's political and military leaders gave the Austrians their full support in their determination to punish Serbia in a short and limited war. But they had miscalculated Russia's determination to stand by its Balkan protégé, and Russia's decision to mobilize on 30 July 1914 began a chain reaction which led to a world war. The first link in this chain was forged in 1890 when the German government abandoned Bismarck's plan of isolating France by remaining on good terms with Russia *and* Austria. The German general staff then drew what was, for them, the inescapable conclusion that war with France was inevitable, and when France and Russia became allies they faced the nightmare prospect of a two-front war. Convinced that the vast spaces of European Russia made a swift victory against Russia impossible, they planned to knock France out first before turning against Russia. Confronted by powerful French fortifications along the Franco-German frontier, Graf Alfred von Schlieffen, the Chief of the General Staff between 1891 and 1906, drew upon Moltke's strategic legacy and decided to outflank them by marching through neutral Belgium. France was to be annihilated within six weeks so that the German army could then turn eastward to deal with the Russians. On 3 August 1914 Germany declared war on France and two days later Britain declared war on Germany, ostensibly to uphold Belgian neutrality, in reality to ensure that Germany did not crush Russia and France, secure hegemony over western Europe, and tilt the balance of power decisively against Britain.

Europe did not plunge into war in 1914 because the great powers had become locked in an arms race. But their competition to create ever more formidable armies and navies did make war more likely by encouraging each of them to fear their neighbours, and did ensure that, once war had begun, it would be appallingly destructive. Thanks to the spread of industrialization throughout Europe, weapons developed out of all recognition in the half-century before 1914, and in doing so they transformed the battlefield. The introduction of smokeless powder bolt-action magazine rifles, quick-firing artillery, and machineguns meant that the tactics, and indeed the uniforms, of 1815 would have been suicidal a hundred years later. The brightly coloured uniforms of the first half of the nineteenth century had been replaced by drab camouflage greys and browns, but the range and increasing lethality of weapons confronted tacticians with a seemingly insoluble problem. If infantry advanced in close order they would be mown down. If they manœuvred in open order, they would become so dispersed that their officers would not be able to control them. Gradually, as the fire grew hotter, more and more of them would go to ground, and the advance would come to a halt.

The success of the Japanese army in Manchuria in 1904–5 seemed to demonstrate that high morale was the only solution. If troops had a sufficiently high morale, infantry attacks could still culminate in a successful bayonet charge. The lesson which most European armies drew was that victory would go to the side whose soldiers had been imbued with a stoicism which amounted to a contempt for death. 'The chances of victory turn entirely upon the spirit of self-sacrifice of those who have to be offered up to gain opportunity for the remainder,' wrote one British military writer in 1905. His words might serve as the bitter epitaph for the generation of 1914.

6

Imperial Wars

*From the Seven Years War to the
First World War*

DOUGLAS PORCH

Imperialism has proved a subject of significant historical controversy. After discarding much, indeed most, of the interpretative framework of imperialism made popular by J. A. Hobson in the wake of the Anglo-Boer War of 1899–1902, and elevated to the status of Marxist dogma by Lenin in his pamphlet 'Imperialism, Highest Stage of Capitalism', historians by dint of diligent research reached conclusions which colonial soldiers of more pragmatic disposition knew instinctively—that trade did not follow the flag, that scant interest in the commercial exploitation or political advantages of imperial expansion existed in Europe. Indeed, imperialism moved forward, not as a result of commercial or political pressure from London, Paris, Berlin, St Petersburg, or even Washington, but mainly because men on the periphery, many of whom were soldiers, pressed to expand the boundaries of empire, often without orders, even against orders. Imperialism, therefore, was essentially a military phenomenon, and, as such, it becomes important to understand the dynamic of imperial expansion—imperial warfare.

From its earliest period, imperial warfare was considered a hazardous and difficult enterprise. Although in the Americas Europeans advanced inland almost from the beginning, their conquest was facilitated as much, if not more, by an avant-garde of disease as by military superiority *per se*. And even then,

Amerindian hostility meant that frontier outposts like Montreal maintained a precarious existence. In the East and in Africa, Europeans remained sea-bound, clutching a tenuous lifeline to the homeland, content to export spices, gold, and slaves from coastal 'factories'. Three things caused this to change over the course of the eighteenth and nineteenth centuries—political instability in Africa and Asia, European rivalries played out in the wider world, and officers and officials driven by patriotism and personal ambition, eager to claim vast stretches of territory for the fatherland. As a result, imperial soldiers faced operational challenges of the sort which had confronted Cortés from the moment he fired his boats at Veracruz—how was a relative handful of Europeans with limited technological means to traverse an inaccessible country, to conquer a numerically superior enemy, and to pacify a new empire? While these challenges remained difficult, over time European soldiers mastered them to the point that imperial conquest came to be regarded as hardly more than a technical problem to be solved. For instance, to the end of his career, Wellington, who had directed what was regarded as Europe's toughest fighting in Spain between 1808 and 1813, who had held Europe's fate in his hands in the cauldron of Waterloo, maintained that Assaye, his 1803 victory over Mahrattan forces, was 'the bloodiest for the numbers that I ever saw', and 'the best thing' that he ever did in the way of fighting. By the turn of the nineteenth century, however, the British Colonel C. E. Callwell's classic *Small Wars* or the less well-known *Observations sur les guerres dans les colonies* by the French Lieutenant-Colonel A. Ditte could adopt a very prescriptive approach to colonial warfare.

What had happened? As in all warfare, European expansion had kindled a competition between European and indigenous forces, a process in which each attempted to respond to the challenges of new foes and conditions, a competition which, over the course of the nineteenth century, the Europeans clearly won. This had not been an automatic process, however, but involved much trial and error. The adaptive response of the Europeans had been more apparent in some areas than others, and gradually accelerated as the nineteenth century drew to a close. This chapter will seek to do three things: first, to examine the problems posed by the conditions of warfare outside Europe on the European military systems, and how European, and eventually American, soldiers adapted to them. As war is an interactive process, European adaptation was conditioned in part by the native response to these invasions. Therefore, one must also ask why, in most cases, indigenous societies failed to organize a successful resistance. Finally, this chapter will argue that, although imperial military success appeared virtually inevitable and unstoppable, in fact it was built on a brittle foundation, both militarily and politically. The tenuous success of imperial conquest before 1914 would become apparent as the Great War was being fought, and even more so in its aftermath.

At home, indifference, even hostility, formed a first constraint on imperial expansion, for the benefits of distant conquests were not altogether apparent to Europeans. As a Continental power, France could never muster sustained interest in its Empire after the death of Colbert, a principal reason why it forfeited its 'old' Empire to England in the Seven Years War. Excesses committed during Bugeaud's campaign against the Arabs in the 1840s earned French colonial soldiers a reputation for brutality, which could be exploited by the political opposition eager for issues through which to attack the government. Politicians who backed far-flung wars ran political risks, as Jules Ferry discovered when hounded from office to cries of 'Ferry Tonkin!' following a French military reversal in 1885 against Chinese forces. Gladstone was severely embarrassed by the plight of Charles 'Chinese' Gordon at Khartoum in 1884–5, while Kitchener's conduct during the Boer War, in particular the grouping of Boer civilians in 'concentration camps' where they died in their thousands from disease, nourished a vocal anti-war movement in Britain. So controversial did German imperialism become after the Berlin Congress of 1885 that Bismarck was forced to camouflage the colonial budget in that of the Foreign Office for fear that it would serve as an excuse to attack his government.

This popular indifference, which might easily slip over into opposition, imposed several constraints on imperial expansion, the most obvious being that governments were reluctant to commit to expensive imperial expeditions. To restrain costs and the requirement to draw extensively on European garrisons, the French and British recruited large numbers of indigenous forces, a tradition which persisted to the end of the imperial era. The French conquest of Algeria in the 1840s was carried out by numbered regiments of the home army. But even then, locally recruited units like the tirailleurs and spahis, or European units specially tailored for imperial service like the zouaves, Foreign Legion, or *chasseurs d'Afrique*, were created. With the founding of the Third Republic in 1870, opposition to the commitment of conscripts to wars in Africa and Asia was such that a separate *armée coloniale* was formed to conquer and police French colonies, to which was joined the *armée d'Afrique*, which occupied North Africa. The traditional British aversion to a large standing army extended to the colonies where, in the eighteenth century, loyal Americans and Hessian mercenaries supplemented British regiments in North America, while India was maintained largely by sepoys in the pay of the East India Company. In the nineteenth century, imperial expansion was the province principally, although not exclusively, of the Indian Army, formed in the aftermath of the 1857 Mutiny, to which in times of crisis, like the Boer War of 1899–1902, were joined colonial volunteers. German colonies were maintained by what was hardly more than a police force. Russians and Americans, dealing basically with continental expansion, relied on their regular armies as instruments of conquest. But lack of support for the US army in general, and opposition to the Indian Wars in particular, kept the army small, recruited largely among foreign immigrants.

A second constraint placed on imperial conquest was that the Europeans could not always press what should have been their strong suit—technology. Until the mid-nineteenth century, Europeans, seldom more advantaged in this area than had been Cortés, were often only equal, even disadvantaged, against an indigenous enemy able in the East to produce his own muskets and artillery. The British had no qualitative technological advantage over their French or American opponents in North America in the eighteenth century. In India, the native opposition matched, and often bested, the British in small arms. The French in Algeria discovered in the 1830s that their short-range muskets offered only a marginal defence against longer-range Arab jezails. Small-arm superiority was seldom a decisive factor in the Russian invasion of the Caucasus.

The situation began to change in the 1860s as European organizational ability, combined with technology, began to give the imperial invaders an edge. However, the change was not a sudden one, and, indeed, organization and technology often cut both ways. On the surface, at least, the introduction in the 1860s of breech-loading rifles and in the 1880s of machine-guns changed the equation of colonial battles. But although Hilaire Belloc could write, 'Whatever happens we have got | the Maxim gun and they have not,' the truth was that firepower gave Europeans an important, but by no means decisive, advantage. No shortage of merchants of death existed to sell modern rifles to indigenous peoples—it is reckoned that over 16 million firearms were imported by Africans in the course of the nineteenth century. Colonial officials, eager to introduce a fatal touch of chaos to African empires which dwelt in conditions of scarcely stifled unrest, might supply weapons to minor chieftains or pretenders to thrones as a means to undermine the position of a local ruler. European rivalries also played a role in arming indigenous resistance—the governor of French Somaliland supplied Menelik with a 'gift' of 100,000 rifles and 2 million tons of ammunition after Britain backed Italy's assertion of a protectorate over Ethiopia in 1891. Although it may safely be consigned to the 'sore loser' category, survivors of the Little Bighorn (1876) charged that Sitting Bull had shot them off the field with Winchester repeaters, while their ability to reply was muted by single-shot Springfields, complaints identical to those of French soldiers in Tonkin in 1885 about their single-shot 1874-model Gras rifles. The French discovered that both the Dahomians in 1892 and the Malagasies in 1895 possessed modern rifles, although they used them badly, when they used them at all. Ethiopians did not lack for rifles at Adowa. The accuracy of Boer Mausers caused the British to alter their tactics in the Boer War of 1899–1902.

The advent of machine-guns did give Europeans firepower advantages in defensive situations. It appears that the Russians and

Americans were the first to add them to the inventories of armed expeditions in central Asia and the West. However, their general use in imperial warfare was impeded by both technical and tactical factors. Early versions like the *mitrailleuse* and Gatling were heavy and unreliable. Most commanders realized that a weapon which jammed at critical moments posed a distinct danger, which was why Custer left his Gatling behind when he departed for the Little Bighorn. Chelmsford carried them into action against the Zulus in 1879, but the Africans learned to work around them and attack on the flank. So firepower did not save him at Isandhlwana. Conventional wisdom in the early days also assigned these weapons to the artillery to be used in batteries, rather than distributed to infantry and cavalry units.

The lighter, more reliable Maxim gun began to appear on colonial battlefields in the 1890s, to be used by the British on the North-West Frontier, and to best effect in the Matabele War of 1893, when armed police of the Chartered Company and volunteers simply laagered their wagons and mowed down the Africans, who charged with reckless courage. But Maxim guns were seldom a battle winner, for at least two reasons. First, they were not well suited for warfare in mountains or jungles where the enemy fought dispersed or was invisible. Pushed too far forward, they might become isolated and their crews be overwhelmed. Second, they remained too few to decide the outcome of a campaign—the British possessed only six Maxims at Omdurman. Maxims were not free of mechanical problems, as the French discovered during the Moroccan attack at Menabba in eastern Morocco in April 1908, when sand jammed the mechanisms of their machine-guns. During the Boer War, the Transvaal government equipped its troops with a number of Maxims, which they regarded as a cheap and efficient form of light artillery, while the British included them in their 'flying' columns. But it was only the Russo-Japanese War of 1904–5 which revealed the value of large numbers of machine-guns, and their tactical use on the offensive as well as the defensive. And even then, the machine-gun remained a relatively scarce item in military inventories well into the Great War.

Artillery might give the invaders an advantage, but not invariably so. Wellington found artillery useful especially in attacking

Indian fortifications, which were often primitive, as were those of central Asia attacked by Russians. It required a considerable siege-train to storm Constantine in 1837, although the defenders inexplicably mined their own curtain wall, thus allowing the French to storm through the breach. But battles were seldom decided on the basis of superior European firepower—Mahrattan and Sikh forces were well supplied with artillery, although heterogeneous and eccentrically organized, and employed European instructors to train their gunners in the latest European techniques. In 1857 the Indian mutineers unsportingly kept the artillery for themselves, so that subsequently the British made certain that the artillery was served only by more reliable white troops. The Chinese used artillery against the French in Tonkin in 1885, although only late in the campaign did it begin to prove its effectiveness. French and Russian advisers were said to have supervised the crews of Emperor Menelik's mountain guns at Adowa. As with small arms, indigenous forces seldom had sufficient artillery ammunition.

The remoteness of imperial battlefields could make artillery a liability, especially the heavier variety employed in the eighteenth and early nineteenth centuries. If the weight of gun carriages was reduced for mobility, only a few rounds could be fired before the wood began to split. If the carriages were solidly designed, mobility became a problem—forty bullocks and a female elephant were required to haul one of Wellington's 18-pounders in India. Bugeaud limited the artillery allowed his 'flying columns' in Algeria to two guns, in part because it was cumbersome, but especially because he found the offensive spirit of his troops diminished in direct proportion to the defensive firepower of their artillery. Light 'mountain guns' carried on the backs of mules or camels and able to be assembled quickly were available from the 1840s. But in areas where pack animals were scarce, like Tonkin, these pieces had to be lashed to bamboo frames carried by forty skittish and unreliable porters. 'Sooner or later the bamboos break, sooner or later the porters fall and roll with the piece over a precipice or into an arroyo,' wrote legionnaire Louis Carpeaux, who complained that columns which required mobility and surprise for success were immobilized by even these light pieces. Artillery might be useful against forts, walled villages, or defensive enclosures. But after taking high casualties in frontal assaults, the French in Tonkin, like the British who stormed Maori pahs in New Zealand, discovered that dynamite or, better still, a manœuvre against the line of retreat was usually sufficient to induce a precipitate evacuation. In any case, it came almost as a relief if the enemy chose to fight from these defensive positions because it lessened the threat of ambushes or surprise attacks, which the European soldiers, especially those fighting in dense jungle, feared most.

In the last quarter of the nineteenth century, small artillery pieces like the Hotchkiss became part of the inventories of expeditionary forces. Larger guns, like Creusot 75s, might be used extensively, especially if the battlefield was not too remote, and the enemy showed a preference for fighting on the defensive, as during the early months of the Boer War. However, the effect of artillery on the enemy, especially on dispersed, irregular forces, was more psychological than physical. The French found that shrapnel had little effect on Moroccans, who sought refuge in palm groves or behind walls of *ksour* (fortified villages). But it was always hard to predict the proper mix of shrapnel and impact shells to be carried on campaign. Firepower might be a factor in victory if the enemy obligingly tried to replicate European methods as did the Indian mutineers or Egyptian troops at Tel-el-Kebir in 1882. Better still if they massed in a 'Holy War' response, as at Omdurman in 1898 or Morocco in 1908 and 1912. But Europeans had prevailed in pitched battles like Assaye in 1803, on the Sikkat River in Algeria in 1836, or at Isly in 1844. It was superior tactics and discipline, rather than firepower, which had assured European victory in these set-piece engagements. When these elements were absent, as with poorly trained and led Italian forces at Adowa in 1896, the result could be disastrous. However, European advantages in firepower, tactics, and discipline might be nullified by geography and by the enemy.

As Callwell observed, while in imperial warfare tactics favour the European, strategy favours the resistance, which, if clever, can control the pace of a war. Operational solutions open to imperial soldiers were determined by what they wished to achieve.

Forts or posts were constructed to defend territory. However, they were seldom useful in themselves because they scattered forces in penny packets, leaving the enemy free to bypass or harass these defenders as he chose. These posts might be extended in a sort of barrier, or 'Lines', approach, such as the Russians carried out to protect the plains from Caucasus raiders or the French in the Sud-Oranais at the turn of the century to stop Moroccan incursions into Algeria. However, these forts could foster escalation as raiders slipped between them or even ambushed supply convoys which lumbered from post to post. Even when mobile units were organized to patrol between the fixed points, they seldom matched the enemy in audacity or speed. So, the solution for imperialists like Hubert Lyautey, commander of the Sud-Oranais between 1903 and 1906, and subsequently Resident General of Morocco, was to lunge forward, chastise an oasis or a town using the justification of 'collective responsibility', and perhaps even occupy it as a gesture of deterrence. This resulted in a vicious circle of conquest, occupation, followed by more conquests, as General O'Connor, commander of the Oran subdivision, recognized in 1902, when he criticized the tactical approach of 'reply to a raid with a counter-raid' current in the French army. 'This never catches the guilty, and draws us into a war of reprisals' which led inexorably to the occupation of more territory. 'Once the conquest is carried out, one must occupy the country, which costs enormous amounts of money' for more posts, which devoured men and left fewer troops available for mobile operations.

All specialists in imperial warfare agreed that, whether the objective was to defend trade, protect territory, or punish a local potentate or tribe, offensive action offered the best method for bringing an indigenous enemy to heel. 'From the days of Clive down to the present time,' insisted Callwell, 'victory has been achieved by vigor and dash rather than by force of numbers.' One major advantage of this approach was a political one—home governments eager for results favoured a 'one blow' approach over more patient strategies which protracted a conflict. This was easier said than done, however, in country which was usually remote and invariably inhospitable. The task

of accumulating supplies, not to mention pack animals, in remote areas was a long and arduous one, which contributed to
the expense of a campaign, a condition which invited opposition, both political and military. From an operational perspective, expeditions which were too large might have their hands
full simply sustaining themselves on the coast, much less be able
to push inland, as was initially the case of the British in
Abyssinia in 1868 and the French in Madagascar in 1895. When
the push into the hinterland began, supply trains slowed the column to a snail's pace, and offered a vulnerable target. This limited the offensive punch of expeditions forced to employ a
disproportionate number of troops and artillery to defend supply trains from hostile attack. For this reason, imperial expeditions were often categorized as 'campaigns against nature'. As
such, no imperial commander could hope for success until he
had solved his logistical problems.

The turning-point for Europeans came in the 1860s and
1870s, when organizational ability allied with technology combined to give them the advantage. While innovative commanders
like Wellington or Bugeaud always attempted to organize expeditions efficiently within the confines of pre-industrial capabilities, the decisive development came, perhaps, with the
Abyssinian expedition of 1868, when the British imported a
complete railway to support the advance into the interior. However, it was General Sir Garnet Wolseley who probably first
achieved the marriage of technology and organization during the
Ashanti campaign of 1873–4. To be sure, Wolseley defeated the
Ashanti in battle thanks to Snider rifles and 7-pounder guns. But
the battle was almost incidental to the success of the campaign,
which had been a triumph of administrative planning. In future,
successful commanders, like Dodds in Dahomey (1892), would
imitate Wolseley by reducing the size of expeditions to around
2,000 men, and take care to provide roads, way stations, porter-
age, pack animals, tinned food, potable water, and quinine for
their troops, all of which would ensure a maximum number of
rifles on line and a rapid conclusion of a campaign.

Admittedly, this lesson was unevenly applied, in part because,
although the Ashanti campaign proved a marvel of technical

organization, its success relied largely on the fact that it was a punitive expedition, not a campaign of conquest. Because Wolseley rapidly withdrew his force after destroying the Ashanti 'capital', the campaign was barren of strategic results. Other commanders seeking more permanent outcomes were obliged to resort to large expeditions, as in the Caucasus where Shamil was able to mass large numbers to hold vital defiles or strategic villages. Russian expeditions in central Asia were essentially expeditions cast into the desert to lay siege to fortified towns, and required what, in effect, were small armies. In Indo-China in 1884–5 the French required a fairly considerable force to take on a Chinese army allied with local Black Flag resistance. Logistics remained the Achilles' heel of all of these operations. When the enemy force was smaller, or fragmented, however, successful commanders like Wellington in India, Bugeaud in Algeria, or General Crook during his 1883 Sierra Madre campaign against Geronimo reduced their baggage train to the absolute minimum by utilizing pack animals like bullocks, camels, mules, or, in Africa and Indo-China, porters, although the latter could usually be recruited only under threat and deserted at the first opportunity. When possible, commanders reduced their dependence on logistics by following river lines, as did the French in Indo-China, Dodds in Dahomey, or Kitchener on the Nile. But the enemy might not necessarily place himself within easy reach, so that roads might have to be constructed; this was done constantly by the French in North Africa, and by Wolseley during the Ashanti campaign. However, it was possible to take the obsession with organization too far, as did General Charles Duchesne during his 1895 invasion of Madagascar; he came within an ace of failure when his forces, employed to construct an invasion road, perished in their thousands from fevers.

Technology and organization were only adjuncts to, not substitutes for, inventive operational solutions. Wellington discovered on his arrival in India that British expeditions there resembled 'migrating people rather than an army', as unitary armies numbering up to 20,000 troops lumbered over the countryside, averaging 10 miles on a good day, but requiring one day's rest in three, forced to meander to find food and fodder. In his campaign against Dhoondiah in Mysore, Wellington divided his forces into four armies, which kept his opponent off balance and allowed the British to march up to 26 miles a day to achieve surprise. Wellington's experience was repeated elsewhere as French, British, and Americans moved to light or 'flying' columns—Hoche used them in the Vendée, Bugeaud in Algeria, the British in Burma, Rhodesia, and against the Boers, and Americans in the West. Callwell cautioned that flying columns were not without their drawbacks, however. They still required substantial logistical support which could slow their advance. Flying columns worked best against an objective like a 'capital' or an enemy army, and could be difficult to co-ordinate with other 'converging' columns. A reversal, even a withdrawal after a successful operation, could be costly. 'If you were forced to re-treat through these people, you could be certain of having them constantly around you,' the Hessian Johann Ewald remembered of the American Revolution. The French discovered as much in Algeria at the Macta Marshes in 1835 and the following year at Constantine, as did the British in Afghanistan in 1844. In the Caucasus, Shamil became expert at allowing Russians to mean-der through valleys, sacking town after deserted town, and then cutting them to ribbons when they attempted to return to base, as was done following the Russian 'victory' at Akhulgo in the eastern Caucasus in 1839. Shamil's greatest triumph, however, came in 1845 as Prince Vorontsov's 'flying' column withdrew through the Chechnian forests towards his base. The Russians were able to cover only 30 miles in one week, in the process abandoning baggage and wounded and losing 4,000 men and 200 officers, including three generals, to Shamil's ambush.

Callwell's clear preference was for small expeditions of mounted men: 'The most brilliant exploits', he believed, 'were carried out by mounted troops alone ... Savages, Asiatics and adversaries of that character have a great dread of the mounted man.' Despite Callwell's praise for 'mounted troops alone', this was not invariably a formula for success, as he recognized. The dilemma for colonial commanders was to achieve the correct balance between mobility and firepower. A large force could vir-tually collapse under the weight of its own logistics. On the other hand, the decision to sacrifice defensive firepower for mobility was not a risk-free one for commanders, as the French found in Mexico, Custer at the Little Bighorn, Chelmsford at Isandhlwana, or Hicks Pasha on the Nile in 1883. As in Europe, cavalry unsupported by infantry was vulnerable, which is why most invaders evolved some type of mounted infantry to fill this gap. But infantry retained an important role in mobile operations, especially in mountainous terrain. One of the points of mobile operations was to wear out the enemy, keep him on the run, until he gave up from weariness. But even when mobility was maximized—especially when it was maximized—these campaigns exacted a terrible toll on white troops, and the drop-out rate on the march, especially for infantry, could be high. Accounts of French soldiers who campaigned under Bugeaud, in Mexico, or in Indo-China against elusive Black Flags, read like a litany of exhaustion. Nor was this exclusively true of the French, for fatigue eroded the efficiency of US forces in the West as well, and was a factor in Custer's defeat.

Spectacular victories, as well as spectacular disasters, were a relatively rare occurrence in imperial warfare, for the simple reason that the problem was not to defeat the enemy, but to get him to fight at all. Callwell counselled offensive action and dramatic battle because he believed it the best way to demonstrate the moral superiority of the European. This worked best against a foe with a fairly cohesive system—a capital, a king, a standing army, a religious bond—some symbol of authority or legitimacy which, once overthrown, discouraged further resistance. But he acknowledged that it was not invariably a formula for success, either because indigenous societies might be too primitive to have a centralized political or military system or to assign value to the seizure of a city like Algiers or Kabul, or because the defeat of the sovereign simply shattered the resistance into a host of petty chieftains who had to be dealt with piecemeal. A third category, more rare but even more troublesome, was that of a leader of a fairly coherent resistance movement who fought in such a way as to deny the invaders the decisive victories which they sought—Abd el-Kader after his defeat by Bugeaud at the Sikkat River in 1836, Shamil in the Caucasus, Samori in West

Africa, or any number of Boer commanders. 'In small wars', Callwell wrote, 'guerrilla operations are almost invariably a feature of some phase of the struggle.'

Guerrilla warfare was the most dreaded form of operation for a regular army for both military and political reasons. As noted, from a military standpoint, regular armies, even those with substantial colonial experience, were poorly equipped to deal with it. An elusive enemy could control the strategic pace of the war, withdraw deep into the country, and nullify the technological and firepower advantage which should naturally be enjoyed by the invaders. To match this, European commanders required a substantial reordering of their military system. This was never easy to do, and officers who advocated such things as light, mobile forces with logistical systems to match were regarded as eccentrics whose innovations seldom survived their departure. A reliable intelligence network was the *sine qua non* of irregular warfare, a field in which commanders of a traditional stamp were usually loath to work. Some of these problems—stamina, mobility, logistics, costs—could be resolved in part by substituting locally recruited soldiers for Europeans. The British and the French evolved a formula of one European for two soldiers of imperial origins. But imperial levies were not an automatic solution, and much ink was spilled by colonial officers on their best utilization. If a commander employed irregular levies of Cossacks, *goums*, or simply tribal formations armed with surplus weapons, he might discover that they were more trouble than they were worth. Part of the problem lay in a different cultural approach to warfare—indigenous levies often could not understand the European preference for frontal assaults and seizing territory or fortresses. For them, battle was an exercise in personal bravery, flirting with danger in exercises like 'counting coups'—that is, getting close enough to touch your enemy. They swarmed all over the battlefield, kicking up dust and getting in the line of fire of European troops who, soon unable to distinguish friend from foe, might come in for some nasty surprises— for instance, during the Bou-Amama revolt of 1881, a French column lost seventy-two soldiers and most of their convoy at Chellala after Arab horsemen, whom the French believed to be part of a French-organized *goum*, were allowed to approach un-contested. Amerindians and Africans went into battle to capture slaves, livestock, or in some cases prisoners for ritualistic sacrifice, rather than to kill people *per se*. For European commanders, this meant that indigenous levies were difficult to control both on and off the battlefield. They might also give imperialism a bad press. Despite Montcalm's attempt to prevent it, the massacre of Anglo-American prisoners by his Amerindian allies following the surrender of Fort William Henry in 1757 caused the British to denounce the French for war crimes. Much of the devastation in the western Sudan occurred because the French relied heavily on tribal levies, or poorly disciplined 'Senegalese' or 'Soudannais' tirailleurs, quick to abandon the firing line to snatch booty and female slaves. Indeed, the practice of arming and leading native irregulars against other tribes led to one of the greatest scandals of French expansion in Africa, the destructive and ultimately mutinous Voulet–Chanoine expedition of 1898.

Nevertheless, it is no exaggeration to say that, without troops recruited in the colonies, the French and British could neither have conquered nor garrisoned their empires. In the American West, Amerindians performed essential service as scouts—Crook's employment of Apache scouts in Arizona in 1872–3 and Miles's use of Crows to hound Sitting Bull after Custer's defeat made the difference between success and failure. 'Nothing breaks them up like turning their own people against them,' wrote Crook. 'It is not merely a question of catching them better with Indians, but of a broader and more enduring aim—their disintegration.' But Crook's successful experiments found few imitators. American officers, like their European counterparts, preferred to oblige native levies to conform to European standards of drill and discipline. Invariably, they got mixed results. While some of these regiments were excellent, commanders who created coloured versions of European regiments might discover that recruitment dried up, and that units lost the rusticity, spontaneity, and resilience which gave them an edge over European troops in mobile operations. To draw the best from these troops also required an officer corps knowledgeable in the languages and customs of their men, and willing on campaign to endure a standard of living which gave new meaning to the concept of misery.

Because imperial warfare, especially irregular warfare, was so indecisive, even the best commanders fell back on economic warfare to bring the enemy to heel. 'In planning a war against an uncivilized nation who has, perhaps, no capital,' Lord Wolseley advised, 'your first object should be the capture of whatever they prize most, and the destruction or deprivation of which will probably bring the war most rapidly to a conclusion.' In desert areas, the party which controlled the wells could often control the war. Wellington burned food and crops and threatened to hang merchants who supplied food to insurgents fighting on amidst the debris of Tipu's empire. Callwell maintained that the trump card of the British in India was that they could always identify and destroy any village which challenged British rule. In Algeria, Bugeaud raised the *razzia* or raid to a strategic concept as his troops destroyed crops, rounded up livestock, and burned villages on the theory that if Algerians could not eat, they could not fight. In the eastern Caucasus, the Russians systematically cut down forests and denied grazing land to insurgents. In the western Caucasus, scorched earth combined with simple eviction forced the migration of the Cherkes population, followed by the resettlement of the area with loyal colonists. The Russian General M. D. Skobelev held to the principle that in Asia, 'the harder you hit them, the longer they will remain quiet afterwards', a philosophy espoused both by Sherman and Sheridan, not only against the rebellious Southern states, but against Amerindians as well. Amerindian troubles would cease, according to Sherman in 1868, only with 'the ringleaders ... hung, their ponies killed, and such destruction of their property as will make them very poor'. Generals Crook and Terry set out to apply precisely this approach to the Sioux in the winter of 1876–7; at Crazy Woman Fork, for instance, a large Sioux settlement was destroyed in sub-zero weather. Marines resorted to harsh measures to pacify the island of Samar in the Philippines in 1901–2. Kitchener followed similar policies against Boer insurgents, as did the Germans against the Herero rebellion in south-west Africa, and some French commanders in Morocco.

This type of economic warfare caused difficulties both on the ground and at home. In the colonies, it served to point up the dilemma which bedevilled western soldiers to the close of the twentieth century—how to distinguish friend from foe. Resistance to European rule was seldom absolute, but involved a very complex reaction in which political, religious, regional, ethnic, tribal, and family loyalties all played a role. The safest solution from a western perspective was simply to treat all natives as enemies until proven otherwise. But even practitioners of this method, like Bugeaud, acknowledged that it created much bad blood, and made reconciliation of a conquered people to colonial rule very difficult. Worse, it might cause one to lose. The Hessian Johann Ewald discovered his inability to distinguish rebel from loyalist in the American Revolution. Yet, he recommended that, in any case, one 'make friends in the middle of enemy country', to avoid 'the revenge of the locals'. As reprisals tended to fall on natives close at hand, rather than on the guilty, indigenous peoples tended to flee when imperial troops appeared on the horizon, which naturally led the Europeans to the conclusion that deserted villages meant war.

Some of the more sensitive commanders realized that the line between 'dissidence' and compliance was a fine one which might be crossed several times. The indigenous population might not be uniformly hostile to the invaders, which is why colonial commanders like Wolseley advocated vigorous offensive actions: 'Irregular armies always count many waverers … even on the battle-field a large proportion of the opposing force consists generally of mere lookers-on … A vigorous offensive has the effect of keeping at home those who hesitate to take up arms and of thereby diminishing the fighting strength of the enemy.' Smashing battlefield success could indeed discourage those living closest to the invaders from continued resistance, though those living further afield whose chattels were less at risk often pressed to continue the fight. Nor did natives see any contradiction in trading with the invaders one moment, and attacking them the next, or working for both at the same time, for that matter, as the French discovered in Mexico, Tonkin, and Morocco, and the Americans in the Philippines. The pacification system in the

American West actually supported continued rebellion by warriors who could confide their women and children to the safe care of the Indian Bureau while they went off raiding. When pressed, they would simply creep back to the reservations, where the army was at a loss to distinguish the guilty from the innocent. In this way, the reservations, alleged repositories of 'pacified' natives, became hotbeds of Amerindian uprisings. Many colonial commanders—Wellington, Lyautey, even the Russians to a certain extent—preferred to co-opt élites as a way to quieting rebellion and winning acceptance for European rule.

If tough methods created problems in the colonies, they were also bound to 'shock the humanitarian', the second drawback of economic warfare. If imperial soldiers like Bugeaud often scoffed at the delicate sentiments of domestic opinion, in fact, European adaptive response was increasingly shaped by attitudes at home as much as, if not more than, by what went on in the colonies. Early on in the Algerian campaign, the brutalities of Algerian soldiers against the Muslim population raised protests in France. 'Humanitarians', led by Quakers, were vocal in their criticism of military methods used against the Amerindians, and conflict between the army and agents of the Indian Bureau became a permanent feature of civil–military relations in the West. French Generals Gallieni and Lyautey developed the *tache d'huile* or 'oil spot' methods of pacification, which encouraged indigenous peoples to rally to the French to receive the benefits of security, trade, and prosperity. However, the advantages of these methods were mixed, in part for reasons already mentioned, but also because, by creating markets where prices for native products were artificially inflated as a matter of policy, they succeeded in disrupting established trading patterns and alienating powerful local economic interests. Lyautey's policy of 'peaceful penetration' in the Sud-Oranais in the early twentieth century contributed in no small measure to the rebellion which fell upon the French in eastern Morocco in 1908. Given its lack of success on the ground, one can only conclude that Lyautey's passionate advocacy of 'peaceful penetration' was done more with an eye to winning domestic support for French imperial expansion generally, and more specifically for the conquest of Morocco, than because it succeeded as a policy.

So far, we have discussed the problems of European adaptation. How does one explain the generally inadequate indigenous response to European invasion? One reason was that the technological revolution in armaments worked against non-Europeans in at least two ways. Unlike the 'intermediate' technology of muskets, later developments meant that they lacked the ability to make spare parts and ammunition. This made them increasingly dependent on European suppliers, part of a general modernizing trend which drove them into debt, and ironically pushed them into the arms of the very Europeans they were trying to resist. The encroachment of European influence stimulated social and political disintegration, especially in Egypt, Tunis, and Morocco. Elsewhere, well-armed minor chiefs with private access to arms merchants challenged central authority. On the battlefield, reliance on outside supply combined with primitive logistical systems usually translated into desperate ammunition shortages.

A second problem was that, in most cases, indigenous forces simply incorporated modern weapons into familiar tactical systems rather than evolving methods which allowed them to be used to advantage. One of the ironies of imperial warfare is that the relative political and military sophistication which made the Zulu, Dahomian, or Ashanti empires so formidable in the African context, or assured Hova domination of Madagascar, rendered them all the more vulnerable to European conquest. In most of these societies, armies and warfare were enmeshed in a very precise social or religious structure. For instance, like the Ashantis, the Dahomian army went into battle in an arc formation, each man's position in the arc determined by the importance of his chief. To change this would have required a social revolution. Furthermore, they were armies designed for slave raiding, or for short campaigns at the end of which the defeated tribe was not annihilated but integrated into the empire. The prospect of fighting a bloody battle, or a series of battles, against a relentless European invader placed intolerable strains on these empires. Even when the indigenous resistance could achieve surprise, like the Ashanti at Amoatu or the Dahomians at Dogba, they were seldom able to profit from it. Defeat invited disintegration as armies whose feudal levies carried about two weeks' rations ran out of food, distant family members, sometimes with European connivance, advanced rival claims to the throne, well-armed minor chiefs declared independence, and subject peoples revolted. Indeed, a combination of these events often did more than European arms to scupper coherent native resistance.

In India, the process of creating armies on a Europeanized model began in imitation of the sepoy units created by Clive and Dupleix during the Seven Years War. Many of these units, under the command of European or half-caste soldiers of fortune, achieved respectable levels of proficiency in the Indian context. But against a European opponent, even one relying to a large degree on its own locally recruited units, they appear to have been at a disadvantage because the Indian potentates proved reluctant to alter their semi-feudal social structure to accommodate a modern army. So Indian armies, though superficially modernized, lacked a coherent officer corps and administrative structure to support them. Worse, in the case of the Sikhs, for example, this new army became such an intrusive political force that some Sikh sirdars or lords actively conspired to have it defeated by the British.

Elsewhere, the very primitiveness of some of the societies, while it may have made them tenacious military opponents, ultimately doomed their resistance. Few of these societies were uniformly hostile to the invader, nor had they a sense of fighting a war of survival. Divided by geography, by rivalries of caste, tribe, clan, or family, their bonds of common culture weak, a unified response based on a shared sense of self-interest, when it could be mustered, seldom survived the first military débâcle. A clever commander with a fine sense of politics like Wellington was able to exploit these differences, co-opt native élites into the imperial system, and lower the morale of those keen to fight by holding up the example of those who were content to submit to the new imperial reality.

Examples of successful resistance are few, and are very much tied to the contingency of local circumstance. The American revolutionaries were victorious ultimately because powerful French intervention gave heart to the insurgents and helped to convince the British that it was no longer in their interests to continue an indecisive war. Other imperial resistance movements, with the possible exception of Afghanistan, were less successful in persuading the invaders that the game was not worth the candle. Abd el-Kader appears to have been a powerful leader, although he may have served more as a symbol to traditionally minded French officers eager to create a single enemy, a unified conspiracy against imperial advance, than as chief of a more-or-less coherent movement. Shamil did enjoy temporary success in uniting the tribes of the eastern Caucasus. But his ability to maintain his coalition was gradually eroded by military defeat and by the reluctance of the fiercely independent-minded mountaineers to submit indefinitely to his authority. Furthermore, while his Murid beliefs served as a unifying ideology, ultimately they irritated his less fanatical Muslim followers and discouraged other inhabitants of the mountains, like the Cherkes in the western Caucasus, from making common cause with him. Samori also managed to unify a remarkable empire which survived for almost a decade by adopting scorched earth and ambush tactics against the French, as well as evolving a social organization which allowed him to shift frontiers to accommodate the need to collect the harvest and the pressures of European encroachment. But as remarkable as were his political and military skills, his longevity appears to owe more to the hesitancy of the French invasion and to military mistakes directly related to French underestimation of their opponent than to the genius of his leadership.

Ethiopian resistance owed much to a semi-successful adaptation to technology, to the incompetence of the enemy, and to luck. The influx of modern arms caused the Ethiopians to abandon their traditional phalanx attack in 1885 in favour of loose formations which approached by fire and encirclement. Nevertheless, their successful resistance at Adowa owed less to the mastery of modern tactics by Menelik's largely feudal levies than to the extraordinary incompetence of General Baratieri, who allowed himself to be goaded into a premature attack by his subordinate officers, and by the stinging rebukes of Italian Prime Minister Francesco Crispi, who had dispatched his successor from Italy. Rather than wait a few days until the Ethiopian soldiers would inevitably have consumed their meagre rations and been forced to disperse, he ordered his 15,000 troops forward in three separate columns to be overwhelmed piecemeal by 100,000 Ethiopians. Boer resistance appears to have been of a tenacity which defies the rule of unsuccessful resistance to imperial rule. On closer examination, however, it adhered more closely to the more common pattern—Amerindian or Algerian—of the fanatical few determined to fight on after the main Boer army had been defeated and most of the Boer people reduced to a state of neutrality. Indeed, the Boer strategy for avoiding national collapse after Bloemfontein was to shed those whose commitment was lukewarm and fight on with only a hard core in the hope that the British would eventually give up.

Though the era of imperial conquest was a successful one for western armies, its achievement contained the seeds of its ultimate demise in the post-1918 era, for at least three reasons. In the pre-1914 era, native resistance was fragmented because it lacked a common ideology or sense of self-interest. This would begin to change as out of an imperial administration and education system, even the experience of serving in European armies, would emerge a nationalism which before had been conspicuously lacking. To this one might add an overlay of Marxist ideology which, in some cases, provided an analytical framework for anti-colonial resistance, and which in the writings of Mao Zedong even discovered a blueprint for revolution which would guide many modern resistance movements.

Second, the Europeans were particularly poorly placed to respond to this emerging nationalism. Imperialism, which had never been popular even in its high renaissance, appeared even more discredited as notions of western cultural and moral superiority were severely shaken by the experience of two world wars. The Marxist nature of some imperial independence movements would make the western response to them even more confused in the Cold War context, and place severe strains on western ability to formulate a coherent response, to make the political concessions which had always been the basis of successful imperial operations. Last, imperial warfare, always seen as a fleeting problem very different from 'real' war, continued to be a neglected area of study for armies. Two world wars had largely destroyed the officer corps which had specialized in colonial service, and with them went the specialized knowledge, the corporate memory required to fight what came to be called 'low-intensity conflict'. As in the earlier era of imperial conquest, western armies would prove slow to adapt to the challenges of unconventional conflicts.

7
Total War I

The Great War

JOHN BOURNE

The First World War was truly 'the Great War'. Its origins were complex. Its scale was vast. Its conduct was intense. Its impact on military operations was revolutionary. Its human and material costs were enormous. And its results were profound.

The war was a global conflict. Thirty-two nations were eventually involved. Twenty-eight of these constituted the Allied and Associated Powers, whose principal belligerents were the British Empire, France, Italy, Russia, Serbia, and the United States of America. They were opposed by the Central Powers: Austria-Hungary, Bulgaria, Germany, and the Ottoman Empire.

The war began in the Balkan cockpit of competing nationalisms and ancient ethnic rivalries. Hopes that it could be contained there proved vain. Expansion of the war was swift. Austria-Hungary declared war on Serbia on 28 July 1914; Germany declared war on Russia on 1 August. Germany declared war on France on 3 August and invaded Belgium. France was invaded on 4 August. German violation of Belgian neutrality provided the British with a convenient excuse to enter the war on the side of France and Russia the same evening. Austria-Hungary declared war on Russia on 6 August. France and Great Britain declared war on Austria-Hungary six days later.

The underlying causes of these events have been intensively researched and debated. Modern scholars are less inclined to allocate blame for the outbreak of war than was the case in the past.

They have sought instead to understand the fears and ambitions of the governing élites of Europe who took the fateful decisions for war, particularly that of imperial Germany.

Fears were more important than ambitions. Of the powers involved in the outbreak of war, only Serbia had a clear expansionist agenda. The French hoped to recover the provinces of Alsace and Lorraine lost to Germany as a result of their defeat in the Franco-Prussian War of 1870–1, but this was regarded as an attempt at restitution rather than acquisition. Otherwise, defensive considerations were paramount. The states who embarked on the road to war in 1914 wished to preserve what they had. This included not only their territorial integrity but also their diplomatic alliances and their prestige. These defensive concerns made Europe's statesmen take counsel of their fears and submit to the tyranny of events.

The Austrians feared for the survival of their multi-racial Empire if they did not confront the threat of Serb nationalism and Panslavism. The Germans feared the consequences to themselves of allowing Austria, their closest and only reliable ally, to be weakened and humiliated. The Russians feared the threat to their prestige and authority as protector of the Slavs if they allowed Austria to defeat and humiliate Serbia. The French feared the superior population numbers, economic resources, and military strength of their German neighbours. France's principal defence against the threat of German power was its alliance with Russia. This it was imperative to defend. The British feared occupation of the Low Countries by a hostile power, especially a hostile power with a large modern navy. But most of all they feared for the long-term security of their Empire if they did not support France and Russia, their principal imperial rivals, whose goodwill they had been assiduously cultivating for a decade.

All governments feared their peoples. Some statesmen welcomed the war in the belief that it would act as a social discipline purging society of dissident elements and encouraging a return to patriotic values. Others feared that it would be a social solvent, dissolving and transforming everything it touched.

The process of expansion did not end in August 1914. Other major belligerents took their time and waited upon events. Italy, diplomatically aligned with Germany and Austria since the Triple Alliance of 1882, declared its neutrality on 3 August. In the following months it was ardently courted by France and Britain. On 23 May 1915 the Italian government succumbed to Allied temptations and declared war on Austria-Hungary in pursuit of territorial aggrandizement in the Trentino. Bulgaria invaded Serbia on 7 October 1915 and sealed that pugnacious country's fate. Serbia was overrun. The road to Constantinople was opened to the Central Powers. Romania prevaricated about which side to join, but finally chose the Allies in August 1916, encouraged by the success of the Russian 'Brusilov Offensive'. It was a fatal miscalculation. The German response was swift and decisive. Romania was rapidly overwhelmed by two invading German armies and its rich supplies of wheat and oil did much to keep Germany in the war for another two years. Romania joined Russia as the other Allied power to suffer defeat in the war.

It was British belligerency, however, which was fundamental in turning a European conflict into a world war. Britain was the world's greatest imperial power. The British had world-wide interests and world-wide dilemmas. They also had world-wide friends. Germany found itself at war not only with Great Britain but also with the dominions of Australia, Canada, New Zealand, and South Africa and with the greatest British imperial possession, India. Concern for the defence of India helped bring the British into conflict with the Ottoman Empire in November 1914 and resulted in a major war in the Middle East. Most important of all, perhaps, Britain's close political, economic, and cultural ties with the United States of America, if they did not ensure that nation's eventual entry into the war, certainly made it possible. The American declaration of war on Germany on 6 April 1917 was a landmark not only in the history of the United States but also in that of Europe and the world, bringing to an end half a millennium of European domination and ushering in 'the American century'.

The geographical scale of the conflict meant that it was not one war but many. On the Western Front in France and Belgium the French and their British allies, reinforced from 1917 onwards by the Americans, were locked in a savage battle of attrition against the German army. Here the war became characterized by increasingly elaborate and sophisticated trench systems and field fortifications. Dense belts of barbed wire, concrete pillboxes, intersecting arcs of machine-gun fire, and accumulating masses of quick-firing field and heavy artillery rendered manœuvre virtually impossible. Casualties were enormous.

The first phase of the war in the west lasted until November 1914. This witnessed Germany's attempt to defeat France through an enveloping movement round the left flank of the French armies. The plan met with initial success. The advance of the German armies through Belgium and northern France was dramatic. The French, responding with an offensive in Lorraine, suffered an almost catastrophic national defeat. France was saved by the iron nerve of its commander-in-chief, General Joseph Joffre, who had not only the intelligence but also the strength of character to extricate himself from the ruin of his plans and order the historic counter-attack against the German right wing, the 'miracle of the Marne'. The German armies were forced to retreat and to entrench. Their last attempt at a breakthrough was stopped by French and British forces near the small Flemish market town of Ypres in November. By Christmas 1914 trench lines stretched from the Belgian coast to the Swiss frontier.

Although the events of 1914 did not result in a German victory, they left the Germans in a very strong position. The German army held the strategic initiative. It was free to retreat to positions of tactical advantage and to reinforce them with all the skill and ingenuity of German military engineering. Enormous losses had been inflicted on France. Two-fifths of France's military casualties were incurred in 1914. These included a tenth of the officer corps. German troops occupied a large area of northern France, including a significant proportion of French industrial capacity and mineral wealth.

These realities dominated the second phase of the war in the west. This lasted from November 1914 until March 1918. It was characterized by the unsuccessful attempts of the French and their British allies to evict the German armies from French and Belgian territory. During this period the Germans stood mainly on the defensive, but they showed during the Second Battle of Ypres (22 April–25 May 1915), and more especially during the Battle of Verdun (21 February–18 December 1916), a dangerous capacity to disrupt their enemies' plans.

The French made three major assaults on the German line: in the spring of 1915 in Artois; in the autumn of 1915 in Champagne; and in the spring of 1917 on the Aisne (the 'Nivelle Offensive'). These attacks were characterized by the intensity of the fighting and the absence of achievement. Little ground was gained. No positions of strategic significance were captured. Casualties were severe. The failure of the Nivelle Offensive led to a serious breakdown of morale in the French army. For much of the rest of 1917 it was incapable of major offensive action.

The British fared little better. Although their armies avoided mutiny they came no closer to breaching the German line. During the battles of the Somme (1 July– 19 November 1916) and the Third Battle of Ypres (31 July–12 November 1917) they inflicted great losses on the German army at great cost to themselves, but the German line held and no end to the war appeared in sight.

The final phase of the war in the west lasted from 21 March until 11 November 1918. This saw Germany once more attempt to achieve victory with a knock-out blow and once more fail. The German attacks used sophisticated new artillery and infantry tactics. They enjoyed spectacular success. The British 5th Army on the Somme suffered a major defeat. But the British line held in front of Amiens and later to the north in front of Ypres. No real strategic damage was done. By midsummer the German attacks had petered out. The German offensive broke the trench deadlock and returned movement and manœuvre to the strategic agenda. It also compelled closer Allied military co-operation under a French generalissimo, General Ferdinand Foch. The Allied counter-offensive began in July. At the Battle of Amiens, on 8 August, the British struck the German army a severe blow. For the rest of the war in the west the Germans were in retreat.

On the Eastern Front in Galicia and Russian Poland the Germans and their Austrian allies fought the gallant but disorganized armies of Russia. Here the distances involved were very great. Artillery densities were correspondingly less. Manœuvre was always possible and cavalry could operate effectively. This did nothing to lessen casualties, which were heavier even than those on the Western Front.

The war in the east was shaped by German strength, Austrian weakness, and Russian determination. German military superiority was apparent from the start of the war. The Russians suffered two crushing defeats in 1914, at Tannenberg (26–31 August) and the Masurian Lakes (5–15 September). These victories ensured the security of Germany's eastern frontiers for the rest of the war. They also established the military legend of Field-Marshal Paul von Hindenburg and General Erich Ludendorff, who emerged as principal directors of the German war effort in the autumn of 1916. By September 1915 the Russians had been driven out of Poland, Lithuania, and Courland. Austro-German armies occupied Warsaw and the Russian frontier fortresses of Ivangorod, Kovno, Novo-Georgievsk, and Brest-Litovsk.

These defeats proved costly to Russia. They also proved costly to Austria. Austria had a disastrous war. Italian entry into the war compelled the Austrians to fight on three fronts: against Serbia in the Balkans; against Russia in Galicia; against Italy in the Trentino. This proved too much for Austrian strength. Their war effort was characterized by dependency on Germany. Germans complained that they were shackled to the 'Austrian corpse'. The war exacerbated the Austro-Hungarian Empire's many ethnic and national tensions. By 1918 Austria was weary of the war and desperate for peace. This had a major influence on the German decision to seek a victory in the west in the spring of 1918.

Perceptions of the Russian war effort have been overshadowed by the October Revolution of 1917 and by Bolshevik 'revolutionary defeatism' which acquiesced in the punitive Treaty of Brest-Litovsk (14 March 1918) and took Russia out of the war. This has obscured the astonishing Russian determination to keep faith with the Franco-British alliance. Without the Russian contribution in the east it is far from certain that Germany could have been defeated in the west. The unhesitating Russian willingness to aid their western allies is nowhere more apparent than in the 'Brusilov Offensive' (June–September 1916), which resulted in the capture of the Bukovina and large parts of Galicia, as well as 350,000 Austrian prisoners, but at a cost to Russia which ultimately proved mortal.

In southern Europe the Italian army fought eleven indecisive battles in an attempt to dislodge the Austrians from their mountain strongholds beyond the Isonzo river. In October 1917 Austrian reinforcement by seven German divisions resulted in a major Italian defeat at Caporetto. The Italians were pushed back beyond the Piave. This defeat produced changes in the Italian high command. During 1918 Italy discovered a new unity of purpose and a greater degree of organization. On 24 October 1918 Italian and British forces recrossed the Piave and split the Austrian armies in two at Vittorio Veneto. Austrian retreat turned into rout and then into surrender.

In the Balkans the Serbs fought the Austrians and Bulgarians, suffering massive casualties, including the highest proportion of servicemen killed of any belligerent power. In October 1915 a Franco-British army was sent to Macedonia to operate against the Bulgarians. It struggled to have any influence on the war. The Germans mocked it and declared Salonika to be the biggest internment camp in Europe, but the French and British eventually broke out of the malarial plains into the mountainous valleys of the Vardar and Struma rivers before inflicting defeat on Bulgaria in the autumn of 1918.

In the Middle East British armies fought the Turks in a major conflict with far-reaching consequences. Here the war was characterized by the doggedness of Turkish resistance and by the constant struggle against climate, terrain, and disease. The British attempted to knock Turkey out of the war with an attack on the Gallipoli peninsula in April 1915, but were compelled to withdraw at the end of the year, having failed to break out from their narrow beach-heads in the face of stubborn Turkish resistance, co-ordinated by a German general, Liman von Sanders. The British also suffered another humiliating reverse in Mesopotamia when a small army commanded by Major-General Sir Charles Townshend advanced to Ctesiphon but outran its supplies and was compelled to surrender at Kut-al-Amara in April 1916. Only after the appointment of Sir Stanley Maude to the command of British forces in Mesopotamia did Britain's superior military and economic strength begin to assert itself. Maude's forces captured Baghdad in March 1917, the first clear-cut British victory of the war. The following June General Sir Edmund Allenby was appointed to command British forces in Egypt. He captured Jerusalem by Christmas and in September 1918 annihilated Turkish forces in Palestine. Turkey surrendered on 31 October 1918.

The war also found its way to tropical Africa. Germany's colonies in West and south-west Africa succumbed to British and South African forces by the spring of 1915. In East Africa, however, a German army of locally raised black African soldiers commanded by Colonel Paul von Lettow-Vorbeck conducted a brilliant guerrilla campaign, leading over 100,000 British and South African troops a merry dance through the bush and surrendering only after the defeat of Germany in Europe became known.

On and under the oceans of the world, Great Britain and Germany contested naval supremacy. Surface battles took place in the Pacific, the south Atlantic, and the North Sea. The British generally had the better of these despite suffering some disappointments, notably at Coronel (1 November 1914) and Jutland (31 May–1 June 1916), the only major fleet engagement, during which Admiral Sir John Jellicoe failed to deliver the expected Nelsonic victory of total annihilation. Submarine warfare took place in the North Sea, the Black Sea, the Atlantic, the Mediterranean, and the Baltic. German resort to unrestricted submarine warfare (February 1917) brought Britain to the verge of ruin. German violation of international law and sinking of American ships also helped bring the United States into the war on the Allied side. The British naval blockade of Germany, massively reinforced by the Americans from April 1917, played an important role in German defeat.

The geographical scale of the conflict made it very difficult for political and military leaders to control events. The obligations of coalition inhibited strategic independence. Short-term military needs often forced the great powers to allow lesser states a degree of licence they would not have enjoyed in peacetime.

Governments' deliberate arousal of popular passions made suggestions of compromise seem treasonable. The ever-rising cost of the military means inflated the political ends. Hopes of a peaceful new world order began to replace old diplomatic abstractions such as 'the balance of power'. Rationality went out of season. War aims were obscured. Strategies were distorted. Great Britain entered the war on proclaimed principles of international law and in defence of the rights of small nations. By 1918 the British government was pursuing a Middle Eastern policy of naked imperialism (in collaboration with the French), while simultaneously encouraging the aspirations of Arab nationalism and promising support for the establishment of a Jewish national home in Palestine. It was truly a war of illusions.

Europe's political and military leaders have been subjected to much retrospective criticism for their belief that the 'war would be over by Christmas'. This belief was not based on complacency. Even those who predicted with chilling accuracy the murderous nature of First World War battlefields, such as the Polish banker Jan Bloch, expected the war to be short. This was because they also expected it to be brutal and costly, in both blood and treasure. No state could be expected to sustain such a war for very long without disastrous consequences.

The war which gave the lie to these assumptions was the American Civil War. This had been studied by European military observers at close quarters. Most, however, dismissed it. This was particularly true of the Prussians. Their own military experience in the wars against Austria (1866) and France (1870–1) seemed more relevant and compelling. These wars were both short. They were also instrumental. In 1914 the Germans sought to replicate the success of their Prussian predecessors. They aimed to fight a 'cabinet war' on the Bismarckian model. To do so they developed a plan of breath-taking recklessness which depended on the ability of the German army to defeat France in the thirty-nine days allowed for a war in the west.

Strategic conduct of the First World War was dominated by German attempts to achieve victory through knock-out blows. Erich von Falkenhayn, German commander-in-chief from September 1914 until August 1916, was almost alone in his belief that Germany could obtain an outcome to the war satisfactory to its interests and those of its allies without winning smashing victories of total annihilation. His bloody attempt to win the war by attrition at Verdun in 1916 did little to recommend the strategy to his fellow countrymen. The preference for knock-out blows remained. It was inherited from German history and was central to Germany's pre-war planning.

Pre-war German strategy was haunted by the fear of a war on two fronts, against France in the west and Russia in the east. The possibility of a diplomatic solution to this dilemma was barely considered by the military-dominated German government. A military solution was sought instead. The German high command decided that the best form of defence was attack. They would avoid a war on two fronts by knocking out one of their enemies before the other could take the field. The enemy with the slowest military mobilization was Russia. The French army would be in the field first. France was therefore chosen to receive the first blow. Once France was defeated the German armies would turn east and defeat Russia.

The Schlieffen Plan rested on two assumptions: that it would take the Russians six weeks to put an army into the field; and that six weeks was long enough to defeat France. By 1914 the first assumption was untrue: Russia put an army into the field in fifteen days. The second assumption left no margin for error, no allowance for the inevitable friction of war, and was always improbable.

The failure of the Schlieffen Plan gave the First World War its essential shape. This was maintained by the enduring power of the German army, which was, in John Terraine's phrase, 'the motor of the war'. The German army was a potent instrument. It had played a historic role in the emergence of the German state. It enjoyed enormous prestige. It was able to recruit men of talent and dedication as officers and NCOs. As a result it was well trained and well led. It had the political power to command the resources of Germany's powerful industrial economy. Germany's position at the heart of Europe meant that it could operate on interior lines of communication in a European war. The efficient German railway network permitted the movement of

German troops quickly from front to front. The superior speed of the locomotive over the ship frustrated Allied attempts to use their command of the sea to operate effectively against the periphery of the Central Powers. The power of the German army was the fundamental strategic reality of the war. 'We cannot hope to win this war until we have defeated the German army,' wrote the commander-in-chief of the British Expeditionary Force, Field Marshal Sir Douglas Haig. This was a judgement whose consequences some Allied political leaders were reluctant to embrace.

The German army suffered from two important strategic difficulties. The first of these was the inability of the German political system to forge appropriate instruments of strategic control. The second was Great Britain. German government rested on the tortured personality of the Kaiser. It was riven by intrigue and indecision. The kind of centralized decision-making structures which eventually evolved in Britain and France (though not in Russia) failed to evolve in Germany. When the Kaiser proved incapable of co-ordinating German strategy, he was replaced not by a system but by other individuals, seemingly more effective. Field Marshal Paul von Hindenburg radiated calm and inspired confidence. This gave him the appearance of a great man but without the substance. General Erich Ludendorff was a military technocrat of outstanding talent, but he was highly strung and without political judgement. In 1918 his offensive strategy brought Germany to ruin.

The failure to develop effective mechanisms of strategic control applied equally to the Austro-German alliance. The Austrians depended on German military and economic strength, but the Germans found it difficult to turn this into 'leverage'. Austria was willing to take German help but not German advice. Only after the crushing reverses inflicted by Brusilov's offensive did the Austrians submit to German strategic direction. By then it was almost certainly too late.

Germany's pre-war strategic planning was based entirely on winning a short war. British belligerency made this unlikely. The British were a naval rather than a military power. They could not be defeated by the German army, at least not quickly. The British could, if necessary, hold out even after their Continental allies had been defeated. They might even have chosen to do this. They had in the past and they would again in the not-too-distant future. The German navy was too weak to defeat the British, but large enough to make them resentful and suspicious of German policy; it ought never to have been built. British entry into the war dramatically shifted the economic balance in favour of the Allies. Britain was one of the world's great industrial powers. Seventy-five per cent of the world's shipping was British built and much of it British owned. London was the world's greatest money and commodities market. British access to world supplies of food and credit and to imperial resources of manpower made them a formidable enemy, despite the 'contemptible little army' which was all they could put into the field on the outbreak of war. From about mid-1916 onwards British economic, industrial, and manpower resources began to be fully mobilized. Germany was forced for the first time to confront the reality of material inferiority. Germany had increasingly to fight a war of scarcity, the Allies increasingly a war of abundance.

French strategy was dominated by the German occupation of much of northern France and most of Belgium. At its closest point the German line was less than 40 miles from Paris. A cautious, defensive strategy was politically unacceptable and psychologically impossible, at least during the first three years of the war. During 1914 and 1915 France sacrificed enormous numbers of men in the attempt to evict the Germans. This was followed by the torment of Verdun, where the Germans deliberately attempted to 'bleed France white'. French fears of military inferiority were confirmed. If France was to prevail its allies would have to contribute in kind. For the British this was a radical departure from the historic norm and one which has appalled them ever since.

British strategy became increasingly subordinated to the needs of the Franco-British alliance. The British fought the war as they had to, not as they wanted to. The British way in warfare envisaged a largely naval war. A naval blockade would weaken Germany economically. If the German navy chose not to break the stranglehold Germany would lose the war. If it did choose to fight it would be annihilated. British maritime superiority would be confirmed. Neutral opinion would be cowed. Fresh allies would be encouraged into the fight. The blockade would be waged with greater ruthlessness. Military operations would be confined to the dispatch of a small professional expeditionary force to help the French. Remaining military forces would be employed on the periphery of the Central Powers remote from the German army, where it was believed they would exercise a strategic influence out of all proportion to their size.

The British never really fought the war they envisaged. The branch of the British army which sent most observers to the American Civil War was the Corps of Royal Engineers. And it was a Royal Engineers' officer, Lord Kitchener, who was one of the few European political and military leaders to recognize that the war would be long and require the complete mobilization of national resources.

Kitchener was appointed Secretary of State for War on 5 August 1914. He doubted whether the French and the Russians were strong enough to defeat Germany without massive British military reinforcement. He immediately sought to raise a mass citizen army. There was an overwhelming popular response to his call to arms. Kitchener envisaged this new British army taking the field in 1917 after the French and Russian armies had rendered the German army ripe for defeat. They would be 'the last million men'. They would win the war and decide the peace. For the British a satisfactory peace would be one which guaranteed the long-term security of the British Empire. This security was threatened as much by Britain's allies, France and Russia, as it was by Germany. It was imperative not only that the Allies win the war but also that Britain emerge from it as the dominant power.

Kitchener's expectations were disappointed. By 1916 it was the French army which was ripe for defeat, not the German. But the obligations of the French alliance were inescapable. The British could not afford to acquiesce in a French defeat. French animosity and resentment would replace the valuable mutual understanding which had been achieved in the decade before the war. The French had a great capacity for making imperial mischief.

And so did the Russians. If they were abandoned they would have every reason for doing so. There seemed no choice. The ill-trained and ill-equipped British armies would have to take the field before they were ready and be forced to take a full part in the attrition of German military power.

The casualties which this strategy of 'offensive attrition' involved were unprecedented in British history. They were also unacceptable to some British political leaders. Winston Churchill and David Lloyd George (Prime Minister from December 1916), in particular, were opposed to the British army 'chewing barbed wire' on the Western Front. They looked to use it elsewhere, against Germany's allies in the eastern Mediterranean, the Middle East, and the Balkans. Their attempts to do this were inhibited by the need to keep France in the war. This could only be done in France and by fighting the German army. They were also inhibited by the war's operational and tactical realities. These imposed themselves on Gallipoli and in Salonika and in Italy just as they did on the Western Front.

Attempts to implement an Allied grand strategy enjoyed some success. Allied political and military leaders met regularly. At Chantilly in December 1915 and December 1916 they determined to stretch the German army to its limits by simultaneous offensive action on the western, eastern, and Italian fronts. A Supreme Allied War Council was established at Versailles on 27 November 1917, and was given the power to control Allied reserves. Franco-British co-operation was especially close. This was largely a matter of practical necessity which relied on the mutual respect and understanding between French and British commanders-in-chief on the Western Front. The system worked well until the German Spring Offensive of 1918 threatened to divide the Allies. Only then was it replaced by a more formal structure. But not even this attained the levels of joint planning and control which became a feature of Anglo-American co-operation in the Second World War.

Allied grand strategy was conceptually sound. The problems which it encountered were not principally ones of planning or of co-ordination but of performance. Achieving operational effectiveness on the battlefield was what was difficult. This has given the war, especially the war in the west, its enduring image of boneheaded commanders wantonly sacrificing the lives of their men in fruitless pursuit of impossibly grandiose strategic designs.

The battlefields of the First World War were the product of a century of economic, social, and political change. Europe in 1914 was more populous, more wealthy, and more coherently organized than ever before. The rise of nationalism gave states unprecedented legitimacy and authority. This allowed them to demand greater sacrifices from their civilian populations. Improvements in agriculture reduced the numbers needed to work on the land and provided a surplus of males of military age. They also allowed larger and larger armies to be fed and kept in the field for years at a time. Changes in administrative practice brought about by the electric telegraph, the telephone, the typewriter, and the growth of railways allowed these armies to be assembled and deployed quickly. Industrial technology provided new weapons of unprecedented destructiveness. Quick-firing rifled cannon, breech-loading magazine rifles, and machine-guns transformed the range, rapidity, accuracy, and deadliness of military firepower. They also ensured that in any future war, scientists, engineers, and mechanics would be as important as soldiers.

These changes did much to make the First World War the first 'modern war'. But it did not begin as one. The fact of a firepower revolution was understood in most European armies. The consequences of it were not. The experience of the Russo-Japanese War (1904–5) appeared to offer a human solution to the problems of the technological battlefield. Victory would go to the side with the best-trained, most disciplined army, commanded by generals of iron resolution, prepared to maintain the offensive in the face of huge losses. As a result the opening battles of the war were closer in conception and execution to those of the Napoleonic era than to the battles of 1916 onwards.

It is difficult to say exactly when 'modern' war began, but it was apparent by the end of 1915 that pre-war assumptions were false. Well-trained, highly disciplined French, German, and Russian soldiers of high morale were repeatedly flung into battle by commanders of iron resolve. The results were barren of strategic

achievement. The human costs were immense. The 'human solution' was not enough. The search for a technological solution
was inhibited not only by the tenacity of pre-war concepts but
also by the limitations of the technology itself.

The principal instrument of education was artillery. And the
mode of instruction was experience. Shell-fire was merciless to
troops in the open. The response was to get out of the open and
into the ground. Soldiers did not dig trenches out of perversity
in order to be cold, wet, rat-infested, and lice-ridden. They dug
them in order to survive. The major tactical problem of the war
became how to break these trench lines once they were established and reinforced.

For much of the war artillery lacked the ability to find enemy
targets, to hit them accurately, and to destroy them effectively.
Contemporary technology failed to provide a man-portable
wireless. Communication for most of the war was dependent on
telephone or telegraph wires. These were always broken by
shell-fire and difficult to protect. Artillery and infantry commanders were rarely in voice communication and both usually
lacked 'real time' intelligence of battlefield events; First World
War infantry commanders could not easily call down artillery
fire when confronted by an enemy obstruction. As a result the
co-ordination of infantry and artillery was always difficult and
often impossible. Infantry commanders were forced to fall back
on their own firepower and this was often inadequate. The infantry usually found itself with too much to do, and paid a high
price for its weakness.

Artillery was not only a major part of the problem, however. It
was also a major part of the solution. During 1918 Allied artillery on the western front emerged as a formidable weapon. Target acquisition was radically improved by aerial photographic
reconnaissance and the sophisticated techniques of flash-spotting
and sound-ranging. These allowed mathematically predicted fire,
or map-shooting. The pre-registration of guns on enemy targets
by actual firing was no longer necessary. The possibility of surprise returned to the battlefield. Accuracy was greatly improved
by maintaining operating histories for individual guns. Battery
commanders were supplied with detailed weather forecasts every

four hours. Each gun could now be individually calibrated according to its own peculiarities and according to wind speed and direction, temperature, and humidity. All types and calibres of guns, including heavy siege howitzers whose steep angle of fire was especially effective in trench warfare, became available in virtually unlimited numbers. Munitions were also improved. Poison gas shells became available for the first time in large numbers. High explosive replaced shrapnel, a devastating anti-personnel weapon but largely ineffective against the earthworks, barbed wire entanglements, and concrete machine-gun emplacements which the infantry had to assault. Instantaneous percussion fuses concentrated the explosive effect of shells more effectively against barbed wire and reduced the cratering of the battlefield which had often rendered the forward movement of supplies and reinforcements difficult if not impossible. Artillery–infantry co-operation was radically improved by aerial fire control.

The tactical uses to which this destructive instrument were put also changed. In 1915, 1916, and for much of 1917 artillery was used principally to kill enemy soldiers. It always did so, sometimes in large numbers. But it always spared some, even in front-line trenches. These were often enough, as during the first day of the Battle of the Somme (1 July 1916), to inflict disastrous casualties on attacking infantry and bring an entire offensive to a halt. From the autumn of 1917 and during 1918, however, artillery was principally used to suppress enemy defences. Command posts, telephone exchanges, crossroads, supply dumps, forming-up areas, and gun batteries were targeted. Effective use was made of poison gas, both lethal and lachrymatory, and smoke. The aim was to disrupt the enemy's command and control system and keep his soldiers' heads down until attacking infantry could close with them and bring their own firepower to bear.

The attacking infantry were also transformed. In 1914 the British soldier went to war dressed like a gamekeeper in a soft cap, armed only with rifle and bayonet. In 1918 he went into battle dressed like an industrial worker in a steel helmet, protected by a respirator against poison gas, armed with automatic weapons and mortars, supported by tanks and ground-attack aircraft, and preceded by a creeping artillery barrage of crushing intensity. Firepower replaced manpower as the instrument of victory. This represented a revolution in the conduct of war.

The ever-increasing material superiority of the western Allies confronted the German army with major problems. Its response was organizational. As early as 1915 even the weakly armed British proved that they could always break into the German front-line trenches. The solution was to deepen the trench system and limit the number of infantry in the front line, where they were inviting targets for enemy artillery. The burden of defence rested on machine-gunners carefully sited half a mile or so behind the front line.

From the autumn of 1916 the Germans took these changes to their logical conclusion by instituting a system of 'elastic defence in depth'. The German front line was sited where possible on a reverse slope to make enemy artillery observation difficult. A formal front-line trench system was abandoned. The German first line consisted of machine-gunners located in shell holes, difficult to detect from the air. Their job was to disrupt an enemy infantry assault. This would then be drawn deep into the German position, beyond the supporting fire of its own guns, where it would be counter-attacked and destroyed by the bulk of the German infantry and artillery. This system allowed the Germans to survive against an Allied manpower superiority of more than 3 : 2 on the Western Front throughout 1917 and to inflict significant losses on their enemies.

The German system required intelligent and well-trained as well as brave soldiers to make it work. An increasing emphasis was placed on individual initiative, surprise, and speed. In 1918 specially trained 'stormtroops', supported by a hurricane bombardment designed to disrupt their enemies' lines of communication and their command and control systems, were ordered to bypass points of resistance and advance deep into the enemy's rear. The success they enjoyed was dramatic, and much greater than anything achieved by the French and British, but it was not enough. Attacking German infantry could not maintain the momentum and inflict upon enemy commanders the kind of moral paralysis that would be achieved by German armoured

forces in 1940. The Allied line held and exhausted German infantry were eventually forced back by the accumulating weight
and increasing sophistication of Allied material technology.

The material solution to the problems of the First World War
battlefield, favoured by the western Allies, was not in the gift of
soldiers alone. It depended on the ability of the armies' host societies to produce improved military technology in ever-greater
amounts. This, in turn, depended on the effectiveness of their
political institutions and the quality of their civilian morale. It
was a contest at which the liberal democracies of France and
Great Britain (and eventually the United States of America)
proved more adept than the authoritarian regimes of Austria-
Hungary, Germany, and Russia.

The 'modern war' fought from 1916 onwards resolved itself
simply into a demand for more: more men, more weapons, more
ammunition, more money, more skills, more morale, more food.
Some of the demands were contradictory. More men meant
more men for the armies and more men for the factories. Balancing the competing demands was never easy. 'Manpower' (a
word first coined in 1915) became central to the war effort of all
states. The Allies were in a much stronger position than Germany. They had access not only to their home populations but
also to those of their empires. 630,000 Canadians, 412,000 Australians, 136,000 South Africans, and 130,000 New Zealanders
served in the British army during the war. Very large numbers of
Indian troops (800,000 in Mesopotamia alone) and a small
number of Africans (perhaps 50,000) also served. (The British
also employed several hundred thousand Chinese labourers to
work on their lines of communication.) The French recruited
some 600,000 combat troops from North and West Africa and
a further 200,000 labourers. And of course there were the Americans. American troops arrived in France at the rate of 150,000
a month in 1918. Truly the new world had come in to redress the
balance of the old.

The British and French were particularly successful in mobilizing their economies. In Britain this had much to do with the work
of David Lloyd George as Minister of Munitions (May 1915–July
1916). The grip of the skilled trade unions on industrial processes

was relaxed. Ancient lines of demarcation were blurred. Women replaced men in the factories. Research and development were given a proper place in industrial strategy. Prodigies of production were achieved. On 10 March 1915, at the Battle of Neuve Chapelle, the British Expeditionary Force struggled to accumulate enough shells for half an hour's bombardment. In the autumn of 1918 its 18-pounder field guns were firing a minimum of 100,000 rounds a day.

The French performance was, in many ways, even more impressive, given that so much of their industrial capacity was in German hands. Not only did the French economy supply the French army with increasing amounts of old and new weaponry, but it also supplied most of the American Expeditionary Force's artillery and aeroplanes. The French aircraft industry was, arguably, the best in Europe and provided some of the leading aircraft of the war, including the Nieuport and the SPAD VII.

Morale was also a key factor. All sides tried to explain and justify the war and used increasingly refined techniques of propaganda to maintain commitment to the cause. Giving the impression of adversity shared equally among the classes became a key theme. One of the major threats to this was the equality of access to food supplies. In Germany this proved increasingly difficult to maintain. Morale deteriorated and industrial efficiency suffered as a result. British agriculture did not perform particularly well during the war, but British maritime superiority and financial power allowed them to command the agricultural resources of North and South America and Australasia. Food was one of the Allies' principal war-winning weapons. The degree of active resistance to the war was low in most countries. But war-weariness set in everywhere by 1917. There were many strikes and much industrial unrest. In Russia this was severe enough to produce a revolution and then a Bolshevik *coup d'état* which took Russia out of the war in 1918.

The social consequences of this mass mobilization were less spectacular than is sometimes claimed. There were advances for the organized working class, especially its trade unions, especially in Britain, and arguably for women, but the working class of Europe paid a high price on the battlefield for social advances at home. And in the defeated states there was very little social advance anyway.

The First World War redrew the map of Europe and the Middle East. Four great empires, the Romanov, the Hohenzollern, the Habsburg, and the Ottoman, were defeated and collapsed. They were replaced by a number of weak and sometimes avaricious successor states. Russia underwent a bloody civil war before the establishment of a Communist Soviet Union which put it beyond the pale of European diplomacy for a generation. Germany became a republic branded at its birth with the stigma of defeat, increasingly weakened by the burden of Allied reparations and by inflation. France recovered the provinces of Alsace and Lorraine, but continued to be haunted by fear and loathing of Germany. Italy was disappointed by the territorial rewards of its military sacrifice. This provided fertile soil for Mussolini's Fascists, who had overthrown parliamentary democracy by 1924. The British maintained the integrity and independence of Belgium. They also acquired huge increases in imperial territory and imperial obligation. But they did not achieve the security for the Empire which they sought. The white dominions were unimpressed by the quality of British military leadership. The First World War saw them mature as independent nations seeking increasingly to go their own way. The stirrings of revolt in India were apparent as soon as the war ended. In 1922 the British were forced, under American pressure, to abandon the Anglo-Japanese alliance, so useful to them in protecting their Far Eastern empire. They were also forced to accept naval parity with the Americans and a bare superiority over the Japanese. 'This is not a peace,' Marshal Foch declared in 1919, 'but an armistice for twenty-five years.'

The cost of all this in human terms was 8.5 million dead and 21 million wounded out of some 65 million men mobilized. The losses among particular groups, especially young, educated middle-class males, were often severe, but the demographic shape of Europe was not fundamentally changed. The real impact was moral. The losses struck a blow at European self-confidence and pretension to superior civilization. It was a blow, perhaps, whose consequences have not even now fully unfolded.

8

Total War II

The Second World War

RICHARD OVERY

The Second World War was a war of extremes. All the powers that fought it were pushed to the very depths of physical and moral endurance. Not since the European wars of religion three centuries before had ideological confrontation provoked such a depth of hatred and military barbarism. No other war in modern times made such demands on the manpower and economic product of the combatants. War was fought by soldiers and civilians; both were its casualties. The 55 million who died in the conflict exceeded the number killed in all the other wars of the modern age together.

It was also a war of extraordinary contrasts. On the Eastern Front both sides fought with large tank armies, but at times reverted to fighting on horseback. In August 1942 two squadrons of Italian cavalry performed their country's last mounted charge, with sabres drawn, against a Soviet infantry division. In the Far East Japanese soldiers fought with knives and the long *samurai* sword side by side with machine-guns. Biplanes saw service throughout a war that generated the first rockets, the first intercontinental bombers, and, at its very end, the first nuclear weapons. Women and children fought in uniform alongside men; 12-year-old boys were drafted into the final frantic defence of the German homeland; regiments of Soviet women fought in the Red Army's advance on Berlin. Hundreds of thousands of women and children died in the front line of the air war in the bombing of Germany and Japan. Throughout the conflict more civilians were killed than soldiers.

The onset of total war

This was the kind of war widely expected in the 1930s. After the experience of the Great War of 1914–18 it was generally assumed that in an age of mass politics and mass production war was waged between whole populations, soldier and civilian alike. The concept of conventional warfare, fought in brief campaigns between rival armed forces, was replaced by the concept of 'total war'. The term was coined by General Erich Ludendorff, the German First Quartermaster General (joint chief of staff), in 1918, but soon gained an international currency. Simply put, total war was a revolutionary departure from traditional theories of conflict. To be able to wage total war states would have to mobilize all the material, intellectual, and moral energies of their peoples; by implication the enemy community as a whole—its scientists, workers, and farmers—became legitimate objects of war. The widespread civilian deaths in the wars of the 1930s in Ethiopia, China, and Spain underscored the change and accustomed populations to the uncomfortable reality that warfare was now indiscriminate.

War preparation in the 1930s was governed everywhere by the imperatives of total war. Economic resources were stockpiled; substitute industries were set up to produce essential raw materials such as oil whose supply might be cut off in war; programmes of civil defence were initiated to prepare home populations for attack by bombs or gas. In the United States an Industrial War College was set up in the 1920s to absorb the lessons of the economic contest in the Great War and to prepare for economic mobilization in the next. In Hitler's Germany the authorities designed propaganda campaigns to prepare the population psychologically for wartime sacrifices.

When the armed forces began to work out the strategy appropriate for total war their views were also shaped by the assumption that high levels of economic mobilization and the maintenance of domestic morale and financial stability were as important as performance on the battlefield. Here the similarities ended. On strictly military issues the differing experiences of the Great War provided the inspiration for very different strategies. German forces wanted to avoid the trench stalemate which had slowly eroded German resources and warwillingness. They returned to the idea of the decisive battlefield engagement, using all the nation's resources, prepared in advance, for a crushing blow at the enemy. The blow was to be inflicted by a combination of armour and aircraft which would act as the spearhead of a rapidly deployed infantry mass. In Britain and France, on the other hand, the idea of a defensive war of attrition, which had eventually produced victory in 1918, was resurrected. When British and French military staffs drew up plans for wartime strategy in the spring of 1939 they decided to stay put in the early stages of war behind a defensive wall, while they wore down German resistance by economic blockade and bombing, before delivering the *coup de grâce* several years later on a weakened and demoralized enemy. It was assumed that the artillery barrage and the machine-gun still gave the military edge to the defender.

When these two differing views of modern warfare were pitted against each other in the summer of 1940 it was shown in six weeks that German choices had been more percipient. Warning had already been given in the first two weeks of war, in September 1939, when the German army and air force tore Polish forces to shreds in a matter of days. The western Allies had expected a campaign of six months. On 10 May 1940 German forces tried again the gamble that had failed in the Spring Offensive of 1918. A fist of ten armoured and motorized divisions—only 7 per cent of the attacking force—drove rapidly across the Low Countries to deliver an annihilating blow against the overstretched French and British line. With good battlefield aviation supporting ground forces, and an effective system of radio communication, the German military made the most of their resources against an enemy whose cast of mind was defensive and whose communication and organization at the front proved woefully deficient. The British and French concept of a war of attrition and blockade, fought partly by bombing aircraft, never materialized. The two western states lost sight in the 1930s of the most basic element of warfare—the ability to fight effectively on the field of battle itself. Both sides possessed comparable resources (the Germans had in fact fewer and poorer-quality tanks) but German military leaders emphasized high standards of training and operational preparation and technical efficiency, the very virtues that brought victory in 1866 over Austria and in 1870 over France.

When France surrendered on 19 June and British forces retreated from Dunkirk back to the home country, it was widely assumed that the war was over. In July Hitler opened the door to an agreement with Britain on German terms. Britain refused to treat with Hitler, and returned for lack of any alternative to the strategy of blockade and bombing adopted in 1939. By this point Germany was not the only enemy. In the wake of German success Mussolini's Italy declared war on Britain and France on 10 June. A few weeks later Japanese forces moved into French Indo-China, threatening Britain's imperial position in the Far East. Unable to get at Hitler's Germany for want of a large Continental army, Britain turned to a form of warfare with which it was much more familiar: small-scale overseas operations supported by naval power and native imperial forces. The defence of the Suez Canal and of India became the focus of British efforts; against Italian forces in North and East Africa the British found an enemy they could defeat.

The war at sea

Until re-entry to continental Europe became possible in force in 1944 Britain fought what was essentially a naval war, supported increasingly by aircraft. Naval power was a critical element in British war-making. The navy kept open the vital trade routes on which Britain's economy and home population depended for survival, and was the instrument which linked together the scattered territories of the Empire and ferried the resources to defend them. Command of the seas was essential to the conduct of any army operation staged outside the motherland. In 1940 the British navy was second only to the American in size, and quite dwarfed the naval forces of Germany and Italy. The threat of its use was sufficient to persuade Hitler that an army invasion of the British Isles in the autumn of 1940 was not yet feasible, even had German air forces been able to contain the RAF sufficiently to provide air cover for an invasion fleet.

From 1940 until the summer of 1943 Britain and Germany fought a contest for control of the Atlantic. German submarines were ordered to strangle British trade and British reinforcement of the Mediterranean and the Far East. With limited numbers of vessels, but with the ability to break British naval ciphers, submarine packs concentrated their efforts in areas where convoys could not be protected by shore-based aircraft. In 1941 submarines sank 1,299 ships; in 1942 1,662, with a total tonnage of almost 8 million. British trade was reduced to less than a third of pre-war volumes. Disaster was avoided only by a vigorous programme to expand domestic agricultural output and a strategy of stockpiling which had begun in the 1930s as a precaution against blockade. In March 1943 the level of attrition experienced by Allied shipping was so high that the British Admiralty feared the collapse of the Atlantic trade routes and, in effect, of Britain's war effort.

The tide in the anti-submarine war was turned not by the old instruments of sea warfare but by the new generation of weapons, radio, radar, and aircraft. Every effort was made to reduce shipping losses as in the First World War by developing a convoy system, providing specially trained escort vessels, and using sonar detection and depth charges. Against modern ocean-going submarines, equipped with advanced radio technology and supplied with intelligence on convoy movements, these methods were ineffective. During 1942 Allied naval forces were supplied with a new generation of radar equipment, based on centimetric frequencies rather than the conventional 1.7 metres, which allowed much more successful tracking of submarines. Great effort was put into breaking German naval codes so that by 1943 submarine strategy could be followed by radio intelligence. Above all the submarine was subjected to more effective air attack.

Though most navies in 1939 were still resistant to the idea

that air power might transform naval strategy, the first years of war demonstrated decisively that sea power, like land power, could only be deployed successfully with adequate air protection. The German battleship *Bismarck* was the most famous victim of air attack, in May 1941, crippled by an airborne torpedo in the Atlantic 700 miles west of Brest; in November 1940 a handful of British biplanes mauled the Italian fleet at Taranto; the German long-range Kondor aircraft sank 150,000 tons of shipping a month in 1941 far out into the Atlantic. Submarines proved particularly vulnerable to air attack. Once aircraft were fitted with the new centimetric radar and effective anti-submarine armament they exacted a high toll. A combination of long-range aircraft hunting over the whole area of the Atlantic in 1943 and of escort carriers sailing with the convoys brought the defeat of the German submarine. In 1943 out of 237 German vessels sunk, 149 were victims of aircraft.

The revolutionary effect of aircraft in sea warfare was demonstrated beyond doubt in the Far East. Japan was one of the few naval powers to recognize the impact of aircraft. When in 1941 Japanese authorities finally decided to use German victories as a shield for their own imperialism in the Pacific, the naval aviators, the élite of Japan's air forces, did to enemy navies what German panzer divisions did to enemy armies. Small in number but technically proficient, Japan's naval air forces formed the spearhead of Japan's war launched on 7 December 1941 against the United States and the colonial powers in the Pacific. At the main American naval base at Pearl Harbor in Hawaii the Japanese air attack almost succeeded in knocking out the American Pacific Fleet at a stroke. Over the following three months British and Dutch naval power was similarly blunted. Without air cover battleships were an expensive liability; without naval aviation an enemy fleet could not be brought to defeat.

It was Japan's misfortune to be confronted in the Pacific by the United States navy, not simply because of its sheer size and the economic potential of American dockyards, but because American seamen had realized sooner than Europeans that aircraft could play a decisive role in naval combat. The US navy possessed large purpose-built aircraft-carriers and a core of marine aviators. American ships also carried radar, and American radio intelligence had access to Japanese codes. These last advantages were vital in the critical naval battles in the summer of 1942. Japan, like Germany, hoped to interrupt Allied supply routes across the ocean to prevent effective reinforcement of the Pacific theatre. In May and June Japanese naval task forces were sent to secure the island bases necessary for this strategy around the Coral Sea, north of Australia, and the American island of Midway, close to Pearl Harbor itself. The Japanese naval commander, Admiral Yamamoto, hoped to lure what was left of the American fleet to a naval battle where Japan's overwhelming preponderance of capital ships could be brought to bear.

The naval engagement never materialized. In both the battles, in the Coral Sea in May 1942, and at Midway on 4–5 June, the conflict was decided entirely by aircraft, which kept the rival surface forces at arm's length. In the Battle of Midway American aircraft-carriers, concealed from the enemy by successful deception, succeeded in sinking the entire Japanese carrier force and destroying half its specialist pilots. The loss was difficult to make good. In 1943 and 1944 Japanese shipyards supplied a further seven carriers; American shipyards produced ninety. American aircraft and submarines, against which Japanese forces had very little effective defence, slowly stripped Japan of its naval and merchant shipping. Over the course of the war air–sea co-operation on the Allied side in the Pacific continually improved with the introduction of high-quality naval dive-bombers, modern radar, and radio communication. The pride of the Japanese battle fleet, the giant battleship *Yamato*, symbol of the traditional age of naval mastery, fell victim in 1945, on its way to the defence of the island of Okinawa, to scores of American aircraft.

The War on Land I: the conflict for Asia

While British and American navies fought for control of the oceans, the armies and air forces of Germany, the USSR, Japan, and China fought for control of the Asian land mass. The German attack on the Soviet Union in June 1941 and the earlier attack by Japan against China, which began in 1931 and turned into a full-scale war in 1937, had much in common. In both states there flourished the belief that their populations needed economic living-space in order to prosper on equal terms with the rich western states; popular ideas on imperialism and race turned both states towards the territories of mainland Asia, whose peoples were regarded as inferior and whose political systems—the Communist Soviet Union and the Chinese dictatorship of Chiang Kaishek—were thought to be both weak and corrupt. The struggle to carve out the new economic and political order in Asia produced total war in its most extreme form. The Soviet Union mobilized its entire population to the limit of physical and moral endurance; Germany and Japan imposed heavier and heavier burdens on their own populations in the effort to secure victory, but, consistent with the ideology of racial exploitation, millions of Koreans, Chinese, and the Soviet nationalities were employed as slave labour. In both the conflict for Eurasia and the war in China an estimated 17 million civilians lost their lives, most from enemy action, some at the hand of their own harsh authorities.

The war between Germany and the Soviet Union which began on 22 June 1941 was waged on an extraordinary scale across a front of 1,000 miles. The war was Hitler's inspiration. Following the success of German forces in 1939 and 1940 he finally decided in December 1940 to launch a quick strike at the Soviet Union using the same war of movement and concentrated armoured/air fighting power that had succeeded until then. Divided into three army groups, North, Centre, and South, three million German and allied forces drove against the unprepared Soviet armies in a series of devastating pincer movements which brought them to the edge of Leningrad and Moscow in four months, and to the economically rich Donets Basin in the southern Ukraine. The winter weather prevented the quick victory Hitler wanted, but the following spring German forces moved forward again in the south to try to capture the whole of the southern industrial and oil region and to swing behind the remaining Soviet forces to the north to complete one final annihilating encirclement. By September German forces had reached Stalingrad on the Volga and the edge of the Caucasus mountains.

The German attack was a model of operational skill and tactical efficiency, but by the late summer of 1942 there were clear signs that the momentum was lost. In November the Soviet armies on either side of Stalingrad inflicted the first major defeat on the invading force. The encirclement and capture of 300,000 men of the German 6th Army in Stalingrad in January 1943 was regarded world-wide as the point at which the tide turned against the aggressor states. The German defeat has often been blamed on Hitler himself, who had taken over direct command of German armies in December 1941. While it is certainly the case that he led his forces into a campaign where they became vulnerably overstretched across the steppe of southern Russia, few German generals even in the autumn of 1942 thought that Soviet forces were capable of very serious resistance in the south. The roots of the German problem go deeper than this. During the first eighteen months of the conflict the German forces underwent a gradual process of 'de-modernization'. The numbers of aircraft and tanks were constantly reduced through high battle losses and the diversion of resources to other fronts. Production in the Reich failed to keep pace. At the end of very long lines of communication the maintenance and repair of vehicles and planes became a logistical nightmare. The severe climate—bitterly cold in winter, hot and dusty in the summer—took a heavy toll of vehicles. Armoured divisions began the war with 328 tanks apiece; by the summer of 1943 they averaged 73; by the end of the war the figure was 54. The German army fell back on the use of horses. During 1942 German industry turned out only 59,000 trucks for an army of 8 million men, but the same year 400,000 horses were sent to the Eastern Front. The German forces concentrated their air and tank power on a few élite divisions; the rest of the army moved like those of the Great War, by rail, horse, or foot.

The Soviet forces experienced entirely the opposite process. From a feeble platform in 1941 Soviet armies and air forces underwent an extraordinary programme of reform and modernization. Soviet military leaders set out deliberately to copy the success of their enemy. Air forces were concentrated in large air armies, centrally co-ordinated for the most flexible response to problems at the front line, and with great improvements in radio communication which made it possible to give effective support to ground forces. Armies were reorganized to match German practice, with a core of heavily armoured and mobile divisions. Small improvements, such as the installation of two-way radios in tanks, supplied from the United States as aid, produced a radical change in fighting power. Stalin gave high priority to supply and logistics, and by 1943 the number of aircraft and tanks produced began to overhaul German production by a wide margin, while the technical quality improved remarkably in the course of two years. The most significant reform came in the attention paid to operational skills. Stalin devolved responsibility for organizing operations to the general staff and his exceptionally talented deputy Marshal Zhukov. Under his leadership the Soviet forces proved capable of planning and executing operations involving millions of men, a feat quite beyond Soviet generals in the early stages of the war.

The effects of these far-reaching reforms were demonstrated in the largest and most significant set-piece battle of the war, at Kursk in July 1943. In an effort to stabilize their front- line German generals planned to lure the Soviet forces into a huge pitched battle on the Kursk steppe where they hoped to encircle and capture the core of the revived Red Army. Zhukov prepared a defensive field of such depth and sophistication that the German armoured spearheads were only able to move a matter of miles before annihilating Soviet counter-offensives broke the German line and drove the invading force back beyond the Dnieper River. In the following eighteen months Soviet offensive tactics succeeded in driving back what had been regarded until then as the finest army and air force in the world. German forces swung on to the defensive, concentrating on using tanks as mobile defensive artillery, and switching to the mass production of anti-tank guns and heavy defensive armament. The growing imbalance of forces in favour of the Red Army disguised the extent to which the balance on the battlefield began to swing back to the defender. In the gruelling advance into Germany both sides suffered extraordinary losses. It was here that the Second World War was won and lost. The Red Army destroyed some 607 divisions of German and allied forces between 1941 and 1945. Two-thirds of German tank losses were inflicted on the Eastern Front.

China was much less successful than the Soviet Union in resisting invasion. By the end of 1941 Japan controlled much of northern China and the key coastal areas of the south. Chinese nationalist forces were in general poorly armed and led, though supplies from the United States flown on the difficult 'Hump' route from India kept a residual resistance alive. In 1944 Japanese forces launched a final major offensive—operation Ichi-Go—which brought them control of much of southern China and linked up their whole empire from Korea in the north to Malaya in the south. The contest resembled more traditional warfare, for neither side had the industrial and technical resources to sustain large-scale air and tank warfare. Japanese troops fought with old-fashioned rifles and small-calibre artillery. Tanks were lightly armed and few in number—400 produced in 1944, 141 in 1945. The more up-to-date weaponry was kept for the fight against American forces in the Pacific. Japanese forces relied on high levels of endurance and a reputation for brutality. Swords, knives, even bows and arrows, were employed alongside guns against a Chinese population whose powers of resistance were drastically impaired by corruption, factionalism, and official incompetence. The feeble nature of the Japanese threat was exposed in August 1945 when Soviet forces swept through Manchuria in ten days. For both the German and Japanese armies the Asian campaigns did not provide the easy victory they anticipated over Asian 'primitivism'. Both their intended victims, China and the Soviet Union, emerged from the war as Asia's major military powers.

The revolution in warfare: air power

The war on land and at sea was transformed by aircraft. The development of tactical aviation, in support of armies on the ground, prevented the Second World War from degenerating into the trench stalemate of the First. Fast monoplane fighters armed with guns and rockets, dive-bombers with 'tank-busting' weapons, medium bombers with high explosives, anti-personnel shells, or napalm, became the standard armoury of battlefield aviation. The moral and material effect of air attack was usually sufficient to blast a way forward for attacking armour except in difficult terrain or against an enemy well dug in in bunkers and trenches. Radio communication was generally adopted at the front line to co-ordinate air and ground attacks, while battlefield radar gave warning of enemy attack.

Aircraft also revolutionized sea warfare in action against surface vessels and against submarines, as well as in the defensive role of protecting convoys and fleet movements. Even in the more mundane areas of supply and reconnaissance aircraft provided a new dimension. Troops in the field were supplied by parachute (on occasion even soldiers were dropped by parachute—the storming of the Eben Emael fortress in Belgium in May 1940, the German capture of Crete in May 1941, and so on), and long air supply routes were established from America to Africa and Europe, for the supply of China and the provisioning of partisan resistance movements. Reconnaissance from the air became a routine source of intelligence on enemy movements or potential military targets. Camera technology was transformed during the war years, and photographic interpretation became one of the key areas of intelligence, less glamorous than the world of codes and spies, but no less essential.

In all these functions aircraft played a supporting or ancillary role. The one area where air forces operated independently—the conduct of so-called 'strategic bombing'—proved the most radical departure of all. Bombing was the supreme instrument of total war. It was directed at the enemy population through attacks on economic targets or domestic morale. It was indiscriminate in its effects because the technology of long-range bombing did not permit the accurate destruction of military targets. Bombing strategy was deliberately aimed not at forces in the field but at the war-willingness and productive capacity of the society behind them.

This form of air warfare featured little on the Eastern Front, partly because of the very long distances involved, but largely because both German and Soviet forces clung to the Clausewitzian view that wars are only won by defeating the enemy's main forces in the field. Strategic bombing was adopted only in Britain and the United States as a central plank in their war-making. This was partly because they expected their enemies to use the air weapon ruthlessly in some kind of first strike (a fear that proved utterly groundless), partly because both states took a very economic view of war rooted in traditions of blockade, partly because bombing would avoid the terrible casualty rates of the Great War which democratic governments hesitated to impose on their own peoples. From the late 1930s the RAF was committed to attacks against German industrial centres and in May 1940 the campaign was officially launched. The United States Army Air Force followed suit in 1941 when plans were drawn up in detail for the precise destruction of a web of vital war industries.

The bombing strategy foundered at first on technical immaturity. The RAF was forced to bomb at night to avoid high losses, but this made accurate bombing almost impossible. The USAAF began in 1942 a campaign of daylight bombing which was more accurate, but was subject to high attrition rates from the waiting fighters and more than 50,000 anti-aircraft guns defending the Reich by 1944. In the winter of 1943/4 both air forces were close to abandoning the campaign because of German defences. The enterprise was rescued by the introduction of improved navigational aids and better bombing tactics, but above all by the introduction of the 'strategic fighter', aircraft equipped with extra fuel tanks to carry them over German airspace. Once the enemy air force was fought on equal terms by Allied fighters German air power was quickly blunted and bombers were much freer to attack industrial targets at will.

The defeat of the German air force coincided with improvements in accuracy and weight of attack which made the combined bomber force a formidable instrument against a highly integrated and tautly stretched war economy. The effects of bombing were twofold. First the bombing campaign diverted a great deal of Germany's war effort away from the war at sea or the main fighting fronts. The fighter force was sucked into the defence of the Reich; German bomber production was cut right back; one-third of the production of heavy guns and electrical and radar equipment went to anti-aircraft defences. Bombing constituted a genuine second front by 1943. The other effects were economic. Bombing placed a ceiling on the expansion of German war potential. In 1944 the production of major weapons and strategic resources such as synthetic oil was cut back sharply because of the bombing. Two million Germans manned the air defences or organized repairs. Bombing undermined the reliability of German workers and forced expensive programmes of evacuation and rehabilitation. It did not end the war on its own, as more outspoken airmen hoped, but bombing distorted the German war effort, demoralized the work-force, and drained the battlefronts of vital resources.

The western states devoted a large fraction of their research and production programme to the bombing campaign. Bomber technology was constantly refined until in the Boeing B29 'superfortress' the USAAF produced the first of the generation of intercontinental bombers which dominated the early Cold War years. Work on the armament of air warfare produced the largest research programme of the war, the 'Manhattan Project' for the production of nuclear weapons. A bomb was not finally developed until after the war with Germany was over. Both the B29 and the first nuclear bombs were turned against Japan. In 1945 a systematic bombing campaign was launched against Japan's major cities. The attacks crippled what was left of Japanese war production and terrified the civil population. By the time two nuclear bombs were dropped on Hiroshima and Nagasaki in August 1945 Japan was already on the point of surrender. The two attacks heralded a new strategic age but they were not the cause of Japan's defeat.

The war on land II: the conflict for Europe

The two western states fought a predominantly air and sea war from 1941 to 1944. Neither Britain nor the United States had large enough armies to force re-entry into Europe and it took two years to recruit, train, and equip an army of sufficient size to risk a direct invasion. So dangerous did the direct assault on

German-held Europe seem that the British preferred a more in-direct route, starting with the defeat of Italy in North Africa and seizing strategic opportunities as they arose throughout south-ern and south-eastern Europe. Since American forces were not ready in 1942 for a direct assault Roosevelt agreed to help Britain reconquer North Africa. So inexperienced were British and American forces that the defeat of Italian armies and the German expeditionary force under Field Marshal Rommel took longer than expected. In October 1942 the British inflicted their first land defeat on Axis forces at El Alamein on the Egyptian border. By May 1943 the whole of northern Africa was secured. The temptation to use existing forces against mainland Italy proved overwhelming, despite the efforts to prepare for an at-tack across the English Channel. Allied invasion of Italy brought Italian surrender on 3 September 1943, but German forces oc-cupied the peninsula and fought a fierce defensive battle which at times threatened the Anglo-American invasion force with de-feat. In Italy the Mediterranean strategy reached stalemate.

The American preference was for a direct attack on the main body of the German army in the west, across the English Chan-nel. The risks of an assault like this from the sea against strongly fortified and defended shores were considerable. Its success de-pended on the victory over the submarine in the Atlantic, and the impact of bombing on the German air force and war production. The cross-Channel attack, codenamed 'Overlord', had to be de-layed until the early summer of 1944, so complex were the preparations and so large the resources employed. Overlord was the first major combined arms operation of the war. It could only be carried out by naval powers. Over 4,000 ships supported the invasion; capital ships played a critical part in bombarding the shore defences and German reinforcements. Over twenty con-voys of supplies crossed the Channel each day after the invasion. The lack of naval power on anything like this scale had pre-vented both Napoleon and Hitler from crossing the Channel.

Overlord also depended on massive air power. The long-range bomber force was used to destroy German communications in northern France and to attack German defences. British air de-fences prevented the German air force from mounting any serious reconnaissance of Allied preparations. Finally, the two western Allies, based on their experiences in North Africa and Italy, built up large tactical air forces to support the ground armies, imitating once again the successful German practice of the early war years. For the first day of Overlord the Allies put 12,000 aircraft into the sky against only 170 serviceable German planes. Throughout the subsequent campaign in France the Allies enjoyed an overwhelming preponderance in the air which helped them to overcome an enemy now practised in defence and armed with weapons—the anti-tank gun, the bazooka, heavy battlefield anti-aircraft batteries—which threatened to restore the initiative to the defence and to recreate the trench stalemate of the Great War.

The plan for Overlord finally agreed between the two western Allies in January 1944 was for an initial assault in Normandy with five divisions and paratroop support, followed by a rapid buildup of forces which would hold the German armies on the east wing at Caen and allow a wide wheeling encirclement by Allied forces further west towards Paris and the Seine. Allied armies were built around high mobility. Thanks to American production both British Commonwealth and American forces were completely motorized and enjoyed a high level of mechanization. Rather than imitate the German practice of an élite armoured core the American army became one vast mechanized instrument, with tanks, trucks, and self-propelled guns assigned to every division. Radio communication was central to the smooth operation both of mechanized armies and of air–ground co-operation. The technical transformation of the American army between 1942 and 1944 made it the most modern army of all the warring powers. This, too, helped to compensate for the low level of military experience among western forces, who came from societies with no tradition of large standing armies. When the Supreme Commander of Overlord, General Dwight Eisenhower, arrived in North Africa to command Allied forces in 1942 he had never before seen armed combat.

For all the advantages enjoyed by the combined arms of the two western states the invasion of Normandy begun on 6 June 1944 depended more than usually on good fortune. The exact time and location was kept from German intelligence by a complex and risky deception plan; the days chosen for invasion were plagued by bad weather, which continued to disrupt Allied plans throughout June and July; German plans to respond to invasion were hesitant and confused. Had German forces—a total of over fifty divisions—been more effectively deployed against the five invading divisions the whole enterprise might well have ended like Gallipoli. As it was the slim foothold gained on the Normandy coastline on 6 June remained insecure for another ten days, and the strategy of the wheeling encirclement took almost seven weeks to launch. During this period Allied firepower imposed an unsupportable rate of attrition on German forces. When the break-out in Normandy came in the last week of July 1944 German resistance crumbled. Within a month Paris was liberated and by September German forces were pinned back on the frontiers of the Reich. The whole of the German western army was destroyed and almost all its equipment lost. This constituted the largest single defeat inflicted on German forces throughout the war. The Allied victory relied on the effective integration of air and land power, on a large and well-organized logistical system, and on exceptional levels of military modernity. Defeat in France did not win the war on its own, but it speeded up German defeat and ensured that any prospect of German revival in 1944 based around new inventions—the rocket, jet aircraft, electric-powered submarines—evaporated. From the autumn of 1944 German defeat became a matter of time. On 7 May German forces in Europe capitulated.

Mobilizing the home front

Warfare between 1939 and 1945 was thoroughly industrialized. The major combatants mobilized between a half and two-thirds of their industrial work-force, and devoted up to three-quarters of their national product to waging war. This was war waged on an unprecedented scale. The economic commitment was partly a result of the nature of modern weaponry, which could be reproduced in mass by utilizing existing production methods and the civilian work-force and management. The cluster of new industries which emerged before 1939—motor vehicles, aviation, radio, chemicals—could easily be converted at speed to produce tanks, fighters, or explosives. The sheer scale, however, was dictated by the shared belief that in total war states should exert their economic strength to the limit consistent with the survival of a minimum living standard on the home front. Only the United States had industrial resources sufficient to produce more war goods than any other power and maintain high levels of export and civilian consumption. In Britain, Germany, Japan, and the Soviet Union trade declined to a fraction and the home population was forced to exist on a narrow band of rationed foodstuffs and household goods.

The mobilization of resources on this scale required extensive planning. Every belligerent power introduced a military command economy in which labour and materials were directly controlled by the state. In the Soviet Union, with recent experience of the Five Year Plans for economic modernization, planning worked to overcome the loss of the bulk of Soviet industrial resources to the German invader. In contrast, despite the existence of a single-party dictatorship, planning remained confused and decentralized in Germany, which failed throughout the war to produce weapons on a scale commensurate with the large economic resources under German control in Europe. With a smaller industrial base the Soviet Union greatly out-produced the German empire throughout the war.

This contrast was partly a reflection of German military preferences. German forces were hostile to mass production and preferred specialist high-quality production with a highly trained work-force. The result was that Germany held a technical lead in most major weapons for much of the war, but could only produce them in relatively small quantities, and had difficulty in maintaining them in the field because of their technical sophistication. A great deal of productive effort in Germany was squandered on the search for new wonder-weapons, or on constant upgrading of existing weapons. Only from 1942 was more effort made to adopt mass-production techniques and from then on bombing began to erode the high potential for expansion contained in the German system.

The Allied powers, Britain, the Soviet Union, and the United States, sought a different balance between technical quality and production. They concentrated on a narrow range of advanced weapons which were then produced in large quantities by modern factory methods and a semi-skilled work-force. A policy of periodic modification ensured that by 1944 Allied aircraft and army weapons were at least a match for German, and existed in vastly greater numbers. The technical threshold was pushed towards jets, rockets, and nuclear weapons during the war, but none was yet capable of having a decisive effect on the contest, which was won with the weapons already well developed by 1939—fast monoplane fighters, radar, heavy bombers, large tanks, and large-calibre mobile artillery.

Every warring society supported with greater or less willingness the sacrifices required by such a level of material and technical mobilization. The level of sacrifice ranged very widely. In the United States the civil population was not directly attacked, and living standards rose by an average of 75 per cent per person. In Japan and Germany bombing destroyed wide areas of the major cities, brought the death of almost 1 million civilians, and contributed to sharp declines in living standards and rising malnutrition. In the Soviet Union many workers were placed under martial law, millions of others ended up in labour camps, and the remainder were subjected to a harsh regime of long hours and meagre rations. In Soviet cities close to the front line, bombing became routine and civilian deaths from enemy action ran into millions.

How civilian populations sustained war-willingness in the face of total war remains one of the central questions of the war. Coercion played a part. In the Soviet Union slacking or absenteeism could be punished by the labour camp or death. In Germany over 7 million forced labourers were made to work at the point of a gun, while the army of slaves in the concentration and extermination camps were literally worked to death for the war effort. But there were limits to coercion even in dictatorships. Ways were found to reward workers with bonuses or extra rations. The apparatus of propaganda preached sacrifice and collective effort, and demonized the enemy. Western populations fought with the conviction that theirs was a very just cause, and their governments made deliberate efforts to present the war as one for freedom and liberal values, despite bombing civilians and despite the alliance with Stalin's Soviet Union. In Japan and Germany the enemy was portrayed as bestial and destructive, bent on annihilating the unique racial culture that sustained the popular sense of superiority. Populations fought from fear of what their enemy might do in an age of total war, when all the conventional constraints on the conduct of military action were apparently in abeyance.

Paradoxically the effort to wage total war between 1939 and 1945 created the conditions which would make it possible to return to the tradition of war fought with limited resources by armed forces. The new generation of weapons developed by the end of the war were too expensive and technically sophisticated to be produced quickly, in mass, by existing civilian industry. Nuclear weapons, though targeted at the civilian urban population, promised a conflict which would be over in seventy-two hours, far too soon to allow the mobilization of national resources. Under these conditions the mass participation of the Second World War would achieve very little. This was a conclusion welcomed by many in the military establishment who disliked the concept of the large civilian army, reliance on domestic civilian resources for effective war-making, and the assault of civilian populations in conventional war. Since 1945 the nature of military technology, together with efforts to tighten up the international rules on the conduct of war and the creation of a narrow 'military-industrial complex' to provide the economic foundation for war, have all contributed to undermining the concept of total war that dominated strategic thinking for a generation after 1918.

9
Cold War

PHILIP TOWLE

The Cold War dominated international affairs for forty-four years from the end of the Second World War until the collapse of the Communist empire in 1989. The confrontation between the Soviet Union and the West was particularly bitter between 1945 and the death of Stalin in 1953. However, even afterwards there were tense crises as the two blocs stormed at each other over the invasion of Hungary in 1956, the building of the Berlin Wall in 1961, and the Cuban Missile Crisis the following year. There was a further and final period of hostility from about 1975 to 1985 marked by growing US disillusionment with the policy of *détente* Washington and Moscow had espoused in the late 1960s.

Fortunately the period of greatest hostility coincided with the time when the two blocs were in the worst position to resort to warfare. In the late 1940s western countries, led by Britain and the USA, not only resented the destruction of all democratic tendencies in the eastern and central European countries, but feared the world-wide expansion of Communism. At that period the West seemed to be on the defensive everywhere from Kuala Lumpur to Athens and from Saigon to Berlin. Yet the Soviet Union and the rest of eastern Europe had been devastated by the Second World War. Many of the Soviets' greatest cities, including Leningrad and Stalingrad, had been largely destroyed and, according to some estimates, up to 20 million of their citizens had died. The Soviets wanted control of eastern Europe to protect them from further invasions from the West but, to the democracies, this seemed to represent another stage in what Marxist rhetoric called the inexorable advance of Communism.

By the time that both sides had recovered from the Second World War, the division of Europe had been largely accepted. An 'iron curtain' in Churchill's phrase stretched from the Baltic to the Mediterranean. Western politicians and newspapers might still rail at the Soviets for their oppression of the Hungarians in 1956 and of the Czechs twelve years later but they knew that they could not give the east Europeans direct assistance without producing a general war. The northern hemisphere had effectively been divided into spheres of influence, with only 'flash points' such as Berlin, Yugoslavia, and Cuba still disputed.

The Cold War involved military preparations and expenditure on an unprecedented scale for a war which never came. Hundreds of thousands of US troops and airmen were based in West Germany, Italy, and Britain. Similar numbers of Soviet servicemen were based in eastern Europe. Each year the military exercises carried out in Europe involved thousands of troops and tanks and hundreds of aircraft and ships. The Cold War led to both a very expensive conventional arms race and the development of hydrogen bombs, intercontinental bombers and ballistic missiles (ICBMs), nuclear-propelled submarines, and reconnaissance satellites. The actual number of men maintained under arms gave a good reflection of tensions at any particular time (see Table 1). US, British, and Soviet forces peaked in the mid-1950s as a result of the Korean War. Then force numbers declined as tensions abated and governments became more budget conscious. The USA reversed this tendency in the 1960s when it became involved in the Vietnam War. The Soviets also began to increase their forces, either to match the USA and to prevent a repetition of the humiliations of the Cuban Missile Crisis, or to counter the Chinese threat from the east. Whatever the reasons, increases in manpower numbers were matched by the expansion of Soviet nuclear forces. The economic effort involved played no small part in exhausting the Soviet economy and bringing about the collapse of the Soviet empire and the end of the Cold War in 1989.

In the early Cold War years Third World guerrillas fought against the restored colonial powers across much of Asia. By the mid-1960s most of Asia and Africa was independent but the

TABLE 1. *Number of men under arms* (thousands)

	USA	UK	West Germany	USSR
1954	3,350	840	15	4,750
1960	2,514	520	270	3,623
1970	3,066	506	466	3,305
1977	2,088	330	489	3,675
1988	2,163	316	488	5,000

weak successor states were themselves torn by guerrilla and civil wars. The Cold War became entangled with these historical processes. It was difficult for western leaders and publics to distinguish between anti-colonial and pro-Communist struggles, particularly when, as in Vietnam, Laos, and Malaya, the independence movements were led by Marxists. After independence the great powers tended to support any Third World governments provided that they backed them in the Cold War; thus they strengthened many of the dictatorial regimes in the developing countries. Both western and Soviet governments also sought to win allies and spread the cost of weapons development by supplying arms to the Third World. Conventional wars were, fortunately, relatively rare during the period but they were generally fought in the Third World with equipment supplied by the Soviet Union and the West.

Nuclear weapons

The extent to which nuclear weapons would alter international politics and military strategy only gradually became clear in the decade after Hiroshima and Nagasaki. Immediately after the surrender of Japan, the US government was alert to the dangers of a nuclear arms race with the Soviet Union. To reduce Soviet suspicions, President Truman and his advisers considered sharing nuclear secrets with the Soviets. After much internal debate, they decided instead to place the so-called Baruch plan before the newly constituted UN. This would have prohibited nuclear weapons and placed key nuclear research centres and facilities directly under UN control. However, the plan would have left the West with the knowledge of how the atomic bombs were made and stopped the Soviets from developing similar skills. It also involved inspection and control within the Soviet Union which was unacceptable to Moscow. Arms control negotiations continued with only a short break during the Korean War but, because of the level of tension, it was not until the 1960s that any agreements were reached.

Meanwhile the USA was continuing atomic experiments and the Soviets were working as fast as possible to produce their own atomic bombs. Western reliance on nuclear weapons increased as conventional forces were rapidly demobilized at the end of the war. Western governments believed that Moscow had not demobilized to anything like the same extent. Consequently, the Soviets would rapidly be able to overrun the occupation troops maintained by the Americans, French, and British in the western zones of Germany. Western plans assumed that there would be nothing to stop a determined Soviet tank thrust towards the Channel, except nuclear weapons, which seemed to offer a relatively cheap way of balancing the assumed Soviet superiority.

This nuclear dependence grew steadily. In the early post-war years the USA had very few nuclear weapons: perhaps seven in 1947, twenty-five in 1948, and fifty the following year. During the Korean War the number grew by some 100 a year as spending on strategic forces quadrupled from $9.6 billion to $43.3 billion. The USA also developed the bombers necessary to attack targets within the Soviet Union. By 1950 it had 289 B29s, 160 B50s, and 38 B36s. Only the B36 had a real intercontinental capability and thus the B29s were based in Europe when the Cold War intensified from the late 1940s onwards.

The Soviets lagged in the nuclear arms race far more than was apparent at the time. Their obsessive secrecy inclined the West to imagine that they were stealing some technological march on NATO. Only occasionally were these fears justified. After titanic efforts the Soviets exploded their first nuclear device in 1949.

Many western officials were surprised, although this coincided with the four-year time-lag which western intelligence had originally predicted between the US and Soviet bombs. The Soviet copy of the B29 bomber, known as the Tu4 or Bull, first flew in 1946. This was followed in the mid-1950s by the Tu16 Badger and the Tu20 Bear. Neither of these provided a really effective intercontinental force. The twin-jet Badger had a range of 3,800 miles and thus could only reach the USA on a one-way mission. The Bear had about twice the range but it was driven by turbo-propellers rather than jets. It would have been an easy target for US fighters even when equipped with stand-off missiles enabling it to attack targets from 100 miles or more. This did not stop the fear of a 'bomber gap' developing in the USA from 1956 onwards, short-lived though this illusion proved to be.

Anxiety about the bomber gap was succeeded in 1960 by concern that a similar missile gap was developing and threatening western security. This was originally sparked by the successful launch by the Soviets of the first ICBM and the first satellite in 1957. In fact, despite these successes, the USA was far ahead in both missiles and bombers at the start of the 1960s. The US bomber force peaked in terms of numbers in 1959 with 1,366 B47s and 488 B52s. Three years later the B47 force was reduced to 880 but the USA now had 639 B52s in service and some 280 ICBMs against some 35 Soviet ICBMs and 100 heavy bombers. It was not until the late 1960s and early 1970s that the Soviet Union first caught up and then surpassed the USA in the number both of its ICBMs and of those missiles launched from submarines (SLBMs) (see Table 2). When the USA stopped adding to its missile stocks in the mid-1960s, Washington assumed that Soviet force levels would peak at around the same level. This supposition proved incorrect and this was one of the main causes of rising tensions in the mid-1970s. But the USA was itself not inactive. It produced the so-called MIRVs or warheads which divided in space after the missile was launched. This made it possible to destroy a number of enemy targets with only one missile and thus made much better use of their destructive potential. The greater sophistication of US missiles, the superiority of their bomber force, and their earlier development of MIRVs

TABLE 2. *US and Soviet missiles*

	1963	1965	1967	1969	1971	1973	1975
US							
ICBM	423	854	1,054	1,054	1,054	1,054	1,054
SLBM	224	496	656	656	656	656	656
Soviet							
ICBM	90	224	570	1,028	1,513	1,527	1,618
SLBM	107	107	107	196	448	628	784

helped offset Soviet numerical superiority. The ratio between the two powers was enshrined in the Strategic Arms Limitation Treaty, signed in 1972, which attempted to halt the nuclear arms race.

Nuclear strategy

Throughout the Cold War years western, and predominantly US, strategists pondered and pontificated about the uses which could be made of nuclear weapons. In the early days they were sometimes seen as simply larger bombs. After all, no greater numbers were killed by the atomic bomb dropped on Hiroshima than in the conventional fire-bomb raids on Tokyo and other cities. Nevertheless, there was, from the beginning, a perception that a turning-point had been reached, that man's very survival was at stake, and this perception increased with the development of the much more destructive hydrogen bombs. The USA tested the first H device in November 1952 and the Soviets followed the next year.

Most strategists started from the premiss that nuclear weapons existed and were unlikely to be abolished in the deadlocked arms control talks. At the same time, if they were used in a war between the Soviet Union and the West, they would cause destruction on an unimaginable scale. Thus they had to be employed to prevent an East–West war altogether through what came to be called nuclear deterrence. The Soviets had to be convinced that the West would use nuclear weapons if its vital interests were threatened, even if this were almost suicidal. They also had to be convinced that US weapons could not be destroyed in an initial Soviet attack. Thus, in the early years, bombers were kept on a very high level of alert, if not actually airborne. Later, missiles were put into concrete silos buried in the earth or sent to sea in submarines which the technology of the time made almost invulnerable.

Deterrence had many critics who argued that a suicidal threat was dangerous, unconvincing, and immoral. Once the Soviets had an effective nuclear force of their own, then nuclear weapons were obsolete even as a threat. Western governments denied that the Soviets could take the risk of overrunning western Europe in the hope that the USA and its allies would leave their nuclear forces unused. The morality of deterrence was also an issue. If the targets designated for western weapons were Soviet missiles and bombers, this would only encourage Moscow to unleash its forces as early as possible in a crisis. If western nuclear forces were actually aimed at Soviet cities, then this threat was both immoral and incredible. It was these arguments, together with changes in technology, which encouraged President Reagan and his advisers to propose the Strategic Defense Initiative or Star Wars programme in the 1980s. This would have protected the United States from nuclear attack by orbiting large numbers of satellites round the earth. These would have contained beam weapons intended to burn holes in Soviet missiles as they rose through the atmosphere. Both the practicality and the affordability of the programme were the subject of intense debate until the end of the Cold War in 1989. Subsequently, the chances of the US Congress voting the billions of dollars involved faded away and the USA and Russia worked together to demobilize many of their nuclear weapons and to prevent them from spreading to other countries.

The Korean war

Militarily and politically the Korean War from 1950 to 1953 was by far the most important conventional conflict to occur during the Cold War years. Militarily it was important because it showed that a nuclear power might fight a war and decide not to use its atomic weapons, even when its forces were losing. It also showed that air power was not as decisive as some air enthusiasts had claimed. Politically the Korean War greatly increased the tensions between East and West, caused a dramatic increase in military expenditure, and transformed NATO from a loose alliance into a tight military coalition.

The war began with an attack by the Communist North Koreans on the non-Communist South Korean forces on 24 June 1950. The southern armies were rapidly overrun or driven back towards the city of Pusan in the extreme south of the country. The USA immediately committed air forces to the conflict and US ground forces landed in Korea on 1 July. Because the Soviet Union had temporarily withdrawn from the Security Council, it was unable to veto western resolutions. Consequently, North Korean aggression was condemned by the United Nations and subsequent military operations were carried out under the UN flag, although the USA provided the bulk of the forces and commanded the operation.

Gradually the USA and South Koreans strengthened their defences round Pusan. At the same time the USA began to build up its forces in Japan. Their commander General MacArthur decided to use these in an amphibious landing behind North Korean lines rather than simply to drive the North Koreans back from Pusan itself. The decision was a considerable gamble because there were few places on the Korean coast where such a landing could be made and the invasion force was highly vulnerable in the early stages. But the gamble paid off. The Inchon landing was so successful in September 1950 that UN forces isolated and destroyed most of the North Korean forces in the southern part of the peninsula. The issue now was whether the UN should cross into North Korea and try to unite the peninsula or simply restore the original border. The fatal decision was taken to cross the frontier, despite indirect warnings from the Communist Chinese government that this would bring them into the war. As UN forces approached the Yalu river in November 1950, the Chinese struck and sent them reeling back down the peninsula. On 4 January 1951 Communist forces took Seoul, the South Korean capital, for the second time.

It was at this stage that General MacArthur asked more and more openly for the use of nuclear weapons against China and for a blockade of the Chinese coast.

The Truman administration did consider the use of nuclear weapons on a number of occasions. It chose not to use them for political and military reasons. It believed that the only 'worthwhile' targets were Chinese cities. Nuclear attacks on Chinese forces spread amongst the North Korean hills might be ineffective and, if they were, they would reduce the impact of nuclear deterrence world-wide. Truman wanted to keep the war limited to the Korean peninsula and to discourage Soviet intervention. He feared that nuclear attacks on China would make this impossible. Later administrations were also to consider the use of nuclear weapons; most notably to assist French forces against Vietnamese guerrillas when the French were besieged at Dien Bien Phu in 1954. But the temptation was always resisted and each time it became that much harder for a later administration to break the 'convention' and initiate the use of nuclear weapons.

Disputes about the use of nuclear weapons and widening the war led Truman to remove General MacArthur from his UN command in April 1951. The Chinese were already being pushed back and the front had stabilized in March 1951 not far from the frontier held when the war began. Peace talks started in July 1951 and continued while the fighting went on for two more years. The Korean peninsula was devastated and hundreds of thousands of civilians and soldiers died. China had established itself as one of the great powers but at the cost of bitterly antagonizing the United States. The limitations both of air power and of nuclear weapons were also exposed. Germany and Japan were encouraged to rearm so that all the weight of defending the West would not fall on the USA, Britain, and France. Thus the confrontation between East and West became increasingly rigid and protracted.

Other conventional wars

More conventional wars took place in the Middle East during the Cold War than in any other part of the world. The region abutted the Soviet Union's vulnerable southern republics and lay across the West's supply lines by ship through the Suez Canal and by air to India and the Far East. It also provided much of the non-Communist world's oil. Foreign interest and involvement complicated divisions within the Arab world and between the Arabs and the newly established state of Israel.

In 1948 the Israelis fought to carve a state out of the old British Mandate of Palestine. Eight years later the British, French, and Israelis attacked Egypt during the crisis over Egypt's nationalization of the Suez Canal. On 25 June 1967 the Israelis surprised the Arab nations, destroyed their aircraft on the ground, and overran Sinai, Jerusalem, and the Golan Heights which separate Israel from Syria. Six years later the Arabs in turn surprised the Israelis; the Egyptians managed to cross the Suez Canal and to establish an army in Sinai, while the Syrians broke through the Golan Heights to the north. In the 1980s the Israelis became bogged down in a semi-guerrilla war in Lebanon, while the Iranians and Iraqis became embroiled in a bloody and fruitless war. In 1990 the Iraqis attacked and captured the Emirate of Kuwait, only to be thrown out six months later by a coalition authorized by the UN and led by the United States.

Militarily the 1967, 1973, and 1991 conflicts were the most significant. The 1967 or Six Day War reminded the world of the importance of surprise and of the dangers of leaving very expensive aircraft marshalled invitingly in rows on airfields. The result was the development of the hardened aircraft shelter made of concrete and steel to protect the ever more expensive fighter-bombers. Over the next two decades such shelters spread across Europe and the Middle East. The war seemed also to suggest that, under the clear Middle Eastern skies, once one side had achieved dominance in the air, enemy ground forces were doomed. In this case the combination of the highly skilled Israeli air force and rapidly moving armoured columns seemed invincible.

In Sinai alone the Egyptians had some 100,000 soldiers and 1,000 tanks in June 1967. They had also been heavily fortifying their lines against possible Israeli attacks. In a classic 'blitzkrieg' campaign, the Israeli General Tal avoided the strongest Egyptian defences in the north of Sinai and threw the Egyptian forces completely off balance by attacking from unexpected directions. Even in the centre, where the Egyptian lines were particularly heavily fortified, General Sharon managed to find weaker sections of the front to penetrate and dropped paratroops behind Egyptian lines to neutralize their artillery. Three days after the beginning of the war, the Israelis had already crossed Sinai and reached the Suez Canal. In order to escape, many Egyptian troops had to go through the Mitla Pass, and it was here that they were ambushed and destroyed by Israeli forces. During the Sinai campaign the Egyptians lost between 10,000 and 15,000 men and perhaps 80 per cent of their equipment.

Meanwhile the Jordanians had unwisely put their forces under Egyptian command. The Jordanian air force was completely destroyed on 5 June and in the next two days Jordanian forces were driven from the part of Jerusalem that they had continued to hold after the establishment of the state of Israel. Again it was the speed and dash of the Israelis, combined with their dominance in the air, which prevented the reinforcement and concentration of Jordanian forces. Not only Jerusalem but the whole of the West Bank of the Jordan fell to the Israeli forces, while the Jordanians lost over 6,000 killed and missing.

In the north the Syrian air force was rapidly knocked out by the Israelis and the Syrian ground forces only attempted a limited offensive. By 9 June the Israelis were able to concentrate their attention on this front and to attack the fortified range of the Golan Heights which separates the two countries. They chose to storm a section of the Heights which was steep enough to be just passable for bulldozers and tanks, but which the Syrians had only lightly fortified, as they had not expected it to be the subject of attack. Despite considerable losses, the Israelis managed to penetrate Syrian lines and on 10 June the Syrian forces began to blow up their fortifications and retreat.

The Israelis had shown on all three fronts what could be achieved by surprise, determination, and speed. The Arabs were thrown completely off balance by the rapidity of the blitzkrieg which they faced. Popular bitterness in the Arab world was increased by the Egyptian mistake of trumpeting imaginary victories, making the reaction all the more extreme when the truth was revealed.

The Israelis had the advantage of occupying interior lines in their struggles against the Arabs. So also the Indians could choose to concentrate their attacks on Pakistani weak points when the two countries went to war in 1971. On their side the Pakistanis tried to emulate the Israeli pre-emptive strike by attacking Indian airfields at dusk on 3 December 1971. However, the Indians had also absorbed the 'lessons' of the June War and many of their aircraft were dispersed or hidden. In the eastern campaign the Indians followed the Israeli strategy of avoiding Pakistani strong points and towns, and moving as rapidly as possible towards their goal, the eastern capital of Dacca. On this front the Indians had total air superiority and the support of the local people who supplied guides and guerrilla fighters. Within twelve days the Pakistani commander had surrendered. In the west the struggle was more evenly balanced but Indian superiority again proved decisive and by the end of the campaign the Indians were entrenched in Pakistani territory. The consequence was the breakup of Pakistan, with east Pakistan forming the new state of Bangladesh and India establishing its hegemony, just as Israel appeared to have done in the Middle East.

The 1973 or Yom Kippur War modified this picture of total Israeli military dominance over its neighbours. The Arabs achieved surprise partly by choosing to attack on 6 October, the Jewish Day of Atonement, and partly by pretending that the reinforcement of the various fronts was just a routine manœuvre. By dint of months of practice the Egyptians developed the techniques necessary to cross the Suez Canal and breach the Israeli Bar Lev line on the other side. Just as the Israelis had done six years before, they avoided the most strongly fortified enemy positions. Once established in Sinai, they set up lines of anti-aircraft guns and missiles to protect themselves against Israeli air attacks. The Israeli armoured columns were also vulnerable to anti-tank missiles and they had to relearn the advantages of combined columns of infantry, artillery, and tanks. The infantry could hunt down enemy anti-tank missiles and the artillery could neutralize them before the tanks were able to operate freely. Even then, whilst the Egyptians remained within their protective screens, the Israeli air and armoured forces found it difficult to evict their forces from Sinai. But the Egyptians felt obliged to stage costly offensives when the Syrians were pressed by the Israelis in the north.

On 16 October Israeli forces again showed their capacity to throw their enemies off balance by the unexpectedness of their actions. They crossed the Suez Canal and established a bridge-head on Egyptian territory. After initially reacting rather slowly, the Egyptians attacked with ever-increasing intensity to expel the invaders, who threatened the communications with their forces in Sinai. By the cease-fire on 22 October the Egyptian position was, indeed, becoming increasingly desperate and they were only saved from the loss of an army by international pressure to end the war.

Meanwhile, in the north, a Syrian force of 1,400 tanks tried to recapture the Golan Heights lost in 1967 and to penetrate deep into Israel. At one stage the Israelis had only a handful of damaged tanks to protect the whole of the northern part of the country. Israeli forces on the frontier were obliterated but they had held on long enough for reserves to take their place. By 10 October these had expelled the invaders and destroyed 867 Syrian tanks. Then they went on to the offensive and began to threaten Damascus itself. The Israeli air force had found ways of dealing with Syrian surface to air missiles and was ranging freely across the country. As with the Egyptians, the Syrians were saved from further humiliation by the cease-fire agreement. Israel remained militarily predominant due to the skill and determination of its armed forces but the margin of its superiority had apparently been narrowed. The campaign in Lebanon was to show that, in guerrilla warfare, it could disappear altogether.

Lebanon became the home of Palestinian guerrilla forces opposing Israel after they were driven out of Jordan between September 1970 and July 1971. Too weak to control the heavily armed Palestinian troops, the Lebanese found their country used as the springboard for armed incursions into Israel itself. When the Israeli ambassador in London, Shlomo Argov, was attacked on 3 June 1982, the Israelis seized the opportunity to invade

Lebanon and to crush the Palestinians. By 4 August they had reached the capital, Beirut, and agreed that a multinational force should be stationed there to oversee the evacuation of the Palestinian troops and subsequently to protect Palestinian civilians. Many of the troops were withdrawn, but the multinational force did not guard the Palestinian women and children, hundreds of whom were butchered by Israel's Lebanese allies. The multinational force itself became the target of suicidal attacks using vehicles loaded with explosive, one of which killed 239 US marines while another blew up 58 French soldiers. Subsequently the multinational force was withdrawn.

Meanwhile, the Israelis were drawn into an ever more ferocious guerrilla war against the Palestinians who had returned or remained, and against Lebanese Shiite militias who had the backing of the Syrians. By May 1985, with no sign that the war would be resolved and with casualties mounting, the Israelis decided to withdraw to a defensive perimeter near their own frontier. For the first time they had failed to achieve their military objectives. The Palestinians were still entrenched in Lebanon, the Shiites had been radicalized, and much of Beirut and of other towns in the south of the country had been destroyed. Mobile warfare, air power, and surprise were effective against Arab conventional armies but counter-insurgency required immense patience, political skill, and the time to build up intelligence. Ruthlessness and military efficiency could not short-circuit the process.

While Israel was embroiled in Lebanon, the Iranians and Iraqis were involved in an equally fruitless and destructive war along their common frontier. Following prolonged friction between the two countries, the Iran–Iraq War began with the Iraqi attack on Iran in September 1980. The Iraqi leader Saddam Hussein calculated that Iran had been substantially weakened by the Islamic Revolution and the overthrow of the Shah in February 1979. This would give Iraq the opportunity of seizing territories which it had long claimed on the frontier. Iran's conventional forces had indeed been undermined by the execution and flight of many of the most senior officers, and only a proportion of their 875 Chieftain tanks and 445 combat aircraft were serviceable. But this was counterbalanced by the grim determination evoked by the Ayatollah Khomeini's revolution, which led tens of thousands of Iranians as young as 13 to volunteer for the front.

Saddam Hussein had indeed made a classic mistake and forgotten how previous revolutions from Cromwell to Lenin had increased the strength of the country involved. Within weeks of the initial Iraqi attack, the Iranians were counter-attacking. The war dragged on inconsequentially until 1988 with Iran insisting that Iraq should compensate it for its aggression and that Saddam Hussein should be replaced. The Iraqis' reintroduction of chemical weapons on to the battlefield on the widest scale since the First World War was technically the most important aspect of the war. The warm climate apparently dispersed the chemical agents rapidly but they still caused thousands of casualties and had a substantial impact on the fighting, which only ended when both states had fought themselves to exhaustion.

The Iran–Iraq War left Iraq deeply indebted to its richer neighbours including the Gulf Emirate of Kuwait. Thus Saddam Hussein's seizure of the oil-rich Emirate in August 1990 was motivated very largely by economics. The UN responded by condemning Iraqi aggression and a US-led coalition gradually assembled forces in Saudi Arabia. When it became clear that the Iraqi leader was unwilling to withdraw peacefully, the USA began the allied offensive with a massive series of air strikes. B52 bombers dropped tens of thousands of pounds of ordnance on Iraqi troops and their tanks dug in around Kuwait. Subsequent investigation showed that these had caused fewer casualties than expected but had had a devastating effect on Iraqi morale. At the same time cruise missiles fired from naval vessels in the Gulf attacked specific government buildings in the capital Baghdad itself.

This represented the most revolutionary development in warfare since Hiroshima. Nuclear weapons were the culmination of a tendency to construct weapons which were ever larger and more imprecise but this led states to be less willing to make use of them. Cruise missiles and laser-guided bombs on aircraft represented the opposite tendency, making weapons more precise and thus employable. This gave the anti-Iraqi coalition a wholly new capability. Mistakes were made; a bunker was attacked in Baghdad under the impression that it was purely a communications centre when, in fact, it was also a harbour for civilians sheltering from the air raids. Other cruise missiles and bombs went astray and killed civilians. But, despite these errors, the Iraqi command system was destroyed with far fewer casualties than would have been caused by earlier generations of weapons. When allied ground forces attacked in February 1991, the Iraqi armed forces simply melted away and Kuwait was liberated within hours.

The war against Iraq was fought, from the US point of view, in near perfect conditions. The anti-Iraqi coalition had five months to build up forces in Saudia Arabia and to prepare to attack. It could also reconnoitre Iraqi targets from aircraft and satellites. The results were inevitable. Iraqi aircraft were driven from the skies and the residue fled to Iraq's former enemy, Iran. Hardened aircraft shelters proved time-consuming and expensive to destroy, but destroyed many were. Terrorist groups allied to Iraq promised reprisals but none of these was effective. Saddam Hussein also used Scud missiles against Saudi Arabia and Israel, hoping thereby to provoke the Israelis into attacking him and thus making the coalition look pro-Zionist. Such attacks with obsolete missiles were hardly different from the German V2 strikes on Britain during the closing stages of the Second World War. Technically more interesting was the use of Patriot antimissile missiles by the USA to intercept a number of the Scuds, but though they had a reassuring psychological effect, later analysis of claimed interceptions showed that few had been successful.

The Falklands war

If the war against Iraq was fought for the UN under the most promising conditions, the opposite could be said for Britain's position in the Falklands War nine years before. The battlefield was thousands of miles from the British Isles and even from the Anglo-American base on Ascension Island, which lies about halfway between. The British had forces trained to fight against the Warsaw Pact in and around Europe, not against Argentine forces at the other end of a long and tenuous supply line.

If the strategic situation contrasted with that in 1991, politically there were some similarities. Just as Iraq had long coveted Iranian and Kuwaiti territory so Argentina asserted a claim to the Falklands going back to the eighteenth century. In March 1982 the ruling Argentine military junta decided that Britain neither could nor would defend the islands against attack. The islands were seized on 2 April. The following day the British House of Commons bitterly attacked the government's failure to protect the islands. The Royal Navy promised that the islands could be retaken—but at a cost. A task force was assembled around the two small aircraft-carriers, *Hermes* and *Invincible*, and rapidly dispatched southwards.

The Falklands War was the most extensive maritime conflict since 1945. The armoured warships of the two world wars had been replaced by delicate frigates and destroyers which were protected from air attack only by their 'active' defences of friendly aircraft, missiles, and chaff. At the same time the threat which aircraft presented to warships had increased with the speed of the aircraft and the accuracy of their weapons. During the fighting the British lost four frigates and destroyers, a large container ship, and a landing ship, to Argentine missiles and aircraft. Even more would have been lost but for the fact that so many Argentine bombs failed to explode after penetrating British ships. But, despite these set-backs, a British force began to land on the islands on 21 May. On 14 June the Argentine forces surrendered.

The war had reminded navies of the vital importance of air superiority if surface forces were to operate safely at sea. The Sea Harriers carried by *Hermes* and *Invincible* gave the British task force some protection but they were without adequate airborne warning of the approach of Argentine aircraft. On the Argentine side their aircraft lacked the range to loiter for any time over the British fleet. The disruption which even a very small submarine force could cause to an amphibious operation was also evident. The British devoted immense effort to protecting the task force against a handful of Argentine submarines. They also drove the

Argentine surface ships from the sea when the nuclear submarine *Conqueror* torpedoed the old cruiser *General Belgrano* on 2 May with the loss of several hundred lives. For land forces the demoralizing effect of remaining inactive in defensive positions, whilst waiting for the arrival of attacking forces, was re-emphasized.

Conclusion

During the Cold War the northern hemisphere was dominated by the threat of nuclear war and the southern by the reality of insurgency. If they interfered in the Third World, the armies of the great powers also found themselves tied down in intractable guerrilla campaigns. The French army was bogged down in Indo-China from 1946 to 1954 and in Algeria from 1954 to 1962. The British were involved in guerrilla wars in Greece, Cyprus, Malaya, and Kenya during the 1940s and 1950s, in Aden and Malaysia in the 1960s, and in Northern Ireland in the 1970s and 1980s. The USA was traumatized by the Vietnam War from 1964 to 1973. All the western powers also had to contend with international terrorism and the Americans, Germans, Italians, French, and British developed specialized combat forces to deal with such problems as hijacked airliners and hostage-taking.

When conventional wars did break out, victory went to the side with the best-trained forces. In the Middle Eastern wars and in the Falklands large numbers of conscripts were rapidly overrun by better-trained armies. Despite their dependence upon reserves, the Israelis in particular established themselves as masters of the art of blitzkrieg and of air combat. When both sides were incompetent, as in the Iran–Iraq War, then the campaign could be prolonged and indecisive. But when one side was sufficiently efficient victory was achieved within a matter of days or weeks rather than months, and the Security Council had to step in to prevent the other side being completely destroyed. There was, however, no experience of warfare between two equally professional combatants and it might be that, in those circumstances, victory would have gone to the side with the largest reserves of equipment and thus the greatest staying power.

Both nuclear weapons and insurgency reduced the propensity of the great powers to use their armed forces. The fate of the Americans in Vietnam, the Soviets in Afghanistan, and the Israelis in Lebanon had a powerful deterrent effect. Generations of conventional weapons were developed, seen in service for ten or fifteen years, and then scrapped or transferred to the Third World without ever having been employed in anger. Paradoxically the great powers spent far more during the Cold War years than in the past on weapons which they fervently hoped would never have to be used and some of which they knew would lead to retaliation and their own destruction. It was predominantly in the Third World where guerrilla strategists could hope to change the situation by military force, and consequently where weapons were used and states were riven by conflict. In the northern hemisphere armed forces became highly conservative institutions dedicated to the avoidance of any measure which could lead to the outbreak of war between the great powers and their own employment in such a conflict.

10

People's War

CHARLES TOWNSHEND

'A people's war in civilized Europe is a phenomenon of the nineteenth century.' Thus Karl von Clausewitz, in the 1820s, in a short but prophetic chapter of his great work *On War*, heralded a new element of modern war. Yet by his careful phrasing he also recognized that the phenomenon was in itself far from new: it was indeed the most primitive, elemental form of war. As a result of the French Revolution, though, this ancient mode had found a place in the world of modern states. Ideology—the potent mixture of nationalism and democracy—not only mobilized manpower for the regular armies, but also inspired ordinary people to fight on their own account. A state which incarnated the national identity of its people, Clausewitz held, would not give up even if its armies suffered defeat: 'however weak a state may be, if it forgoes a last supreme effort, we must say there is no soul left in it.'

Clausewitz was remembering the humiliating contrast between the rapid and total collapse of his own country, Prussia, under attack by Napoleon in 1806–7, and the refusal of other countries—most notably Spain and Russia—to give in. In Spain, for four bruising years after Napoleon's invasion of 1808, local resistance fighters wore away the French garrison and defied all efforts to suppress them. The 'Spanish ulcer', as the occupiers vividly called it, the most impressive people's war of the period, showed the limits to the capacity of even the most dominant army in Europe. An even more spectacular demonstration of the vulnerability of regular armies to a hostile people was provided by the destruction of the *Grande Armée* in Russia in 1812.

The local Spanish resistance fighters were called *partidos*, or partisans, the same name usually given to their Russian counterparts. It was the French label for their style of operations, *la petite guerre*, which in its Spanish translation, *guerrilla*, was most widely attached to the phenomenon which Clausewitz identified. But 'little war' is in a sense a misnomer: it may suggest that people's war is a form of 'limited war', whereas its spirit belongs much more to what Clausewitz called 'absolute war'. The means may be small, but the ends are not. People lacking the armament and training of regular armies had to use methods which would exploit the weak points of large-scale military organization. Small, part-time forces would harass rather than confront the enemy. Sabotage and ambush, a compound of physical and mental attrition, would replace the decisive battle. Partisans needed to avoid taking big risks, Clausewitz saw, if they were to convince ordinary people that resistance could be effective. Thus the process would be diffuse and slow—the polar opposite of the rapid, decisive Napoleonic strategic manoeuvre. What Mao Zedong would, a century later, call 'protracted war', would depend on the moral commitment of the people to the struggle. For Clausewitz, this commitment would be generated by national spirit: the people would fight for freedom from foreign domination. And they repeatedly have; but besides nationalism, other ideologies and beliefs have also fuelled modern people's wars.

This was already clear from the first example which Clausewitz knew: not an international war, but an internal conflict within revolutionary France. In the early spring of 1793 the peasants of the Vendée took arms against the republican government in the name of the Crown and the Church. Though the immediate provocation was conscription, the real motivation of the Royal and Catholic Army, as the Vendean rebels entitled themselves, was to resist the Republic's attempt to subordinate the clergy to the state. After a number of early rebel victories, such as the overwhelming of General de Marce's column marching from La Rochelle to Nantes on 19 March, the rising became a ferocious war in which neither side would compromise. The Republic made little effort to win back the loyalty of the rebels,

Napoleon at the Battle of Wagram. Although Vernet's painting presented the classical image of the great commander at the decisive moment, the long drawn-out offensive against the Austrian army on the Danube was a foretaste of attritional battles of the future rather than one of the brilliant victories which had marked Napoleon's earlier career: his *Grande Armée* lost almost a quarter of its combat strength.

Penetrating power of guns. By about 1870, when this comparative chart was drawn up, firepower was being decisively transformed by the introduction of breech-loading mechanisms. German arms manufacturers pioneered this technology first for infantry rifles and then artillery guns, achieving greater muzzle velocities as well as higher rates of fire.

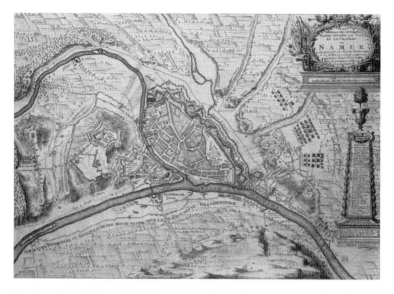

The Great Siege of Namur, 1695. Namur was an immensely strong fortress at the confluence of the Sambre-Meuse. Besieged by the French in 1692, its recapture in 1695 by the Confederate Army under William III of Orange was the major military event of the Nine Years' War (1688–97). The Great Siege has entered literary folklore through the deeds of Uncle Toby and Corporal Trim in Laurence Sterne's *Tristram Shandy*.

Some of the 622,000 soldiers who lost their lives during the American Civil War. European soldiers who discounted the battlefield experiences of the Union and Confederate Armies did so at their peril.

French mounted infantry in Morocco in 1912. European commanders sought ways to achieve mobility without sacrificing cohesion and firepower, their strong suits against indigenous resistance. The French developed mounted infantry in the 1880s to support vulnerable cavalry in North Africa. In the American West, the cavalry preserved their character as mounted infantry developed during the Civil War.

War 1918 style. Scenes of devastation in the Ypres Salient, February 1918. A shattered British tank lies in the centre of the picture. The featureless and empty battlefield came increasingly to characterize the war on the Western Front from 1915 onwards.

The largest set-piece battle of the war took place around the steppe city of Kursk in July 1943, where more than 2 million men and 6,000 tanks clashed in a week of furious fighting. Soviet infantry, operating here with the famous T-34 tank, inflicted a major defeat on the cream of the German army.

Balloon site, Coventry. Laura Knight created a powerful image of women's service in an 'auxiliary' role which had in effect become the front line: in November 1940 Coventry was the target of one of the most destructive air attacks of the Blitz. The anchor cables of these captive balloons formed a simple defensive weapon.

Left: **Boer fighters** caught crossing a railway. The ability of the irreconcilable Boer 'bitter-enders' (*bittereinders*) to keep up a guerrilla campaign long after the surrender of the main Boer armies depended on their extraordinary mobility and fieldcraft. After fruitless attempts to pursue and pin them down, the British resorted to building a network of iron blockhouses to interdict the movements of the *commandos*, as in this dramatic (but not inaccurate) representation.

Right: **The machine-gun—** 'the concentrated essence of infantry'—came of age in the First World War. Most modern machine-guns, like this M-60 used by United States troops in the Vietnam war, are belt-fed and have air-cooled barrels that can be changed quickly when they become too hot.

Left: **After making a 1,000-mile 'hop'** in the Pacific, the first wave of 127,571 troops land from some 535 ships at Saipan on 15 June 1944. While troops had often landed from ships before, it was not until specialized landing craft and support ships were built in the Second World War that amphibious landings against a defended shore became a successful form of warfare.

The British science-fiction writer H. G. Wells predicted before the First World War the mass bombing of Europe's cities. In this still from the 1930s film of Wells's *Things to Come* bombers are seen streaming towards their target. Fear of bomb attack played an important part in the growth of pacifism in the inter-war years.

During the Second World War air power came of age. Every air force produced its crop of air aces, top pilots who brought down large numbers of enemy planes. Here the Soviet ace Alexander Pokryshkin stands in front of his aircraft on which every 'kill' has been recorded.

Civilians leaving the burning city of Königsberg after surrender to the Red Army. On 26 January 1945 Soviet troops reached Königsberg in East Prussia, a town already full of refugees fleeing from places further east. Whilst a good portion of the population managed to escape before the town finally fell in April, some 100,000 civilians were left behind. Königsberg was in the territory not returned to Germany after the war, and its surviving German inhabitants later joined the more than 12 million expellees and refugees driven westwards.

Women's peace activism has a long history. The First World War created widespread revulsion against the carnage of modern war and spurred multiple peace efforts, including 'No More War' pledge movements. Here a group of American women in 1922 are campaigning for the National Council for Reduction of Armaments.

An atomic explosion over Bikini, 1946. From 1945, the development of weapons too powerful to use has prevented their owners from fighting each other in earnest.

relying on naked force and terror, and confident in the superiority of patriotic armies over priest-ridden peasants. As a result, the people treated the *bleus* as invaders, and gave them no information about rebel movements.

Here was a total war in miniature, replete with atrocity and counter-atrocity. Though the rebels captured Saumur and Angers, internal rivalries prevented them from establishing a unified strategy. In the end their campaign was defensive, but their local knowledge made them formidable guerrilla fighters, and several republican generals were sent to the guillotine for failing to overcome them. Saint-Just's chilling call for the extermination of everything that opposed the Republic gave a deadly licence to the attempt at final pacification carried out by the twelve mobile columns, the so-called 'infernal columns' (*colonnes infernales*), commanded by General Turreau. Their systematic devastation of the countryside through the spring of 1794, including forced evacuation of loyal citizens, prefigured many future internal wars. The immediate result was to alienate the surviving peasantry completely, so that it took Turreau's wiser successor Lazare Hoche—who told his government, 'for the twentieth time I repeat, if you do not grant religious tolerance, you must give up the idea of peace' – another two years to end the conflict. By then, some 160,000 out of 800,000 inhabitants of the rebel area had perished.

The message delivered by the Vendéan revolt, that popular forces had a remarkable capacity to survive, and could inflict serious cumulative damage on better armed and trained regular armies, was amplified in Spain and Russia. But these wars also bore out the point made by Clausewitz, that the power of guerrilla action was limited. Irregulars could weaken but not decisively defeat a strong and determined enemy; to achieve victory they must act as auxiliaries to conventional forces. The ascendancy of conventional military logic was not to be broken for a hundred years after the Napoleonic Wars. Although guerrilla fighting added a significant dimension to a number of major nineteenth-century wars, in none of them was it decisive. The campaign of France and Piedmont to drive the Habsburg Empire out of Italy in 1859 was preceded and accompanied by several attempts to conjure up a popular revolt of the kind brilliantly envisioned by Giuseppe Mazzini. 'Insurrection—by means of guerrilla bands—is the true method of warfare for all nations which desire to emancipate themselves from a foreign yoke.' Mazzini grasped the point that guerrilla warfare 'opens a field of activity for every local capacity, forces the enemy into an unaccustomed method of combat, avoids the evil consequences of a great defeat, secures the national war from the risk of treason, and does not confine it within any restricted basis of operations. It is invincible, indestructible.' Yet this ringing call to arms was only weakly answered in Italy itself. Giuseppe Garibaldi was its best hope: an inspirational revolutionary leader, who made his reputation in Uruguay, in one of the great liberation struggles of Latin America. During the revolutions of 1848 he led the defence of the Roman Republic, and by 1859 he was an international liberal icon, yet none of his efforts had come near success. Only on the back of the French victory in 1859 did he launch his astonishing invasion of Sicily, which triumphed mainly because of local peasant grievances, not Italian national feeling.

The vastly greater scale and intensity of the American Civil War foreshadowed the appearance of modern total war, reaching down to the roots of social life. For instance, a proposal at the start of the war to demilitarize Missouri, a deeply divided state, was uncompromisingly rejected by the Union military commander: 'Rather than concede to the state of Missouri for one single instant the right to dictate to my Government in any matter, I would see you and every man, woman and child in the State dead and buried. This means war.' Alongside the struggles of the huge Union and Confederate regular armies, irregular operations were carried out by partisans mainly affiliated to the Confederacy. In the Shenandoah Valley, Mosby conducted a systematic guerrilla campaign. In the Midwest, nastier gangs of self-proclaimed guerrillas conducted vicious vendettas, in which the burning of Lawrence, Kansas, by the Missourian William C. Quantrill in August 1863 was merely the most spectacular of thousands of acts of indiscriminate destruction, rapine, and murder. The response was also extreme. In 1861 General Fremont announced that all captured guerrillas would be executed (though President Lincoln revoked the order). General Ewing's Order No. 11 after the Lawrence raid depopulated the border counties, expelling 20,000 people from their homes. Sheridan systematically devastated the Shenandoah Valley to starve out the guerillas. In the end, this grim irregular war remained marginal to the final military decision; and attempts to use guerrilla action as a direct auxiliary to regular action, such as Sterling Price's invasion of Missouri in late 1863, proved ineffective. Recognizing this, the Confederacy formally disbanded all its partisan forces and disclaimed all other guerrilla action (denounced by Robert E. Lee as 'an unmixed evil') in April 1864.

The spectre of people's war rose again in France to haunt the victorious German armies after the surrender of Napoleon III in September 1870. In a few weeks of conventional war, almost all the French regular forces had been captured at Sedan or besieged in Metz and Paris, yet the new republican government refused to admit defeat. Leon Gambetta, modelling himself on the Jacobins of 1793, called for 'war to the knife', organizing new armies and urging the people in occupied areas to form *franc-tireur* resistance units. 'Harass the enemy's detachments without pause or relaxation, prevent him from deploying, restrict the area of his requisitions, disturb him day and night, always and everywhere.' The people's response did not live up to his expectations; as in America, the partisans were sometimes unpopular — 'the terror and ruin of the country which they should have protected', as one observer put it. But they kept the Germans in check for four months. Garibaldi himself brought volunteers to help the Republic, fighting to some effect (if in the main conventionally) around Autun. If the government had been ready to stake everything on 'people's war' (the phrase was widely applied at the time), the outcome might have been different. Instead it held to the conventional belief that conventional armies were needed to break the siege of Paris, and committed nearly all its resources to this doomed attempt.

Only in South Africa at the end of the century did people's war begin to show its fully developed characteristics. What the British called the Second Boer War — the Second War of

Independence (*Tweede Vryheidsorlog*) for the Boer republics themselves—once again conformed to the Clausewitzian pattern. A period of conventional warfare ended, after many British setbacks, in the comprehensive elimination of the main Boer armies, but thousands of *burghers* continued to resist. For them, the transition to partisan war was quite natural. The Boer forces had always been at best semi-regular armies, citizen militias held together by voluntary co-operation, loosely organized in 'commandos' rather than regular units. They were natural guerrilla fighters. The *volk* had a strong sense of community, and the determination to defend its rural way of life against the *uitlanders* remained resolute. The leaders were well aware of the likely costs of irregular warfare: their farms would be destroyed, and they might fail in the end. Louis Botha, for instance, counselled negotiation after the fall of Pretoria, but Marthinus Steyn (President of Orange Free State) was determined to fight on, and was joined by Botha, Jacobus De La Rey, Christian De Wet, Jan Smuts, and others, who proved to be inspiring and resourceful guerrilla strategists.

But did their campaign offer any realistic chance of success? The great hope was a true people's war—a rising of the whole Afrikaner population including the Cape Dutch, which might have swept the British bodily out of South Africa. Many of the most ambitious guerrilla operations were designed to trigger such a rising, but it never came. Without it, the Boer commandos were effectively confined to defensive operations: most of their energies went on sabotage—especially cutting communications—and evading British pursuit. British attempts to pin down their elusive opponents were initially futile. Slow-moving 'flying columns', raising clouds of dust on the veld, had little chance of engaging adept horsemen helped by the local inhabitants. Gradually more systematic and ruthless methods were adopted, beginning with the burning of crops, and relocation of partisans' families in the infamous concentration camps. Eventually a network of blockhouses and wire fences criss-crossing the country crippled guerrilla mobility, reducing the natural advantage of the commandos in the bare veld.

Slowly the resistance of the *bittereinders* petered out. The irregular war lasted nearly four times as long as the conventional phase, forcing Britain to deploy unprecedentedly large forces, accompanied by a fearsome upsurge of public hatred (euphemistically called 'jingoism'). But the apparent defeat of the guerrillas, and the unique nature of the war in the remote veld, allowed regular soldiers to underestimate the wider significance of the Boer achievement. The potential impact of people's war was finally spelt out by a confluence of two national movements, the Arab revolt of 1916–18 and the Irish war of independence in 1919–21.

The Arab revolt is a central moment in the history of modern Arab nationalism, though for those fighting on the Western Front it was 'a sideshow of a sideshow'. The British advance from Egypt into Palestine and Syria was assisted, to an extent disputed then and since, by Arab guerrilla forces led by the Emir Faisal, son of the Sharif of Mecca. That these forces harassed the Turkish supply lines in the Hejaz, captured Aqaba, and were the first to enter Damascus when the Turks retreated, were important symbolic facts. Faisal was advised by a remarkable British officer, T. E. Lawrence, who became a world celebrity as 'Lawrence of Arabia', and whose romantic account of the revolt, *Seven Pillars of Wisdom*, was hailed as a literary masterpiece. In Lawrence's picture, it was the Arabs who had achieved victory with a little help from the British, not the other way round. The revolt was a popular insurgency, and his short article in the *Army Quarterly* in 1920 argued its irresistible potential. 'Granted mobility, security, time, and doctrine, victory will rest with the insurgents.' This was a truly revolutionary doctrine.

Of the four key factors identified by Lawrence, mobility and security were essential aspects of guerrilla operations. He held that irregular action could turn the qualities of organization and discipline so prized by regular armies into liabilities. Security was guaranteed by public support, whether active or merely passive, which would ensure that the enemy was deprived of information and had to operate in the dark. He avoided discussing the issue of space, considered vital by Clausewitz, and did not acknowledge that the peculiar conditions of the desert—and the near-absence of aircraft—were crucial to the invulnerability of the Arab forces. He preferred to focus on time, which was on the insurgents' side, and ideology. National consciousness was the real key: the survival and gradual success of the insurgents, publicized by skilful propaganda, would build up the demand for freedom; 'a province would be won when we had taught the civilians in it to die for our ideal of freedom'. The real war would take place in the hearts and minds of the people. 'The printing press', Lawrence wrote, 'is the greatest weapon in the armoury of the modern commander.'

This message fell on the ears of a world that was now prepared to believe it. The Great War had expanded the field of combat far beyond the battlefronts, reaching down to the everyday sphere of industry and public life. Total war created the 'home front', where civilian morale was the foundation of the war effort. Propaganda was believed to have played a vital part in the Allied victory by undermining German morale. The sense of ideological struggle was heightened by the Russian Revolution and the civil war which followed it, carrying popular mobilization to new extremes. The possibility that unconventional methods could produce decisive victories provided the inspiration for a sequence of revolutionary struggles and national liberation wars in the twentieth century, changing the power structure of the world.

The examples of South Africa and Arabia might still be dismissed as peripheral cases, but the Irish war of independence brought the process firmly back into Europe. The republican campaign also put together all the elements of the modern people's war to convince the British government that the insurgents were backed by the Irish people as a whole. Ireland had a tradition of armed nationalist rebellion, but the risings up to and including that of Easter 1916 had been old-fashioned insurrections, usually planned in secret by small revolutionary groups, and failing precisely because they could not mobilize the people. After 1916 a much more diffuse and slow-burning campaign of resistance evolved under the banner of Sinn Féin, the party which swept the Irish constituencies in the general election at the end of the First World War. Sinn Féin's political strategy was to issue a unilateral Declaration of Independence and form an Irish national assembly (Dáil Éireann). It launched a wide-ranging campaign of civil resistance, together with guerrilla action by the Irish Republican Army. The IRA's primary target was the armed police force, the strongest agency of the British administration, which was first of all subjected to a boycott, and later to assassination, sniping, and eventually ambushes and attacks on police stations. Intimidation of witnesses and jurors paralysed the legal system, so that the republican forces could only be countered by military methods.

The IRA demonstrated, however, that effective military countermeasures were difficult if the guerrilla forces remained dispersed in small units, and enjoyed—as they mainly did in Ireland—the support (if sometimes grudging) of 'the people'. Most of the republican forces operated part-time, usually at night. Above the local (company and battalion) level, brigade organizations existed mainly to devise policy, not to dispose larger forces. Eventually, under increasing British military pressure, some full-time 'Active Service Units' were created—colloquially called 'flying columns'—with men who had gone on the run. These could attempt more ambitious and time-consuming ambushes. In the last analysis, though, the scale of operations was determined by the scarce supply of weapons, ammunition, and explosives. Thus the relative invulnerability of the IRA had both positive and negative aspects: its survival was a great propaganda blow against British rule, yet its capacity to inflict direct damage on British forces was limited. The balance was psychological, and was tilted in the end by the violent reaction of the British forces themselves, especially the temporary police recruited from war veterans (the 'Black and Tans'), to the provocation of the elusive enemy. British reprisals were perhaps mild by the standards set in Napoleonic Spain, or German-occupied Belgium, but they were enough to convince British public opinion that such a conflict was unacceptable.

The Irish war of independence produced several gifted guerrilla leaders, and an organizer of genius, Michael Collins. But although the IRA had a tireless and effective publicity department, it did not produce a writer of Lawrence's stature to formulate its lessons. The guerrilla concept remained marginal. The Russian civil war, most importantly, was won by conventional means, although it witnessed an extraordinary guerrilla campaign led by the anarchist Nestor Makhno in the southern Ukraine. Makhno's peasant 'Insurgent Army' fought first against the Whites and, eventually, the Reds in the name of land and liberty. It was probably more successful than either of its larger opponents in mobilizing the peasantry, though as pressure mounted its recruiting methods became more coercive, and it lost its democratic character. Still, Makhno remained committed to resisting state authority, whether conservative or Bolshevik, and his own power rested on traditional rural bonds: his followers called him *batko*, father. His operations were astonishingly flexible, largely due to adventurous use of light, sprung farm carts (*tachanki*)—a local peculiarity—which enabled his infantry to move at cavalry pace, and to concentrate and disperse at speed. On at least one occasion he inflicted a major strategic reverse on the White army of General Denikin, cutting his supply line during his advance on Moscow in September 1919 and precipitating his retreat. The *Makhnovschina*, the two-year period of loosely organized anarchist power from early 1919 to late 1920—'a republic on tachanki' as one Makhnovite called it—ultimately needed a political vacuum to survive in. Once Trotsky's Red Army finally won out over the Whites, it was able to crush anarchist resistance with overwhelming force.

The Spanish Civil War, too, was undoubtedly a people's war, especially in the Republican defence of Madrid; but it was fought by conventional strategy. The anarchist movement, uniquely strong in Spain, and uniquely suited (as Makhno had proved) to guerrilla warfare, was condemned there to failure in a campaign of fixed positions. In the same period (1936–9) the rebellion of the Palestinian Arabs took guerrilla form but lacked a coherent doctrine. The man who finally gave definitive shape to the idea of people's war was Mao Zedong. Mao was a socialist with a commitment to the total transformation of Chinese society as part of a world revolution. But he had to bring the Chinese Communist Party round to the idea of people's war by a circuitous route, beginning in the 1920s with the attempt to organize insurrection amongst the workers in China's few industrial cities. The failure of these, and the assault launched on the Communists by the Nationalist (Guomindang) government under Chiang Kaishek, led to the creation of the rural Jiangxi Soviet which fought off several Nationalist attacks—the so-called 'bandit extermination campaigns'—in the early 1930s. The last offensive in October 1934, however, drove the Communists into a protracted retreat from the south-east of China to the north-west, taking twelve months; in this 'Long March' only some 10,000 out of the 90,000 who set out reached their destination. Mao's reputation was enhanced by this epic, and in a series of theoretical tracts he laid out the structure of what he called 'protracted war'.

The strategic and tactical aspects of these writings would not have surprised anyone familiar with Clausewitz and Lawrence, even though Mao added some memorable metaphors—most famously, perhaps, that of the people as the water in which the guerrilla fish could swim. What was distinctly new was Mao's ideology: instead of a war of national liberation, he was organizing the people for an internal class war. This accounts for the prominence in Mao's military writings of 'base areas', both as proto-states which could demonstrate that Communism would bring visible improvements, and as industrial springboards for the full-scale open warfare of the final showdown. Mao was under no illusions that the Nationalists would give way to the force of public opinion alone. He held that guerrilla warfare must prepare the way for conventional war. It was a transitional process, in which the spread of irregular fighting would steadily enlarge the people's confidence and solidarity. Its central strength was the capacity to take time, but Mao also saw that dispersion contained the danger of degeneration into local banditry: discipline was essential to hold the campaign together.

The Communist victory in the Chinese civil war was generally taken to confirm Mao's contention that class solidarity provided the strongest basis for people's war, though later scholars have found this less convincing, and have argued that the real key to Communist success was nationalism. Ironically, perhaps, the Communists were able to convince the Chinese people that they, not the Nationalists, were the most determined and effective opponents of the Japanese invasion which began in 1937. The Long March had put them in a position where they were fairly distant from the coastal areas which Japan occupied, so that the Nationalists bore the brunt of resistance. This, aggravating the deep-seated corruption and inefficiency of the Guomindang regime, fatally undermined the government's capacity to survive.

The impact of Mao's writings was none the less tremendous, and was amplified by the experience of the Second World War. An unprecedented number of resistance struggles in Europe and Asia brought belief in the concept of people's war to a new level, and the war was followed by a spate of national liberation movements, most of which were led by Communists. South-east Asia, where Japanese conquests had broken the invincible image of the European empires, was the epicentre of this earthquake.

In Vietnam the systematic application of Mao's theory produced results as spectacular in their own way as those in China. Shortly before the Japanese withdrew, the nationalist Vietminh proclaimed a republic in Hanoi. When the French drove them into the northern hills, they began a widespread guerrilla campaign using units of their already substantial regular army. French regular troops were unable to do more than keep the Vietminh guerrilla forces out of the capital city, and to hold a line of forts along the frontier with China. Even with the benefits of full motorization and some air support—though with few helicopters—the French could only just dominate the main highways in daylight, and could neither bring their enemy to battle on their own terms nor prevent the steady erosion of their local control. This *pourrissement* (rotting), as one observer pungently labelled it, was the result of an immensely energetic, many-layered Vietminh political campaign, mixing both inspiration and intimidation. Vietminh military leaders produced such classic pamphlets as Truong Chinh's terse 'The Resistance War Will Win', and Vo Nguyen Giap's more rhetorical 'People's War, People's Army', applying Mao's theoretical framework to Vietnamese conditions. They elaborated a new concept, 'mobile warfare', to make the transition from defensive guerrilla fighting to large-scale offensive operations ('To keep itself alive and to grow, guerrilla warfare necessarily has to develop into mobile warfare.').

Yet this transition proved hazardous, and the Vietminh suffered several major set-backs. After five years of fighting there was a situation of stalemate which might well have lasted indefinitely, but for the persistent belief of French military commanders in the inherent superiority of their regular soldiers. This overconfidence, and failure to grasp the principles on which their enemy was working, led to the risky and ultimately disastrous attempt to regain control of the western region by occupying Dien Bien Phu late in 1953. After a long battle, in which the Vietminh astounded the French by bringing in and supplying (by bicycle) the heaviest Chinese 155mm artillery, the besieged French garrison was overwhelmed in May 1954 by 'human wave' attacks—a sharp contrast with the 'nebulous vapoury essence' of guerrilla action advocated by Clausewitz, but politically decisive. Giap's greatest achievement was perhaps to persuade the world that the virtually professional army which won this victory was really the people in arms.

The parallel attempt of Communist insurgents to drive the British out of Malaya failed, in part because the Malayan People's Liberation Army was rooted in the Chinese rather than the Malay population, and was not able to create a unified 'Malayan people', in part because the British showed a greater readiness than the French to make political concessions. Independence was formally promised at an early stage. A rural resettlement programme was successful because it was widely regarded as bringing an improvement in the quality of life, not merely herding people into fortified villages. But the British campaign also sank to depths of brutality which drove the Chinese into the arms of the MPLA, and ensured that for them, at least, the struggle became a real people's war. And though the defeat of the 'Communist Terrorists' became a beacon to counter-insurgency experts the world over, it did not prove easy to repeat elsewhere. More characteristic of the post-war pattern was the remarkable success of the Jewish guerrilla insurgency in Palestine.

In one sense the Zionist insurgents, mainly members of the Irgun Zvai Leumi (the other 'revisionist' group, Lohamei Heruth Israel or the 'Stern Gang', being much smaller), faced the same problem as the MPLA. The Jewish community (*Yishuv*) formed less than half the population of Palestine, and was subject to even greater suspicion on the part of the majority than were the Chinese 'squatters' in Malaya. But the Irgun were hard-line Zionists whose object was to create a Jewish state, not a multi-ethnic Palestinian political system. They made no effort to appeal to Arab opinion, and indeed were ready to attack Arabs as well as the British administrators of Palestine. Britain exercised a League of Nations Mandate on the basis of its commitment (in the Balfour Declaration of 1917) to establish a 'national home for the Jewish people in Palestine', but by the Second World War this had proved an impossible compromise. Arabs believed they would be subjugated by a Jewish state; hard-line Zionists believed that Britain was abandoning them in face of Arab protest.

Still, when the Irgun's campaign began, most of the *Yishuv* still relied on Britain, and disapproved of violence. The Irgun was a small organization, capable only of intermittent attacks on police, military, and government targets. But it showed great skill in selecting these targets, and carrying through attacks. Moderate Jews sheltered the guerrilla fighters from security force pursuit. Irgun attacks on British (as distinct from Arab) targets were usually highly discriminate. The most spectacular exception was the destruction of the south-west corner of the King David Hotel, which housed the British government secretariat, in July 1946. Amongst the 91 victims of this urban bombing were 41 Arabs and 17 Jews as well as 28 British administrative and clerical staff. Even this did not reverse the flow of Jewish opinion towards the armed campaign; indeed the severity of British repressive action tended to drive moderates into the arms of the extremists. Increasingly large-scale military search operations, coupled with martial law restrictions, were designed to put pressure on ordinary people to co-operate with the authorities. 'Collective punishments' were seen by some administrators as a means of building a sense of civic responsibility and preventing the insurgency from being legitimized as a 'people's war'; others believed they would have the opposite effect. The division highlights the dilemma of government in the face of political violence.

Many people's wars have been won because the incumbent government either failed or refused to see the seriousness of the challenge. There are often good reasons for both failure and refusal: the early manifestations of an underground movement are typically sporadic and trivial in physical scale; their psychological impact is cumulative. Politically, governments have an interest in minimizing the significance of resistance, and preserving the appearance of 'normality'. By the time that the power of the insurgents is unmistakable, much more drastic action will be required, and will generate a sense of political crisis which may accelerate the erosion of legitimacy. The struggle for 'the hearts and minds of the people'—the phrase coined in Malaya—becomes much rougher. The danger to the security forces drives them to take short cuts, to coerce rather than to persuade.

The ferocity this can engender was demonstrated in the Algerian war of independence. Immediately after its Vietnam disaster, France was confronted by a similar challenge initiated by Algerian veterans returning home from service in the colonial forces in Indo-China. The FLN (Front de la Libération Nationale) was able to pick up a blueprint of people's war ready-made, although the war they fought was rather different. Lacking the Vietminh's regular military strength and its Chinese sanctuary and support, the FLN's campaign was more strongly marked by terrorism. The war began in 1954 with one of the most spectacularly deadly urban bombings yet seen, and was largely sustained by similar means. The French responded in kind, with a counter-terror intensified by a new doctine of 'revolutionary war'. The French army had bitterly concluded that defeat in Vietnam had been due to its failure to match the ruthlessness and conviction of the Communists. The key to victory in *la guerre révolutionnaire* was propaganda, which if skilfully conducted could pull public opinion free from Communist influence. 'Brainwashing' was widely believed to be the reason for Communist successes, so the task was to find a way of reversing the process.

In theory this might have produced a sophisticated political campaign, mixing judicious reforms with anti-Communist propaganda, but in practice the French aim of keeping Algeria as an integral part of France left little room for political concessions. Even the possibility of building up support by just and progressive administration was eliminated by the pervasive sense of racial superiority which denied equal rights to Arabs, and by French insistence that they were fighting not against nationalism but against Communism. The conduct of the military campaign was shaped by simple military logic; as Colonel Roger Trinquier wrote, 'We know that the *sine qua non* of victory in modern war is the unconditional support of a population. If it does not exist, it must be secured by every possible means, the most effective of which is terrorism.' But the kind of control envisaged by these theorists called for resources which the government could not provide. The army was unable to carry through the large-scale measures, such as resettlement, which its policy required, though at least a million people were moved into military-administered camps, and many more were simply ejected from their homes. One crucial process, the creation of village self-defence forces, went ahead so slowly that it was still far from complete when the war was ended. The only measures which went on unchecked were constant raids, searches, collective punishments, interrogations, and torture.

The so-called 'Battle of Algiers' in 1956–7 was the culmination of this war. After a series of setbacks in the desert, the FLN concentrated on intensifying operations in the capital city. When the campaign quickly outstripped the power of the gendarmerie, the Governor-General called in military aid in the form of the parachute troops of General Massu. This martial law regime was highly effective in one sense: the systematic combing-out of the city section by section—*quadrillage*—eventually destroyed the urban FLN. But most of the information through which the *paras* broke into the FLN organization was got by torture, and military success brought a political disaster as French public opinion turned against the 'dirty war'. This did not seem to be 'battle' or even 'war' in any recognizable sense.

The general historical tendency of modern people's wars has been to dissolve the traditional distinction between combatants and 'civilians', and engulf populations in formless and uncontrolled violence. If this is a regression from civilization, it seems to be an inescapable consequence of mass politicization under the banner of ideologies like nationalism and Communism. Exceptions to this spiral of violence have been rare (and maybe legendary). The Cuban revolutionary war established a romantic guerrilla legend which inspired many unsuccessful imitators. Fidel Castro originally attempted a Garibaldian military adventure, leading eighty-three men ashore from a dangerously overloaded motorboat in the south of Cuba in December 1956. But the miracle of Garibaldi's early victory in Sicily was not repeated: instead the rebels were crushed and dispersed within a few days. It was this apparent disaster which forced the survivors to adopt a strategy of operating in extremely small groups. What was eventually to be called the *foco insurreccional* was only a dozen strong. Its survival over two years in the southern mountains depended on the help of the people as much as on its operational skills, though it was the latter which became an international commodity after the publication in 1969 of Che Guevara's sensational book *Guerrilla Warfare*. Guevara's thesis was much closer to the romanticism of Lawrence than to the materialism of Mao, suggesting that a dedicated revolutionary group could cause the shift in mass opinion which would precipitate a social revolution.

The vital qualities of the *foco*, as Guevara set them out, were moral rather than ideological. Castro himself was a romantic socialist rather than a strict Marxist; only after taking power, and in face of fierce American hostility, did he become a pillar of the Communist bloc. Dedication to the liberation of the people in a vague, populist sense, coupled with heroic machismo, were the keynotes of the revolutionary movement. One of its most dramatic motifs was the release of captured government troops—as on one occasion witnessed by a US marine officer, when Raul Castro announced, 'We took you this time. We can take you again. And when we do, we will not frighten or torture or kill you. If you are captured a second time or even a third, we will again return you exactly as we are doing now.' The propaganda effect of such gestures was heightened by contrast with the nastiness of the Batista government, but its practical effect might have been different had the conscript soldiers not been so demoralized and badly led.

Later attempts to apply Guevara's *foco* theory in other circumstances, against governments less inefficient and unpopular, revealed the limits of what Régis Debray famously called the 'Revolution in the Revolution'. Guevara himself died in the Bolivian jungle in 1967, trying vainly to mobilize the peasantry against a regime which had already carried out a land redistribution programme. In the year following his death, a revolutionary current swept across the world. The prominence of major rural guerrilla wars in Guatemala, Venezuela, Colombia, Nicaragua, and Angola (as well of course as Vietnam) was gradually eclipsed by a shift of revolutionary warfare to the cities.

The idea of 'urban guerrilla warfare' adapted the notion of the *foco* to the circumstances of modern or modernizing countries in which the rural population was less significant, and the real power lay in rapidly growing cities. In Brazil, Carlos Marighela argued that the mobilization of the people could be begun by a kind of gangster action—bank robberies and kidnappings—which would sharpen up the revolutionary forces and provoke the government into repressive action, which in turn would antagonize the people. The idea that the people would eventually support the provokers of violence was common to nearly all urban guerrilla organizations. In practice, governments were often successful in branding the would-be guerrillas as 'terrorists'—a much more negative label which effectively robbed them of legitimacy. This process was illustrated at an early stage in Uruguay, where the Tupamaros (named after the last Indian resistance leader, Tupac Amaru) initially won widespread public support for their 'Robin Hood' style social banditry, including the seizure and distribution of food, but in the early 1970s were crushed by an intense campaign of repression backed by a massive swing of public opinion to the right. The revolutionaries merely became, in the dispirited phrase of Régis Debray, 'the gravediggers of liberal Uruguay'.

Whether or not urban guerrilla warfare was seen as a decorous label for terrorism, it reinforced the general tendency of people's war to dissolve the boundary between combatants and civilians. This was belatedly recognized in an attempt, initiated by the International Committee of the Red Cross, to extend the protection of international law to civilians in internal as well as international wars. The resulting Geneva protocol (Geneva Additional Protocol II, 1977) was really designed for conventional civil war, however, rather than 'irregular' people's war (whilst it referred to 'armed conflicts' rather than wars, it was declared to be applicable only to 'armed groups in sufficient control of part of the territory to enable such groups to carry out sustained and concerted military operations'). It banned such time-honoured features of counter-insurgency action as collective punishments and the taking of hostages, as well as pillage, terrorism, and 'outrages upon personal dignity'. But in view of the sad fact that such outrages have appeared even more frequently in people's wars than in wars between states, the Geneva agreement did not offer much real hope of enforcement.

The two decades after it have witnessed a succession of what may be called 'total people's wars', where all conventional restraints have been broken. In Cambodia, 1975 was 'Year Zero' for the new Kampuchea which the Khmer Rouge set out to create after their victory in a thirty-year guerrilla struggle: they aimed at nothing less than eliminating bourgeois attitudes, if necessary by eliminating the entire middle class. At the same time the carefully balanced political structure of Lebanon collapsed into a civil war that was to last, with minor remissions, well into the 1980s. The Lebanese catastrophe was particularly shocking because Lebanon had been regarded as a model of ethnic compromise. During the Second World War the Christian Maronites of Mount Lebanon, the dominant community under the French Mandate, had conceded some political ground to Muslims in a power-sharing constitution. But even before this, the tradition of organizing paramilitary militias had been started by the Maronite Pierre Gemayel in frank imitation of Hitler's brownshirts. Though these *Ketaeb* remained a loose set of local groups until they were combined into the Lebanese Forces in 1976, their Fascist ideological origins led to an emphasis on Maronite identity at the expense of Lebanese federalism.

The *Ketaeb* provided a vehicle for armed action when that identity seemed to be threatened by the Arab nationalist movement reinvigorated by Nasser's Suez triumph. As in most such cases, the first Lebanese civil war of 1958 was fought—in the Maronite view—in self-defence; their exaggeration of the Arab (Muslim) threat typified the paranoid tendency latent in all modern ethnic nationalism. Though the first civil war was ended fairly quickly, because of continuing public belief in the old constitution, a second and bloodier breakdown was increasingly likely. The influx of Palestinian refugees and the Palestine Liberation Organization after the 1967 Arab–Israeli war finally destroyed the uniquely balanced Lebanese civic culture. The great civil war began in April 1975 with the killing of twenty-seven Palestinians travelling to Tel-al-Zaatar refugee camp in east Beirut. After five months of armed clashes, the *Ketaeb* in central Beirut turned the conflict into all-out war by wrecking the Arab market area in a four-day artillery bombardment.

The centralization of the Maronite militias under Bashir Jumayyil (Gemayel) in 1976 laid the basis for something more like people's war. The combined Lebanese Forces became a social as well as a military organization, fostering public transport and housing schemes, and constructing a revolutionary—and in Muslim eyes distinctly western—state within a state in the Maronite enclave. Bashir Jumayyil himself personified this tendency by breaking a deeply ingrained local tradition, taking control of the Maronite people from both his father (the founder of the *Ketaeb*) and his elder brother. Though the situation was complicated by external intervention, first by the USA and then, most destructively, by Israel in 1982, it was this radicalization of the Maronites which fatally undermined the tradition of compromise in Lebanese politics.

Indeed, the picture presented by the 1990s was one of drift towards armed struggle to assert ethnic identity. Even more shocking, perhaps, than the breakdown of Lebanon—to European eyes at least—was the disintegration of Yugoslavia, an ethnic war whose grim roster of rape, starvation, and massacre eclipsed the brief sunburst of optimism which followed the end of the Cold War. The determination of Orthodox Bosnian Serbs to separate themselves from Muslims, either by becoming part of a Greater Serbia or by establishing their own state, not only created a human disaster but revealed the fragility of international institutions like the United Nations to mitigate the armed expression of ethnic hostility. In Rwanda, even worse happened, and the limitations of the UN were even more cruelly highlighted. In such conflicts, the proportion of 'the people' directly engaged in violence is impossible to gauge exactly. But it need not be large (Lawrence suggested '2 per cent active and 98 per cent passively sympathetic'), and as Chechen attacks have once again demonstrated, ruthless desperation can push conflict beyond all moral bounds. People may wish it otherwise, but 'the people' can be the most destructive of all military forces.

Part II

Elements of Modern War

11

Technology and War I

To 1945

MARTIN VAN CREVELD

This chapter rests on one very simple premiss, which serves as its starting-point, argument, and *raison d'être* rolled into one. It is that war is completely permeated by technology and governed by it. The causes that lead to wars and the goals for which they are fought; the blows with which campaigns open and the victories with which they (sometimes) end; the relationship between the armed forces and the societies that they serve; operations and intelligence and organization and supply; objectives and methods and capabilities and missions; command and control and strategy and tactics—not one of these is immune to the impact that technology has had and always will have.

Pre-modern military technology

Ours is a world where technological progress in general, and military-technological progress in particular, is often taken for granted. For as long as any individual alive today can remember, new devices have been coming off the assembly lines in an uninterrupted stream; as a result, it has become very difficult to imagine a world in which such advances did not take place and in which old, rather than new, was usually better. And yet, if we go back before 1500, that is precisely the world in which we find ourselves.

Alexander the Great at the beginning of his campaigns was

presented with a suit of armour guaranteed to be of Trojan War vintage; which supposedly 900-year-old contraption he then proceeded to wear in battle until it became so dented that it had to be replaced. The warriors whom we meet in the early medieval *chansons de geste* did not appreciate new weapons either. Quite the contrary; very often the best weapons were considered to be old ones which supposedly had belonged to famous heroes now dead; and indeed the longer the 'genealogy' associated with any sword, the higher the value which was attached to it and the higher also the price that it could command.

On a less anecdotal level, consider the history of fortification. Looking at the reliefs made for the Assyrian King Sanherib in order to commemorate the siege of Lachish in Judaea in 701 BC, we see a city perched on a hill; an enclosed space surrounded by double walls, the innermost of which overlooks and dominates the outer one; towers, projecting from the walls, whose function is to permit flanking fire and eliminate dead ground; crenellation providing shelter for the defenders; fortified gates dominating the entrance road, which characteristically makes a right turn so as to expose the flanks of a would-be attacker; and a central stronghold taller than the rest and meant to serve as a last refuge. Without exception, all these elements were still present in medieval fortresses, such as those constructed by Edward I in Wales around AD 1300.

What is true for the art of fortification is, not surprisingly, also true of siege technology. In the hands of the Greeks and Romans, this technology advanced rapidly between 400 and 200 BC, after which it stagnated. By that time battering-rams, catapults, ballistae, mobile towers, and cranes—not to mention the much earlier bores, mines, scaling ladders, grappling hooks, and mantelets—had all been invented and were to remain basically unchanged for almost a millennium and a half. The only new device added by the Middle Ages was the trebuchet; and even that was simply another stone-throwing machine, more powerful than, but not basically different from, those that already existed. As a result, a capable Roman military engineer of the time of Marcellus (*c.*210 BC) or Scipio Aemilianus (*c.*150 BC) or Julius Caesar (*c.*50 BC) or Marcellinus Ammelianus (*c.* AD 360) would have felt himself quite at home in any siege operation before the invention of artillery; and might, indeed, have had something to teach his generally less competent successors.

Passing from sieges to field warfare, we likewise find that the most important iron-made weapons—the mace, the sword, the spear, the lance, the pike, the javelin, and the axe in its various forms—had all been invented by 600 BC (at the latest) and changed little thereafter. So had the bow in its various forms; and, of course, the various forms of body armour, such as shields, breastplates, helmets, greaves. Depending on tactical needs as well as cultural factors, all these weapons and devices were to assume a bewildering variety of forms and shapes. However, from pre-classical Greek to late medieval times not one of them underwent fundamental changes, and the great majority even remained in use right down to the dawn of the modern age.

Sixteenth- and even seventeenth-century commanders such as Gonsalvo de Córdoba, Machiavelli, Maurice of Nassau, and Gustavus Adolphus all received a classical education. Consequently they were well aware of these similarities, as indeed they were supposed to be: given that the weapons that they used were sometimes almost identical to those of the ancients, they deliberately attempted to model their own armies on those of the Greeks and the Romans. Such was the case of the Swiss and German pikemen, the Spanish sword-and-buckler men, and the Dutch battalions. So obvious were the parallels, and so slow and sporadic (owing to the absence of a good theoretical framework) the technological progress, that even as late as 1724 a Frenchman, the chevalier de Folard, could write a famous textbook on tactics in which he advocated a return to the Macedonian formation of pikemen.

The acceleration of military-technological change

What were the factors which brought this age-old situation to an end, and how did modern technological progress—including military-technological progress—begin? While the literature on this question is vast, basically it can be divided into two schools.

Some, following Karl Marx, have argued that technological progress was the result of economic factors: such as the rise of cities, bourgeois capitalism, the early forms of industry, commerce, and exchange, free enterprise, and the like. Others, following Max Weber and Robert Merton in particular, acknowledge the role of economic factors but put greater emphasis on the changes in mental outlook that accompanied them and, perhaps, caused them: such as the shift from medieval religious and scholastic thought to a modern scientific approach based on goal-oriented rationality, experimentation, and mathematics.

Military-technological progress would, of course, have been absolutely inconceivable except against the background provided by technological progress in general. At the same time, it is necessary to recognize some specific developments which, beginning some time in the sixteenth century, put an end to stagnation and promoted the steady development of military weapons and equipment. Chief among these factors was the state-owned, regular, standing army, the *militum perpetuum* as it was known. From the fall of the Roman Empire on, European societies had not known the standing army; instead they had relied first on tribal and feudal levies and then, increasingly, on mercenaries. The former two were part-time fighters light-years removed from any preoccupation with technological development as we understand that term; the latter, although professional (and often highly competent) soldiers, only served for the duration of a war and were dismissed at its end. Neither type of army provided the kind of stable, permanent framework that is necessary for military-technological progress to take hold, become self-sustaining, and flourish.

In other words, men from Eilmer the Lame (the reputed inventor of a flying machine) through Roger Bacon (the first European to propose a formula for gunpowder) to Leonardo da Vinci (the inventor of many military engines most of which remained on paper) had never lacked inventive genius. Similarly, from the time of Homer on fighting men had always been able to recognize a good weapon when they saw it and, acting as individuals, were often prepared to pay a high price for it. What was lacking was neither inventiveness nor motivation, but rather the kind of *institutional* environment which could promote the prolonged, and often immensely expensive, process of development, testing, and deployment; which process could only take root where concentrated, long-term, relatively steady, economic demand existed.

The first European standing army was the one established by King Charles VII of France towards the end of the Hundred Years War. Other rulers followed suit, albeit slowly at first; even as late as the end of the sixteenth century, the famous Dutch political scientist Justus Lipsius could write that a standing force of two 'legions' (13,200 men, to be exact) sufficed for the needs of a 'large' state such as France or Spain. Although, during the Thirty Years War, the standing armies on all sides were still quite small (in the case of Sweden, perhaps 30,000 out of a maximum of 200,000 under arms at one time), after 1648 they began to grow by leaps and bounds. Around 1690 the strongest monarchs, that is, the Holy Roman Emperor and Louis XIV of France, maintained forces numbering 100,000–200,000 men at all times, rising to as many as 350,000–400,000 in wartime. Other countries such as Britain, Spain, and Prussia did the best they could, maintaining tens of thousands of troops in peacetime and as many as 100,000 in wartime. By creating a demand that was much steadier, larger, more concentrated, and more centralized than anything seen in history until then, these military establishments offered plenty of scope for technological experimentation and innovation. What is more, for the first time in European history there appeared a class of men — professional officers — whose one purpose in life was to find better and better ways of waging war.

Whereas military-technological progress during the eighteenth century was still quite slow, with the coming of the industrial revolution it accelerated. Invention followed invention at a rapid pace, causing armed forces to be revolutionized every few years. The armies of the French Revolution, albeit commanded by a Napoleon, would have been swept away by the armies of the Crimean War under even a Lord Raglan. The latter would have been overwhelmed by the Prussian forces of 1866–71; these, in turn, would have been destroyed even by a relatively small 1914-type force. Whereas previously commanders had been able to look into the past for guidance, now to do so became much more problematic. Whereas previously it had usually been possible to take existing weapons for granted, now to do so was often tantamount to suicide. Thus the characteristic modern situation was created whereby all armies find themselves on a technological treadmill and have to keep constantly running in order to remain in the same place; and war, instead of repeating itself, became an exercise in managing the future.

After 1870 or so, the nature of the process by which new weapons and devices were incorporated changed. On the one hand, demand continued to grow; on the other, so complicated were the newly invented devices and so huge the resources needed for their development that the place of individual inventors was increasingly taken by engineering departments operating collectively. Often funded by giant corporations (Krupp, Rheinmetall, and Mann in Germany, Vickers in Britain, Schneider-Creusot in France, and Dupont in the USA), these organizations were capable of bringing out new weapons every few months: or, at any rate, introducing improvements into existing ones. For example, the first dreadnought-class battleship was launched in 1906 and at once made all existing warships obsolete; yet it was only eight years before that battleship itself had been replaced by others whose size, and the weight of the broadsides that they fired, were at least 50 per cent greater. Similarly, the aircraft with which the main military powers opened the war of 1914–18 were entirely useless by the time that it ended. By 1918 one of the most important ground weapons (certainly the one with the greatest promise for the future) was the tank, a machine which had only been conceived three years earlier.

Until 1918 military-technological progress usually originated outside the military establishments proper, first at the hands of individual inventors and then—as we just saw—at those of industrial corporations. Generally speaking, the sense that victory in war depended on technological progress only slowly made its way up the military-political hierarchy; when it did so, however, the state took over with a vengeance. During the inter-war years many of the leading armies established colleges specifically devoted to the problems of industrial technology and mobilization. By the Second World War every self-respecting president, prime minister, and commanding general appointed a scientific adviser whose function was to tell, as best he could, which of the endless flow of new ideas and inventions were practicable and which ones should be developed. New devices coming into service—radar, computers, jet engines, rockets, nuclear energy, to mention but a few—were force-fed by the state, which provided them with virtually unlimited amounts of funding, technicians, and raw materials. The result was another unprecedented spurt in the power of weapons, and their cost; once again, many classes of ships, aircraft, tanks, and artillery pieces with which the various powers had begun the war were almost if not entirely out of date by the time that it ended.

Since 1945 the defence departments of many advanced countries have become important sources of technological innovation, helping to produce not merely military devices but, by way of the so-called 'spin-off' effect, civilian technology as well. Particularly after 1970, more and more small, developing countries the world over have sought to imitate the great powers, and started their own independent military R. & D. programmes; always at very great economic cost, and often to no apparent 'defence' benefit. Yet perceptions, whether right or wrong, represent powerful social forces in themselves. The idea that armed might is critically dependent on having the most advanced military technology at one's disposal was probably expressed for the first time by Francis Bacon in the seventeenth century. As a general maxim it dates back approximately to the industrial revolution. For good or ill, it has become one of the most important driving assumptions of the modern world. Whether it is still correct, or whether it is itself obsolete, is a question to which we shall return in the final chapter of this book.

The military impact of technology 1500–1830

In discussing the relationship between technology and war during the period 1500–1830, it is impossible not to begin with the introduction of gunpowder. Gunpowder seems to have been invented during the eleventh century in China, where it was used in small rockets and grenades as a means of scaring away demons (sometimes, perhaps, demons in human form). Over the next 200 years it reached Europe via the Mongols or the Arabs, or both. At first, its progress was slow. As late as 1475 during the siege of Neuss by Charles the Bold, crossbows and firearms were used interchangeably; some armies, notably the English, even clung to the bow and arrow until the first quarter of the seventeenth century.

A hundred years earlier, nevertheless, the dominant type of hand-gun in use—known as the arquebus—already looked more or less like the modern rifle, with wooden stock, long metal barrel, lock, trigger, and sometimes trigger guard. The weapon weighed perhaps 5 to 6 kilograms; detonated by a burning fuse which the trigger brought into contact with the charge, it relied on black powder to fire a lead ball weighing around one-twelfth of a pound to an effective range of perhaps 100–25 yards. The rate of fire was one shot per minute at most (without counting the frequent misfires), far too slow for fighting at close quarters or for holding off cavalry. To provide the arquebusiers with staying power, commanders used to interlace them with pikemen. Large blocks of pikemen, carrying light body armour (breastplates and helmets, but usually no shields or greaves), formed the main tactical units on sixteenth-century battlefields. They in turn were protected by 'sleeves' of arquebusiers deployed on each of their four corners.

Owing to its length, and the way in which it had to be loaded, the arquebus was difficult if not impossible to employ on horseback. Special shorter weapons, known as pistols, were accordingly developed for the latter use; however, finding the optimum way for cavalry to use both firearms and edged weapons represented a difficult problem that took time to solve. The sixteenth century favoured a manœuvre known as the *caracole*, in which the riders gingerly approached the opposing infantry, fired their pistols, and withdrew to reload, making way for the next rank. This system was relatively ineffective, given that it sacrificed the cavalry's most important characteristic, its mobility. Beginning with Gustavus Adolphus in the Thirty Years War, there was a return to cold steel in the form of the sword and, increasingly, the sabre. Thereafter, heavy cavalry, now wearing breastplates instead of the older full armour, was able to regain much of its medieval status as a battle-winning arm. As Murat was to show at the Battle of Friedland (1808), it retained this role until Napoleonic times. Even thereafter its final decline was slow, uneven, and reluctant.

The weapon which often enabled seventeenth- and eighteenth-century cavalry to press home attacks on infantry equipped with firearms was field artillery. The development of artillery had initially been even slower than that of hand-guns. For the first hundred and fifty years or so, cannon, being heavy and cumbersome, were not even provided with wheels, and were used principally in siege operations. Towards 1500, however, this situation was gradually transformed. Better powder and improved metallurgy permitted the size of guns to be reduced. The place of the giant *muurbraeckers* (wall-busters) was taken by a collection of much smaller (5–12 pounder) sakers and culverins; from the 1760s on, horse artillery made it possible for guns to be moved while in action. Deployed, as far as possible, on ridges giving a clear field of fire, artillery was capable of blowing heavy formations of infantry apart; either they took cover, as was recommended by Machiavelli in his *L'arte della guerra*, or else they scattered. Taking cover was, of course, only practicable in places where the terrain was suitable. Scattering would leave them at the mercy of cavalry (especially light cavalry) which, by reason of speed and mass, continued to hold a very great advantage over individual infantrymen however brave. Thus tactics became nothing so much as a question of properly co-ordinating the three arms. The enemy was to be put in a situation where he was damned if he did and damned if he did not; and so it remained until after the Battle of Waterloo in 1815.

Soon after 1600 the arquebus was gradually replaced, first by the heavier musket (fired either by a matchlock or, more rarely, by the complicated and expensive wheel-lock) and then by the flintlock. While effective range remained much as it had been, the rate of fire rose to perhaps two to three rounds a minute on the part of the best-trained troops. Thanks to the addition of sights, accuracy also improved. The increasing rate of fire caused the number of pikemen in infantry formations to fall from perhaps 80 per cent at the time of the Battle of Pavia (1525) to less than 50 per cent a hundred years later. Around 1660, the invention of the bayonet permitted the remainder to be abolished, and with them went the last vestiges of armour worn by men on foot. As uniforms replaced armour, there came into being the 'line' infantry typical of the eighteenth century—homogeneous and suitable for most operational purposes, except perhaps small-scale irregular warfare.

As of 1620, infantrymen usually no longer fired their weapons individually but on the word of command by platoon, company, or demi-battalion. They thus produced devastating volleys, capable of shredding entire ranks, and requiring a ferocious discipline to withstand. Another outcome of the technological improvements being made was that the time required for reloading continued to drop steadily; hence the number of ranks required to stand behind each other could also be reduced, from eight to ten in the time of Maurice of Nassau and Gustavus Adolphus, to four to five in the time of Marlborough, three to four under Frederick the Great, and two to three under Napoleon. By the end of the period, as many as one-third of the infantrymen in the most advanced armies were no longer fighting in formation at all. Instead they acted as skirmishers, preceding the main body of troops and firing at will from cover.

The declining number of ranks in infantry formations, together with the constant growth in the size of armies, caused battlefields to spread out in breadth from perhaps 2–3 kilometres at the beginning of the period to 6–7 at its end. Yet the nature of battle was not thereby changed. In 1815, as in 1500 (and indeed in 500 BC), a battle was a kind of tournament. Arranged by tacit, and sometimes explicit, consent between the opposing commanders, it saw their main forces engaging each other at close quarters. Taking up no more than a few square kilometres of space, battles were almost always over within a day or less. Since formations took a long time to alter from marching to tactical order, often it was a question of one afternoon only: a few hours of concentrated slaughter in which as many as one-third of the troops on both sides might fall on the field, either dead or dying. The fact that the nature of battle, as opposed to the techniques by which it was fought, remained constant has led at least one modern authority to divide the whole of military history into two periods—before and after Waterloo.

If the spreading use of gunpowder left the nature of battle unchanged, the same can be said of siege warfare. The development of siege artillery was initially very slow; it was only in 1453 that the fall of Constantinople, considered the strongest city in the world and the survivor of many previous sieges, gave notice to a horrified world that a new age had dawned. The tall, narrow curtain so characteristic of pre-modern fortifications could neither resist artillery nor be used as a platform for it. Accordingly, from the middle of the fifteenth century onwards, a desperate search for new types of fortification developed. As might be expected, this search led to many strange experiments—among them the imaginary castles drawn by Albrecht Dürer as well as the barely serviceable structures built by King Henry VIII along the coast of England to resist a possible French or Spanish invasion.

Towards 1520 a new system of fortification seems to have been worked out by an Italian military engineer, Michele San Michele. The *trace italienne*, as it became known, consisted of an immensely broad ditch; thick, straight, angular walls; and equally thick bastions at the corners, designed to provide flanking fire for the walls and for each other, and endowing the entire structure with its characteristic star-shaped form. Above all, the new fortifications differed from all their predecessors from neolithic times onwards in that they did not stand high above the ground—on the contrary, the whole idea was to build them as low as possible so as to avoid presenting a target to artillery. A revolution of this magnitude took time to be understood, but from 1550 on we can follow the new style of fortification as it spread into France, the Low Countries, Germany, England (as at Berwick-on-Tweed), and Poland.

The original 'Italian' fortresses were comparatively simple structures. During the seventeenth century, however, the growing power of the cannon with which they were confronted, as well as their own logic, caused them to grow and become more complicated. At first, outlying or detached structures would be built to protect the corners of the bastions; next, those structures themselves would require protection, and the whole lot would have to be linked with the main fortress, at which point the process repeated itself. Thus first-class fortresses, such as those constructed by Vauban or Coehoorn around 1690, became ever larger. They acquired ravelins and redoubts, bonnettes and lunettes, tenailles and tenaillons, counterguards and crownworks and hornworks and cuvettes and fausse brayes and scarps and cordons and banquettes and counterscarps, that baroque profusion lampooned in Laurence Sterne's *Tristram Shandy* (1760–8).

With the elements of fortification thus modified, the procedures of siege warfare followed suit. As before, a siege would start by throwing out a perimeter cordon—possibly a double one—designed to keep the defenders in and relieving forces out. Next, a reconnaissance would be conducted to find the weakest spot in the defences. A trench would be opened parallel to the walls, perhaps 700–800 metres away from them, and the siege guns, protected by mantelets, placed inside it. Once one section of the fortifications had been cleared of defenders, another trench would be opened closer to the walls, connected to the first by zigzagging communication trenches. The guns would be dragged forward, and the process repeated. Normally it was necessary to dig yet a third trench, 200–300 metres from the walls, to enable the guns to be fired at point-blank range and open a breach. Counting from the cutting of the first trench, most firstclass fortresses could be taken in roughly six to eight weeks. Unless a relief force appeared, or the besiegers ran out of ammunition, or winter put an end to the enterprise, the outcome of a well-conducted siege was almost certain. As a result a regular procedure developed for surrendering fortresses with honour by means of so-called *belles capitulations*.

The rise of artillery obviously led to important changes in the techniques of early modern siege warfare, leading to the disappearance of most earlier devices (except, be it noted, mining).

Still, as in the case of battle, gunpowder altered neither the basic nature of the siege nor the fundamental distinction between it and field warfare. The latter remained a question of tactics, the former, one of engineering. The latter depended on *coup d'œil* and impetuosity; the former on technical skill, persistence, and sheer donkey work. The two types of operation required different kinds of troops, and, increasingly as the calibre of field artillery diminished, different kinds of cannon as well.

Furthermore, the new devices so far described only modified one part of warfare—fighting; their effect on other elements, such as supply, communications, and strategy, was much more limited. While firearms did require powder and ammunition, the quantities involved were fairly small at this stage; measuring by weight, the great bulk of all military supplies continued to consist of food, and in particular of fodder for the horses that carried the cavalrymen, moved the cannon, and hauled every possible kind of equipment. Though some of the best-organized states began to set up magazines of grain from the late seventeenth century onwards, on the whole armies remained as dependent on local supplies as they had always been. Either the soldiers bought their food directly from the civilian population, or the army did so, using money extracted from that same population by means of so-called 'contributions'. Otherwise requisitioning was resorted to, or else it became plunder pure and simple.

Since plunder represented the most wasteful and least efficient method of all, after 1648 it tended to disappear except in emergencies, or when control broke down. Often enough, none the less, the goal of warfare remained the same: namely, in the words of Frederick the Great, to eat all there was to eat in one province before moving on to the next one and repeating the process. Because of the need for fodder, hostilities were generally restricted to the summer season; moreover the dependence of armies on the countryside for their supplies tended to canalize their operations into certain well-defined, densely populated areas like the southern Netherlands, northern Italy, and south-central Germany. Finally, since most if not all ammunition would be taken along at the outset of a campaign, there was no question of lines of communication in the modern sense of that term. As the operations of Gustavus Adolphus and Marlborough show clearly enough, early modern armies, so long as they were able to dominate or intimidate the surrounding countryside, were almost as free to move around as ships at sea. Normally, logistic difficulties were only to be expected during a prolonged siege, which made it necessary to stay in one place until it was eaten bare. Under such circumstances, the meaning of strategy was also entirely different, and indeed it was not until shortly before the Napoleonic Wars that the term, in anything like its modern sense, even came into use.

Last but not least, military-technological progress during this period left the means of command, control, and communication much as they had always been. On the battlefield, these means comprised the spoken (more often shouted) word; auditory signals produced by drums, trumpets, or bugles; and visual signals in the form of flags, banners, and standards being raised, lowered, or waved about. Long-distance communications likewise developed very little. They consisted almost entirely of mounted messengers combined, very infrequently, with optic telegraphs or prearranged signals in the form of cannon shots. These technical means imposed strict limits on the size of tactical units; the distance from headquarters at which they might operate; the maximum strength of armies; the extent to which their separate parts could co-operate against a single enemy; and the ability of rulers to control their commanders in the field, or even maintain an adequate knowledge of what they were doing. In this way they ensured that, the invention of gunpowder notwithstanding, the period from 1500 to 1830 probably had more in common with the age that preceded it than with the one that was to follow.

The military impact of technology 1830–1945

War-related technological progress after 1830 differed from what had gone before. Hitherto it had been weapons that developed, albeit slowly by modern standards. Now it was transport and communications that took the lead, bringing about profound changes not merely in strategy and tactics, but also in the infrastructure on which they are based. Accordingly this section will focus on the infrastructure first; only then will it march from weapon to weapon until arriving finally at the most powerful weapon of all.

The first major improvement in transport to make its effect on war felt was the railway. The practice of making wagons move on rails, chiefly in connection with mining operations, originated in the late sixteenth century, but it was only the industrial revolution which permitted the manufacture of iron rails and made available the steam-driven locomotive. Once the first public railway between Liverpool and Manchester was opened in 1830, attempts to use the new device for moving troops towards threatened areas began almost immediately in France, Austria, Prussia, and Russia. The first 'operational' use of railways seems to have been in the summer of 1848, when the defeated anti-Prussian revolutionaries in Baden seized a train and drove it to Switzerland and exile; among those who made their escape in this way was Marx's lifelong friend Friedrich Engels.

Using railways to transport large bodies of troops sounds simple in theory. In practice it is very complicated, and requires meticulous planning to prevent loading and unloading stations from becoming clogged, lines congested, trains stuck (or even lost!) in the traffic, and accidents happening. Initially, the leaders in the field of military railway administration were the French. In 1859 they displayed their mastery by moving a quarter of a million troops into northern Italy within six weeks. Next it was the Prussians under Moltke who came to the fore; their mobilizations against Austria in 1866 and against France in 1870 represented masterpieces of planning which astonished the world. These events, plus the equally spectacular use made of railroads during the American Civil War of 1861–5, were observed by general staffs the world over. They concluded that in the next war the side with the superior railway system would be able to mobilize first, and hence gain a critical advantage which it might not be possible to overcome thereafter.

The rise of the railways was accompanied by that of the electric telegraph, another non-military technology whose effect on war was far-reaching. Without the telegraph the railways themselves could operate, if at all, only at a fraction of their capacity. More important still, without the telegraph it was impossible to command the armies moving over immense distances by rail. Wires and tracks accordingly co-operated in transforming strategy. Whereas formerly even a Napoleon had only been able to command his corps as long as they were not much more than 25 miles away from headquarters, now it became possible to co-ordinate forces scattered across hundreds of miles against a single enemy. Whereas previously strategy had operated in terms of provinces, now it came to embrace countries, and before long entire continents. Armies moving on such broad fronts could bypass any fortress; this fact, together with the growing power of cannon, caused siege warfare as traditionally understood to disappear. Finally, railways and telegraphs for the first time in history enabled large countries to mobilize as efficiently as small ones. In this way they not only led to a vast increase in the size of armies deployed—from hundreds of thousands in 1861–71 to millions in 1914—but accentuated the gap between the 'great powers' and the rest.

The growing role of railways and telegraphs was accompanied by equally far-reaching developments in the field of weapons. As late as the Napoleonic Wars, the basic weapons had been the flintlock and the muzzle-loading cannon. In 1831 the transformation of the former began with the invention of the breechloading Dreyse 'needle gun'; from this point on scarcely a decade passed without armies being forced to rid themselves of their old arms and purchase new ones, complete with all the expense and administrative disruption such a process entails. By 1890 percussion caps, rifled barrels, bolt-action loading mechanisms, all-metal cartridges, magazines, and smokeless powder had been added. The result was to increase the rate of fire of the basic infantry weapon by a factor of three or four, effective range by a factor of four or five, accuracy by the same amount, all this while enabling troops to fire from behind cover. And still to come was the machine-gun, which was to enable a crew of two or three to produce firepower equal to, if not greater than, that of a Napoleonic battalion.

The development of artillery was equally spectacular. From 1850 onwards inventors such as John Armstrong in Britain and Alfred Krupp in Prussia began to replace bronze and cast-iron pieces with steel ones; add rifled barrels as well as breech-loading mechanisms; provide explosive ammunition (shrapnel and high explosive) instead of the old solid iron balls; and, by way of a final touch, add recoil mechanisms which made it unnecessary to resight the guns each time they were fired. These developments increased the rate of artillery fire from perhaps one round per minute in Napoleon's time to a (theoretical) maximum of ten or twelve. By the First World War, ordinary field guns, relying on indirect fire, possessed an effective range of 6 to 8 kilometres; heavy cannon could do much better, reaching targets up to 30, and in one case 120, kilometres distant. Since such ranges made sighting with the naked eye no longer possible, increasing reliance was placed on complicated mathematical calculations combined with meteorological data and, at sea, the first mechanical computers. Alternatively, laying and aiming the guns was done with the aid of those new inventions the balloon and the aircraft.

Among the first victims of the immense increase in firepower was the heavy cavalry. Already during the American Civil War such cavalry was conspicuously absent from most major battlefields, though units of light horsemen whose principal weapon was the carbine did play a very important role in scouting, screening, foraging, and deep raiding into the enemy's rear. On western European battlefields, the last substantial mounted charge was the famous 'death ride' of the Prussian hussars at Mars-la-Tour in 1870. With that, the death-knell of heavy cavalry had sounded; from then on it disappeared, and light cavalry served only in less important theatres of war, where modern weapons were either absent or thin on the ground, such as the British campaign in the Sudan (1898), the Boer War (1899–1902), the Eastern Front (1914–18), Palestine (1917–18), the Russian Civil War (1918–19), and the Russo-Polish War (1919–20), which seems to have been the last in history to see cavalry of any kind manoeuvring in mass.

Even in combat between infantry forces, the effect of growing firepower was to make the tactical defensive much stronger than the offensive. At Gettysburg in 1863, as at Königgrätz in 1866, attempts by the infantry to close with its entrenched opponents merely led to row upon row of casualties amongst the attackers. Infantrymen began to abandon the close formations in which they had hitherto fought, and to disperse. Instead of fighting erect (and wearing uniforms intended to emphasize their height) they found themselves crouching, lying down, and leaping from one shelter to the next. From the great Moltke down, most commanders did not welcome these changes. As fronts became longer and soldiers (aided by the new camouflaged uniforms which were coming into use) literally disappeared into the ground, those commanders found it hard to exercise control or even to know what was going on. Some tried to rely on discipline, forcing soldiers to fight as if technology had stood still since Waterloo; the result was disasters such as the first day of the Battle of the Somme in 1916, when 60,000 British troops were cut down. Others, more prescient, responded by decentralizing command to company level. By so doing, they pointed the way to the future.

By the time of the First World War, the preceding developments had created a situation where armies numbered in the millions were confronting each other in fortified trenches across wide fronts. A combination of defensive firepower with that simple invention, barbed wire, prevented them from breaking through; when they occasionally did so, the wire-bound means of communication at their disposal (the telegraph and telephone) were usually unable to follow up, making the advancing spearheads impossible to control, and causing the attack to stall. Furthermore, the new weapons which entered service after 1870 had led to a vast increase in the logistic requirements of armies. The daily consumption per soldier had been multiplied three or four times; taking account of the growth in the size of armies, the figure is closer to twelve or fifteen. But apart from the few motor vehicles coming into service, no new means of transporting such quantities were available. The result, once again, was a sharp decline in mobility. Even when armies successfully took the offensive, supplies were unable to follow up, and sooner or later the result was stalemate.

By 1916 it began to look as if the stalemate thus created might last forever. Vast battles such as Verdun and the Somme were being fought, lasting months and costing hundreds of thousands of casualties, for the gain of little if any ground. On both sides of the front, the protection afforded by the trenches provided belligerents with the time needed to mobilize resources on a scale that dwarfed all previous wars combined. Not only the troops, but entire populations were harnessed to war work in factories, fields, and offices. To direct the effort, huge bureaucratic machines were constructed as if by magic. Before long they assumed responsibility for every aspect of national life, from individuals' daily calorie intake through the allocation of fuel and raw materials all the way to the qualifications that skilled workers had to possess and the pay they would receive. Though the advent of peace caused much of this machinery to be dismantled, the blueprints remained in government files. The Second World War caused it to be rebuilt, and this time it was not dismantled but used as a framework for the welfare state to come.

By the middle of the First World War, two new technologies began to indicate possible ways out of the impasse. The first, the tank, was developed simultaneously in Britain and France. Early tanks were essentially motorized, bullet-proof boxes moving on tracks; they were armed with machine-guns and cannon, and intended above all as trench-crossing vehicles. In this role they were quite successful at an early stage. However, mechanical limitations—low speed, short range, unreliability, extreme discomfort for the crew, and lack of communications with the outside—meant that exploiting success was usually impossible, and left the machines themselves vulnerable to counter-attack, as happened at Cambrai in October 1917. Had the war gone on, some of these limitations might have been overcome, and indeed the famous 'Plan 1919' drawn up by the then Colonel J. F. C. Fuller already pointed to the use of armour in its future role, a modern version of deep-thrusting heavy cavalry. As it was, hostilities came to an end and the Plan came to nothing.

The other novel weapon that made its début in the First World War was of course air power. The idea of putting flying devices to military use was not new—its appearance dates from 1793 when it was suggested that hot air balloons could be used to land French troops in England. Throughout the nineteenth century balloons were employed for observation; during the siege of Paris in 1870–1 they served to get passengers and mail out of the city (though not back in). Serious progress, however, had to await the invention of powered heavier-than-air machines, first successfully flown by the Wright brothers in North Carolina in 1903.

The first to use aircraft in war were the Italians in Libya (1911). By 1914 all leading armies had incorporated the machines in their order of battle, expecting to use them for reconnaissance and liaison. Such missions soon led to encounters; the pilots took pot shots at each other, using first pistols, then carbines, and finally machine-guns aligned with the airframe and synchronized with the propeller. As hostilities intensified, the number and variety of missions assigned to aircraft grew and grew. To reconnaissance and liaison were added artillery-spotting, close ground support, interdiction of communications, attacks on airfields, 'strategic' bombing far behind the front, and, of course, air combat. By the time the war ended, specialized aircraft had been developed for many of these missions, and air forces which initially had numbered a few thousand men had expanded a hundredfold.

The coming of peace in 1918 did not put an end to military technological progress. On the contrary, it led to a lively debate as to how the new weapons ought to be employed in the future and, above all, how their role would relate to the traditional ones. The first to hit on an answer, not just on paper but in the form of a functioning organization, were the Germans who, having been defeated, were more open-minded than the victors. By the second half of the 1930s they were using another technical instrument, radio, to tie tanks and aircraft into an integrated team. Tanks were grouped into armoured divisions consisting, besides the *Panzerkampfwagen* themselves, of motorized infantry, artillery, anti-tank troops, combat engineers, signals, and a headquarters to co-ordinate the lot; aircraft, now made of stressed aluminium rather than wood and canvas, were organized into *Luftflotten* (air fleets) consisting of all types of machines and trained to operate ahead of the ground forces, opening the way for them and providing support. Then, as now, the entire operation ran on huge numbers of motor vehicles which provided mobility and brought up supplies (as much as 300 tons a day per armoured division in 1939–41, twice as much by 1945). This in turn meant that oil became the most important war-winning strategic commodity of all.

The early operations of the tactical air force cum armoured division were brilliantly successful, enabling the Germans to overrun entire countries at comparatively small cost in the first two years of the Second World War. An offensive would now open with a paralysing blow by the air force at the enemy's air bases, anti-aircraft defences, communications and mobilization centres, and transportation system. Next the armoured divisions, after tearing a gap in the front, would thrust deep into the enemy's rear, overrun his depots and headquarters, cut off chunks of his forces, and enclose them in pockets. The armour would be followed by other forces which consolidated the breakthrough, defended the flanks against counter-attacks, and mopped up the trapped enemy forces. Such methods blurred the traditional distinction between front and rear, leading war to spread across zones dozens or even hundreds of kilometres deep. Continuing a trend that had started with the advent of modern firepower in the nineteenth century, they also led to a sharp decline in the density of troop concentrations until the battlefield took on its characteristically modern empty and eerie look.

War, however, is an imitative activity. By 1943 the German methods were well understood, and on the way to being effectively copied: the very success of blitzkrieg brought its limitations to light. First, since it depended on motor vehicles for its supplies, its operational reach was limited to about 300 kilometres; not enough to secure a quick decision in very large theatres of war such as North Africa or Russia, or western Europe in 1944–5. Second, the armoured division, initially created for the offensive, turned out to be almost equally potent on the defensive. In particular, tanks proved vulnerable to a lethal combination of anti-tank artillery, minefields, and, increasingly, even infantry firing shoulder-held rockets with 'hollow' warheads.

From 1943 onwards these factors led to a decline in the pre-eminent role of tanks within the division; in attack and defence alike, they became increasingly dependent on other forces, including engineers to open the way, artillery to deal with enemy infantry and anti-tank guns, and anti-tank artillery to counter enemy tanks. Thus the doctrine of combined arms took the place of blitzkrieg. In essence, it has remained dominant in all major armies from the middle of the Second World War to the present day.

By 1943-5 the most powerful forces everywhere were either armoured, or mechanized—that is, riding in armoured personnel carriers—or, at the very least, motorized—that is, made road-mobile by means of large-scale motor transport. Horses had disappeared from combat, although the poorer armies like the *Wehrmacht* and the Red Army still used them in large numbers for transport and supply. The skies above the armies swarmed with fighter-bombers, launching deadly attacks on transport, communications, rear echelons, and in some cases enemy fortifications as well as armoured vehicles. But the most powerful air forces—those of Britain and the USA—did not content themselves with supporting the ground forces: they also developed vast fleets of heavy bombers employed on independent missions deep in enemy territory, smashing industries and cities, causing the death and injury of millions of civilians. Neither the Soviets nor the Japanese (who, as an island people, concentrated on naval aviation) had anything comparable. Only the Germans tried to counter strategic bombing by means of ballistic missiles; these came too late in the war, however, and possessed neither the payload nor the accuracy to have decisive effect.

Meanwhile, hidden in the south-western American desert, far away from the centres of hostilities, a new weapon was being forged which would ultimately render all its predecessors obsolete. The possibility of atomic weapons had been foreseen by H. G. Wells even before 1914. By 1938, laboratory experiments in Berlin had proved that they were technically feasible, and by mid-1942 construction was in progress under the control of the US army. In less than three years a combination of first-class scientific work, brilliant engineering, astonishing organizational skills, and the unlimited resources made available by total war mobilization had borne fruit. In Hiroshima, in southern Japan, 6 August 1945 was a fine summer day, with a clear sky and excellent visibility. Against this background the first atomic bomb was dropped from a B29 heavy bomber; a thousand suns shone, and large-scale conventional modern war, as it had evolved since 1500, abolished itself.

12

Battle

The Experience of Modern Combat

RICHARD HOLMES

At the very heart of war, wrapped in layers of boredom and anticipation, veiled by confusion, and eerily lit by terror, anguish, and savagery, lies the experience of combat. Yet war and battle are not synonymous. There were always strategic thinkers and practical commanders who recognized that battle was usually bloody and often indecisive. If an opponent could be psychologically unhinged, rendered helpless by subtle manœuvre, or simply deprived of material means of resistance by the severance of his logistic sinews, so much the better. Indeed, B. H. Liddell Hart argued that 'In most campaigns the dislocation of the enemy's psychological and physical balance has been the vital prelude to a successful attempt at his overthrow.'

But other thinkers, most notably Karl von Clausewitz, insisted that combat was 'the central military art: all other activities merely support it.' Clausewitz emphasized that, although battle was 'the bloodiest solution', a general ought not to flinch from it, for it was only by defeating the enemy's army in the field that he could bring about those conditions which made possible victorious peace. Still, many generals did shrink from it. There were no certainties in combat, which was as damaging to reputations as to life and limb, and, especially during the eighteenth and nineteenth centuries, it was all too easy to see the results of years of laborious peacetime training knocked to pieces in an unlucky afternoon.

It was not only military theory and cautious campaigning which contributed to the rarity of battle. For much of history pitched battle depended on the consent of both adversaries, and Clausewitz went so far as to say that 'There can be no engagement unless both sides are willing.' Inadequate maps, poor communications, and unforgiving terrain often made it difficult for even the most aggressive commanders to bring their opponents to battle. And even when great armies did clash, many of their soldiers found themselves in the wrong place at the crucial time. Napoleon's *Grande Armée* began the Austerlitz campaign with an effective strength of over 210,000 men, but only 73,000 were at Austerlitz, and by no means all of them were actively engaged. The Battle of Mons, the British Expeditionary Force's opening action of the First World War, involved one of the BEF's two corps. Only one of this corps's two divisions was seriously engaged, and well over half the British casualties that day were incurred by three battalions in a single brigade.

The proliferation of supporting services at the expense of combat arms—in itself one of the characteristics of modern war—made it increasingly easy for a soldier to experience war but never to see combat. By November 1918 the American Expeditionary Force in France had over a million men, many of them cooks, drivers, or quartermasters, in its forward zone, supported by 855,600 in the rear area. In mid-1966, when there were 276,000 Americans in Vietnam, with another 30,000 South Koreans and Australians, there were only 44,800 infantrymen in theatre, up to 35,000 of whom were actually available for operations away from bases. It is small wonder that combat soldiers of various armies and different generations have coined their own derogatory nicknames for these denizens of the world of the rear: *Etappenschweine* in the First World War German army, REMFs (Rear Echelon Mother-Fuckers) in Vietnam, and PONTI (People of No Tactical Importance) in the Gulf.

This tension between those whose primary function is to engage the enemy and those who support them underlines the fact that, for so many cultures, combat has been much more than a simple military necessity. For the medieval knight, scion of a caste bred to the sword, it was the supreme justification of his existence. 'It is a joyous thing, a war,' proclaimed Jean de Bueil in the mid-fifteenth-century *Le Jouvencel*. It gave the Zulu warrior the opportunity of distinguishing himself and being rewarded with cattle by his king. 'War was important and bravery essential,' writes Robert Edgerton, 'but the basic reason for life was cattle.' To the nineteenth-century product of the teeming towns of Britain's industrial Midlands, it provided an almost unique opportunity for social advancement. 'Well, boys, here goes death or a commission,' shouted a cavalry sergeant, setting his horse at a Sikh square whose point-blank musketry confirmed the sombre side of his prophecy.

Across history, hundreds of thousands of men have been impelled into military service by legal compulsion or sheer economic necessity. John Parrish, facing conscription as a medical officer during the Vietnam War, thought that he had three choices: Canada for life, three years in prison, or a year in Vietnam. 'My free country was forcing me to leave home for an undeclared war in a distant country,' he wrote. 'To what lengths was I in honour bound to serve my country? Where was my freedom of choice?' Stanley Goff, a black man from a blue-collar background, felt that he had no real alternative. 'I got my draft greetings,' he recalled. 'I just succumbed. What else could I do.'

A lad's empty belly (or his girlfriend's unmistakably full one) often drove him to enlist. Wellington analysed the raw material of his own incomparable army in Spain.

People talk of their enlisting from their fine military feeling—all stuff— no such thing. Some of our men enlist from having got bastard children—some for minor offences—many more for drink; but you can hardly conceive such a set brought together, and it really is wonderful that we should have made them the fine fellows they are.

In Second Empire France, Maurice Fleury was a well-educated young man who squandered his inheritance. Faced with a choice between 'jumping in the Seine or joining some regiment', he enlisted without delay and ended his days a general and a count.

Dismissive though Wellington was, we should not underrate the appeal of military service for young men bored by humdrum civilian lives. 'We were tired of fathers, of advice from relations, of bottled coffee essence, of school, of newspaper offices,' remembered John Lucy, who enlisted into the Royal Irish Rifles on the eve of the First World War. 'The soft accents and slow movements of the small farmers who swarmed in the streets of our dull southern Irish town, the cattle, fowl, eggs, butter, bacon and the talk of politics filled us with loathing.' The fact that enlistment was frequently a precursor to combat only sharpened its appeal. 'I wanted to go to war,' recalled an American soldier of the Vietnam era. 'It was a test that I wanted to pass. It was a manhood test, no question about it.' Christopher Isherwood, who grew up in England during the First World War, admitted that:

Like most of my generation, I was obsessed by a complex of terror and longings connected with the idea 'War'. War in this purely neurotic sense meant The Test. The test of your courage, your maturity, your sexual prowess; 'are you really a man?' Subconsciously, I believe, I longed to be subjected to this test; but I also dreaded failure. I dreaded failure so much—indeed, I was so certain that I should fail—that, consciously, I denied my longing to be tested altogether.

The transformation of recruit, willing or unwilling, suspicious or enthusiastic, into trained soldier is a process which, like so many other facets of military life, has both physical and psychological aspects. The recruit is sworn in, often using an oath whose public affirmation of allegiance and brave conduct harks back to the military oath taken by Roman legionaries. The full majesty of the ritual was not always readily understood by those involved. The Swiss poet Ulrich Bräker, impressed into the Prussian army in the reign of Frederick the Great, remembered that:

They ... brought up several badly-holed colours and ordered each of us to take a corner. An adjutant, or whoever he was, read a whole screed of articles of war and pronounced a few formulae ... Lastly he swung a colour over our heads and dismissed us.

The recruit's appearance is transformed by the issue of uniform, which marks him off, not only from the civilian society of which he was until recently a member, but also from other subtribes within the same army. The costume historian James Laver suggested that the design of uniform was based on three key principles. The utilitarian principle demanded that uniform should be practical; the hierarchical principle that it should mark out the graduations of rank, and the seduction principle that it should make its wearer as attractive as possible to the opposite sex. In this half-flippant proposition we see the essential ingredients of uniform through the ages. Much to the regret of its wearers, it has often been more showy than utilitarian. Cavalrymen wore brain-boiling brass helmets or elaborate millinery which was incompatible with fractious horses. The long-tailed double-breasted coat characteristic of eighteenth-century infantry uniform was often skimpily cut from cheap cloth which shrank into the bargain. The complete panoply of packs, knapsacks, crossbelts, and pouches looked splendid in dress regulations but felt ghastly after an hour or two on a cobbled road under a blazing sun. When the unlucky Ulrich Bräker prised his coat open beneath its constricting mass of straps he saw steam burst out as if from a boiling kettle.

The development of breech-loading weapons and smokeless powder accelerated the drift towards functionalism. As late as 1914, however, the officers of the contending armies carried swords, underlining the knightly origins of their profession. French infantry wore the traditional blue coat and red trousers—attempts to replace the latter with something more utilitarian had produced the firm ministerial statement: 'the red trouser *is* France.' It was not until 1916 that peacetime headdress was generally replaced by the steel helmet, and even then national differences were explained as much by culture as by science.

There is something of the peacock in most soldiers, especially when a distinctive item of uniform hints at individual prowess or tribal achievement. A British regiment which killed many Continental soldiers, in controversial circumstances, at Brandywine Creek in 1777 dyed its white plumes red so that the Americans would know upon whom they might seek to take revenge. The tradition was preserved in the 'Brandywine patch' worn behind the cap-badge of the Royal Berkshire Regiment. Such baubles matter more than we might think. The Prussian Regiment of

Anhalt-Bernberg was subject to collective punishment for failure in battle in 1760: common soldiers lost their swords and officers and NCOs the braid on their hats. A month later the regiment, anxious to efface the stain on its character, spearheaded the breakthough which won the Battle of Liegnitz.

The training which follows enlistment gives soldiers a grasp of individual and collective skills, and begins the process of bonding them together into groups which emphasize co-operative values and loyalties. Many of history's most distinguished commanders recognized that performance in action was founded on sound training and administration rather than on more cerebral qualities. Lord Hopton, a Royalist general in the English Civil War, declared that a good general ought to 'command well, pay well and hang well'. The last point emphasized that the discipline which kept men together at times of mortal danger was often robust, although the changing nature of battle and of western society more generally has tended to make such discipline harder to apply within the army and to justify outside it. We should not, however, lose sight of the fact that at least one of the motives which persuaded the warriors of history to face death in battle was the possibility that failure in combat would result in an ignominious death from rope or firing-squad. Italian military law long included the provision that soldiers executed for cowardice would be shot in the back.

The nature of combat is itself one of the characteristics which define modern war. In ancient times battle was essentially a compendium of single combats as men hewed with bronze or iron as long as their strength allowed. Homer catches the dreadful essence of it:

The son of Telamon, sweeping in through the mass of the fighters, struck him at close quarters through the brazen cheeks of his helmet and the helm crested with horse-hair was riven about the spearhead to the impact of the huge spear and the weight of the hand behind it and the brain ran from the wound along the spear by the eye-hole ...

To be sure, there were missile weapons which killed at a distance—the javelin, the *pilum* of the Roman legionary, or the English longbow. But their ranges were short, and the men they

slew fell within sight—and sound and smell too—of their enemies. And though some weapons, like the mangonels and tre-
buchets used in sieges, were what we would now term
crew-served, the overwhelming majority were individual, their
motive power the strength of a man's arm, their point of aim a
target within his view. And unspeakably dreadful though the cut
and thrust business of battle was, a man's survival still depended,
to a great extent, upon the strength of his arm and speed of his
reactions: it was not altogether unreasonable for song and story
to cast the warrior in the role of hero.

The advent of gunpowder did not change this at a stroke. Indeed, early firearms were less effective—in range, accuracy, and
rate of fire—than a longbow in skilled hands. But with them
came developments which have come to distinguish modern war.
First was the deepening of the battlefield, whose dangerous edge
widened from the spear's cast or arrow's flight of ancient times,
through the hundreds of yards made deadly by the bounding
cannon-ball, to the horizon-distant lethality that came with the
breech-loaders of the late nineteenth century and on to the air-
delivered death of the twentieth.

As battlefields became deeper, so they seemed increasingly empty
to those who strove to survive on them. Captain Alfred Wirth, a
German staff officer, found the early clashes of the First World War
'like being on manœuvres; one could actually see the troops taking
part. In the later fighting all that disappeared, and, in the three day
battle on the Marne especially, we experienced the truth of "the
emptiness of the battlefield".' P. J. Campbell, a British artillery officer, described the view from his observation post.

I learnt the names of every wood and all the villages. I knew the con-
tours of the hills and the shapes of the lakes in the valley. To see so
much and to see nothing. We might have been the only men alive, my
two signallers and I. And yet I knew there were thousands of hidden
men in front of me ... but no one moved, and everyone was waiting for
the safety of darkness.

This emptiness had several causes. In part it bears witness to
the blinkering effect of danger on a combatant's field of view.
Captain Cavalié Mercer, a horse artillery officer at Waterloo,

could see little but his own battery and infantry squares on either flank, while Captain Anthony Farrar-Hockley, adjutant of a British battalion in Korea, became fascinated with a black and yellow beetle crawling up the wall of his trench.

In part it reflects the obscuration caused by smoke, dust, and debris. The hoplite infantry of ancient Greece stamped blinding dust into the air. Black powder, in use until its replacement by smokeless powder at the end of the nineteenth century, covered the battlefield with clouds of foul-smelling sulphurous smoke. When Captain Richard Atkyns rode up Lansdown Hill in search of a body of Royalist horse on 5 June 1643 he

saw Sir Bevill Grinvill's stand of pikes, which certainly preserved our army from a total rout, with the loss of his most precious life; they stood as upon the eaves of an house for steepness, but as unmovable as a rock; on which side of this stand of pikes our horse were, I could not discover, for the air was so darkened by the smoke of the powder that for a quarter of an hour together (I dare say) there was no light seen, but what the fire of the volleys of shot gave.

A Union officer summed up his vision of Chancellorsville as one of 'smoke and bushes', a phrase which could equally well do duty for the caption of photographs of the Battle of Goose Green (1982), though in the latter case the smoke was produced by burning gorse, ignited by tracer bullets. Trenches and armoured vehicles also restrict their occupants' field of vision, as do some weapon sights and night-vision devices which often produce the ultimate vacuity by reducing the adversary to a symbol glowing amidst the surrounding murk.

The growing emptiness of the battlefield brought to the fore one of the most acute problems of modern war, that of maintaining the individual's motivation at a time when he may be out of sight of leaders and comrades. The massed formations which had been typical of combat up to the end of the nineteenth century had both tactical and psychological purpose. Tactically, they encouraged the effective employment of weapons which were loaded and fired in a sequence of set movements, and enabled units to be moved quickly and efficiently, usually in column, and then to be deployed for battle, usually in line.

Their psychological impact was no less important. Soldiers in battle are gregarious, and close, instinctively, on their comrades. Shoulder-to-shoulder formations gave men facing death or mutilation the moral prop of companions to left and right. No less significantly, it exposed them to the surveillance of comrades, whose respect they hoped to earn or maintain, and leaders, who would punish failure. Frederick the Great decreed that a soldier who turned round in the ranks under fire was to be run through by the NCO behind him, and even Major-General James Wolfe, an officer of liberal views on leadership who fell in the moment of victory at Quebec in 1759, issued draconian orders when commanding the 20th Foot in 1755: 'A soldier who quits his rank, or offers to flag, is instantly to be put to death by the officer who commands that platoon, or by the officer or sergeant in the rear of that platoon; a soldier does not deserve to live who won't fight for his king and country.'

Many contemporaries recognized that the proliferation of breech-loading infantry weapons and rifled artillery in the second half of the nineteenth century created particular difficulties. Looser, more flexible formations would mean that, as Colonel Charles Ardant du Picq, killed in the Franco-Prussian War of 1870–1, put it, solidarity would no longer have the sanction of mutual surveillance. Indeed, despite the fact that units in close order had suffered appalling casualties when they entered the zone swept by enemy fire—the Prussian Guard, attacking a French position at Saint-Privat on 18 August 1870, lost over 8,000 men, most of them in twenty minutes—soon after the war tactical regulations, which had briefly reflected the war's hard lessons, once again prescribed close-order formations. Even the British army, with a long tradition of colonial war and recent experience of fighting Boer irregulars in South Africa, emphasized, in *Infantry Training* 1914, that

The main essential to success in battle is to close with the enemy cost what it may ... The object of infantry in attack is therefore to get to close quarters as quickly as possible, and the leading lines must not delay the advance by halting to fire until compelled by the enemy to do so ... [When the charge is sounded] the call will be taken up by all buglers, and all neighbouring units will join in the charge as quickly as possible. During the delivery of the assault the men will cheer, bugles be sounded, and pipes played.

This emphasis on inspiring sounds catches another of the eternal truths of combat. Battlefields are noisy places. Hand-to-hand fighting was far from quiet. There was a distinctive thud, unmistakable to the experienced, the product of shield smashing into shield, weapons striking armour and piercing flesh, that marked the impact of one body of armoured infantry upon another. Virgil wrote of how 'the trumpet crashed out its dreadful note ... Shouting followed, and the sky roared back the echo.' An account of medieval battle declared that 'The din was so frightful that one could not have heard even God's thunder.' This sort of noise survived well into modern times, as long as men hacked and thrust with cold steel. A British sergeant was reminded of a thousand coppersmiths at work as he listened to British and French cavalrymen at handstrokes at Waterloo. Men shout, grunt, groan, and shriek in agony. War-cries follow national preferences, from the yodelled 'eleleleu' of Athenian phalangists, the barking 'Out, out' of the Saxon fyrd, the spine-chilling 'wild, weird falsetto' of the Confederate rebel yell, the Zulu howl of 'uSuthu', and the Russian shout of 'Urra' to the Vietnamese 'Tiên-Lên.'

Songs and music were a feature of many of the great battles of history. They helped keep up men's spirits as they set off towards that distant smudge of colour tipped with glitter that marked the enemy's line of battle. A Protestant pastor serving in the Russian ranks at Zorndorf in 1758 watched Frederick's battalions stepping out to the tap of drum.

Then the menacing beat of the Prussian drums was carried to our ears. For a time their woodwind was inaudible, but as the Prussians approached, we could hear the oboes playing the well-known hymn 'Ich bin ja, Herr, in deiner Macht!' I cannot express what I felt at that instant, but I do not consider that people will think it odd when I say that never since in the course of my long life have I heard that tune without experiencing the utmost emotion.

The musicians faced all the perils of a soldier, but perhaps their preoccupation with the task in hand helped take their mind off the risks they ran. A Napoleonic officer saw a regimental band hit squarely by cannon fire, but noted approvingly that the remaining fifers did not miss a single note. When the advance of 7th King's Own Scottish Borderers faltered at Loos on 25 September 1915, Piper Laidlaw played 'Blue Bonnets over the Border', inspiring his comrades and winning the Victoria Cross. Battle is often a bizarre mixture of ancient and modern, and Loos was a classic case in point. It was fought amongst the slagheaps, winding-gear, and miners' cottages of a coalfield in smoke and clouds of poison gas by men who could hear the shriek of bagpipes through the drizzle.

The noise of small arms and artillery drenches the modern battlefield. The thump and crash of black-powder muskets and cannon was unsettling enough, but with smokeless powder and high-velocity weapons came the vicious cracks that have made high-frequency deafness and tinnitus almost identifying features of combat soldiers from the two world wars. Weapons have their own distinctive sounds. Charles Carrington, a British infantry officer in the First World War, wrote of how

Every gun and every kind of projectile had its own personality ... Sometimes a field-gun shell would leap jubilantly with the pop of a Champagne cork from its muzzle, fly over with a steady buzzing crescendo, and burst with a fully expected bang; sometimes a shell would be released from a distant battery of heavies to roll across a huge arc of sky, gathering speed and noise like an approaching express train, ponderous and certain ... Some shells whistled, others shrieked, others wobbled through space gurgling like water poured from a decanter.

The subdued thump of repeating cannon earned them the nickname pom-poms; massed infantry fire sounded like tearing calico; fast-firing Second World War German machine-guns resembled motor bikes or power-saws. The second half of the twentieth century has brought sounds of its own. The throaty roar of engines, the squeaky rattle of tank tracks, the clang of long-rod penetrators hitting armour, and the reverberating boom of ground-attack aircraft all combine to assault the soldier's ears.

It is small wonder that the battlefield seems lonely and confusing, and that its events are often remembered in an unreal and
disjointed way. William Manchester, a US marine NCO in the
Second World War, retained only snatches of the fighting on Okinawa. 'Some flickers of unreal recollection remain,' he wrote;
'standing at the foot of the hill, arms akimbo, quavering with
senseless excitement and grinning maniacally.' Guy Sajer, who
served with the German army on the Eastern Front, found it 'difficult even to try to remember moments during which nothing is
considered, foreseen or understood, when there is nothing under
a steel helmet but an astonishingly empty head and a pair of eyes
which translate nothing more than would the eyes of an animal
facing mortal danger'.

Noise assaults a body already wearied by load-carrying and
lack of sleep. C. E. Montague thought that 'For most of his time
the average private was tired. Fairly often he was so tired as no
man at home ever is in the common run of his work.' He was
writing of the First World War, but his point has wider validity.
Nor is it fair to assume that sleep, like pay, is distributed according to rank. Sometimes middle-rank officers, majors and
lieutenant-colonels, find the burden hardest to bear. They are no
longer in the first flush of youth, the contrast between peace and
war strikes them hard, and the unremitting pressure of staff
work may remind them that they have become more worriers
than warriors. When the French 5th Army fell back after its defeat in the Battle of the Frontiers in August 1914, its brigade and
divisional staffs, whose manning reflected no provision for 24-
hour working, were exhausted: they spent their days in the sad-
dle and their nights writing and issuing orders.

The men under their command, who did at least manage to
snatch an hour or two's sleep, albeit with 'the furrow for mat-
tress and the pack for pillow', may even have been more fortu-
nate. But their good luck would scarcely have been apparent to
them as they lurched on through a fog of exhaustion. An infantryman described sensations which so many soldiers would
have remembered all too well. 'We slogged on,' wrote Stephen
Westman of the German 113th Infantry Regiment, 'living, as it
were, in a coma, often sleeping while we marched, and when the

column came to a sudden halt we ran with our noses against the billycans of the men in front of us.' This strikes a chord with Max Hastings's description of British paratroops and marines crossing East Falkland in 1982.

The men marched in long files, 10 yards apart so that a moving commando stretched across 5 miles of East Falkland. Even if they managed to dry their feet during the night, each morning within a few minutes they had squelched through a marsh in the darkness, waded a stream or merely endured a torrential rain shower. Their canvas webbing stiffened and shrank on their shoulders, their hair hung matted on their skulls, the strain of stumbling across the hillside with grenades, weapons and linked-belt ammunition across their chests was etched into each face long before evening.

This physical and mental strain often falls upon a body weakened by hunger. Logistics—the practical art of moving armies and keeping them supplied—generally receives less attention from historians than it deserves. But this ought not to conceal the fact that combat is entirely dependent on logistics. Soldiers need around 3,000 calories a day, and without it their usefulness sharply declines. Brigadier Bernard Fergusson, who commanded a column behind Japanese lines in Second World War Burma, reckoned that 'lack of food constitutes the single biggest assault upon morale', while Jean Morval, writing of Napoleon's army, declared that 'when food was lacking, veterans complained, conscripts groaned, guardsmen killed themselves, linesmen decamped'. It is not simply that lack of food weakens soldiers. It also loosens the bonds of discipline, encouraging looting, and, by removing the need for the comfortable rituals of cooking and eating, strikes a telling blow at the cohesion of those little communities upon which so much effectiveness in combat depends.

Tobacco, in its way, is scarcely less important. The Napoleonic cavalry theorist F. de Brack advised his readers to 'smoke, and make your men smoke'. The smoker would have the means of striking a light to hand, which was always a good thing in bivouacs, and the need to attend to his pipe would encourage him to stay awake on sentry-duty. Bernard Fergusson thought that cigarettes literally 'saved men's lives', in part because they were appetite-suppressants, and smokers worried less about food than non-smokers. A Royal Marine company commander in the Falklands acknowledged that cigarettes were not good for one's health, but an officer in battle was not doing too badly if he kept his men alive long enough to be at risk from lung disease.

Drink and drugs have also played their part in enabling soldiers to cope with 'rainy marching in the painful field' and to face the iron glare of battle. Communal drinking fostered the small-group bonding process in the Anglo-Saxon hall, and has done ever since. The rum ration helped British soldiers through the repetitive drudgery of trench life by giving them something to look forward to at dawn stand-to. Soldiers across history have enlisted drink or drugs to help them through combat. Corporal Shaw of the Life Guards, one of the heroes of Waterloo, had been drinking heavily before he hewed nine Frenchmen through steel and bone, and a British officer of the First World War remembered that the air smelt of 'rum and blood' during an attack. Drug abuse in Vietnam, frequent though it was, should be placed in context. The easy availability of drugs meant that soldiers were likely to seek solace in them, and the drug problem was more serious in the world of the rear than in units in contact with the foe.

Contact. The word, in British military parlance, has a quite specific meaning: an encounter with the enemy. It is the moment to which all the soldier's training has led, and towards which he has looked with a mixture of emotions, summed up by one veteran as 'apprehensive enthusiasm'. Lieutenant Frederick Hitchcock, going into action at Antietam on 17 September 1862, admitted that he

felt most uncomfortable. Lest there might be some undue manifestation of this feeling in my conduct, I said to myself, this is the duty you have undertaken to perform for my country, and now I'll do it, and leave the results to God. My greater fear was not that I might be killed, but that I might be grievously wounded and left a victim of suffering on the field.

Lieutenant Raleigh Trevelyan, in Second World War Italy, prayed: 'God give me strength for tomorrow, for I can think of nothing else.' A marine in the Falklands caught one of the eternal truths of combat when he remarked that 'people were frightened before it began rather than while it was going on'. Those with status to lose find it easier to master themselves while waiting tugs at their soul. 'Everyone is horrified', remembered a Second World War company sergeant-major, 'but so many including myself are driven on by pride, one cannot show oneself to be afraid in front of others. Subordinates look to their leaders for example.'

First contact is often puzzling and unreal. Training and war films alike strive to divide the business of battle into phases, but reality gives the lie to such neatness. Combat is confusing and untidy. Its sounds, sights, and smells are unsettling to the uninitiated, and the notion that a complete stranger is trying to kill them seems bewildering. Philip Caputo, a US marine officer in Vietnam, asked himself: 'Why does he want to kill *me*? What did I ever do to *him*? A moment later, I realised that there was nothing personal about it. All he saw was a man in the wrong uniform. He was trying to kill me and he would try again because that was his job.' Often the very fact that action has come at last elbows fear into the sidelines. An Australian described the scene in his boat, making for the beach at Gallipoli in 1915. 'The key was being turned in the lock of the lid of hell. Some men crouched in the crowded boat, some sat up nonchalantly, some laughed and joked, others cursed with ferocious delight … Fear was not at home.'

The sight of dead and wounded, defined as 'casualties', that blandest of collective euphemisms, shocks many. Charles Carrington saw an NCO die on the Somme as he watched.

I was looking straight at him as the bullet struck him and was profoundly affected by the remembrance of his face, though at the time I hardly thought of it. He was alive, and then he was dead, and there was nothing human left in him. He fell with a neat round hole in his forehead and the back of his head blown out.

Death is often more barbarous. Ensign Leeke, clutching his regiment's colour at Waterloo, received a painful blow on the thumb from a fragment of a soldier's skull, and a British platoon commander in Italy 1944 recalled being temporarily stunned when hit in the face by a flying forearm, easily identifiable from its tattoos.

The shocking effects of high explosive and spinning metal strip dignity from death in battle. The crews of burnt-out tanks are reduced to hunched, simian homunculi, and infantry who suffer direct hits from shells may vanish as if they had never existed, or have their passing marked by the discovery of disconnected tatters of mortality. A sergeant in the King's Liverpool Regiment recalled 8 September 1914 as 'The most awful day I have had. Shells bursting on all sides, bullets within a foot. Before entering firing line prayed and had a look at [a photograph of] Flo ... I was in charge of the burial party. Terrible sights. Jakes had to be picked up in pieces and buried in a ground sheet.'

One of the many depressing things about death in battle is that many soldiers fall victim to their friends rather than their enemies. Even in the ranks of the Greek phalanx, where telling friend from foe might have been a simple matter, men were slain when front-rank soldiers drew back their spears to strike, stabbing comrades to the rear. As weapon ranges have increased so the capacity for error and misunderstanding has grown. Worn barrels, miscalculations on the gun position, incorrect grid-references, and errors by forward observation officers have made artillery a capricious weapon. General Charles Percin, author of *Le Massacre de notre infanterie*, reckoned that 75,000 French infantrymen were killed by French gunners in the First World War. Air power is sometimes double-edged: the highest-ranking American fatality of the Second World War, Lieutenant-General Lesley J. McNair, was killed in Normandy by an American air strike which killed 111 US soldiers and wounded another 490.

Survival in this alien environment is often a matter of luck: Frederick the Great recognized that much depended on 'His Sacred Majesty Chance'. The deepening of the battlefield has increased its capriciousness. The influential British military historian Colonel G. F. R. Henderson, writing a century ago, observed that 'The battlefield in the old days was a comparatively safe locality except at close quarters; but today death has a wider range and ... the strain on the nerves is far more severe.' This strain breaks some men swiftly, and almost all if they are compelled to endure it for long enough. Lord Moran, who served as a regimental medical officer during the First World War, developed the notion of a 'well of courage' which a man might steadily drain by repeated sips or suddenly empty with one long, deep draught.

Sometimes there is collective panic, often the product of a sudden, unexpected shock. A First World War British infantryman described how a delicate operation to relieve another unit in the line near Ypres in 1917 went desperately wrong when a German aircraft appeared. 'Never before, despite my capacity for fear, had I felt myself in the grip of a terror so absolute. All around us was the continuing threat of instant death. Yet I saw no one fall ... The company that night was in the grip of a sort of communal terror, a hundred men running like rabbits.' But sometime the failure is individual, and individuals bolt, freeze, or withdraw into a trance. It took medical science some time to recognize that such men were often ill, psychiatric rather than physical casualties. The surgeon-general of the Union army in the American Civil War wrote of a dazed, withdrawn state he called 'nostalgia', while First World War doctors identified 'shell-shock', so called because it was initially believed to originate in the concussion inflicted by a shell bursting nearby.

There are several types of combat-induced psychiatric illness, from the numbing battle-shock, through hysterical conversion syndrome, in which a soldier develops a psychosomatic paralysis, to post-traumatic stress disorder (PTSD), in which survivor guilt—'why did I survive when so many good men perished'— plays a large part. Numerous factors, such as the effectiveness of screening and training, the intensity and duration of battle, the stresses imposed by terrain and climate, and the state of morale more generally, influence the incidence of psychiatric casualties. They are often very numerous. During the Second World War Allied troops sustained psychiatric casualties which ran from about 8 per cent of all battle casualties (for the British 2nd Army in the spring of 1945) to 54 per cent (for the US 2nd Armoured Division in forty-four days of gruelling continuous operations in

Italy in 1944). Recent attention has focused on PTSD, with some estimates for the Vietnam War running at up to 1,500,000.

There can be no doubt that many of those who survive modern combat apparently unscathed bear invisible scars for the rest of their days. But the whole question of psychiatric casualties is a complex one. While most armies recognize that there is indeed a clear difference between cowardice and breakdown, the distinction is less easy to draw in practice than in theory, especially when the first rough diagnosis lies in the hands, not of a trained psychiatrist, but of a line officer applying the age-old mix of stick and carrot to keep his men at their task. Sway too far towards being permissive, and soldiers are presented with a cheap ticket out of combat: swing too far in the other direction, and sick men are pilloried.

Despite combat's manifold assaults on courage, resourcefulness, and dignity, most soldiers cope with it, some with relatively little difficulty, others at the cost of a burden of stress which they are never able to jettison. A few enjoy it all, and many more enjoy fragments of the experience. 'I *adore* war,' wrote Captain Julian Grenfell. 'It is like a big picnic without the objectlessness of a picnic. I have never been so well or happy.' He was killed in early 1915, before his enthusiasm had been buried deep in the mud: few infantry officers who floundered in the slime of Passchendaele would have echoed his comments. But some are attracted by the sheer anarchy of war; the excitement that comes from being able to call in an air strike or unleash the fire of an artillery battery; the challenge of beating a cunning opponent at the most dangerous game of all.

Hatred for this enemy nerves surprisingly few soldiers. It may figure prominently if an opponent is so different, in terms of race or culture, that he may in effect be deprived of his common humanity. Second World War Allied soldiers felt very differently towards the Germans, for whose soldierly qualities many of them had a grudging respect, and the Japanese, whose behaviour aroused, for many, the deepest disgust. An Australian sergeant entitled his memoirs *The Brave Japanese*, arguing that, whatever else the Japanese might be, they were unfailingly and obdurately courageous, but respect for Japanese bravery was, for most of their opponents, simply drowned in a tide of hostility. However, soldiers sometimes feel closer to their opponents, comrades in suffering, than they do to their own superiors. There were times and places on the Western Front in the First World War when men adopted the 'live and let live' philosophy, and it took real pressure from the chain of command to inject hostility into men for whom staying alive in the trenches was challenge enough.

Politics, too, has sharp limitations as a motivator. Soldiers certainly feel more comfortable if they believe that their cause is the right one: a study of Second World War American combat performance identified 'a tacit and fairly deep conviction that we were on the right side and that the war, once we were in it, was necessary'. Most analysts now suggest that what one Australian called 'the bonds of mateship'—the ties linking man and man in combat primary groups—are a far more important source of battle morale. Writing of the First World War, C. E. Montague declared that

Our total host might be two millions strong, or ten millions, but whatever its size a man's world was his section—at most, his platoon; all that mattered to him was the one little boatload of castaways with whom he was marooned on a desert island making shift to keep off the weather and any sudden attack of wild beasts.

But this is no simple, universal truth. As Omer Bartov has shown in his brilliant study of motivation on the Eastern Front in the Second World War, the personnel turnover in German units was so high that there was little opportunity for these bonds to be tied. He suggests that German soldiers welcomed political indoctrination, and the frequently repeated assertions that the Russians were barbarian subhumans both helped maintain morale and, at the same time, lent a rough edge of barbarism to the conflict.

Most soldiers are impelled across the battlefield by no single dominant force. A mixture of generalized patriotism, professional pride, comradely respect and affection, discipline, brave and competent leadership, and the unvarnished imperatives of survival play their part, though proportions inevitably vary between individuals, nations, and conflicts. Donald Featherstone, an NCO in the Second World War, sums up the issue well. He fought

Certainly for my country—a deep sense of patriotism and chauvinism has always sustained me. I was immensely proud and sustained by being in the Royal Tank Regiment, and my own group were good. The lads around me—with whom I am still in regular contact—were first class ... The fight for survival was not the most conscious aspect, more an innate ever-present background.

Religion has often played a part in enabling men to cope with battle. It may be a cliché to say that 'there are no atheists in fox-holes', but it was certainly true that troops sailing to the Falklands in 1982 attended church services in ever-increasing quantities. Father Willie Doyle, killed in 1917, believed that the Irishmen of his battalion fought all the better for the comfort of their Church. 'It is an admitted fact', he wrote, 'that the Irish Catholic soldier is the bravest and best in a fight, but few know that he draws his courage from the strong faith with which he is filled.'

Often it is spiritual comfort, rather than religion in the strictly theological sense, that helps lift men's spirits. The Second World War American soldier-cartoonist Bill Mauldin was by no means uncritical of the military establishment, but he had 'a lot of respect for those chaplains who keep up the spirits of the combat guys. They often give the troops a firm anchor to hang onto.' John Parrish, who served as a medical officer in Vietnam, recalled that his unit's chaplain 'didn't push religion but somehow made it known that comfort and support and talk and God and all that sort of stuff were available if we needed them'.

Islam, too, can bestow a conviction which enables a man to face death with equanimity: the driver of the explosives-packed truck that blew up the US marine base in Beirut in 1983 was seen to smile moments before he blew himself to pieces. His was a relatively recent example of the courage buttressed by belief in the certainty of salvation for those who die fighting the unbeliever in holy war. When the dervishes, most of them armed with sword and spear, attacked the Anglo-Egyptian army, with its rifles, machine-guns, and artillery, at Omdurman in 1898 they persevered in the face of a fire which hit almost half of them: 9,700 were killed and 16,000 wounded.

Combat is a watershed even in the lives of those who survive it unscathed. Few of them regard war as anything other than an evil, unavoidable perhaps, but an evil nevertheless. Their experiences bind them inextricably to those who shared them: Jacques Meyer wrote of the First World War as 'our buried, secret youth'. There is often an air of ambivalence about the remembrance of war. A First World War company sergeant-major told me: 'When I left France wounded after two years there I felt and still feel that war is a vile, soul-destroying and uncivilising evil. But if I were a younger man I would fight again.' An Israeli paratrooper who fought in the Six Day War summed up war as 'Murder and Fear', but thought that his experience had changed him, not necessarily for the worse. A Vietnam veteran summed up the whole bewildering paradox. 'Thinking about Vietnam,' he reflected, 'once in a while, in a crazy kind of way, I wish that for just an hour I could be there. And then be transported back. Maybe just to be there so I'd wish I was back here again.'

13
Sea Warfare

JOHN B. HATTENDORF

Since the creation of state navies in the mid-seventeenth century, the form and character of sea warfare have changed dramatically. Yet, despite those changes, the general range of naval functions and the uses of naval power have remained largely the same.

The elements of effective naval power

There has been a wide variation in the kinds of navies that different nations have built and the effect that they have had on world affairs. These differences have depended on the particular situations that derive from the complex interaction of a variety of factors. Amongst these are a country's vulnerability to an enemy at sea, the relative importance of sea-borne activity including trade and transportation, a country's position in the structure of international power including its aspirations for international prestige, its financial, industrial, and technological capacity to build a navy, its bureaucratic capacity to control and to direct a navy to achieve specific ends, its logistical means to support a navy, the relative skills of its people to operate and to fight ships in the uncertain conditions that are normal at sea, and the relationship and timeliness of those operations to the employment of other aspects of national power. These many factors create both the necessary elements and the inherent limitations on effective naval power. Beyond them, human decency, tradition, the commonly accepted practice of nations, along with formal international agreements, place further restraints on sea warfare.

The roles of navies

In this context, warships have served a variety of roles. The ultimate purpose of a warship has been to use armed force in order simultaneously to assert one's own use of the sea and to control an enemy's use of it. Because of this, historians and commentators have made much of the drama surrounding fleet battles in history. Indeed, battles and the blockade of war fleets have been the two traditional means by which one opponent has achieved control over another, preventing an enemy from interfering in its own use of the sea. However, focusing on this one element of sea warfare alone can conceal the less glamorous, but far more important, ways in which the sea has been used for maintaining control or for limiting the actions of an enemy.

In wartime, there have been many military uses of the sea for this purpose. Among the most important wartime functions have been protecting and facilitating one's own merchant shipping and military supplies at sea, denying an enemy effective use of commercial shipping, protecting the coast and offshore resources, acquiring advanced bases, moving and supporting troops, gaining or maintaining local air and sea control in support of air or land operations.

Thus, the fundamental focus of maritime strategy governing sea warfare has centred on the control of human activity at sea. There are two aspects to this. On the one hand, there has been the effort to establish control for oneself or to deny it to an enemy. There have been gradations to understanding this kind of control that range from the abstract ideal to the practical and the possible: whether control was general or limited, absolute or merely conditional, widespread or local, permanent or temporary. On the other hand, control has been used to achieve specific ends. The effort to control, by itself, means nothing unless it has an effect within a wider sphere of human affairs. Most important, in the wide spectrum of activity involved, has been the use of control at sea to influence and, ultimately, to help in controlling events on land.

The fundamental characteristics of these two broad aspects of sea warfare stress their sequential and cumulative relationships: the need to obtain some degree of control before using that control to obtain the important ends that one seeks. This, of course, has not excluded the simultaneous pursuit of these objects. Whatever the relative and temporal character of the control achieved, it has necessarily affected the nature of the end-result.

From a narrowly defined perspective, these are uniquely maritime and naval functions, but in a wider understanding of modern warfare, all these broad functions closely relate to other aspects of national power. In particular, the navy has operated in its own element, at sea. It has used its specialized skills and equipment in a manner that is not in any way divorced from, but very closely tied to, the parallel and complementary functions of diplomacy, of land and air warfare, and of economic warfare.

In peacetime, in operations short of open warfare, and in the non-war functions of naval power, many of which have continued even during wartime, naval operations have involved many other considerations. These may be categorized under three headings: a diplomatic and international role, a policing role, and a military role. The fact that naval ships are armed has been, of course, the basis for the other two roles of navies, but a navy's peacetime functions have ranged from modern strategic nuclear deterrence to both past and present conventional deterrence. They have included developing the bases, shore facilities, and procedures that are prudent and necessary to prepare in peacetime in case of war. The military role has involved protecting the lives, property, and interests of one's national citizens on the high seas, in distant waters, and in offshore possessions in time of natural disaster.

Related to their military capability, navies have a policing function that in the past has involved such duties as the maintenance of law and order, the control of piracy, and the enforcement of customs duties. As a minor subsidiary function under the policing role, navies have also contributed to a smaller and newer country's internal stability and to its internal development. For obvious geographical reasons, this type of peaceful use of naval force in giving assistance to the civil community is limited, but the presence of naval shore facilities and active bases can act as a symbol of a nation, contributing to national solidarity while also contributing to the local economy by employing civil workers who lived in the region.

The third peacetime role for navies has been the diplomatic role, influencing perceptions. From a position of naval strength, nations have employed warships in this way, to influence action, to show interest and concern by maintaining presence and by using warships as symbols of national prestige.

All three roles are based upon the ability to put armed forces to sea and the potential that they have, even in peacetime, to use force when necessary. Naval ships and seamen have appeared offshore or entered ports around the world as ambassadors and diplomats—and even as benign helpers in times of catastrophe. In this, the fundamental relationship of navies to national economies, through the protection of commercial shipping and other national maritime activities beyond land boundaries, has given naval forces a unique character, tying naval men and women to the larger community of peaceful seafarers. Thus, navies have shown capabilities and functions that have derived from two complementary, but quite different, spheres of tradition, one civil and one military, providing them with resources for important roles in both peace and war. In this, the uses of navies in peace and in war have been closely interrelated.

The development of navies

In the early and middle seventeenth century, there was a shift in maritime warfare from the dominance of armed merchant shipping to that of regular naval forces. Up to this point in history, sovereigns had often hired vessels or depended upon merchants and cities to provide the temporary use of armed vessels for the Crown when the king called for it. At the same time, they relied heavily upon privateering for attacking the enemy. The development from private warfare to war conducted by the naval forces of the state was a gradual one; privateering did not disappear for more than two centuries. While the interchangeability of merchant and naval ships was gradually decreasing, technological changes in warships brought slowly increasing specialization in design, armament, and other equipment that gradually made it more difficult to convert back and forth between the roles of merchant and warship.

In the course of this transition, there was an intermediate stage during which overseas commercial trading companies, such as the various East India Companies, operated by the Dutch, English, French, and others, took up the responsibility for arming ships and protecting their own trade. This was part of several larger developments that were occurring at this time. Evolving sovereign states were taking on the responsibilities of private groups within the state. During this period, the state began to pay more attention to the interests of its citizens working or trading in distant foreign places, protecting them from foreign depredations. This development in sea warfare resulted in increased restrictions on private warfare, the extension of admiralty jurisdiction, and the stabilization and more rigorous enforcement of the law in relation to captures made at sea.

Coinciding with the English Civil War and continuing into the period of general peace during the 1650s, the new republican government in England invested heavily in a large navy as a means of giving the new regime credibility in international politics and, also, to support English mercantile development. As part of this, the first of three Anglo-Dutch Wars broke out in 1652–4 in a purely naval and maritime struggle over the control and use of rival sea-borne trade routes in the Channel and North Sea area.

The period of the Anglo-Dutch Wars marks several important developments in naval warfare. In the area of naval tactics, there was the development of the disciplined line of battle to concentrate effective gunfire. These wars marked, too, the period when general European naval warfare expanded out from the coastal areas of belligerents and spread to distant seas; in this case, to the Mediterranean, the Baltic, and American waters. Simultaneously, naval bureaucracies emerged and began to devise methods of controlling and regulating state navies. These changes brought with them permanent regulations, career officers, and permanent institutions.

The law of war at sea

Paralleling these changes, the laws of naval warfare became more clearly defined through the decisions of admiralty courts, marking this out as a key period in the development of maritime law. From the mid-seventeenth century to the early years of the eighteenth century, England, the Dutch Republic, Denmark, Sweden, Portugal, France, Spain, and Venice reorganized their navies, and Russia created an entirely new navy, marked by these general features.

The creation of state navies along these lines was a major step, tending to control violence at sea through a state monopoly. The legal process that paralleled it moved slowly and tended to focus on particular issues. For example, to avoid the suspicion of carrying enemy goods in neutral ships, Sweden and the Dutch Republic suggested that ships carry passports that would exempt neutral ships from search in wartime. Englishmen disagreed, arguing that the system did not give sufficient assurance; they preferred to rely on the right of visit and search. The question was whether a belligerent naval vessel could attack when enemy goods were in neutral ships or when neutral goods were in an enemy ship. By 1668, a series of treaties established some generally accepted rules. At first, practice was not rigid, but it soon became clear that, without a passport, only a neutral ship carrying neutral goods was immune from capture.

Another related issue was the nature of cargoes that were subject to capture. Here one encounters the idea of contraband or a prohibition on trade in particular commodities with an enemy: especially munitions, naval supplies, and victuals. Nations accepted the general idea that neutral trade prevented a warring nation from cutting off all supplies to an enemy by banning all trade. A belligerent could, at least, ban selected articles that were most useful to prosecuting a war, though for a long period there was no consensus on the details of such bans. The debate between belligerents and neutrals on the matter was unresolved, and it remained an issue of give and take in concessions, but without any fundamental compromise. Belligerents understandably wanted to destroy *all* the vital supplies of their enemy, while neutrals preferred to continue *all* their trade.

In the same period, the issue of blockade came under negotiation. Nearly every commercial treaty had a more or less standard provision on blockade, listing free and non-contraband goods permitted for trade to enemy ports, except to those cities and places under siege or blockade. Thus, nations recognized blockade as a special circumstance. Only in 1742, in a treaty between France and Denmark, does one find the first reference to the legal principle that a blockade must be an effective one if it is to be regarded as a blockade at all. Oddly, the law of blockade was recognized in treaties for more than 150 years before it first became the basis of a legal decision in a prize court in 1798.

While each European war of the seventeenth and eighteenth centuries added to the range of admiralty court cases, the strategic and naval situations in each war provided differing aspects of larger issues. For example, France's shift of strategy from naval fleet combat to *guerre de course* in 1694, during the Nine Years War, showed the potential efficacy of a commerce raiding strategy in combating an opposing strategy based on naval fleets and illustrated why some were reluctant to agree to constraints on such warfare.

Two nearly simultaneous wars, the War of the Spanish Succession (1701–14) and the Great Northern War (1700–21), raised the practical problem of neutral rights in circumstances when a nation was a belligerent in one war, but a neutral in the other. The years that followed leading up to the Seven Years War produced a legal principle that came to be called 'The Rule of the War of 1756'. In fact, it was not a legal rule, but the British government's attempt to relieve some earlier restrictions on capturing neutrals. With it, British Admiralty courts held that neutrals lost their immunity to capture when they carried on a trade with the enemy that was not normally permitted in peacetime.

The structure of modern naval war

The development of European navies throughout the late seventeenth and eighteenth centuries was closely tied to the processes of individual state-building, national geographical position, and the role of individual states in international relations. In contrast to an earlier period, maritime power was not only associated with the commercial interests that supported long-distance trade and the directly related development of overseas empires, but now also with co-operation between maritime and non-maritime elements, both internally and externally. Thus, navies became a product of broader internal support while also obtaining the backing of non-maritime interests that encouraged their external activities. Thus, the development of overseas empires was not entirely forced upon other peoples, but often tied to co-operation with rulers representing local political and economic interests.

This period also demonstrated the capacity of maritime powers to intervene in foreign affairs, without the necessity of imperial control, allowing a maritime state to support another that lacked naval strength. While there were geographical limits as to where they could operate, a strong naval power like Great Britain gained in such a way a new flexibility in European politics that was not otherwise obtainable. The development of such naval roles was important in driving the technological refinements beyond the earlier demand for fast warships to attack commerce, towards the development of fast fleets capable of staying at sea in virtually all seasons of the year.

Military historians often single out the French Revolution and the Napoleonic Wars to mark the beginning of warfare in the modern age. However true this was of land warfare, it was not the same at sea. Technological changes had begun earlier in the eighteenth century and their effects on naval strategy had already become apparent. Nevertheless, naval commanders in the 1775–1840 period did make some incremental changes in controlling their fleets through improved signalling systems, in ship design with diagonal framing to increase longitudinal strength, in gunnery with the use of flintlocks, and by being more innovative in their tactics.

Like other wars, however, those wars, both at sea and on land, illustrated the fact that nations with the power to enforce restraints determine them. While France posed as the champion of neutral rights and freedom of the sea, it more often than not gave way to Britain's belligerent rights when the Royal Navy controlled the sea. Napoleon's Berlin Decree of 1806 and Britain's countering Orders-in-Council the following year temporarily shifted the flow of trade during the war. From 1793 to 1812, neutrals reaped their profits, while belligerents were reluctant to attack neutral trade for fear of creating a new enemy. Yet, as the war spread and the coalitions formed, neutrality itself was largely snuffed out. By 1812, when the United States went to war with Britain, the last important maritime neutral joined the conflict. For the moment, restraint in maritime warfare vanished.

By the early decades of the nineteenth century, national investment in the bureaucracies and technologies surrounding sails, wooden ships, and smooth-bore cannon had become an obstacle to change, but the economic forces connected with wider industrial development soon overwhelmed this resistance. This change paralleled the general decline in world-wide naval strengths from 1815 to 1840, and the rapid growth that occurred in the 1840s and 1850s, which brought world-wide naval strength levels to a point higher than the earlier peak in the 1790s. Throughout these years, one sees a variety of technological innovation with steam-powered vessels, with the use of iron hulls, with gunnery refinements, and even with experiments in submersible vessels.

As these changes occurred in the first half of the nineteenth century, nations had clearly chosen sides in the arguments over the law of naval warfare, but few were consistent in their views, and they resolved few major disputes. In general, England opposed the principle of 'free ships, free goods'. On the other hand, the Dutch, the Danes, and the Swedes, and sometimes France and Spain, objected to the English view of contraband that included naval stores as well as food supplies. Britain continued to argue that a superior sea power had the right to close the seas to its enemies, and that its use of blockade, with the rules of contraband, continuous voyage, and enemy property, was a justifiable right for a belligerent in preventing neutrals from helping an enemy. Opposing this, the United States continued to maintain that the British position was a violation of freedom of the seas and the sovereignty of neutrals. Despite such fundamental disagreement, these issues did not lead to another war as they had in 1812. Conflicting national interests and strategies, as well as changing technologies, were closely intertwined in these legal questions. Belligerents and neutrals were forced to balance contradictory interests at sea against pragmatic policies and strategies.

During this period, navies moved into the sphere of humanitarian operations, leading eventually to multinational cooperation in this area. The abolition of slavery created a body of human rights law that provided for the peacetime use of naval force on the high seas. In this instance, law justified and guided an entirely new area of naval operations, searching and seizing vessels engaged in the slave trade. In the 1820s, the United States and Britain enacted laws declaring that the slave trade was a form of piracy punishable by death. At first, each nation sent out its own warships for the purpose. In 1842, the United States and Britain agreed to maintain two squadrons for the suppression of piracy, operating separately but co-operatively. Later, during the American Civil War, Britain and America finally agreed on a mutually acceptable approach to search and boarding, while also establishing three Anglo-American Mixed Courts of Justice to adjudicate slave-trading cases at Sierra Leone, Cape Town, and New York. Although these courts lasted for less than a decade, and the anti-slavery patrols themselves were never fully effective and became ancillary to other strategic and political objectives, they provided a valuable precedent in the use of law to channel naval force.

Technological change and naval strategy

When Russian warships destroyed the Turkish fleet at the Battle of Sinope in 1854, their victory confirmed the importance of shell-firing naval artillery and led to widespread changes in naval ordnance that included breech-loading, rifled gun barrels, cylindrical shapes in projectiles and powder charges, with increased range and accuracy of gunfire at sea. These innovations in offensive naval capability quickly led to innovation in defence, including an emphasis on armour and innovative hull designs.

While these changes in technology were just beginning to take effect, the peace settlement following the Crimean War in 1856 resulted in a major step toward resolving some knottier issues in the law of naval warfare. In the Declaration of Paris, the European powers agreed to outlaw privateering, France abandoned the doctrine of 'enemy ships, enemy goods', and Britain recognized the doctrine of 'free ships, free goods', thus abandoning the Rule of 1756 and agreeing that non-contraband goods could not be seized on neutral ships. Britain formally accepted in practice the principle that blockades had to be real and effective to be legally binding. These were major concessions that severely reduced the advantages of naval supremacy. One can trace the reasons for this sudden change, on issues that had lain unresolved for so long, to the dramatic increase in technology and the specialized knowledge needed to man naval vessels. These were the leading factors that made privateering and the impressment of merchant seamen far less attractive enterprises. Prevailing opinion, predisposed towards economic liberalism and free trade, also militated in favour of the doctrine of 'free ships, free goods'. Moreover, the diplomatic situation made it profitable for each side to make concessions to the other in order to preserve other diplomatic alignments. Although, for its own constitutional reasons, the United States could not easily sign the Declaration of Paris in 1856, it showed that it accepted it as international law.

Following the new technological trends, France matched the gains it had made at the Paris peace conference by launching an innovative new type of warship in 1859, *La Gloire*. This wooden, propeller-driven warship protected with a belt of iron armour plate sparked off a peacetime naval race. Britain responded with HMS *Warrior*, the first iron-hulled warship and one that had watertight compartments and armoured protection for its guns, boilers, and engines. Shortly after that, the Swedish inventor John Ericsson provided a radically designed armoured ship for the US navy with a revolving turret and forced air ventilation below decks, the USS *Monitor*. Demonstrating her potential in combat at Hampton Roads in 1862 during the American Civil War, *Monitor* stimulated a widespread acceleration of ship construction among the world's navies. This encouraged further development, throughout the remaining years of the nineteenth century, in propulsion, gunnery, and armour, along with related work in the use of electricity, wireless telegraphy, and the self-propelled underwater torpedo. All these inventions brought bureaucratic changes to control, develop, and apply them as new classes of ships developed.

As the new technological applications arrived, a new structure of international politics began to appear in the latter half of the nineteenth century. For the moment it seemed that Britain had moved away from the issues of European balance of power politics and redefined its interests in broad imperial terms. Thus, it apparently lacked interest in defending the types of broad belligerent rights that it had earlier demanded. The development of technology continued to reduce the importance of the dispute between belligerent and neutral rights. The railway, for example, provided an alternative means of transportation that seemed to make navies a less effective tool in halting enemy commerce on the Continent. Finally, many believed that the nature of war itself had changed. Prussia's experience in the 1860s and 1870s suggested that wars would be determined by short, decisive conflicts on land, following national mobilization. These new conditions seemed to undermine the importance of old issues such as blockade, neutral rights, and contraband. Combined with the new transformations in technology, many assumed that the old methods were entirely irrelevant to the future. However, a small group of thinkers began to examine the nature and character of naval warfare in the context of this change, leading to the first abstract writings on naval warfare.

The pioneers in this area of professional thinking were Captain Sir John Colomb, Vice-Admiral Sir Philip Colomb, and Professor Sir John Knox Laughton in the Royal Navy. Together, they provided early insights for analysing the broad uses of naval power, examining issues through historical examples. Adopting this approach, Rear-Admiral Stephen B. Luce in the US Navy combined it with a comparative study of military thought, bearing in mind both the ideas of Jomini and the experience of the Prussian general staff in the 1860s and 1870s. As a result of this,

Luce established the Naval War College in Newport, Rhode Island, as the world's first establishment to research and to teach to senior officers the highest aspects of naval warfare. Including international law and the development of naval war-gaming in its syllabus, the College's first and most influential product was the work of Captain Alfred Thayer Mahan. In 1890 he published his college lectures under the title *The Influence of Sea Power upon History, 1660–1783*. This book and others that followed it created a distinctive philosophy of sea warfare that many nations, including Germany and Japan, used in the following half-century. For naval leaders in his time, the most attractive aspect of Mahan's work was his emphasis on command of the sea, and his related ideas on the primacy of battleships, decisive battle, imperial competition and struggle for national survival, and the development of bases and colonies along lines of sea communication. Sir Julian Corbett, working in England two decades later, provided a systematic understanding of naval warfare through a more profound study of naval history that gave further depth and refinement to Mahan's pioneer work in *Some Principles of Maritime Strategy*.

In 1898 the Spanish-American War reinforced Mahan's ideas as well as the growing perceptions about the new character of naval warfare. Illustrating the idea that naval warfare had demonstrably changed from the days of commerce raiding, the President of the United States proposed to the Hague Conference in 1899 that all private property should be immune from capture at sea. In the same year, the US Secretary of the Navy ordered the US Naval War College to prepare a draft code of naval warfare. Incorporating ideas from the Hague Convention of 1899, the College's law expert, Charles Stockton, went further and based his proposed naval code on the 1863 rules for land warfare that Francis Lieber had written. The United States adopted the code in June 1900, and it remained in effect for nearly four years, applying to the maritime sphere virtually everything that regulated land warfare. Among other things, it narrowed the limits for bombarding unfortified and undefended towns, forbade reprisals for an offence, exempted coastal fishing vessels from capture, provided definitively that free ships make free goods, exempted mail steamers from capture, excepted neutral convoys from search, and classified contraband goods in a way that general international principles could agree upon. Certainly idealistic in its attempt to get international support to restrain naval warfare, the United States withdrew the code in February 1904, so that it should not be at a disadvantage in case of war with a less principled state, and so American negotiators could have a free hand at the Hague Conference in 1907.

Although concerned about the continued rise of German naval power, influential leaders in Britain and the United States continued to follow policies designed to restrict belligerent rights further. Both countries approved the German proposal for an international prize court and agreed at the London Conference in 1909 to reach compromise on other issues. At the time, many observers heralded these events as substantial steps towards world peace through international law. Most important, the Declaration of London preserved the ideas behind the 1856 Paris Declaration, and it extended neutral rights and immunity by specifying a list that restricted contraband to a short list of munitions and war supplies, while at the same time establishing a much longer list of free goods, including raw materials for industry.

The reforms in international maritime law along these lines ran directly counter to the contingency plans that naval officers were making simultaneously for the possibility of an economic blockade of Germany. In the end, neither the 1907 Hague Convention agreement for an international prize court nor the 1909 Declaration of London went into effect, although many accepted the provisions of the Declaration as customary law.

The Twentieth Century

In the years between 1898 and 1914, Britain and Germany, as well as small naval powers, developed remarkable naval establishments through technological innovation that was closely associated with general scientific, technological, economic and industrial, and bureaucratic capacities. Technological applications moved in several directions, involving battleships and submarines, and the beginnings of naval aviation. On the one hand, the Royal Navy, under Admiral Sir John Fisher, developed a concept of fast, heavily armed battle-cruisers, a new type of ship exemplified by HMS *Invincible*, which was the centre-piece of his plan to replace his own earlier innovation for heavy battleships in HMS *Dreadnought*. The tactical stalemate that occurred in the Battle of Jutland in 1916, and Germany's subsequent shift to an innovative, unrestricted use of submarines for a highly damaging war on commerce, demonstrated the impact of technological innovations. At the same time, however, the conduct of sea warfare in the First World War displayed an equally remarkable rigidity in strategic and tactical thought, showing the difficulties involved in dealing with rapidly changing technological alternatives.

The events of the two world wars in 1914–18 and 1939–45 destroyed the prevailing assumptions and expectations about the nature of world politics and the role of international law that had developed in the waning years of the preceding century. While Germany's use of U-boats ultimately failed, it nevertheless succeeded in terrorizing merchant shipping, reducing the world's tonnage by more than 3 million tons in only three months in 1917 and, again, in the first forty months of the Second World War sinking 2,177 ships totalling more than 11 million tons. This, in itself, was a campaign that brought hardship to civil populations dependent on the peaceful exchange of goods. At the opening of the First World War, the British government began a maritime blockade that was as harsh as anything imagined in the Napoleonic Wars. This involved several new aspects, among them the British declaration in November 1914 that the whole North Sea was a military area and that all merchant ships, whatever their cargoes, were subject to danger from mines as well as to search. In this dramatic change from previous practice, the British government justified its action as retaliation for Germany's indiscriminate mining of the main trade routes north of Ireland between Liverpool and North America. Similarly, in February 1915, the German government announced that it would destroy every enemy merchant ship found within the war zone surrounding the British Isles, giving no recognition of neutral rights or the safe passage of goods within the war zone.

Following the First World War, diplomats made several attempts to deal with the broad issues of naval warfare through the naval disarmament negotiations held in Washington in 1921-2 and, later, in London in 1930 and 1936. Attempting to prohibit unrestricted submarine warfare against merchant ships, the delegates to the Second London Naval Conference issued a special protocol on the subject. By the time that the war broke out in 1939, more than forty countries had ratified or acceded to it, including all the major maritime powers. Meanwhile, naval thinkers such as Admirals Sir Herbert Richmond in England and Raoul Castex in France gave thought to more restrained methods of naval warfare.

Yet none of this affected the actual practice of war at sea in 1939-45. The restraints on naval construction in the inter-war period had only been diverted into other methods for making naval warfare a more effective and decisive tool. The belligerents employed much the same policies in the Second World War as they had in the First, although the Second was surely the largest and most violent naval war in history. Both sides used the idea of war zones in which unrestricted combat took place. In 1940 Germany declared an unrestricted war zone in the North Atlantic against merchant shipping and the United States followed suit in the Pacific with its declaration of unrestricted submarine warfare against Japan. As the war progressed, clearly the tactical centre-piece of fleet operations in sea warfare shifted from the battleship to the aircraft-carrier. Simultaneously, navies and armies found the means to work together in a series of amphibious operations stretching all the way across the Pacific Ocean as well as on North African, Italian, and French coasts. While there had been earlier signs of the coming trend, the Second World War clearly showed the necessity for co-operation between air, land, and sea forces.

In the years immediately following the Second World War, the various naval powers experienced the typical decline in naval strength that had followed all the major wars in the past. Yet this time there was a major difference. The employment of nuclear weapons had changed the context for thinking about future warfare. At first, navies were entirely left out of the picture, but by the 1950s the US Navy had adapted to the situation by effectively showing a way in which nuclear weapons could be employed at sea from aircraft-carriers and through ballistic missiles launched from submarines. The last development, in particular, was extremely important in helping to link navies with the broad issues of nuclear deterrence. Slowly, this also brought navies into the realm of conventional deterrence and the broad new application of naval force for peacetime political purposes.

As navies became active in local and regional crises in the years between 1950 and the 1990s, many naval leaders returned to the older ideas about the range and functions of navies, extending wartime tasks into peacetime duties. In the same period, the advance of technology continued to change the face of navies. Guided missiles, electronic sensors, satellite communication and surveillance systems, underwater sound technology, new propulsion systems, new aircraft design, and detection countermeasure designs have all helped to change the way navies look.

The changes involve vast new technologies, requiring different and far more sophisticated skills. They appear to have changed the nature of navies. To a degree, they have done just that. Yet the fundamental role of navies has remained to establish control for oneself at sea or to deny it to an enemy, linking that control to broad political and economic issues ashore. In peacetime, navies continue to have a diplomatic and international role, a policing role, and a military role. As one peers towards the twenty-first century, naval leaders confidently predict that sea warfare in the future will continue to deal with the traditional issues while expanding in terms of multilateral naval co-operation to deal with such new issues as environmental threats, protection of precious natural resources, terrorism, illicit drug traffic, and enforcement of international law.

14
Air Warfare

RICHARD OVERY

At the end of October 1911 Second Lieutenant Giulio Gavotti, one of a handful of Italian aviators fighting with Italy's forces against the Turks in Libya, flew his small Austrian-built Taube aircraft to the towns of Taguira and Ain Zara, where he dropped four small bombs. His flight marked the start of modern air warfare. It contributed almost nothing to Italy's eventual victory in 1912, but bomb attack was quickly imitated. Bombs were used by French flyers in Morocco a year later; in the Balkan Wars Serb forces flying aircraft supplied by France resorted to small-scale bombing; and both sides in the Mexican civil war did the same in 1913.

The revolutionary potential of aircraft in war was hardly evident in these feeble experiments. None the less before the First World War, even before the first unassisted powered flight in 1903, there had already emerged a popular notion of how air power might transform war. Military thinkers, science-fiction writers, and the press vied with each other to produce lurid visions of some future apocalypse brought about by aircraft. The British novelist H. G. Wells in *The War in the Air* portrayed a terrifying fantasy of bomber aircraft unleashed indiscriminately against urban areas. He foresaw the utter collapse of modern civilization without the intervention of sea or land forces. His novel helped to shape the attitude of a whole generation of Europeans to modern war, in his assumptions that aircraft could end wars on their own, and that they would be directed by an unscrupulous enemy against hapless civilians rather than soldiers.

The Great War

Neither of these propositions was seriously tested in the war which broke out in 1914. Nevertheless air warfare made remarkable strides in just four years. In 1914 air forces were small and technically immature, flying aircraft that were flimsy, low-powered, and unsafe. The French army possessed 141 planes at the onset of the Great War; the British Expeditionary Force arrived in France with 63. By the end of the war the major powers had produced over 215,000 aircraft between them. In 1914 most aircraft were light, single-seat biplanes used for reconnaissance or 'scouting' missions. In 1918 each air force had a range of aircraft types designed to perform specialized functions — fighters to combat enemy air forces, ground-attack planes to support army operations, bombers for battlefield support or for longer-range attacks.

In the early stages of the war most army leaders believed that aircraft were useful mainly for reconnaissance, providing more accurate and up-to-date evidence of enemy troop movements or artillery emplacements than could be got from spying or scouting on the ground. This function remained an important one throughout the conflict. Specialized units were established on both sides to carry out artillery-spotting, to report on enemy troop movements and dispositions, and to discover quickly the current course of battle. Early radio communication was primitive, and much of the reconnaissance information was scribbled down and thrown over the side of the aircraft to the waiting infantry. Each army had to develop a sophisticated signalling system to let friendly aircraft overhead know the position and unit numbers of the forces below them.

It soon became clear that aircraft were capable of a good deal more than this. In the early weeks of the campaign on the Western Front aircraft began to carry guns in order to shoot down enemy reconnaissance aircraft, or bombs and grenades to disrupt the supply trains and troop movements of the opposing army. By 1915 purpose-built fighter aircraft, equipped with machine-guns firing through the moving propeller, appeared in large numbers over the battlefront, strafing ground troops from close range, but more usually fighting other fighters for the achievement of what soon came to be termed 'air superiority'. In the pre-parachute age air combat took a high toll. In 1918 losses of British fighter pilots ran at 75 per cent per month. Over 40,000 aircrew died between 1914 and 1918, including most of the élite of fighter aces whose popularity with the wider public brought a regular stream of young volunteers into the fledgeling air forces. Fighter pilots were seen as modern aerial knights, elevating modern warfare above the mud and squalor of trench combat.

Air superiority—the ability to operate freely in a particular air space without insupportable losses—was difficult to maintain without effective radio communication and in a context of rapidly evolving technology. But it was seen to be the key to pursuing other forms of air combat. Without the neutralization of the enemy fighter force, slower ground-attack or bombing aircraft were vulnerable to high losses. Neither side in the Great War proved capable of maintaining permanent air superiority, though by 1918 the balance had shifted towards the western Allies partly from sheer weight of numbers, partly because the German army began to place much greater emphasis on the direct support of its ground forces.

The most effective contribution made by air power to the conduct of war between 1914 and 1918 was in tactical support, using ground-attack aircraft or bombers to break up enemy attacks, destroy artillery, disrupt reinforcement of the battlefield, and bomb or strafe rear communications and supply depots. Aircraft designed for this purpose began to appear in quantity in 1917. The German army created so-called 'Battle Squadrons' (*Schlacht-Staffeln*) trained to attack ground targets, and directed to them by liaison officers assigned to ground units. By 1918 it was possible to use radio to direct air attacks—radio was installed on the formidable all-metal Junkers JI aircraft used in the German March Offensive—while both cannon and rockets were developed to replace the machine-gun. These developments were carried furthest in the German air force, which by 1918 used aircraft in support of a heavily armed infantry fist aimed at weak points in the enemy line, a strategy that lived on into the next war. The use of aircraft in support of tank attack was also introduced late in the conflict. In November 1917 at Cambrai aircraft helped to ease the path of British tanks whose attack threatened to collapse under accurate German artillery fire. In 1918 the western Allies routinely used aircraft and armour together. This tactic did not add a great deal to Allied firepower, but the moral impact was considerable. Against even seasoned troops air attack initially created panic quite out of proportion to the actual threat.

It was this moral impact that first tempted both sides to explore the use of long-range bombing against civilian targets far from the battlefronts. The first attacks were made by German Zeppelin airships, with the object of creating widespread panic sufficiently strong to encourage the enemy government to capitulate. Airship attacks on Britain began in 1914, but they achieved little. Over the war they dropped a mere 196 tons of bombs, killed 557 Britons, and suffered unacceptable levels of loss. Not until 1917 did the state of aviation technology support a more serious attempt to use bomber aircraft for long-range attacks. In 1917, armed with the Gotha IV bomber, the German high command ordered bomb attacks on British cities to 'destroy the morale of the British people' and take Britain out of the war. They mounted twenty-seven raids, dropped 110 tons of bombs, and created widespread popular alarm in London. But the strategic effects were negligible, and the German army insisted on a return to battlefront priorities.

Neither Britain nor France gave much heed to long-range or 'strategic' bombing. But the Gotha attacks stimulated British action. Against French objections that distant attacks would do almost nothing to assist the fighting fronts, the British created an independent air force in 1917, the RAF, one of whose objects was to mount a campaign of destruction with 2,000 heavy bombers against the German war economy and the morale of the German work-force. In June 1918 an Independent Force was set up for the bombing mission and detailed plans drawn up for a major strategic offensive against the German war effort in 1919. The Armistice in November 1918 left the bombing offensive in limbo, its potential untested. Only limited attacks were made in 1918 against Rhineland cities, using at most 120 aircraft. Post-war bombing surveys in 1919 concluded that the destructive power of bombing was meagre with the existing technology, but asserted that the raids had exerted a 'tremendous moral effect'. This assertion left open the inviting question of what air power might have achieved in the Great War if bombing had been the primary mission.

The search for a doctrine

The post-war stocktaking of air power demonstrated a widening gulf between what air power had actually done, which was modest both tactically and strategically, and popular perception of its potential. There were a number of airmen who argued the maximum case, that air power had revolutionized war and could now finish conflicts in a matter of days. The most famous exponent of this view was an Italian aviator, General Guilio Douhet, whose book *The Command of the Air* was published in 1921. Douhet was the most outspoken supporter of the argument that bombers were the key instrument of future warfare, capable of delivering a 'knock-out blow' with gas, incendiaries, and high explosive which would terrorize the enemy's urban population and bring about surrender in a few days. It was a seductive argument, echoed world-wide by airmen who wanted a strategy which gave them greater independence from the senior services and matched the self-consciously modern image of air warfare.

Yet Douhet's influence is easy to exaggerate. There were other air power thinkers—such as the British Chief of Air Staff Sir Hugh Trenchard, and the American airman General Billy Mitchell—who were better known than Douhet in the 1920s. Air power theory moved forward on a broad front. Moreover most professional soldiers, sailors, and even airmen were sceptical of air power. They did not regard aircraft as war winners on their own, and indeed sought to make aviation a subordinate service, assisting, but not supplanting, armies and navies. The view of air power as auxiliary was more widespread in the inter-war years than belief in the knock-out blow. In Germany and France the lessons of the Great War encouraged an air doctrine which emphasized the ground-support role and the search for air superiority over the battlefield. These priorities reflected the interests of powerful armies with considerable political influence, but there were also strong strategic arguments in favour of the limited use of air power. During the Great War aircraft had only produced demonstrable military advantage when used in conjunction with ground forces, or to interrupt the immediate reinforcement of the battlefront. German and French air doctrine focused on these functions, in combination with attacks on the enemy air force to secure an aerial umbrella over their own army. When the German air force re-emerged in 1935 in violation of the Peace Settlement of 1919, its manual of employment could have been written by Clausewitz: concentrate air forces against the enemy air force, and when that has been destroyed attack the enemy ground forces and supplies. This simple but effective use of air power was practised with exceptional success in the first campaigns of the Second World War.

The tactical deployment of air power was adopted by almost every major air force in the inter-war years, in support of both armies and navies. The exception was the RAF, which, together with the Italian *Regia Aeronautica*, was the only organizationally independent air force after the Great War. This very independence explains the inclination of many RAF leaders to look for a strategy that was also doctrinally independent of the other services. The theory of strategic air power was developed on the foundation of the wartime Independent Force. The RAF War Manual published in 1936 stated baldly that 'the bomb is the chief weapon of an air force'. The main objective of bombing was to destroy the enemy's capacity to make war by destroying the economy and moral reserves that sustained it. There was little attention paid in British air circles to counter-force strategy, or to co-operation with armies and navies. The bomber fleet, whose progress to its target was widely regarded as unstoppable in the 1920s, became the central instrument in British air theory, capable, it was argued, of deciding the outcome of a war on its own.

The reasons for this British choice are many. Britain had no powerful standing army, keen to exert its authority. Bombing fitted with British traditions of economic warfare and blockade. It was seen as a cost-effective way of avoiding the misery of the trenches and high casualties. Bombing also fitted with Britain's geopolitical outlook, at the centre of a global empire, with potential enemies thousands of miles from the home country. It was a modern version of sea power, congenial to the world's foremost naval state. Bombing was used for what was called 'imperial policing', and its success in forcing native rebels into line in Iraq, northern India, and southern Africa (though such actions bore no relation to European combat) encouraged a British cast of mind that saw bombing as cheap and effective.

The emphasis on low casualties and cost-effectiveness appealed to American airmen too, but they were attracted to the British idea of bombing because of its evident modernity. It was reliant on the most advanced large-scale aircraft designs, in which America had a clear lead, while the emphasis on destroying the economic power of the enemy seemed to make strategic sense in a country absorbed in industrial and technical modernization, and in which there was no tradition of the European standing army. By the 1930s American air leaders had developed a clear strategic conception of air power as a form of warfare distinct from ground war, one more compatible with emerging ideas of total war in which states committed all their economic and social resources to the struggle. In the United States, however, there was strong resistance from both the army and the navy to the independent use of air power, and air forces were tied in the 1930s to a support role. At the high point of American disarmament, and with no perceivable enemy within range of American aircraft, bombing remained theory rather than fact.

In truth, for all the enthusiasm for bombing, the RAF was poorly prepared for independent air power. Little thought went into the operational preparations. The bomber force was small and armed with light or medium bombers whose range was so limited they could barely reach the Ruhr cities, even from European bases. There was no adequate bombsight, bombs were small and stocks low, and until 1938 no serious plans existed for strategic bombing. Bombing was, in the words of the British airman John Slessor, 'a matter of faith'. When serious analysis of bombing strategy began in 1938 in the face of German air re-armament, that faith was found wanting. The head of RAF Bomber Command, created in 1936, was compelled to admit that his force was capable of almost no serious attacks on the German industrial system. An effort was made to draw up clear plans for such attacks, but it proved difficult to decide which economic branches were most vulnerable to attack, and which might affect the German war effort decisively. A priority list was drawn up, headed by oil, chemicals, iron and steel, and machinery, but it was recognized that with existing technology not much more could be hoped for than general attacks on the Ruhr area on clear days. This remained the core of Britain's 'independent' air strategy when war broke out in 1939.

The inadequacy of the bombing threat was compounded with the development of air defence. Paradoxically enough it was in Britain, pioneer of the bombing offensive, that the most sophisticated system of air defence was developed in the 1930s. This was an aspect of air warfare largely neglected in the Great War, though a system of observers, barrage balloons, and anti-aircraft guns was set up around London in 1917 to combat the Gotha threat. This system had achieved few results. The assumption arose in the 1920s that bombers could not be prevented from reaching their targets. 'The bomber', Stanley Baldwin warned the British Parliament in 1932, 'will always get through.' By the mid-1930s this was no longer true. Fast all-metal monoplane fighters created a wide disparity in speed and performance between fighter and bomber; the development of radar permitted the early warning of air attack; anti-aircraft batteries and civil defence preparations reduced the risk to urban populations. When light British bombers were used against German targets in 1940 there were occasions when not a single bomber returned.

By the outbreak of war in Europe in September 1939 no air force was yet adequately equipped or prepared for an independent air strategy, least of all Britain, where Bomber Command was ordered to hold fire for fear of provoking an annihilating German attack on London. British fears were entirely unfounded. Both their enemy and their allies stuck with the prevailing doctrine of using air forces in combination with surface forces to maximize military effectiveness. The German air force was instructed to bomb open cities to terrorize the population only as a last resort in retaliation for attacks on the German home population. The real strength of German air power was illustrated in the campaign in Poland where, against weak resistance, it was used with almost model precision; first destroying the tiny Polish air force, then helping the army batter a way through, and finally turning German bombers on the defended Polish capital when it refused to surrender. It was this campaign that demonstrated how far air power had come since the Great War.

Air power comes of age

There is a much better case for arguing that the Second World War was the point at which aircraft transformed the nature of warfare, though not quite in the way that Douhet, whose book was finally translated into English in 1942, had expected. There was no aerial knock-out blow. Air warfare proved to be a war of attrition, both at the battlefront and in the bombing campaigns which developed in the later stages of the conflict.

The Polish campaign set the pattern of tactical air power. Aircraft gave surface forces much greater flexibility and striking power, but only where they were concentrated together, as German air forces were, into large air fleets, and where communication between air and ground forces was technically sophisticated enough to co-ordinate air and ground attacks and to call up air assistance in minutes. The failure of French and British air forces to concentrate in mass in 1940, and the poor state of command and communication, which forced British soldiers to follow a lengthy procedure of requesting air support via headquarters in England, contributed greatly to the defeat in France in June. The same errors cost the Soviet Union dear a year later. The German assault in June 1941 faced Soviet air forces which were spread out in small clusters throughout the Red Army, with poor radio communication and no central control of air units. Though the Red Army had developed a doctrine of close air support in the 1930s, it compared poorly with its German counterpart. Every army division had its complement of aircraft which were tied in-flexibly to the front line, and could communicate only poorly with other air forces, or with the soldiers on the ground they were supposed to be supporting. In four months just over 3,000 German aircraft destroyed an estimated 10,000 Soviet planes.

German success compelled imitation. Over the next two years Soviet, British, and American air forces reorganized their tactical force in order to achieve both higher concentration of effort and better co-ordination with ground forces. The Red Army developed air armies in 1942. Each one contained fighter, ground-attack, and bomber aircraft, linked to a central control station by radio, and to the ground armies by radio and liaison officer. In 1942 they mustered 800–900 aircraft each; by 1945 they could number 2,500–3,000. The USSR was supplied through American Lend-Lease with almost one million miles of telephone cable, and 35,000 radio stations. The technical edge enjoyed by German aircraft in 1941 was quickly eroded through a crash programme of development and production. The tactical immaturity of Soviet pilots was reduced through close observation of German practice. Air power became a major element in the revival of Soviet military fortunes; without it the long struggle to Berlin would have been slower and riskier.

Britain and America were also strongly influenced by German success. The rudimentary ideas on tactical air power in the RAF were refined in the struggle in North Africa in 1941 and 1942. It was here that the western powers learned the obvious lesson that the first requirement for any bombing or ground-attack strategy was to win air superiority. Under Air Marshal Arthur Tedder the RAF in the Middle East concentrated on counter-force attacks as a prelude to supporting ground troops with accurate and swift operations by ground-attack or medium bomber aircraft. Liaison officers were posted with ground armies to co-ordinate these attacks, while special 'spotter' aircraft, first used on the Western Front in 1916, hovered over the battlefield to direct artillery fire or to draw aircraft to troublespots. The RAF and, later, the United States Army Air Force both favoured heavy bombing behind the front line against enemy transport, supplies, ports of embarkation, and reinforcements. By D-Day there was available to the western Allies a flexible and numerous tactical air force which contributed more than any other single factor to the success of the Normandy invasion.

Aircraft were just as important in transforming the war at sea. The vulnerability of warships to air attack was demonstrated as early as 1923 when the American General Billy Mitchell staged a display in which a handful of biplanes sank two battleship hulks in a matter of minutes. The powerful American navy did not like the object lesson, but during the 1920s a naval air arm, and two giant aircraft-carriers, were added to the fleet. Japan was the only other naval power to adopt carrier aircraft as an integral part of naval strategy. There was less doctrinal argument about what aircraft at sea could do. Their object was to protect ships from enemy attack and to mount attacks with bombs and torpedoes against the opponent's fleet. The effectiveness of air power at sea was dramatically demonstrated in the Japanese attack on the American Pacific Fleet at Pearl Harbor on 7 December 1941. Six months later, in the Battle of the Coral Sea and the Battle of Midway, Japanese expansion in the Pacific was ended by American naval aviators who succeeded with just ten bomb hits in sinking all four Japanese aircraft-carriers committed to the conflict. In neither battle was a shot fired by a naval gun; the outcome was decided by aircraft.

A further hazard was added to old-fashioned sea power by attacks from shore-based aircraft. Wherever naval vessels were within range of air attack from the land they were vulnerable in the extreme. In the Mediterranean and in the Battle of the Atlantic aircraft dominated the sea war. The submarine threat to Allied shipping lines was finally eliminated by the introduction of very-long-range aircraft (modified B24 Liberator bombers) which could patrol the whole ocean, and by the development of effective airborne radar. The only way to counter the impact of land-based aircraft was to introduce radar and anti-aircraft guns on to all naval vessels, and to provide fighter defence to establish air superiority over the fleet. By the end of the Second World War naval power functioned only in combination with offensive and defensive air power.

The strides made by tactical aviation during the war were

demonstrated to great effect in the invasion of France in June 1944. The Overlord operation was a model of combined arms combat; neither the naval operations nor the landing and break-out in France could have been mounted without the role of aircraft. Over 12,000 were assigned to the operation. Some protected the fleet from air and submarine attack; others bombed the enemy fortifications and forward positions; fighters kept enemy aircraft away from the battlefield; fighter-bombers relentlessly attacked troops, supplies, and transport; gliders flew in with supplies and troops; three divisions of Allied forces dropped by parachute on D-Day. The operation demonstrated the flexibility and versatility of aircraft, and the unity necessary to the exercise of air power. Each element of the air force complemented the activity of the others, and was combined with the requirements of surface forces. The concept of unitary air power exploited in combined operations eventually came to dominate the post-war evolution of air doctrine.

Strategic bombing

The successful development of tactical aviation threw into sharp relief the whole issue of strategic bombing. This was a form of air combat in which aircraft undertook operations independent of surface forces, indeed a form of air power in which aircraft might, in the view of many airmen, bring the war to an end on their own. In the early years of the war this was a view hard to sustain. For all the fears of apocalypse generated by the air power writing of the inter-war years, bombing made little impact on the early stages of the conflict.

This was partly the result of the deterrent effect. Neither side was willing to risk retaliation against its own population for attacks on enemy cities. The decision to unleash British bombers to attack German industry, taken in May 1940, was a result of the German air attack on Rotterdam undertaken in the advance into France. Even then German bombers did not retaliate against British cities until the autumn when Hitler, infuriated by two small attacks on Berlin, ordered the German air force to attack London. But the real barrier to a bombing war was technical.

The German air force had not been prepared for a strategic campaign. Its role in the summer of 1940 was tactical: to defeat the RAF over southern England as a prelude to the invasion planned for September 1940. The German failure in the Battle of Britain made invasion impossible. The attacks on London, and other British urban centres, became a substitute for invasion in the hope that Britain might be terrorized into surrender. The winter blitz of 1940/1 carried out by medium bombers with small bombloads failed to dent British resolve. Hitler concluded that strategic bombing was a waste of effort. The airmen agreed. The German air force returned to the tactical role which had brought rich dividends in the campaigns of 1940.

Britain persisted with the bombing of Germany for want of an alternative strategy. But the campaign suffered from the lack of large bombers and bombloads, poor navigation and bomb-aiming, and the rapid development of a German defensive system which was to become effective enough by the autumn of 1943 to bring the bombing campaign virtually to a halt. Only in 1942 did heavy four-engined bombers arrive in quantity. Not until 1943 did improved navigational aids allow more bombers to meet over the target area. To avoid German defences the RAF flew missions at night, which made accuracy even harder to achieve. In 1942 Bomber Command was joined by an American bombing force, equipped with high-performance heavy bombers, advanced Norden bombsights, and a strategy for attacking a web of industrial targets deemed to be vital to the German war effort. In 1943 both forces were capable of mounting large raids against targets far into Germany. The RAF was directed to attack urban areas in order to disrupt transport and services, hit industrial sites, and 'de-house' the work-force. The American 8th air force concentrated its efforts against specific industrial targets by day. The central aim of both forces was to erode German economic strength to a point where the ability and willingness to fight were critically reduced.

This aim could not be realized as long as the German air force was capable of defending German airspace. The bombing mission was only possible with air superiority. In the spring of 1944 long-range fighter aircraft were introduced into the conflict to convoy the bombers to their targets. The German fighter force was defeated in a matter of months, and the bombers' subsequent attacks on the aircraft industry and aviation fuel production made it impossible for the German air force to contest air superiority again. For the last year of the war the Allied bomber forces were free to attack the German economy and German morale. German tank, truck, and aircraft production was reduced by roughly one-third; explosives output sank by two-thirds. The industrial economy fragmented into smaller regions; the transport network was fatally weakened. German battle-fronts were starved of weapons and supplies. Bombing made it impossible to sustain or expand the German war effort, though it did not force capitulation. That came about through the physical occupation of Germany by Allied armies.

During the war Allied air forces dropped almost 2 million tons of bombs on European targets; over 400,000 Germans were killed. Bombing by its nature eroded entirely the distinction between civilian and military in war. Even the precision bombing strategy practised by the US 8th air force involved a high level of civilian casualty. The social impact of bomb destruction in Germany was extensive. Over 4 million houses were destroyed; 8 million Germans were evacuated and rehabilitated; welfare programmes were instituted to keep essential amenities going and to provide food for bomb victims. The persistent bombing led to widespread absenteeism, which reached levels of 20 to 25 per cent in the Ruhr area. Demoralization was undoubtedly caused by bombing (this was evident on the battlefield, too, where soldiers were subjected to attack by heavy bombers), but it was never expressed, as pre-war strategists had suggested, in terms of social resentment or political unrest. Bombing produced apathy and despair and fear, not revolution.

The age of the bomber

From 1943/4, when bombing became a serious component of Allied strategy, down to the 1970s when American bombers attacked Communist forces in Cambodia, air war was identified with the heavy bomber and the doctrine of strategic air power.

Yet the whole bombing strategy was riddled with ambiguities. Arguments developed about the nature of the bombing achievement even before the war ended. A post-war bombing survey conducted by American intelligence showed that bombing had not halted German production, nor had it produced insupportable demoralization. Critics of bombing strategy seized on these arguments to show that the campaign had been an expensive waste of effort, and the expectation that air power could end wars on its own was now exposed as wilful exaggeration. Bombing also aroused deep moral concerns after the war. Objections to bombing civilians were muted before 1945, but the evidence of civilian casualties (over a million in Germany and Japan together), and the growing realization that the RAF had deliberately pursued attacks on whole urban targets, rather than just factories, provoked a backlash against bombing in the western states.

Those who supported bombing strategy could point to the success of bombing in the Pacific war, where city attacks brought Japan to the point of surrender without the need for costly assault on the Japanese home islands. But there were more significant grounds for the continued pursuit of bombing strategy. The assumption was made in the West in the years immediately following the end of the war that total war, directed against home populations and economic resources, as well as military targets, was now the characteristic form of modern conflict. The bomber was regarded as the key instrument in the attack on the enemy home front in any conflict which did not involve atomic weapons. By the late 1940s bomber technology had moved on to a new stage. Very large, jet-powered intercontinental aircraft, capable of lifting bombloads many times greater than the bombers of the Second World War, offered a technical capability well beyond that of 1945.

Bombing also offered air forces the prospect of independence from the embrace of armies and navies. In the United States a new Strategic Air Command was set up in 1948 under the bomber general Curtis LeMay. The following year a Presidential Air Policy Commission recommended that America make its air striking force the central plank in its future military strategy. The

force was capable of using both conventional and nuclear armament and could operate quite independently of the other services. The commitment to bombing in the American air force
was tested in both the Korean War and Vietnam. In Korea
bombing sorties comprised almost half the air activity of United
Nations aircraft. Bombers aimed at North Korean industry and
transport, but although a considerable amount of damage was
inflicted the attacks did little to impede the flow of troops and
supplies for North Korean forces, which moved through open
country rather than by road or rail, and were supplied not by
their own industry, but by Chinese and Soviet aid. North Korean
forces were considerably better equipped by the end of the
period of intensive bombing than at the start.

Bombing enjoyed equally mixed fortunes in the Vietnam War.
Throughout American involvement in the war over 8 million
tons of bombs were dropped on North Vietnam and the Viet-
cong guerrilla forces, twice as much as the quantity dropped by
all combatants in the Second World War. The effect was again
considerable. The Linebacker I and II attacks launched in 1972
brought the North Vietnamese war effort to a critical point. But
the bombing campaign was directed with no clear purpose. At
different stages in the war the attack on morale was given priority; at others the emphasis was on the industrial and transport
system of the North; there was great pressure from American
politicians and public opinion to confine attacks to demonstrably military targets. The bombing was also more costly than expected. Persistent losses of B52 bombers in attacks on the North
were expensive in men and equipment, but also called into question the whole credibility of the bombing campaign. When President Nixon finally suspended bomb attacks in 1973 air power
had gained nothing decisive. Two years later the North Vietnamese triumphed.

The relative failure of bombing in both campaigns exposed the
entire strategy once again to serious criticism. In practice bombing in mass was so expensive by the 1950s that only the United
States could seriously contemplate employing it. Moreover the
heavy bomber proved to be a blunt instrument; it could obliterate
urban areas, but it could not hit smaller military targets reliably,

and was itself more vulnerable by the 1960s to anti-aircraft weaponry, particularly the ground-to-air missiles with which North Vietnamese forces were armed by their Communist allies. In both Korea and Vietnam, and in the Arab–Israeli wars of 1967 and 1973, tactical air power proved to be a more cost-effective and militarily useful way of deploying aircraft.

During the period of the Vietnam War the balance in air power technology shifted away from bombers towards fighters and anti-aircraft defences. This was a process already evident in the last stages of the Second World War with the development of jet aircraft, ground-to-air missiles, rocket-firing aircraft, and advanced radar-guided anti-aircraft artillery. The anti-aircraft armoury could be developed by states with relatively modest resources. The development of fast, heavily armed fighters helped to solve the problem of providing both firepower and accuracy in air attacks on surface targets. By the 1960s the frontier of aviation technology lay not with heavy bombers but with fighter-bombers, capable of performing multiple roles in reconnaissance, in engaging enemy aircraft, and in providing accurate and heavy fire against ground targets. Equipped with advanced radar and electronic guidance, capable of supersonic speeds, highly flexible both in terms of role and armament, the generation of tactical aircraft which emerged in the 1960s and 1970s created a revolution in air power theory. The tactical mission was no longer an auxiliary one, but was central to any conception of air power strategy.

After the bomber

The decline of the strategic bomber after the failure in Vietnam brought to an end a long period, stretching back to before the First World War, during which there flourished the popular belief that bombing would transform modern war. The idea of total war was bound up with the idea of bombing cities, and the two rose and fell together. After the Second World War bombing was compromised by the development of nuclear weapons and the missiles to deliver them. As long as the mass destruction of enemy cities and industrial centres remained a strategic contingency, as it did throughout the period of the Cold War, nuclear weapons were both cheaper and more deadly means to achieving these ends than conventional bombing. At the same time popular hostility to the idea of civilian targeting and rejection of the idea of total war as anything but a military fantasy, given the nature and expense of modern weaponry, undermined the credibility of strategic bombing.

This shift in popular perception in the West about what was strategically desirable (and affordable) and morally acceptable was evident in the widespread protests against American bombing of Vietnam between 1968 and 1973, and the profound public concern about air targets in the Falklands War and the conflict in the Persian Gulf in 1991. Rejection of mass bombing as an acceptable instrument of war, and of the idea that civilians were legitimate targets, coincided with a shift in doctrinal preferences within air forces themselves. Since with modern high-cost technology no air force other than the American and Soviet could afford a large bomber force, mass bombing was no longer a serious strategic option. Hence the emphasis shifted towards tactical aviation employing small numbers of high-quality, multi-role aircraft in combination with naval and ground forces. In the Gulf War Britain fielded only 76 combat aircraft; at the end of the Second World War the RAF had had a strength of over 8,000 planes. With smaller numbers of technically sophisticated and expensive aircraft the choice of objective became more important. Air power was once again, as in 1918, directed at strong points on the battlefield, at the enemy air force, and at the supplies and communications feeding the battle zone. Modern aircraft performed such functions with pin-point accuracy, high mobility, and formidable firepower, but without revolutionizing the principles of military combat. By the 1990s air warfare had become more effective militarily, but less radical in its strategic impact, than the pioneers of air power theory could ever have expected.

15

War and the People

The Social Impact of Total War

MARK ROSEMAN

Twice in this century European societies have been engulfed by the tidal wave of total war. Every region and every social group was affected by the unprecedented dislocation and destruction of industrial warfare. Yet once the deluge was over, how different was the social landscape it left behind? For contemporaries, it often seemed as if the war had changed everything. For one thing, wartime memories lived on, with a vibrancy and vigour unmatched by peacetime recollections. Moreover, the wars appeared to be not just the source of powerful personal experience but also major turning-points in the collective life of the societies which waged them. One observer noted subsequently that 'in the summer of 1940 the British people found themselves again, after twenty years of indecision. They turned away from past regrets and faced the future unafraid.' In France, too, the period 1940–4 has often been seen as a crucial period of reorientation, when the static France of the Third Republic gave way to the dynamic society of the post-war years.

It is surprising to discover, however, that historians have recently begun to be impressed more by the degree of similarity between pre- and post-war societies than by change. And they argue that where significant social change took place it was not the product of war but part of long-term processes originating ultimately in peacetime society. So how far *did* the participant societies change during the two world wars and what were the mechanisms for such change? How significant was it in the longer term? Finally, if the *perception* of wars as turning-points or as crucibles for social development really is belied by the evidence, what should we make of the (mis-)perception? How did it arise, and what historical significance does it have?

Societies at war

Mobilizing society. During the two world wars the human and material resources of the European powers were mobilized with unparalleled intensity and comprehensiveness. The most obvious manifestation was the size of the military call-up. Five and a quarter million men served in the British army between 1914 and 1918, a figure equal to almost 50 per cent of all men aged between 15 and 49 in 1911. In France, almost 8 million men were mobilized—79 per cent of all Frenchmen aged between 15 and 49 in 1911. During the Second World War a staggering 30 million Soviet citizens were called to arms. Enrolment on this scale was accompanied by massive occupational mobility. Huge retraining programmes were carried out to equip yesterday's garment worker to become the munitions producer of tomorrow. And new reserves of labour needed to be tapped, which meant above all the incorporation of female labour into sectors of the economy previously regarded as male bastions. Contemporaries found this perhaps the most dramatic social change wrought by war. Whereas in 1914 women accounted for 23 per cent of the British work-force in industry and transport and 27 per cent in trade and finance, those proportions had increased to 34 per cent and 53 per cent by 1918. During the Second World War female employment in Britain grew by 1.5 million from 6,250,000 to 7,750,000. By 1943 almost half of all government employees in Britain were female. Only Germany, of the major combatants in the Second World War, was for ideological reasons restrained in its efforts to mobilize additional female workers (female participation rates were in any case quite high in 1939) or at any rate those classified as racially pure. Instead the Nazis preferred to use foreign labour; by 1944 there were 7.1 million foreign labourers employed on German soil.

During the Second World War such occupational changes were only one factor in the truly massive levels of population mobility. There were the millions of families evacuated from cities subject to bombing raids. And there were the huge number of people in eastern Europe thrown into flight by the advancing front line. As many as 25 million Soviet workers were involved in eastward movements from the western territories to the Urals and beyond. As the tide of war turned so did the flow of humanity: millions of German refugees now fled the Red Army back into German territory. One estimate is that in spring 1945 two-fifths of the German population was on the move in some direction or other. And apart from such directly war-related movements, there were millions more involved in ethnic resettlement programmes in eastern Europe. Whilst the Nazis displaced and murdered Slavs to make way for ethnic Germans, the Soviets were, for example, uprooting the entire German population of the Volga region and resettling it in Siberia and central Asia.

In the process of this massive mobilization, the trenches and frontiers of social and economic life were moved or opened up or sometimes obliterated altogether—between town and country, between one economic sector and another, between the social classes, between skilled and unskilled, and between the sexes. Disruption to existing trade patterns and new national priorities meant that some industries were deprived of labour or raw materials whilst other sectors rapidly expanded. Changes were required to customary work procedures and demarcation lines as previously skilled occupations were offered to hastily trained unskilled or semi-skilled workers. Gender barriers were dropped and roles redefined as women upped tools in hallowed halls of male manual labour. Evacuated working-class children were placed with middle-class mums; upper-class volunteers in the army found themselves side by side with the great unwashed. And almost everywhere the boundary line between state and society was redrawn. After all, wartime mobilization entailed not just dislocation and change to the lives of millions of people, but also the adoption by the state of powers and responsibilities previously left with the individual or private groups within society.

The crucial prerequisite of mobilization on this scale was the competence, size, and authority of modern bureaucracies. It was no easy task, for instance, to identify and enlist army reserves on the scale required, to transport them to the front, and to ensure that military demands were balanced against those of industry and agriculture. Indeed, initially in the First World War, most states failed to do the job very efficiently—in France industrial production almost came to a standstill. Particularly during the First World War states found themselves on a voyage of discovery, uncovering and refining their awesome potential for harnessing human and material resources. The French government, for example, initially preferred to rely on the market to meet wartime needs. It was only in 1916 that the government began to organize businesses into consortia to control raw materials and imports, only in 1917 that it began to control prices (though rents had been fixed since 1914), and only in the last year of the war that it introduced rationing of basic foodstuffs. Though states went into the Second World War with a far greater grasp of the requirements of total war, here too there was a gradual evolution and it was only in 1942 that the war economy was fully established. In that year Britain created a Ministry of Production, the Germans passed control over the economy to Speer's Armaments Ministry, and the USA created the War Production Board and War Manpower Commission.

Apart from the need to organize the military call-up and to ration scarce labour, it was the disruption war brought to foreign trade which was often most influential in initially forcing the state to extend its powers over the economy. Governments found themselves involved in exercising import and export controls, rationing scarce materials, and controlling price and wages. They withheld raw materials and extracted labour from consumer goods industries and other inessential civilian sectors and diverted those resources to the war effort. They also became heavily involved in promoting innovation—whether to achieve more effective use of scarce resources, to find substitutes for missing raw materials, or to surpass the enemy's weapons technology. Radar, sonar, jet engines, long-range heavy aircraft, nuclear weaponry, synthetic oil and rubber, penicillin, synthetic quinine, and DDT were all developed in the course of the Second World War.

Thus from reluctant beginnings both wars saw a transition to what has been called the 'exuberance of the state'. A great many proposals emerged, from both wartime state administrations and other sources, for extensive state involvement in peacetime. In 1917 and 1918, for example, the French Ministry of Commerce proposed for the post-war period a powerful Ministry of National Economy and a Production Office, in effect an incipient planning agency. Similarly, during the Second World War, France was host to a whole series of proposals for post-war planning. In Nazi Germany, too, the early stages of the Second World War saw some ambitious planning for a new European economic order under German control, though here the emphasis was more on establishing economic structures for German hegemony over Europe rather than learning from wartime experience *per se*. As the war neared its end, however, German and Italian economists began—unlike those in Britain or France—to react against wartime experience and propose an economy freed not only from wartime controls but also from the corporatist regulation of the pre-war period.

Conflict and corporatism. Although the scale of total war was predicated upon the new capacity of the modern state, in fact the civil services of the combatant nations were rarely in a position to run society and economy on their own. In a number of countries during the First World War the army itself assumed many direct civil administrative responsibilities, in lieu of a functioning civil service. In Germany and Russia, where emperors not up to the task were nominally in control, the army developed *de facto* into a powerful independent agency, requisitioning men and materials and, increasingly, exercising overall political power as well. During the Second World War, however, all the principal combatant nations had far more powerful state governments, denying the army a serious autonomous role.

In almost all cases, the state's ability to manage the economy depended on close links with business. Everywhere except the Soviet Union, both wars but particularly the Second World War engendered new forms of corporatist co-operation between civil servant and businessman. In some countries, notably the USA and Canada in the Second World War, the state brought industrialists in to run its wartime agencies, ensuring harmonization of state and business agendas. Elsewhere the civil service retained its distinctness, but licensed trade associations to perform important allocative tasks—something which not only strengthened the state–business relationship but also increased the associations' power within industry. Even in Nazi Germany, the Wehrmacht, the Four Year Plan organization, and the Speer Ministry all co-opted senior businessmen to help run the war economy.

If co-operating with business was seen as crucial for meeting economic targets, state administrations were also keenly aware of the need to avoid labour protest. For one thing, war brought full employment and that in turn gave labour more power. In First World War Britain, for example, union membership doubled from 4 to 8 million. States thus sought to minimize the threat of disruption by a mixture of incorporation, concession, and control. The Labour Party was included in Asquith's coalition of 1915 and across the Channel in that same year the socialist Albert Thomas became the French Secretary for Munitions. In Britain, in the absence of conscription laws and with a well-organized labour movement, labour gained unprecedented rights to scrutinize and oversee the regulation of production. Even the military call-up of skilled men became subject to trade union negotiation. In Germany, where labour had been fiercely excluded from the system, the Auxiliary Service Law of 1916 forced employers for the first time to recognize the unions. The pattern in the Second World War was in some ways similar, though more uneven. In the case of the totalitarian states in particular, labour had already been so powerfully suppressed that it no longer figured as an organized group. However, as we will see, even the Nazis felt under pressure to offer labour important concessions.

War and welfare. In many combatant nations, the First World War saw the state implementing or planning extensive new measures in the field of welfare and social policy. The sacrifices by the population on the battle and home front put moral pressure on the state to ensure a just distribution of resources—all the more so given the diminishing share of the cake available for civilian consumption as a whole. Quite apart from the moral claim of the combatant, growing state responsibility for economic management meant that it was the government which was now liable to be blamed for any material hardship. That too stimulated official interest in matters of social policy—as did the fact that in many cases organized labour had gained access to policy discussions. Finally, wartime also confronted the state with the needs of the family. This was partly because new kinds of family support were required to make it possible and attractive for women to work or to provide support when men went away to the front. But also, by killing so many young men, both wars encouraged measures to improve the birth rate.

States thus introduced crèches to take responsibility for children off working mothers. They provided free lunchtime meals for workers and for schoolchildren. Ration cards, which were issued on the basis of perceived need, contained a strongly redistributive element—provided they were supported by a functioning allocative system. In many countries rent controls were introduced during the war to alleviate the hardships suffered by soldiers' families. Maternity benefits and family income supplements were provided to compensate for the missing soldier's wage. By the end of the First World War, the British Treasury was spending over £100 million a year on separation allowances alone. The redistributive impact can be gauged from the fact that by 1917 the separation allowance for a woman with four children was higher than the average earnings of an agricultural worker. In addition, a large amount of specialist advice was provided. In wartime Belgium, for example, consultation offices were established even in small villages to advise young mothers on healthy feeding and to supply them with food. The state's interest in public health also grew. Medical checks during call-up provided a first means of vetting and where necessary treating a large minority of the population.

Alongside the implementation of such practical measures,

wartime also saw the formulation of ambitious plans or position papers on the course of the future social policy. Perhaps the most famous was the 1942 Beveridge Report, the result of an interdepartmental committee appointed in June 1941 to look into social insurance and allied services in Britain. The report, which laid down a blueprint for the welfare state, encompassing child benefits and sickness and accident insurance, was followed up by a series of white papers on a national health service (February 1944), full employment (May 1944), national insurance (September 1944), and housing (March 1945). The year 1944 also saw the National Education Act. In the occupied countries similarly ambitious plans were being hatched by resistance leaders, governments in exile, and other interested parties. It is perhaps less well known that Nazi Germany, too, felt obliged to hold out the promise of major welfare state reform. In 1940 the German Labour Front produced a blueprint for comprehensive social insurance that bore considerable resemblance to the Beveridge Report. It should be remembered, however, that these welfare plans were merely part of a wider programme of racial engineering. The Nazis saw in war the opportunity to radicalize their racial programme, culminating in the mass murder of millions of Jews and Slavs.

War, ideology, and rethinking society. So far the main explanation offered for wartime institutional and policy changes has been the demands of mobilization. However, in many instances the issues of allegiance and identity thrown up by war—war's unparalleled capacity for forcing individuals and groups to take sides—were just as potent a source of change. For the Continental labour movement in the First World War, having to make the 'choice of 1914' (to remain true to internationalism and accept vilification as national traitors or to forsake international brotherhood and support *la patrie*) probably had a greater impact on its development than any of the new wartime committees which followed. In many cases the labour movement split between patriotic majorities and internationalist minorities—splits that were to become institutionalized in divisions between socialist and Communists in the post-1917 period. For the patriotic majority the break with the rhetoric of internationalism opened up new vistas—new possibilities of reformist co-operation with the state, for example—a process that both supported and was re-inforced by the state's desire to draw labour into the war effort.

The Second World War was still more a struggle not so much between nations as between philosophies. As a result the war polarized or displaced ideological differences within societies, virtually eradicating, to take one example, the substantial section of the British right that had held some sympathies for the authoritarian corporatism of the Fascist regimes. But it was the occupied countries of western Europe where the war's impact on ideologies and agendas was greatest. Left–right struggles were sometimes reinforced, sometimes muddled by conflicts between collaborationists and resisters—a confusion with profound consequences for the development of political identities at home. Moreover for some occupied societies—Vichy France above all—the Nazi occupation led to major shifts in the ideological balance of power. Vichy's social and economic policies were, to be sure, partly dictated by circumstances rather than ideology—the need to husband scarce resources and respond to German wartime demands. But Vichy also represented a particular synthesis of authoritarian and anti-liberal attempts to solve the perceived problems of the 1930s and create a new France. It is probable that the electorate would never have voted a government into power with these politics. Instead German power and the threat of civil war shifted power to the protagonists of compromises, appeasement, and anti-liberal renewal.

As the war progressed it became clear to all that the future would not have a swastika hanging from the balcony. Now it was the right which in France and elsewhere had cause to rethink its position. Employers tainted by collaboration felt under moral and political pressure to come to an agreement with labour. Few went as far as Agostino Rocca, an Italian managing director who distributed to all his managers a copy of the Soviet constitution in August 1943, annotated with approving comments! But in Belgium, too, employers were busy building bridges with trade unionists, elaborating a Social Pact under the occupation. Thus during the Second World War it was often the ideological fall-out of the encounter with Fascism as much as the demands of mobilisation *per se* that encouraged a restructuring of relations between state, capital, and labour.

The uneven burden of war. The social impact of war was, of course, not just a matter of institutional changes or new directions in social and economic policy but also of economic rigours, destruction, and death. The degree to which living standards suffered as a result of war varied enormously. At one extreme, millions more Soviet civilians succumbed during the Second World War to hunger, cold, diseases, and exhaustion than to direct enemy action. At the other end of the scale, the US economy grew so fast during the Second World War that despite being the world's largest armaments manufacturer it was still able to send ever larger numbers of Hershey bars and refrigerators off the production line. In between were those countries like Britain and France during the First World War and Britain during the Second World War, where the relative imperviousness to blockade, the efficiency and fairness of state rationing, and the influence of unions at shop-floor and national levels all contributed to an improvement in real wages, living standards, and public health and, within the working class, to a relative levelling up of living standards. The First World War was actually associated in Britain and France with a *reduction* in mortality levels for women and older men.

One group of nations which suffered particularly badly was those occupied by the Germans. During the Second World War, the exploitation of labour and material resources was most savage in the east. By 1941 Polish national income had fallen to one-third of its pre-war level—and it was to fall much further in the course of the conflict. Where they were not being systematically liquidated, Polish men were recruited as slave labour to work for the German war economy. But western European countries too were expected to staff German factories and put bread and sausage on the German dinner table. Between 1942 and 1944 some 650,000 workers were extracted from France by the so-called Sauckel Actions and these, coupled with the 1.5 million French prisoners of war, were sorely missed from the

French economy, particularly from French agriculture. By 1943, France was transferring resources to Germany equivalent to over one-third of its national income in 1938.

It is usually the poorest in society who are least able to counterbalance declining rations by purchases on the black market. However, during the First World War, as we have seen, the Allied countries largely succeeded in protecting and indeed raising working-class living standards. In Germany and Russia, by contrast, the rationing system, with its dominance by the army in the case of Russia and by a military industrial complex, in the case of Germany, was unable to guarantee fair or efficient distribution of foodstuffs and basic necessities. In Germany, even so crucial a group as armaments workers saw a 25 per cent cut in their real income in the course of the war. Yet for understanding the legacy of the conflict it is crucial to note that they were better able to protect their living standards than white-collar workers, who saw a 50 per cent cut in their living standards. The fact that manual labour outside the armaments industries also saw a similar cut did not prevent clerks, teachers, small traders, and other middle- and lower middle-class groups in Germany from feeling that they were being sacrificed on the altar of agreements between big unions and big industry. Elsewhere during the First World War, wartime corporatism often aroused a feeling of exclusion and indignation on the part of the middle class.

One group often relatively protected from the worst of the shortages was the farmers. The new inequality between town and country emerged most sharply where rationing systems failed to ensure equal distribution of foodstuffs, either because of rural distrust of the official forms of remuneration, or because of the authorities' failure to force farmers into line. The collapse of Russian and German urban morale was closely associated with the failure to force peasants to provide the towns with sufficient food. In the Second World War, by contrast, both Nazi Germany and Stalinist Russia applied so much pressure and control that farmers were denied the chance to profiteer from food surpluses. In Stalinist Russia the countryside sometimes starved so that the towns could produce and the soldiers fight. But even in less well-organized Fascist Italy, farmers were made to give up an increasing share of their food produce.

Even more than hunger and poverty, it was the sheer destructiveness of war that seared itself on the European soul. In France, one of the chief battlegrounds of the First World War, some ten departments of the north and east were completely laid waste and a proud regional centre such as Reims saw its pre-war population of 117,000 reduced to a mere 17,000 by the end of the war. The Second World War was even more destructive than the first. Aerial bombing, long-range artillery and rockets, the depredations of tank and troop movements, and the scorched earth policies of retreating armies collectively saw to it that massive swathes of arable land, large parts of European cities, railways and communication lines, shipping and ports were destroyed. By 1945 some 4 million British houses had sustained some damage. In the Soviet territory which had been occupied by the Germans, and indeed in Germany itself, almost *half* of all urban living space was destroyed or badly damaged. US troops entering Berlin in 1945 likened what they found to a lunar landscape. For Hiroshima and Nagasaki, there was no metaphor at all.

Most shattering of all for contemporaries of both wars was the tribute taken in terms of human life. No one could have imagined in 1914 that in the course of the war some 30 million soldiers would be killed or maimed. And even that horrific total was eclipsed by the 55 million people who died as a result of the Second World War. In both wars Continental powers with larger armies lost more than maritime powers using naval and economic means to win wars. Britain's casualties were thus smaller as a proportion of its population than those of its continental neighbours, with Germany alone accounting for 2 million of the 10 million troops killed in the First World War. During the Second World War, while Britain and the USA lost some 300,000 troops each, German troop losses amounted to some 4.5 million and those of the Soviet Union were twice as much again. As these figures imply, the Second World War saw even more savage distinctions between the theatres than the First World War, with the western fronts in Africa and France a pale shadow of the merciless killing in the east. Two-thirds of all German service deaths took place on the Eastern Front. It was a mark of how variable was this aspect of wartime experience that for the USA—the nation whose input of resources was most decisive in ending the war—troop losses during the Second World War were always far below traffic accident fatalities at home.

Apart from bad driving in the USA, there was another more sinister reason why the safety margin between civilian and troop life had narrowed: the civilian was now in the enemy's sights as much as the soldier. Whilst the Soviet Union lost at least 9 million soldiers in the Second World War, estimates of civilian losses range between 10 and 19 million war-related deaths. According to official statistics 70,000 Soviet villages and 1,710 Soviet towns were obliterated. The Allies' growing air supremacy meant that Axis civilian losses were also immense. German civilian losses amounted to some 1.5 million. Yet for the western Allies, too, a quarter of British losses were civilians whilst two-thirds of the 600,000 French men and women who died as a result of the war were civilian victims of reprisals, bombing raids, deportations, and so on. But the most sinister reason of all for massive civilian casualties was of course the Nazis' use of wartime to carry out a programme of systematic mass murder. The vast majority of the staggering 6 million Polish citizens (including some 3 million Jews) who died during the war—in addition to a further 3 million Jews and many hundreds of thousands of Gypsies and other groups—were the victims of racially motivated killings. As the full reality of the Holocaust became clear to post-war generations, the scale of these killings and the combination of system and irrationality in their implementation were to leave an aftertaste even more bitter than that of the fierce and wanton destructiveness of combat.

War and long-term social change

The short world wars. After this dramatic story of dislocation, mobilization, destruction, and death, it is striking in the longer term how many changes wrought by war were reversed or absorbed into pre-existing trends. Modern economies proved to be enormously resilient. Though economic performance in the inter-war period was to say the least patchy, nevertheless those economies which had been hardest hit by the war were the ones which grew fastest in the course of the 1920s. And the even greater damage wrought by the Second World War was, in western Europe at least, even more rapidly repaired. By dint of the dispersal of industrial production, the inaccuracy of night-time bombing raids, and the rapid rebuilding during the war of damaged plant, Germany, for example, emerged in 1945 with almost as much industrial capacity as it had possessed at the beginning of the war. Taken in conjunction with the human capital flooding in from the East (see below), the basic productive capacity of the economy was in astonishingly good shape. For Britain, the wars unquestionably saw the destruction or exhaustion of a considerable proportion of its national wealth. It has been argued that the overall loss of overseas assets, incurring of foreign debt, and run-down of domestic capital left Britain no richer in 1945 than in 1914. Yet in terms of its productive capacity Britain confirms the picture of the ability of a modern economy rapidly to reverse wartime destruction both during and after the conflict. In 1945 British output was 13 per cent above pre-war levels and it continued to grow thereafter.

Much of wartime structural change was also rapidly undone. The temporary shifts away from consumer goods to heavy goods production were reversed in the post-war periods. It is true that in the inter-war period war-induced surplus capacity in some heavy goods industries proved a burden on the economy. However, the failure to convert this capacity or redeploy the labour was—as the very rapid structural change achieved after the Second World War suggests—more a *consequence* of low growth than a fundamental cause of Britain's or Europe's inter-war economic problems. Conversely, there is little evidence that innovation and structural change during the Second World War hold the key to the success of the post-1945 era. There is some evidence, though, for a more enduring structural effect if we turn to foreign trade. Disruption during the First World War to British exports, in particular, allowed the USA to step into Latin American markets and the Japanese to extend their toehold in Asia. Indian manufacturers substituted for what had previously been imported goods. Britain's poor export growth in the early 1920s was at least partially the result of the loss of overseas markets. But in general the changing division of labour in the world market was governed by longer-term trends.

Even the enormous population losses had less impact than might have been expected. For their loved ones and families, the dead of course could not be replaced. In political and psychological terms inter-war Europe was indeed haunted by its fallen heroes. Moreover, the enormous troop losses of the First World War, concentrated in such a narrow cohort of young men, undoubtedly had some economic effects. In France, for example, getting on for one-seventh of all men aged 15–49 were killed, the number of survivors who had lost at least one limb equalled the population of a medium-sized town, and another small town could be peopled with men blinded by the war. These and the 600,000 war widows and three-quarters of a million orphans represented a significant financial burden for the post-war state. Of equal economic significance was the fact that as a result of the war there were in 1938 only half the normal number of 19–21-year-olds, relative to the rest of the population. However, it is hard to quantify the economic impact of these developments, particularly as the biggest problem of the inter-war period was the under-utilization of available labour capacities.

But for post-1945 Western Europe the demographic impact of war was surprisingly limited. For France, this time around war losses were more than compensated for by the population explosion of the post-war period. The French population, which had stuck at around 40 million for half a century, now rose to 55 million in the space of forty years, an increase of 40 per cent. The German experience is even more remarkable. Between 1939 and 1946 the population of the territory of the former German Reich lost some 6 million citizens through war, emigration, mass murder of German Jews, and so on. Yet through surplus of births over deaths (1.5 million), and refugee migrations of 4.3 million, the losses were compensated for in statistical terms. In the West German part of the former Reich, the population actually *increased* by 9 per cent over the same period. It was only in eastern Europe and the Soviet Union that the war's demographic effects were to have enduring economic consequences.

Our sense of the transience of wartime change is reinforced when we turn to the peacetime fate of the new policies and reform initiatives of wartime. By 1920 the British government, for example, had largely withdrawn from intervention in the domestic economy and by 1922 the entire control apparatus had been dismantled. Most of the innovative social policies adopted in the First World War were abandoned afterwards. The ambitious plans for social reform were largely consigned to the scrap heap. After the Second World War, too, the hopes for a new corporatist order in Belgium corresponded as little to the reality of post-war experience as did those aspirations to creating a 'third way' between Communism and capitalism which in post-Fascist Italy and Germany had been held by many groups on the left. In those countries the specifically Fascist quality of wartime state intervention produced a powerful reaction against extending the role of the state; a neo-liberal economic ideology became the dominant one. Elsewhere even undoubted innovations in the post-war era—such as the British National Health Service—fell far short of the dreams and hopes of wartime.

Where labour had gained in influence during the First World War, this was often short-lived. Particularly after the First World War, it was usually the end of the post-war boom and the return of unemployment that signalled the turning-point. Employers began to renege on wartime or immediate post-war negotiating arrangements, union power began to fall away, the state lost its will or ability to act as even-handed mediator. Rationalization in the course of the 1920s and mass unemployment in the 1930s only underlined labour's precarious position. In Britain, France, and Germany, labour reformists' hopes that they might work in tandem with the state to change the nature of the political system were replaced by a far narrower and more defensive attempt to preserve jobs and union power. In most countries radical alternatives became increasingly popular among rank and file workers as the depression bit. In the post-1945 period, too, many of labour's hopes and gains during the war years came to nothing. In both France and Italy the working-class parties, from having been major participants in the resistance and the coalitions of the immediate post-war years, found themselves playing second fiddle in increasingly conservative coalitions after 1947. The Communists, whose national appeal had been massively enhanced by resistance activity, were politically sidelined. In the USA, labour was already being squeezed out of national policy-making during the war itself. In Germany, of course, labour had made no wartime gains.

After both wars there were powerful ideological and social pressures on women to leave their wartime employment and return home. Everywhere the nurseries and communal restaurants were closed down. In Britain in both world wars, but particularly in the first, the power of unions and the weakness of women ensured that the expansion of women's employment was organized in a way which explicitly envisaged the removal of women after the war. In France, within two years of the 1918 armistice, the return of enlisted men brought the proportion of women in factory work down to roughly the 1914 level. Paradoxically, the war marked the end of a trend of increasing participation rates in France. And in the Second World War too women's employment increased in Britain by 1.5 million from 1939–43 only to fall by 1,750,000 in the period 1943–7. The 35 per cent of adult women in paid employment in 1951 was virtually identical with the 34 per cent twenty years earlier. Of course, some changes did endure. In Britain after the Second World War far more older married women worked than had done before (while their younger married counterparts moved out of industry and had children). And the structure of employment was changing. Women made up 10 per cent of the engineering workforce in 1939 but 34 per cent in 1950. And in most countries war, particularly the First World War, does seem markedly to have accelerated the decline in domestic service.

Dislocation and stability: the two post-war eras in comparison.
It would be foolish to argue that the wars brought no significant lasting social and economic changes. Most commentators are agreed, for example, that the First World War had a destabilizing effect on the economy in the inter-war period. This was due

not least to government monetary and fiscal policies during the war: most governments, believing initially that the war would last no more than a few months, had financed the war by short-term loans. The result was that France, for example, saw government debt quintuple during the war and prices increase fourfold. In Britain, government debt rose from £700 million to £7.5 billion 1914–19. Short-term debt increased from £16 million to £1.4 billion. It was certainly of significance for Europe's slow recovery that the two biggest European economies, Britain and Germany, both suffered from the legacy of this debt. Germany allowed the inflation to continue into the post-war period, leading ultimately to hyper-inflation, a condition which also befell Russia, Poland, Austria, and Hungary. For its part, Britain got its inflation and debt under control, but only at the price of a savage recession in the early post-war years.

The war's disruptive legacy was not restricted to the economy. All across Europe there were signs of social and political unrest. For Russia and Germany there was clearly a close connection between war and revolution. The inability of wartime rationing systems to deliver fair and sufficient supplies of foodstuffs was, in conjunction with failures on the battlefield (in the German case defeat), a decisive cause of the revolutions of 1917 and 1918. In Russia, the revolution, as we know, led to a permanent transformation of the political system. In Germany the revolution added little to the constitutional reform process under way, but left behind roving paramilitary bands as well as a climate of fear and division within German society, both of which were to bedevil the Weimar Republic.

If recovery was much smoother after the Second World War, society more stable, one reason for this was that the European powers had learned so much from the First World War about how not to wage war and carry out demobilization. For one thing, both the Soviet Union and Nazi Germany had learned from the wartime failures of their predecessors the necessity of vigorously suppressing an independent working class and containing revolt. For another, most governments recognized in the Second World War the need to finance the war properly and to control inflation. In the post-1945 period, governments also took steps more rapidly to correct imbalances between monetary values and the state of real economy. Thus the western German Zones of Occupation only had to wait three years for a currency reform, whereas their Weimar predecessor had waited six. And the post-1945 British Treasury pushed for a sterling devaluation in September 1949, whereas in the 1920s it had fought hard and damagingly to restore pre-war parities. Finally, the victorious powers did not make the mistake of leaving the vanquished to stew in their own juice. Instead the defeated powers were occupied for lengthy periods, and their post-war evolution tightly controlled.

It is also incontestable that both world wars played at least some part in developing the new styles of governance and economic and social policy which were such an important part of the post-Second World War success story. In France, the commitment to economic modernization and indicative planning policies had taken shape in wartime discussions among the resistance groups and Free French. In Britain it was the wartime white papers which laid the foundations for the post-war welfare state. Belgium's post-war Social Pact between employers and labour and the setting up of a General Parity Commission led on from wartime initiatives between the two sides. Similarly, the war had clearly helped to bring the labour movement into the centre of political life—even if many hopes and ambitions were disappointed in the process. In Britain, the Labour Party's power and its attitude towards government had both been shaped by involvement in the wartime coalition. The momentum gained by the union grass roots during the war was sustained, thanks to the full employment of the post-war years. In the liberated countries and Italy, the labour movement's role in resistance had enormously enhanced its prestige, even if it was to achieve much less than it sought in the post-war period. In the eyes of potential supporters and of many of the leaders themselves the labour movement was now seen as a core part of the nation, rather than being at odds with it. Of course, many of the economic and social policies developed during the Second World War had, in turn, been first rehearsed during the First War. Indeed it was arguably the 1914–18 conflict that had been the most innovative. It was surely no accident, to take just one example, that Jean Monnet—the architect of planning in post-1945 France—had during the First World War been part of the pioneering team at the Ministry of Commerce under Étienne Clémentel.

And yet even a cursory glance at the wider contexts of the two post-war eras reminds us that the social and economic consequences of war were only minor tributaries in the flow of long-term social development. From the end of the nineteenth century, the more far-sighted members of Europe's élites had been wrestling with ways to legitimize capitalist society and tame its wild fluctuations and rough edges. The long-term evolution of the modern welfare state began well before the First World War and in many respects showed a remarkably consistent long-term trend. A similar consistency is shown in the progressive increase in the state's share of GDP—from 12 per cent before 1914 to 25 per cent on average in the inter-war years to 36 per cent in 1963 and 49 per cent in 1975 in Britain. In so far as there was a major turning-point, it was arguably the depression, rather more than the war, which was the real crucible for the emergence of new ideas on the government's role in the economy, on labour relations, and so on. Keynes, Monnet, Fiat, the neo-liberals in Germany, and many other principal players in the twentieth-century drama of stabilizing European capitalism made their key proposals in response to the perceived policy failures of the inter-war period rather than to the war. For social policy too, the late 1920s and 1930s were fertile ground. The Second World War thus came at a time when in a number of societies strategies for stabilizing and legitimizing capitalism were beginning to evolve as a result of the shock of depression. The First World War, on the other hand, came 'too early'. It produced great innovations in government policy but these changes required a whole series of psychological and social readjustments which failed to take place. Moreover the cataclysmic nature of war itself deterred many from further change and created a powerful desire to return to older familiar ways. It took the experiences of the 1920s and 1930s to create the broad consensus in the 1940s for social change.

The other crucial difference between the two post-war periods was, of course, the geopolitical context. Indeed, we might well conclude that the wars' most important contribution to societal change was indirectly through changing the international environment in which reconstruction took place. The point was not just that the US and Soviet military umbrellas after 1945 created stable environments in which the two European subsystems could achieve social stability and prosperity in the one, modest growth in the other. It was also that the economic instability of the inter-war period was very much related to the absence of a stable international trading system and to the corrosive effects of Britain's loss of hegemony. The result had been tension, protectionism, poor economic performance, and the fostering of nationalist political agendas in many European countries. After 1945, however, US tutelage and loans helped to create the confidence for transition from protectionism to a liberal multilateral trading system.

To sum up then, what made the Second World War, in particular, seem such a watershed was the fact that the crystallization of lessons drawn from the 1930s, the resolution of a number of pressing geopolitical problems of rivalry, hegemony, and structural adjustment, *and* the undeniable psychological impact of war itself all impressed themselves on European society at the same time. It was the simultaneity of these nevertheless separate processes which made 1945 seem such a defining moment in the evolution of European societies.

The long World Wars

Those who have lived through one or both of the two post-war eras may well feel that this account fails to encompass the shadows the First and Second World Wars cast over the two post-war eras. How can we resolve the discrepancy between the conclusions ventured above and contemporaries' perception of the war's overwhelming importance?

Let us take as an example the 'Front Generation' which became a defining idea in inter-war German politics. On the face of it the Front Generation was a clear example of wartime experience invading peacetime society. The persistence of paramilitary politics, the style and ideology of groups such as the Stahlhelm or writers like Ernst Jünger, and the outlook and background of Nazi leaders all helped to create the public sense that here was a generation that had been cast by war into something new, something which could not be accommodated into post-war bourgeois society, and whose militaristic values paved the way for Hitler. Yet when we look at those who espoused paramilitary politics and saw themselves or were seen as members of the Front Generation, we find that they were largely too young to have served at the front. Furthermore the majority of those who *had* served did not support this kind of politics. The wartime memories even of figures such as Jünger were initially very critical of war. It was only later, under the impact of post-war events, that Jünger's characteristic 'Front Generation' tone emerged. (A similar pattern was observable in France, where the huge number of ex-servicemen's leagues were initially predominantly anti-war. It was only much later that the *Croix de feu* took on a more martial tone.) A further indication that the 'Front Generation' was not the product of war was that its supposed qualities were in fact only a modest evolution of dreams common in pre-war Germany about the role youth might play in shaping future society. And yet for all that, it is hard to imagine the enduring paramilitary style of politics without the experience of the First World War.

As historians in general are learning to discard the more mechanical notions of social history, the challenge is thus to think in terms of a dialogue between war and the post-war period, as memories and experiences were marshalled and regrouped by the needs and demands of post-war society. There is no doubt that what it was to be British in the years after 1945 — as indeed what it was to be German — was decisively shaped by the sense of having gone through the war, and by the narratives and explanations post-war groups found to fit and make sense of the war experience. The shock and test of war was so great, the simple, shared fact of having won or lost was so powerful, that the war hung over post-war politics, demanding to be explained and integrated into political argument and social identities. But it was up to post-war society to make sense of it and the war in it-self was not the decisive agent of change.

One kind of narrative that emerged after 1945 to make sense of the sacrifice was precisely that of war as social leveller. By presenting war as the midwife of the welfare state, for example, British élites could vindicate even a costly victory that had seen Britain's power eclipsed and its Empire undermined. Thus for the historian the task now is to analyse the way post-war society interrogated and re-evaluated the war. Only in this way can we resolve the paradox that for at least three generations the war experience dominated European societies and culture while at the same time leaving the broad sweep of social development remarkably unaffected.

16

Women and War

JEAN BETHKE ELSHTAIN

Women have been history's designated non-combatants. Thus, the story of women and war would seem to be a story of how women have either directly or indirectly been war's victims despite their status as those who mourned or cheered or stalwartly persevered rather than those who fought. As with all historical truisms, however, the story of the female non-combatant is not a simple one. There are the inevitable exceptions to the rule—with mythic examples of Amazonian terrors and Joan of Arc saints lurking in the background. Here Second World War partisans, resistance fighters, and Soviet women tactical fighter pilots; anti-colonial guerrillas; and American women loading ordnance or, now, piloting navy fighter aircraft come to mind most immediately. But these exceptions *remain* exceptions and that is why we take note of them. Nevertheless, there is a story to be told about women and modern war, and it is rather more complex than the story of non-combatants and those we take note of as exceptions. In order to bring conceptual clarity to the tale, it will be necessary to step back, briefly, to look at antique and medieval antecedents to women and modern warfare.

Trojan women, Spartan mothers, and the Madonna

Myth aside, women were very much part of the war story of antiquity. For the Greeks, war was a natural state and the basis of society. The Greek city-state was a community of warriors. The funeral oration of Pericles enshrines the warrior who as the true Athenian has died to protect the city. The Greek citizen army was the expression of the *polis*; indeed, the creation of such armies served as a catalyst to create and to sustain the *polis* as a civic form. How did women figure in this ancient story of war? As non-combatants, to be sure, but the female non-combatant comes in several varieties, as we shall learn. No more than the 'soldier' is she a generic figure. Non-combatant roles and identities are profoundly shaped by quite particular historical patterns and forces. Two forceful and prototypical collective female representations from Greek antiquity will help to drive home this point. The central theme, remember, is that warrioring is a male affair. A woman may seek private vengeance (for example, when Clytemnestra murders her husband Agamemnon) but it is the maternal Hecuba mourning the death of son and grandson that figures more prominently in subsequent stories of women and war. The tears and mourning of women here dominate: they suffer war but they, too, regard it as both inevitable and an arena of male combat and honour.

A fiercer non-combatant alternative is that embodied in the Spartan Mother. The Spartan Mother does not give way to tears and lamentations: she is the goad who urges her son to return with his shield or on it. In volume 3 of his *Moralia*, Plutarch recounts tales, anecdotes, and epigrams that constructed the Spartan woman as a mother who rears her sons to be sacrificed on the altar of civic need. Such a martial mother, for example, is better pleased to hear that her son died 'in a manner worthy of herself, his country, and his ancestors than if he had lived for all time a coward'. Sons who failed to measure up were reviled. One woman whose son was the sole survivor of a disastrous battle killed him with a tile, in Plutarch's account: the appropriate punishment for his obvious cowardice. Spartan women shook off expressions of sympathy in words that bespeak an unshakeable civic identity. Plutarch recounts a woman, as she buried her son, telling a would-be sympathizer that she has had 'good luck', not bad: 'I bore him that he might die for Sparta, and this is the very thing that has come to pass for me.' This story of the determined Spartan Mother, a civic militant, devoted above all else to *polis* or *la patrie*, is one enduring feature in the western story of women and war.

But there are other figures who rise to dominance with the triumph of Christianity in the West. The warrior's task becomes a more ambivalent one, at least theologically and theoretically speaking. The woman's mission is powerfully shaped by the image of the Madonna, the *mater dolorosa*, suffering the loss of her son rather than cheering him to glory. Unlike the stern Spartan Mother, the suffering mother is cast in the role of a victim of war. She may support the war of her country but she mourns rather than exults over the deaths of sons. Over the long sweep of western history, the mourning mother is one who may, in her own way, be mobilized for combat, that is to say, become available in the early modern era as a civic republican mother whose call is to buttress and to sustain the call to arms.

But this Spartan Mother figure is now haunted by the more pacific figure of the Mother as Beautiful Soul, she who embodies verities and virtues at odds with the clamour and killing of war. This is the Mother who laments and protects and regrets and mourns. Finding in the paths of peace the most desirable way of being, she exalts a pacific alternative. Ironically, of course, she does so from a stance that has historically been civically deprived. Absent from the ranks of warriors and leaders, her influence had to be exerted in other ways and through other forms, often religious, sometimes sentimental. No doubt the anthropologist would also remind us of the fact that the imperative to protect the childbearers is a deep exigency of the human race. That is, there are some good evolutionary reasons to keep women out of the thick of things. But with modern war much of this was to change. To be sure, women remained noncombatants, overwhelmingly so, but they could now be attacked not just by marauding bands and occupying forces but by long-range weapons of siege warfare and, in our own century, by bombs dropped on cities. Even as warfare grew more total, women's involvement in war fragmented into multiple possibilities—all of them, however, making contact, one way or another, with the exemplars deeded from antique and medieval models.

Renaissance and early modern warfare

With Spartan Mothers and Beautiful Souls framing the story, the historic development of warfare in the Renaissance and early modern periods contains few surprises. Women play their multiple parts. But they are still very much peripheral to the main story. For example, a quick check of the index of historian J. R. Hale's *Artists and Warfare in the Renaissance* for 'Women' reads '(see Atrocities, Baggage Train, Camp Followers, Encampment Scenes, Sex, Wives)'. Following up these hints one encounters a few specifics of an old tale: women as victims of war (atrocities); as sufferers of their men's wars (wives); and as the disreputable but ever-present provisioners of material supplies and sexual possibilities (baggage train, camp followers, encampment scenes, sex). These latter do not occupy an honourable place in the iconography and dominant narratives of the western way of war. From the rape of the Sabine women to modern use of rape as a weapon of war in the Balkans, the dark underside of women and war is a persistent counterpoint but, like the rare female combatant, is regarded by most military historians more as the exception than the rule. This, of course, is a controversial point. There are authors who claim that rape is a normal strategy of war-fighting, perhaps even a major *casus belli*. A more credible way to analyse the matter is to distinguish between rape in wartime as an explicit war-fighting strategy; as a by-product of victory, part of general plunder and pillage; and as random and opportunistic. After all, it is the case that the Geneva Protocols as well as the Uniform Code of Military Justice place rape under their punitive articles and, under the standards of the UCMJ, it may be punishable by death. Clearly, all of this points to the pervasive presence of women *in* war or, at least, in the general field over which the drama of war is played.

Baggage train depictions by Renaissance artists feature women routinely as dispensers of drink, medicines, food, and solace of both a maternal and a carnal nature. Wives followed husbands in campaigns and wherever there were soldiers there were camp followers. With the coming of state-dominated, conscripted, disciplined, and standing armies, the loose congeries that characterized pre-modern warfare—a ragtag agglomeration of fighting men, speculators, provisioners, wives, prostitutes, animals, a kind of vagabond social system of its own—gave way to a far more restrictive enterprise. Wives were kept out of it. Sex never could be, of course, but attempts were made to restrict 'fraternization' and to discourage lingering or long-term relationships with off-base women, whether domestic or foreign. Women in war were there to serve the men, one way or another, but they were overshadowed by the prototypical figures I have already discussed.

The modern state, women, and war

Once one arrives at the nation-state in its modern form, one finds congealed in it the notion of the woman as a collective noncombatant, and by the late eighteenth century strong distinctions between men and women in regard to violence were the prevailing norm. Male violence had been moralized into just war-fighting—the rules of war—but female violence lay outside the boundary of normal expectation. When the latter occurred, it was seen as disruptive and personal whereas male violence in time of war could be orderly and rule-governed. At the same time, very sharp cleavages emerged between personal life and public life; between family and state. Women were the guardians of the family; men, the protectors of the state. Viewed through the lens of these constructions, men saw edifying tales of courage, duty, honour, and glory as they engaged in acts of protection and defence and daring: heroic deed-doing. Women saw edifying stories of nobility, sacrifice, duty, quiet immortality as they engaged in defensive acts of protection, the non-heroics of taking-care-of. To be sure, the emergence of total war in the modern era threw irritants into the refinements of this picture, scenes of levelled cities, refugees clogging highways, starvation, and disease. But the force of received understandings never lost its resonance. To this day the phrase 'the deaths of innocent women and children' springs to the lips of observers when they want to tell a tale of authentic horror concerning wartime destruction. Women, then, remain the prototypical noncombatants, outside the circle of collective violence, even as the history of twentieth-century warfare places them at the epicentre of war's destruction—quite literally in the case of the terror bombing of German cities in the Second World War and the

dropping of the atomic bombs on Hiroshima and Nagasaki—
and, as well, women bring themselves more forcefully into the
picture not as they were in the pre-modern era but as irregulars
and partisans; as bomb-throwers and assassins; as *provocateurs*
and spies; and, finally, as themselves combatants in uniform,
subject to military requirements and discipline.

Women and modern war

The story of women mobilized for modern war pre-dates the
First World War. Much of the American Civil War—particularly
for women of the Confederacy—is a story of stolid suffering and
indefatigable patriotism, all necessary to pursue the war effort.
Indeed, General Sherman notoriously insisted that, in order to
pursue the American Civil War to a successful conclusion for the
forces of the Union, it would be necessary to 'make the women
of Georgia howl'. The point was to break the will of the South
and it was necessary to demoralize Southern women, Spartan
Mothers of and for their time, in order to undermine the war effort overall. Southern women cursed the foe, agitated the home
front, 'rushed out of their homes' to champion the Confederate
cause by stimulating enlistments (one historian notes that 'the
cowards were between two fires ... the Federals at the front and
... the women in the rear'), created relief and soldier's aid societies, provided individual and collective examples of martial enthusiasm and religious faith in the Southern cause, and received
the 'enemy' with hatred and invective. Perhaps the most famous
embodiment of the Spartan Mother on the Northern side was
one Mrs Bixby, who received a letter from President Abraham
Lincoln that became classic; he wrote to this mother of five slain
soldier sons of 'the solemn pride that must be yours to have laid
so costly a sacrifice upon the altar of freedom'.

When the opening salvoes of the First World War were fired,
women no less than men were swept up in patriotic fervour. In
Great Britain, women queued in long lines to sign up for the
Women's Emergency Corps. Relief committees were set up all
over the country. Young women could be seen shaming young
men not in uniform by handing out white feathers as a symbol

of their cowardice. Solid Spartan Mothers sprang up every-where, trouncing pacifism and faint-heartedness. One Mrs F. S. Hallowes, in her 1918 book *Mothers of Men and Militarism*, noted women's equally 'passionate love of mother-country. . . . Though we loathe slaughter we find that after men have done their best to kill and wound, women are ever ready to mend the broken bodies, soothe the dying, and weep over nameless graves.' The suffrage cause in England and the United States, where these efforts were most visible and highly developed, gave itself over to the war effort—with a few notable exceptions. The newspaper of the Women's Social and Political Union in Britain was renamed *Britannia* and dedicated to king and country. The National American Woman Suffrage Association in the United States prepared itself for American entry into the war as early as 1914 by proclaiming its members' professed readiness to serve in a variety of detailed capacities in event of war. Among the de-partments of work the association declared its willingness to un-dertake were employment bureaux for women's war work, increase of the food supply, the Red Cross, and Americanization aimed at integrating 'eight millions of aliens' into the American way of life. Politically active women of the Triple Entente pow-ers often justified the war on liberal internationalist grounds: the world will be safe only when democracy defeats autocracy, a somewhat tricky proposition given Romanov Russia's alliance with the western democracies in this particular struggle.

Although women were separated from combat, they did serve in a variety of capacities, most notably as field nurses, a job cre-ated as honourable and necessary in the nineteenth century. This put many women closer to the point of actual war-fighting but simultaneously reaffirmed the prototypical view of them as heal-ers not fighters. Women also served as couriers and the occa-sional notorious spy turned up (Mata-Hari being the most infamous and glamorous). At the same time, the war occasioned an outburst of anti-war activity by women as well. To such ac-tivists, opposition to war was a logical continuance of the suf-frage campaign, which, to their minds, meant the humanizing of governments by extending the vote to women. For example, in the United States a Women's Peace Party was formed. At its height some 40,000 women were involved. The Women's Peace Party was one section of the Women's International Committee for Permanent Peace, later to become the Women's International League for Peace and Freedom. After the war, women were influential in pressing for the Kellogg–Briand Pact of 1928 declaring war illegal and served as members of the National Committee on the Cause and Cure of War which collected 10 million signatures on a disarmament petition in 1932.

Women advance to the foreground in yet more dramatic ways in the Second World War. Nobody knows how many women participated actively in resistance movements in Nazi-occupied Europe. Some estimates go as high as claiming that 'tens of thousands' of women were involved in the French Resistance alone, operating as 'couriers, spies, saboteurs and armed fighters'. In France in the Second World War, 'in the tradition of Joan of Arc, women led partisan units into battle . . . . During the liberation of Paris women fought in the streets with men.' Some women members of the armed services, recalling events many years later, remain vexed by restrictions on what they could and could not do—for example, women pilots for Britain's Air Transport Auxiliary—as others detail wartime camaraderie and equality with men. French Resistance fighters and Soviet women regulars alike thought of themselves as 'comrades . . . soldiers . . . just the same as them [the men]'.

One of the least-known histories of the Second World War is that of Soviet women in combat. Soviet women formed the only regular female combat forces during the war, serving as snipers, machine-gunners, artillery women, and tank women. Their peak strength was reached at the end of 1943, at which time it was estimated at 800,000 to 1,000,000 or some 8 per cent of the total number of military personnel. Soviet women also formed three air regiments and participated in minesweeping actions. According to a recent historian, the women's 'instruction, equipment, and ultimate assignment were identical to those of their male counterparts. There is nothing in the designation of the regiments that were later formed out of the 122nd [the women's air group]—the 586th Fighter Regiment, the 587th Bomber Regiment, and the 588th Air Regiment—to indicate that these were female units.' Ground crews attached to these regiments included large numbers of women as well. In the aftermath of the war ninety-two women combatants received the title Hero of the Soviet Union and one-third of these were airwomen. It should be noted that women who served in this capacity were volunteers but, unlike their American counterparts—the WASPS, or Women Airforce Service Pilots—they were not restricted to non-combat activity. One of these Soviet bomber pilots, when asked to recount her wartime experience, deploys classic language of force, familiar to all soldiers in all wars: 'They were destroying us and we were destroying them . ... That is the logic of war . ... I killed many men, but I stayed alive. War requires the ability to kill, among other skills. But I don't think you should equate killing with cruelty. I think the risks we took and the sacrifices we made for each other made us kinder rather than cruel.' Despite this quite rare experiment—given the numbers of women involved and the tasks to which they were assigned—after the war the Soviet Union returned to the standard model, with women designated as non-combatants. At the time of the demise of the Soviet Union as a geopolitical entity, women played a marginal role in its army, primarily in secretarial capacities.

Far more important in the Second World War were those women called upon to manage the home front. Some women were direct victims of the war—women in bombed-out Germany, occupied France, and eastern Europe—but nearly all women in the combatant nations found their lives touched by this most extensive of all modern wars. Women entered factory war work to make up for the 'manpower shortage' with so many men off to combat. Women had to make do through shortages and deprivations of all kinds. Meeting adversity head-on signified what the home front helpmeet was all about. Mothers who sacrificed their sons to the war were honoured in all combatant nations. In the United States, for example, women who lost a son received a 'gold star' insignia from their government and were designated officially as gold-star mothers. Dramatic imagery of 'mother-home-homeland' was part of the rhetoric and propaganda arsenal of all nations as ancient myths and memories mingled with modern realities. Perhaps the most dramatic instance was Stalin's call to his people to fight the 'Fascist invader' not in the name of Communism but for 'Holy Mother Russia'. There was little doubt in Stalin's mind, it seems, about what icon carried the most patriotic clout.

Women and war since the Second World War

The story of women and war in the past fifty years is not a single story but many. Europe, worn out by bellicist excess, turned to commerce and Cold War politics under the nuclear umbrella of the United States. It was difficult to generate any enthusiasm for war, and the question of women's role in combat was not an urgent one. More exigent by far, for many women, was fear of nuclear war. Criss-crossing with forms of feminist protest, large numbers of women protested against nuclear dangers, often in flamboyant and dramatic ways by creating 'Women's Peace Camps' in Britain and the United States, for example. As we have already seen, women in the Soviet Union were demobilized, and political circumstances did not permit their political mobilization whether to support war or to oppose it. In the United States, feminism cut a number of ways—both for and against war and women's participation in it. This latter story, together with the participation in anti-colonial struggles and, more recently, nationalistic upheavals, is surely the most important and interesting of post-1945 developments in the saga of women and war.

The story of women's deepening involvement in the armed services of the world's one remaining superpower is a tangled tale of competing forms of feminist (and anti-feminist) politics. The United States now has a higher percentage of women in its armed forces than does any other industrial nation, around 12 per cent of an overall force of nearly 2 million. This rise in the number of female soldiers is extraordinary. By the middle of 1948, the numbers of women were down to approximately 8,000—about 0.25 per cent of the total, given post-war demobilization. The 1991 Persian Gulf War not only put more women in uniform closer to combat than ever before in the history of the United States, it also marked a definitive signal that the United

States is more willing to put women officially in war danger zones than is any other major industrial country.

Israel, for example, often thought of as a country with 'women soldiers', exempts all married women from the military and reserves, and women in the Israeli Defence Forces have no combat duties on land or sea. It should be noted that American society near century's end is divided in this matter. Although at the time of the Gulf War 74 per cent of women and 71 per cent of men favoured sending women on combat missions, 64 per cent overall rejected sending mothers of young children into the war zone. But mothers of children as young as six weeks were called up and deployed to the Gulf. This prompted a debate concerning the welfare of children, especially infants, and what baneful effects might result if they are torn from the primary parent. (The estimate is that some 17,500 children were left without a custodial parent during the Gulf War.) But that debate was largely short-circuited in the general American fervour concerning 'our men and women in the Gulf'.

The figures on actual female participation show a lopsided rotation in favour of men. Women were 6 per cent of the overall force in Operation Desert Storm, some 32,350 out of a total force of about 540,000. Women served as supply pilots, mechanics, police officers, ordnance workers, and the usual array of clerical, nursing, and support services. Several women were taken prisoner and lived to tell the tale, in language familiar to all students of war. For example, one Major Rhonda Cornum, a surgeon and helicopter pilot, discussed her own views of participation in war: 'Being killed doing an honorable thing like defending my country wasn't the worst end I could envision.' She did not want to be a coward, she said, and she feared that her own daughter would think she 'was a wimp if I stayed home'. Perhaps, after the humiliation and distress occasioned by the Vietnam débâcle, Americans were prepared to hear upbeat tales of heroism from women who were fighting the enemy rather than mending mangled and broken bodies in often unbearable circumstances—the stories Vietnam-era nurses brought back with them.

Although the Persian Gulf participation of women was limited and, going by the actual numbers, quite small by comparison to the men deployed and put in harm's way, enthusiasm for eliminating nearly all extant 'combat exclusion' rules waxed in 1992 and 1993. The result is that the United States navy began integrating women into its combat fleet in March 1994. Although women make up less than 10 per cent of the 5,500-member crew of the aircraft-carrier USS *Eisenhower*, they paved the way for further infusion of women into the combat fleet. The air force and navy also opened the door for female combat pilots—another first—in 1994. At the moment, women are not yet permitted to serve as ground combat troops or in the special forces. These final limitations, based on mission philosophy and necessary physical ability, especially upper body strength, are unacceptable to those most committed to seeing women in every combat role.

Will the next century see the curtain close on the male/female, combatant/ non-combatant divide so strenuously interwoven with the way in which modern nations have made war; so earnestly reincoded from generation to generation; so clearly etched into the legal codes of nations and the ethical codes of peoples? That is unlikely. Even in the United States, embarked as it is on a nearly unprecedented experiment in this regard, ambivalence runs deep. Although some servicewomen see combat slots as a way to move up the ranks to senior positions, only 10 per cent of military women overall consider ineligibility for combat roles a 'very important' issue and only 'one in nine would volunteer for such duty'. For the vast majority of women in the American All Volunteer Force, the risks of combat far outweigh any potential benefits. Undoubtedly this has been the case for the overwhelming majority of young men historically, too. The difference, of course, is that they have had little or no choice in the matter.

There have always been those who declared that war would one day, perhaps soon, become obsolete, in part because human beings would simply cease to be able to bear the destruction that war trailed in its wake. That seems not to have deterred the human race and there is little likelihood that it will in the twenty-first century. In fact, if anything, there are now doctrines generating a gender politics that would eradicate traditional ways societies had of trying to limit war's damage—by erecting a barrier between combatants and non-combatants. If women are no longer designated non-combatants, a designation that did not spare them altogether but did have a discernible effect in moderating war's fury, what new barriers might arise? Perhaps one between 'civilians' and 'war fighters' whatever the gender. This distinction, of course, lacks the texture and depth of the centuries-old division by gender. It will probably not yield iconography, myth, story, and song to the same extent but it may one day operate as well as the old gender divide. It is very difficult to say.

What is easier to conjure with is the fact that in the matter of women and war a vast array of options, many of them unattractive, will continue to present themselves. Women were not spared in the mass killings by machete in Rwanda. Women have not been killed in as large numbers as men in the war raging in the Balkans but, whether as non-combatants being shelled in cities, or as victims singled out for brutalization, war has been forced upon them in the most horrendous ways. Palestinian women are in the forefront now, as they have long been, in the fight for full-fledged statehood for their people. In the successor micro-states to the Soviet empire, women, so far as one can tell, are no less nationalist or chauvinistic than men, whether in the name of defence or offence. Ironically, it is in the post-industrial western democracies that, at one and the same time, a highly developed 'peace politics' generated by religious women and one strand of feminism clashes with a *realpolitik* sustained by yet another strand of feminism. Although at one point citizen and soldier were tightly tethered in western history, this is no longer the case. But we continue to honour soldiers who behave honourably. The difference is that we can expect women to number among them in a way we could not in the past. Whether this is progress or not is a judgement I prefer not to make. That it is change one can hardly doubt. But how significant the change is remains to be seen. One is struck, looking back on this long history, by the ways in which symbols and themes recur and by the fact that the numbers of women involved as official combatants in the armies of nation-states is minuscule compared with the number who continue to carry on as they carry out those daily tasks of sustenance, care, and perseverance with which women have always been associated.

17

Against War

ADAM ROBERTS

How can war be prevented, opposed, or at least restrained? What can take the place of such functions as it serves? Since at least the time of the European Renaissance there has been a continuous stream of proposals for tackling the problem. In each generation, thinkers and political movements have approached it in their own ways, reflecting their society's particular experience of the ever-changing phenomenon of war. In the nineteenth and twentieth centuries ideas about limiting, abolishing, or replacing war have been more numerous and more politically influential than in earlier eras, but have not in every case been more successful.

Proposals for tackling war have been based on a bewilderingly wide variety of approaches, which can be classified thus:

1. legal restraints on the resort to, or the conduct of, war;
2. systems of international organization and collective security;
3. measures of bilateral or multilateral arms control and disarmament;
4. pacifism (refusal of individuals and groups to participate in war) and unilateralism (proposals for disarmament by a single state);
5. peaceful methods of pressure and struggle (including economic sanctions and non-violent forms of resistance) as substitutes for war in resisting foreign or dictatorial control.

There are obvious elements of compatibility between these approaches; and the work of any given thinker, statesman, or institution may contain several of them. Yet they retain distinctive elements. Each approach has been based on a particular view of the causes and character of war; and each has created a particular image of an international society in which war might be controlled or eliminated.

The approaches listed above are among the most direct attempts to tackle the problem of war in the last few centuries, but they are not the only ones. Many different groups—women, the working class, churches, psychologists, and academics among them—have believed that they had a unique perspective from which to address the problem. For those who have seen war as the outgrowth of a particular type of society, fundamental social reform to remove the causes of war constitutes the most effective way of opposing war. Philosophical anarchists, believing that the state is the central problem of modern politics and a prime cause of war, see the abolition of the state as a means of preventing war. Some democratic theories, based on the idea that wars are caused by dictatorial and autocratic regimes, suggest active measures to remove such regimes as the surest road to peace. Similarly, Communist movements and states derived much of their moral strength and political appeal from their promise to eliminate the class divisions, and systems of imperialism, that had created countless wars. States with such an overarching world-view, seeing themselves as bearers of an ideal of cosmic significance, are sometimes less inclined than others to take seriously more limited and mundane (or in some cases old-fashioned) approaches to the control and limitation of war.

Legal restraints on the conduct of war

In most cultures, and in most ages, the organized violence of war has been seen as requiring special justification, its initiation as requiring special authority, and its conduct as having to accord with certain principles and practices. Such ideas can be found, for example, in ancient Rome, when they began as part of the *jus sacrum* associated with the college of priests, and then became associated more with the idea of natural law: of a 'law' which emanated from nature itself, and could be perceived or deduced by man through the use of his reason. They can also be found in the Christian tradition, in the works of such writers as St Augustine (354–430) and St Thomas Aquinas (1226–74). They also had a place in poetry and drama, a good example being Shakespeare's *Henry V*, first published in about 1600.

The precise content of the broad body of principles, rules, and rituals relating to war has varied greatly over time and across cultures. Yet three broad areas of universal concern can be identified, which overlap and interrelate with each other in many ways:

1. rules regarding who has legitimate authority to wage war;
2. rules relating to the justification for resort to war (*jus ad bellum*);
3. rules relating to the conduct of war (*jus in bello*).

From the beginnings of the modern system of sovereign states in the sixteenth and seventeenth centuries, these areas were a major concern of the principal writers about international law, including Francisco de Vitoria (*c.*1486–1546), Alberico Gentili (1552–1608), and Hugo Grotius (1583–1645). It is a strange paradox that the first area of international law to be developed was that which concerned war. Part of the reason is that peaceful relations could often be regulated on an *ad hoc* basis (for example by bilateral treaties on commercial, diplomatic, or other matters). By contrast, the wars of the period threw up complex questions of a general character which could not be settled at the time by agreement between adversaries. The following examples are typical: were belligerents entitled to impound the ships and property of non-combatants trading with the enemy? How were prisoners to be treated? Was it legitimate to wage war to bring heathens under Christian rule?

The 'law of nations' that was expounded by pre-nineteenth-century writers was not for the most part treaty law. Rather it was based on an idea of *jus*, of principles underlying law; and it drew on a rich and informal range of sources, including moral philosophy and the history of classical antiquity. Some of it was expounded in terms of natural law, some as divine law (the law of God), and some as law created by human volition.

It was only in 1789 that Jeremy Bentham gave the law of nations its contemporary name, 'international law'; and only in the second half of the nineteenth century did the idea of the multilateral treaty, open to any state to accept, move to the centre stage of international law-making. Once again the law of war had a pioneering part in this process. The 1856 Paris Declaration on Maritime Law, concluded at the end of the Crimean War, laid down general rules on relations between belligerent and neutral shipping in wartime. Within a year forty-nine states had become parties. In 1864 the first of what was to be a long stream of Geneva Conventions was concluded, for the 'Amelioration of the Condition of the Wounded in Armies in the Field'. This spelt out the principle that those helping the wounded, on or off the battlefield, were to be recognized as neutral and to be protected from attack. The Red Cross was to be used as a symbol of humanitarian work and to ensure freedom from attack.

One of the clearest statements ever of the purposes of the laws of war was in the preamble of the 1868 St Petersburg Declaration, prohibiting explosive bullets. This said that 'the only legitimate object which States should endeavour to accomplish during war is to weaken the military forces of the enemy'. Here is a clear idea, which also influenced much subsequent law-making, of war as a struggle between states, rather than between peoples; this is true enough in some cases, but by no means fully captures the complexity of civilian involvement in many wars both civil and international. The law relating to conduct in war was further developed at large international conferences held at The Hague in 1899 and 1907. These were especially notable for the conclusion of a Convention on the Laws and Customs of War on Land, covering such matters as treatment of prisoners of war, protection of hospitals, truce negotiations, and the conduct of armies in occupied territories. The 1907 version remains formally in force today.

The First World War cast a shadow over this process of making law on the conduct of war. The many violations of the law had exposed its fragility, and the propaganda war about atrocities had shown how law could in some circumstances exacerbate mutual hostility. More fundamentally, much of the terrible slaughter of the trenches in the war had been technically in accord with the Hague regulations, exposing law as an inadequate means of limiting war. No wonder that, at the end of the war, governments were not interested in further refining the *jus in bello*, but sought rather to prevent war altogether through the mechanisms of the League of Nations, including disarmament and collective security (discussed further below).

In the inter-war years, there were some other efforts to use international legal agreements to limit the use of force. The 1925 Geneva Protocol prohibiting the use of gas and bacteriological weapons in war may have played some part, along with threats of retaliation in kind, in limiting the resort to these weapons in major international conflicts, including the Second World War; and it has remained in force since. There were many expensive failures. In the 1928 General Treaty for the Renunciation of War as an Instrument of National Policy, otherwise known as the Kellogg–Briand Pact, the major powers of the day stated that they renounced war 'as an instrument of national policy in their relations with one another'. Subsequent experience showed the limited value of this paper promise. In 1939 Germany clearly saw war precisely as an instrument of national policy.

In the Second World War, many of the principles of the laws of war were violated, especially by the bombing of cities, the ruthless treatment of many prisoners of war, and the appalling treatment of Jews, Gypsies, and others in many of the Axis-occupied territories. The International Military Tribunals held at Nuremberg and Tokyo immediately after the war, and many other courts as well, sought to punish leading Axis figures involved. Allied war practices, though less terrible by far than those of the Axis powers, went largely unexamined.

The United Nations Charter, concluded in 1945, sought to prevent war by a multi-faceted approach which included formal legal commitments by states to refrain from the use of force except in cases of individual or collective self-defence, or in actions approved by the Security Council. In practice there has been a tendency for states in the UN era to justify their uses of force by expanding the meaning of self-defence beyond the core idea of defence of national territory from actual attack. (UN efforts at collective security are discussed further below.)

If the use of force was effectively prohibited, there would be no need for the *jus in bello*. In reality, in the years since the Second World War, there has been a succession of wars, major and minor: in consequence, governments have felt the need to bring law to bear on the changed faces of war. Ten major agreements on the laws of war have been concluded in the UN era. The best known are the four 1949 Geneva Conventions seeking to protect four categories of victims of war who come under the power of the enemy: wounded and sick on land; wounded, sick, and shipwrecked at sea; prisoners of war; and civilians. Virtually all states in the world have acceded to these four conventions: the number of adherents was 185 at 1 January 1995—the same number as the membership of the United Nations, though the two lists are not quite identical. Two Additional Protocols, concluded in 1977, supplemented the terms of the 1949 Conventions: they sought to bring the laws of war to bear more directly on some aspects of guerrilla war, and generally enunciated significant limits on the conduct of war. Other post-1945 agreements have dealt with the prevention of genocide, the protection of cultural property, restrictions on the use of some conventional weapons including mines, and protection of UN peacekeeping forces.

Observance of this body of rules in the conflicts of the post-1945 era has been uneven. Often one side was unwilling to admit the legitimacy of the adversary's existence or status as a belligerent. Many struggles were at least partly civil wars, about which states have been able to agree far fewer rules than those governing international wars. The distinction between the soldier and the civilian, basic to the modern laws of war, was not nearly as clear in practice as it was in theory. Extreme nationalism and ideological zeal militated against observing rules of moderation. Many violations of basic rules went unpunished. The establishment of an International Criminal Tribunal for the Former Yugoslavia in 1993 exposed some of the difficulties of trying to apply the law supra-nationally.

Yet it was also true that many limits were observed. In most wars, military prisoners received reasonable treatment and lived to tell the tale. In the 1982 Falklands War, and the 1991 Gulf

War, there was much (though not complete) observance of the rules. On the whole this did not hamper, and may have positively assisted, those who did observe them: evidence that the law is by no means incompatible with the efficient conduct of military operations. What is clear is that narrowly legal efforts to restrict the use of armed force have had only limited impact, and need to be complemented by other approaches.

In general, the relation of war to law is deeply ambiguous. There is hardly a war in modern times that has not been justified, sometimes by both sides, as a necessary response to an allegedly illegal action of the adversary. The part of law that in the end contributed most to limiting the use of force may have been not that which addresses war and peace directly, but rather the large body of agreements on trading, transport, border demarcation, and a host of other matters. This web of treaties, both general and bilateral, has generated ingrained habits of cooperation. The comparative success of Latin American states in avoiding the outbreak of war in that continent for most of this century may be due in part to their strong traditions of interest in international law.

International organization and collective security

'International organizations', in the sense of structures for formal and continuous communication and decision-making between states, can serve many purposes, one of which is to make possible co-ordinated responses to outbreaks and threats of war. Since at least the seventeenth century, schemes for international organization have been regularly advanced as means of discouraging resort to war and creating conditions for a measure of disarmament. In 1693, for example, William Penn in *An Essay towards the Present and Future Peace of Europe* proposed 'the Sovereign or Imperial Diet, Parliament, or State of Europe'.

The term 'collective security' normally refers to a system, regional or global, in which each participating state accepts that the security of one is the concern of all, and agrees to join in a collective response to aggression. Cardinal Richelieu of France proposed such a system in 1629, and a pale reflection of his proposal survived in the Peace of Westphalia, concluded in 1648 at the end of the Thirty Years War.

In the eighteenth and nineteenth centuries, ideas of collective security were periodically revived. In 1713 the abbé de Saint-Pierre, a prolific writer on French law and society, published his *Projet de paix perpetuelle*, proposing a complete freezing of all political arrangements in Europe, the establishment of a union between sovereigns, a system of mediation between states, and common military action against any state failing to observe the rules of the new system.

The idea of common military action was raised again in 1815, in the wake of Napoleon's defeat by a coalition of powers. Several of them, including Great Britain, were reluctant to commit themselves to a system of joint action if it meant underwriting the existing political and territorial arrangements in Europe. Throughout the nineteenth century, although states remained unwilling to create anything like a general system of collective security, the idea of the Concert of Europe—of the major powers gathering and working out common action in respect of threats to the peace—repeatedly spurred governments to coordinate their policies. Further, the rapid growth in the number and importance of functional international organizations, starting with the International Telegraph Bureau in 1868, inspired thoughts that the problem of war, too, should be addressed though international organization.

The First World War revived ideas about collective security, but in a peculiar way. The idea that peace could be based on a more or less natural 'balance of power' between states had been undermined catastrophically in 1914. The fact that the war was made worse by the rough balance between the two sides did not help. An alternative basis for international security had to be found. However, the same terrible experience of war made governments reluctant to contemplate the possibility, however remote, of having to commit their populations to war once again. The result was the League of Nations Covenant. This implied that a system of collective security was to be developed, but the procedures by which states were to be committed to resist an act of aggression were unsatisfactory (requiring, as they did, unanimity of the League's Council); and the type of action to be taken was not spelt out with any precision. In practice, in the entire period of existence of the League of Nations (1920–46) it never achieved anything like universal membership, nor did its members ever agree on military action against Japanese, Italian, German, or any other state's acts of military expansionism. Its one effort at organizing economic sanctions, against Italy following its 1935 invasion of Abyssinia, was a failure. It did, however, encourage the further growth of international functional organizations, including the International Labour Organization. The Permanent Court of International Justice (since 1945, International Court of Justice) was established in The Hague in 1920.

The United Nations system, established in 1945 with the adoption of the UN Charter, was intended to eliminate the causes of war by promoting social progress and human rights, extending the network and the reach of international functional bodies, and strengthening arrangements for peaceful settlement of disputes. As to preventive action against threats to the peace, the Charter reflected a compromise between a system of collective security and an acceptance of a continuing role for national and regional defence arrangements.

The Charter provisions for the UN Security Council (originally eleven strong, enlarged to fifteen in 1965) provided a much more realistic structure for reaching decisions than their equivalents in the League Covenant. In the UN Security Council, Britain, China, France, USSR/Russia, and the USA have permanent membership and the power to veto resolutions, but otherwise resolutions are passed by three-fifths majority vote. This means that decisions can sometimes be reached. On the other hand, because of the veto, military actions by any of the 'Permanent Five' cannot be effectively opposed by the UN itself. Hence the Cold War was conducted largely outside the UN framework.

In the half-century after 1945 the UN achieved and maintained virtually universal membership of all states recognized to exist at any given time—a scope that had eluded the League of Nations. It provided one, but by no means the only, forum for deliberating on common responses to military threats. It authorized certain uses of force by US-led coalitions of states in what were perceived as important international causes, including in Korea in 1950, in the Iraq–Kuwait Crisis of 1990–1, and over Somalia in 1992. It also introduced a new type of military activity, UN peacekeeping missions. These are impartial multinational military presences to help the parties to a conflict to implement cease-fires and peace agreements, and to assist with humanitarian work. Thirty-eight such operations were established between 1948 and 1995, mainly in post-colonial (and latterly also post-Communist) states. Although the record of such operations was mixed, many of them did help to shore up vulnerable cease-fires, assist political settlements, and isolate conflicts from the rivalries of great powers or neighbouring powers.

During the Cold War years, the UN was often unable to act owing to the veto in the Security Council; and states often brought to it issues on which they wanted rhetoric more than action. In the years from 1990 to 1995, when the veto virtually ceased to be used, there were hopes that the UN might at last emerge as the centre of a post-Cold War system of collective security and international peace. The success of the UN-led coalition in expelling Iraq from Kuwait in 1991 reinforced such hopes. However, certain central weaknesses of collective security proposals resurfaced. Faced with complex crises in former Yugoslavia, the former Soviet Union, Africa, and elsewhere, there simply was not enough agreement among states about which crises should be tackled, and what action should be taken. When the Security Council did propose action, there was often a reluctance on the part of states to provide the necessary forces and resources, or to take risks with their soldiers' lives.

The UN has not achieved anything like a general system of collective security, but it has provided a forum for co-ordinating responses to at least some problems, and has given important symbolic recognition to the ideas of the equality of states and of peoples. If it has not abolished war, it has sometimes been perceived, even by some belligerents, as strengthening presumptions against the use of force.

Some international organizations have been intended to eliminate war, not by providing for common action against aggression, but rather by developing patterns of interaction between states and peoples so as to make resort to war unlikely or impossible. In western Europe after the Second World War, much of the thinking that went into the creation of European institutions in the 1940s and 1950s was along precisely these lines. Aware that the United Nations might not succeed, European leaders established what eventually became the European Union with the idea in mind that a high degree of mutual co-operation and interdependence would reduce the likelihood of another catastrophic European war. For many decades, European institutions such as the European Community had no direct security functions, yet the abolition of war was the ultimate rationale for their existence. The European experience has strengthened the hand of those who argue that, on a global level, a transnational society is beginning to emerge, based on the increasing number and complexity of cross-border interactions, and characterized by the spread of political and economic liberalism. This is an enticing vision, but it seems to be based on an assumption that reversions into narrow nationalism—a common response to headlong advances into modernity—are mere temporary aberrations. Such integrationist visions also sometimes neglect the phenomenon of civil wars, whose outbreak generally confounds the idea that more interaction is necessarily good for peace.

Agreements for disarmament and arms control

The idea that war can be abolished by agreed measures of disarmament among states has a long history. In 1816, directly after the final defeat of the Napoleonic Empire, Tsar Alexander I of Russia proposed 'a simultaneous reduction of armed forces of all kinds which the powers have brought into being to preserve the safety and independence of their peoples'. In reply the British Foreign Minister, Lord Castlereagh, expressed elegantly the realist critique of such ambitious schemes: 'It is impossible not to perceive that the settlement of a scale of force for so many powers, under such different circumstances as to their relative means, frontiers, positions and faculties for rearming, presents a very complicated question for negotiation.'

When he convened the 1899 Hague Peace Conference, Tsar Nicholas II was concerned about the cost and dangers of arms competition, and also about Russia's technical inferiority. He wanted to bring about major reductions in armaments, but actually the two Hague Peace Conferences, while reaching agreement on some other matters, failed to achieve any significant arms reductions.

After the First World War, the Covenant of the League of Nations called for 'the reduction of national armaments to the lowest point consistent with national safety and the enforcement by common action of international obligations'. Some measures of arms limitation were achieved in the inter-war years, including the 1922 Washington Naval Treaty and the 1930 London Naval Treaty. However, the ambitious disarmament aims of the League were not translated into reality. In November 1927 Maxim Litvinov, head of the Soviet delegation to a League disarmament commission in Geneva, made the first ever formal diplomatic proposal for 'complete and general disarmament'—the 'complete' referring to all armaments, the 'general' to all countries. There is some question about how serious he and his government were in advancing this proposal. At all events it gained little support. Subsequently the League convened the much-heralded Conference for the Reduction and Limitation of Armaments: held in Geneva in 1932–4, at the very time of increasing challenge from Japan and Germany, this failed to achieve any significant results. Overall, the League's combination of high aspiration in the disarmament field and poor performance contributed to the perception of the organization as hopelessly unrealistic.

On disarmament as on other matters, the United Nations was based on more realistic assumptions than the League. Articles 11 and 26 of the Charter make only cautious references to disarmament and the regulation of armaments. As the Cold War developed and East–West arms competition intensified, there were increasing calls for disarmament, especially from the nonaligned countries which came to form a majority of the UN's membership. Both the Soviet Union and the United States put forward schemes for general and complete disarmament in 1959–60, and they never explicitly renounced this approach.

The UN General Assembly held Special Sessions on Disarmament in 1978, 1982, and 1988, which were long on rhetoric but short on achievement.

In the UN era, a sharp distinction came increasingly to be drawn between general and complete disarmament on the one hand, and arms limitation on the other. The former was widely criticized as unattainable. Some argued that the idea of all countries agreeing to disarm at the same time was not credible; that arms still had a function within societies, and in their defence against external enemies; and that inspection of disarmament would be very difficult, especially as nuclear weapons, so large in their effects, were relatively easy to conceal. Against a background of such pessimistic arguments, advocacy of more modest measures of arms limitation gained much ground, especially from about 1960 onwards. The main international arms limitation agreements concluded since 1945 are:

1963 Partial Nuclear Test Ban Treaty (PTBT);

1967 Latin American Nuclear-Free Zone Treaty (Treaty of Tlatelolco);

1968 Treaty on the Non-proliferation of Nuclear Weapons (NPT);

1972 Biological Weapons Treaty (BW Convention);

1972 Accords resulting from US–Soviet Strategic Arms Limitation Talks placing limits on long-range nuclear delivery vehicles and on anti-ballistic missile systems (SALT-I);

1985 South Pacific Nuclear Free Zone Treaty (Treaty of Rarotonga);

1987 US–Soviet Treaty eliminating intermediate-range nuclear forces (INF Treaty);

1990 Treaty on Conventional Armed Forces in Europe (CFE Treaty);

1991 US–USSR Strategic Arms Reduction Treaty (START Treaty);

1993 Convention on the Prohibition of the Development, Production, and Use of Chemical Weapons and on their Destruction (CW Convention).

The purpose of these and other agreements was not to eliminate all possibility of war, but rather to reduce the costs of armed confrontation, to make it more predictable, and to circumscribe weapons systems and activities that were seen as particularly offensive or provocative in character. A further underlying purpose of arms control discussions was to build up a degree of mutual understanding between adversaries. This did not always work: arms control conferences were often the scene of polemical statements, including complaints about the adversary's allegedly poor record of implementation. Sometimes arms limitation negotiations were criticized as failing to tackle the qualitative arms race, or more generally for being too mildly reformist when more fundamental change was needed. Local wars with an East–West dimension, including that in Vietnam, continued despite the simultaneous conclusion of arms control agreements between the USA and USSR. Yet the habit of mutual consultation, and the emergence of some elements of common understanding of strategic problems, may have contributed to the process of change in the Soviet Union that resulted, in 1989–91, in the end of the Cold War and the collapse of the Soviet Union itself.

Pacifism and unilateralism

Throughout recorded history, the rejection of organized mass violence has been a feature of many religious systems and sects, including Buddhism. Since the time of the Reformation, many of the smaller Christian sects have been pacifist, including Anabaptists, Mennonites, and Quakers. Many writers advanced essentially pacifist positions. Erasmus wrote in *A Complaint of Peace Spurned and Rejected by the Whole World* (1517): 'You see that hitherto nothing has been achieved by treaties, nothing advanced by alliances, nothing by violence or revenge. Now try instead what conciliation and kindness can do. War springs from war, revenge brings further revenge. Now let generosity breed generosity, kind actions invite further kindness, and true royalty be measured by willingness to concede sovereignty.' Writing in similar vein over three centuries later, Leo Tolstoy, author of *War and Peace*, was doubtful about all attempts to humanize or limit war: it had to be opposed outright, and from below.

In the nineteenth century, many movements, both liberal and socialist, were highly critical of uses of armed force by states. Many advocated arbitration, the setting up of international courts, and reductions of armaments. They were not necessarily completely pacifist in the modern sense, and are perhaps better described by the term 'pacificist', which implies exploring all possibilities of peace but not necessarily rejecting all uses of violence in all circumstances. An awareness that there was a common civilization among European countries, or common interests between the working classes of different countries, powerfully strengthened such movements. In the First World War, militant nationalism proved stronger than such internationalist ideas, and projects for a general strike against war collapsed.

Since the First World War, the word 'pacifism' has come to be used mainly to refer to the belief that all waging of war, and the participation in war by individuals, is wrong. Twentieth-century pacifism has differed from its religious forebears in three main ways. First, it has included a stronger element of rationalism, basing itself more on pragmatic arguments about the alleged futility of war than on absolute religious prescriptions. Second, in some countries it has become a basis of political movements seeking to bring about a radical change in government policy. Third, it has been associated with movements for conscientious objection (i.e. a principled refusal to be inducted for military service). A distinction has persisted between policy-minded pacifists who have argued optimistically that if states abandoned military preparations, they would thereby reduce the danger of war; and more pessimistic pacifists, who have seen their role in more limited terms as maintaining their integrity and distancing themselves from the state.

Pacifist movements sprang up in many countries in the 1930s, and were particularly strong in Great Britain and the USA. They were a reaction to the terrible experience of the First World War, in which the number of lives lost seemed out of proportion to the results achieved. In many countries, a deep fear of full-scale air attacks further strengthened pacifist arguments that it was time to make a break from the vicious spiral of arms races and war. The slogan of the Peace Pledge Union, 'Wars Will Cease When Men Refuse to Fight', logical if simplistic, exemplified the pacifist argument.

In the 1930s, as in more recent times, pacifists were often asked how they intended to defend their family, their country, or their political system. The emerging menace of Fascism in Italy, Spain, and Germany added weight to such questions. In response, pacifists sometimes urged the value of negotiations as an alternative to war—an answer which was rapidly discredited as policies of appeasement (especially by France and Britain) failed completely to contain Nazism. Sometimes they stressed the value of non-violent resistance (discussed in the next section) as a means of countering violence, but their vague and general approach did not inspire confidence. After the outbreak of the Second World War in 1939, there was a tendency (rightly or wrongly) to blame pacifists for having contributed to the lack of military preparedness of several states, and for having helped Hitler to believe that he could attack certain countries with impunity. During the war, some former pacifists decided to support the war effort, but thousands of men, in Britain and the USA as well as some other countries, refused to be conscripted.

Pacifist movements, and the cause of conscientious objection to military service which they had espoused, emerged much weakened from the Second World War. The events of 1939–45 had shown that military methods were not, after all, entirely outmoded and ineffective. The aggression and inhumanity at the heart of German policy forced many to the conclusion that, against powers as evil as those of the Axis, the use of force was legitimate. While pacifist opinion continued to exist, it had lost some of its salience and moral force. Further, some saw the emerging possibilities of force being used under United Nations auspices as calling into question absolute pacifist objections to the use of force.

The development of nuclear weapons from 1945 onwards stimulated, eventually, the emergence of a new kind of pacifism. In the late 1950s and early 1960s, when both the Soviet Union and the United States had developed thermonuclear (H-bomb) weapons and the means to deliver them, there was a new wave of revulsion against war and weaponry in many countries. This took largely the form of 'nuclear pacifism'—i.e. the rejection of all preparation and threats of use of nuclear weapons, leading logically to calls for unilateral nuclear disarmament. In Britain the change from pacifism to nuclear pacifism was symbolized by the philosopher Bertrand Russell, who had been a conscientious objector to military service in the First World War, and then, while not supporting complete pacifism in later years, became a leading figure in British campaigns against nuclear weapons from 1958 until his death in 1970. As East–West tensions declined in the late 1960s and the 1970s, peace movements also lost their sense of urgency and mission.

The December 1979 decision by NATO to deploy land-based, nuclear-armed, intermediate-range missiles in several member states led to a revival of nuclear pacifism in many countries, especially in western Europe. The campaign against the missile deployments had a strongly international aspect: some of its leading figures sought to develop parallel movements in the eastern European Warsaw Pact states. Moscow and its allies supported the movements in the West, while naturally opposing their emergence in the East. The demonstrations in western countries caused great concern to some of their governments, but did not prevent the deployment of the missiles in 1983.

Nuclear pacifism addressed an important issue, but was vulnerable to criticism. Many supporters of unilateral nuclear disarmament by western European countries could not agree on whether they also supported a comparable act of disarmament by the USA. Many conceded, publicly or privately, that nuclear weapons did have some deterrent value and could not be totally renounced at one go. While everyone had an idea of what advocates of unilateral nuclear disarmament opposed, it was by no means always clear what defence policy, if any, they favoured.

In the late 1980s, efforts to remedy this weakness led to a series of proposals, especially strongly advanced in European NATO member states, for a system of mainly conventional 'non-offensive defence': manifestly defensive military systems that would deter attack without causing the adversary to feel threatened. This approach, it was hoped, would overcome the action–reaction spiral that was seen as a cause of arms races and wars. It revived older ideas, important in socialist movements in the late nineteenth and early twentieth centuries, that the key to international peace was to replace the armies of princes with armies of the people, which would be inherently defensive in character.

The balance-sheet of the various pacifist and nuclear-pacifist movements of the twentieth century is not encouraging. On the positive side, such movements played some part in bringing about an awareness of the futility of many wars, and the dangers of nuclear weapons. They constituted one of the many pressures that contributed to the conclusion of such key arms control measures as the 1963 Partial Nuclear Test Ban Treaty. There were some effective campaigns against participation in particular wars: in France against the Algerian War (1954–61), and in the USA against the intervention in South Vietnam and other parts of Indo-China (for over a decade up to 1973). On the other hand, on their central issue of concern, the renunciation of military preparations by states, peace movements have not been successful. In no major state has anything approaching a majority of popular opinion been persuaded of the case for complete unilateral disarmament. While many states (including Sweden, Switzerland, and Japan) had not developed nuclear weapons despite having the technical capacity to do so, such states have generally followed a non-nuclear approach for pragmatic reasons or on account of legal constraints. They have maintained large conventional forces, or allied themselves with a nuclear power, or both.

Perhaps the most enduring effect of western anti-nuclear movements was the most paradoxical. They contributed to the larger series of processes which ended the Cold War by having two generally unanticipated effects in the Soviet bloc. First, their very failure to stop the implementation of NATO's 1979 decision on intermediate-range missiles compelled the new Soviet leadership under Mikhail Gorbachev (who became General Secretary in 1985) to conduct a fundamental reappraisal of the

Soviet Union's relations with the West. Second, the ideas of 'defensive defence' which they had used in fundamental criticism of NATO's conventional and nuclear postures actually became a framework within which the 'new thinkers' who were close to Gorbachev criticized and began to change the Soviet Union's military posture. The gradual move away from the ideas of conventional and nuclear overkill on which Soviet defence policy had previously been based had many causes: but to some extent at least it was a reverberation from anti-nuclear developments in the West.

Methods of peaceful pressure and struggle

The idea that the use of armed force could be replaced by peaceful methods of struggle has a long history. In this approach, armed force is recognized as having served some important functions, including in defence of societies against armed attack; but peaceful means of struggle are seen as capable of providing a partial or total substitute—and as overcoming some of the terrible costs of reliance on destructive power.

Two main types of peaceful pressure are economic sanctions and civil resistance. Sanctions are primarily (but by no means exclusively) an instrument of governments and international bodies; while civil resistance (i.e. popular resistance conducted by largely or entirely non-violent means) often arises from below, but has at times been used or encouraged by governments.

Economic sanctions have long been seen as a possible alternative to war. In 1793 Thomas Jefferson said that he hoped America would set

another precious example to the world, by showing that nations may be brought to do justice by appeals to their interests as well as by appeals to arms. I should hope that Congress ... would instantly exclude from our ports all the manufactures, produce, vessels and subjects of the nations committing this aggression ... This would work well in many ways, safely in all, and introduces between nations another umpire than arms. It would relieve us too from the risks and horrors of cutting throats.

Similarly President Woodrow Wilson stated in 1919, when arguing for US membership of the League of Nations:

If any member of the League breaks or ignores these promises with regard to arbitration and discussion, what happens, war? No, not war but something more tremendous than war. Apply this economic, peaceful, silent, deadly remedy and there will be no need for force.

The UN Charter, like the League Covenant before it, provided for the imposition of economic sanctions against states deemed guilty of aggression; but it realistically conceded that such measures might be inadequate. General economic sanctions were applied by the UN Security Council to Rhodesia following its unilateral declaration of independence (1966–79); Iraq following its invasion of Kuwait (1990–); and Serbia and Montenegro (1992–). The UN also imposed more limited sanctions, such as arms and air traffic embargoes, in many other cases, especially in the 1990s.

The use of international economic sanctions, whether by states or groups of states, has always been controversial. There has been concern about their exact purposes, their effects and effectiveness. As many of the cases in the UN era demonstrate, sanctions have symbolic functions, and are often used as a form of communication of international values. They can be a means of warning an adversary of the seriousness with which a particular matter is viewed, and of the prospect of more forceful action: however, where (as over Kuwait in 1991) their use is accompanied by a resort to armed force, there are bound to be arguments that sanctions should have been tried harder or for longer. Sanctions may also be used with the rather different purpose of assuaging domestic opinion in states taking part, often with the intention of avoiding military action or other unpalatable options. Further, sanctions may at one and the same time be completely effective and a total failure: they may stop the target country's international trade and hurt its citizenry, but fail to achieve the intended change of its policy. There can in some cases be serious questions about their compatibility with the human rights of the target state population. A report issued by the UN Secretary-

General in January 1995 expressed some of these concerns: 'Sanctions, as is generally recognized, are a blunt instrument. They raise the ethical question of whether suffering inflicted on vulnerable groups in the target country is a legitimate means of exerting pressure on political leaders whose behaviour is unlikely to be affected by the plight of their subjects.' A further problem of sanctions is that they are sometimes seen to require near-universal support (and thus to be organized in a UN rather than regional framework) if they are to be in any way effective. Yet there are relatively few security issues on which all countries agree to the point of being willing to take action. In short, for a collective action to work, sanctions are seldom enough: military means are therefore likely to be seen as necessary.

The phenomenon of civil resistance is much older than the twentieth century: cases of strikes, and passive resistance of various types, can be found in the history of most countries at most times. In its modern form, however, civil resistance begins to emerge in the nineteenth century. It was then that terms such as 'the strike' (which seems to have originated in the USA at the beginning of the century), 'boycott' (which originated in Ireland in the autumn of 1880), and 'passive resistance' made their appearance. The growth of civil resistance since the mid-nineteenth century has been comparable to the growth of guerrilla warfare, and had some of the same causes: an increase in political consciousness and national aspirations; and disparities of military power, combined with increased destructiveness, which led many political movements to avoid direct military confrontation.

Civil resistance has often been used in circumstances where the alternative might have seemed to be war. In the nineteenth century, for example, several nationalist movements used methods of non-cooperation against external imperial control. One such example was the Hungarian struggle between 1849 and 1867 against Habsburg rule. As so often, civil resistance was engaged in because of the necessities of the situation, after military action in 1849 had failed to defend the gains of Hungary's 1848 revolution. There was tax refusal, economic and political non-cooperation, and resistance to conscription. The ultimate outcome was that in 1867 the Hungarian constitution was restored. However, although the Hungarian struggle had remained largely non-violent, war may still have served as the midwife of history: it is at least a question whether the 1867 outcome would have been reached but for the Habsburgs' defeat in war in 1866 at the hands of the Prussians. In a similar case, between 1898 and 1905 there was strong popular resistance in Finland against Russian control, leading to major Russian concessions in 1905 and 1917: again, in each case the outcome may have owed something to Russia's involvement at the time in wars, against Japan and Germany respectively.

In the twentieth century, civil resistance played an important part in many anti-colonial struggles. In India from 1907 onwards it was the principal means of struggle against British rule. M. K. Gandhi's extraordinary leadership of many of the campaigns of the Indian National Congress from 1919 onwards involved developing a general doctrine of non-violence, and conducting numerous mass actions such as defiance of certain British-imposed laws and taxes. The problem of communal violence, against which Gandhi acted heroically, led him to interrupt some of the campaigns. He did not succeed in his proclaimed objective of making British rule physically impossible by completely withdrawing all the co-operation on which it depended. However, the campaigns he led did hasten British plans for self-rule, leading to independence in 1947.

There were elements of non-violent struggle (sometimes accompanied by violent incidents or threats) in movements for independence in many other countries, including Egypt (1919–22), China (anti-Japanese boycotts, 1906–19), and the Gold Coast (the 'positive action' campaign, 1950). In Europe, the Franco-Belgian occupation of the Ruhr area of Germany in 1923–5 faced a campaign of 'passive resistance' which had to be called off after eight months.

In the Second World War there were some important cases of civil resistance in Nazi-occupied territories. For example, in Norway in 1942 principled non-cooperation by teachers defeated plans to impose Nazi educational ideas on the schools. In

Denmark in 1943 some 6,500 of the country's 7,000 Jews were spirited out of the country to neutral Sweden. For the most part such resistance was not based on any doctrinal opposition to war in general or the Allied war effort in particular, but rather seemed the most appropriate form of action to take in particular circumstances. Gandhi's 1940 exhortation to Britons to 'fight Nazism without arms' had no impact in Britain or Europe, and indeed he himself had retreated from this extreme view by 1942.

The nuclear age has seen extensive development of civil resistance. In the USA, the civil rights movement of the 1960s, headed by the Revd Martin Luther King, demonstrated how principled non-violent mass action could buttress and stimulate a process of federal legislative change in support of equal rights for all regardless of race. From the 1950s to the 1980s civil resistance was an important component of successive struggles against Communist regimes and Soviet domination in East Germany, Hungary, Czechoslovakia, and Poland. In 1989, in all these countries, such resistance played a crucial part in the peaceful revolutions that led to the end of Communist rule. Strikes, mass emigration, and popular protests in the streets all helped to undermine weak Communist regimes lacking serious outside support, and to bring in more open political systems. In the Philippines in February 1986 a movement of 'people power' led to the ending of President Ferdinand Marcos's rule, and his replacement by Mrs Corazon Aquino.

The increase in the use of civil resistance world-wide did not establish that it was anything like a complete substitute for war. This was not so much because some movements of civil resistance suffered serious defeats at the hands of armed forces (as happened in many cases, such as anti-authoritarian movements in Burma in 1988 and in China in 1989), but rather because it appeared that civil resistance did not operate entirely on its own as an independent means of bringing pressure to bear on violent adversaries. Those engaging in civil resistance in eastern Europe, for example, often expressed their appreciation of a strong and defended western Europe, whose very existence helped to undermine Communist regimes.

Conclusion

The phenomenon of war has proved extraordinarily resilient and multi-faceted. Throughout the centuries since the Renaissance the recurrence of wars has been a challenge to the rationalist spirit that has played so important a part in public life and political theory. The efforts of mankind to bring war under control have had less effect than was hoped. Sometimes, indeed, movements, states, and ideologies seeking to eliminate war can themselves become part of the problem. In so far as major war between the big powers has been avoided since 1945, credit may be due at least in part to nuclear weapons, which have carried military technology to its *reductio ad absurdum*.

Yet the story of the various efforts to oppose war or at least control it is by no means one of complete failure. If they have not eliminated war entirely from the world, and if their effects have sometimes been the opposite of what was intended, they have nevertheless had a real impact. They have contributed to the avoidance of war in some countries and continents, and to the ending of the French war in Algeria and of the US involvement in the war in Indo-China; and they had a key role in the uprisings that ended Communist Party rule in eastern Europe. They have played some part in shaping popular views of war, effectively restricting the circumstances in which it is accepted as legitimate; and they have stimulated the development of a range of institutions and modes of action which, while not eliminating war completely, have provided useful experience in how it may—and how it may not—be prevented, limited, and at least partially replaced.

18

Technology and War II

From Nuclear Stalemate to Terrorism

MARTIN VAN CREVELD

As the Second World War approached its climax in 1944, military history appeared to be firmly established on the track set for it during the previous three centuries. By far the most important players were mighty sovereign states, operating either on their own or else in coalitions, most of them fairly loose. Having grown steadily, the armed forces fielded by those states totaled between 40 and 45 million men; armed with tens of thousands of heavy, motorized weapons, they dwarfed anything in history before or—in spite of the unprecedented growth of both population and industry—since. To judge by the number of countries that had been conquered or were in the process of being reconquered, the only organizations capable of resisting these armed forces were others roughly similar to themselves. And yet, looking back from the perspective of the early twenty-first century, we can see that these armed forces with all their modern technology were approaching the end of their historical lives. In fact, one reason why they were coming to the end of their lives was precisely *because* of their unlimited trust in, and dependence on, modern technology.

The advent of nuclear weapons

As mentioned in an earlier chapter, the first atomic bomb exploded over Hiroshima on 6 August 1945. With a yield of

14,000 tons of TNT, it was a thousand times as powerful as any previous weapon; yet in less than ten years advancing technology made it possible to build weapons more powerful than all the arms ever used in all wars since the beginning of history. The race towards greater and greater destructive power led through the hydrogen bomb of 1953. It peaked in 1961, when the USSR exploded a device with an estimated yield of 58 *million* tons of TNT—the equivalent of over 4,000 Hiroshima-type bombs. By that time research into the development of larger weapons still had come to a virtual halt. Not because it could not be done, but because, in Winston Churchill's words, all they would do was to make the rubble bounce.

The first country to build nuclear weapons was the USA. Driven by Stalin, who during his last years in power spared no expense and no effort, the USSR took only four years to follow suit. From this point on, the two so-called 'superpowers' engaged in a neck and neck race to see who could design better weapons, manufacture them *en masse*, and put them into delivery vehicles which themselves were becoming more and more sophisticated. To focus on the better-documented USA, initially the number of bombs was so small that a Japanese refusal to surrender after Nagasaki could not have been followed up immediately by dropping more of them. However, it rose fast. By the end of the 1940s it was in the low hundreds; by the end of the 1950s in the low thousands; and by the end of the 1960s around 10,000. By 1985 there were probably 30,000—including devices of every size from 5 megaton to 500 kiloton or less.

Originally the bombs were so large and cumbersome that they could only be delivered to their targets by the heaviest available bombers. However, subsequent technological breakthroughs led to much smaller and lighter devices; this enabled them to be carried, or launched, or fired, by an extraordinary range of delivery vehicles. The constantly developing heavy bombers apart, nuclear weapons were put on top of Inter Continental Ballistic Missiles (ICBMs), each of which was capable of reaching from one side of the globe to the other and putting several warheads on different targets. Others were put in submarines capable of launching them on top of missiles without having to surface first; or were delivered by intermediate-, medium-, and short-range ballistic missiles; or by cruise missiles, air-breathing, subsonic devices that could be launched either from the ground, or from the air, or from the sea; or by the new, jet-engined fighter bombers that came into service from 1950 on; or by being fired by heavy artillery. Some could even be launched from a jeep, using a device manned by three soldiers and known, somewhat facetiously, as the atomic bazooka.

During the years immediately after 1945 statesmen, soldiers, and the scientists who worked for them and provided them with ideas could still delude themselves that the next war would be like the previous one—give or take a few cities turned into smoking radiating ruins. However, after 1955 or so the arrival of so-called 'nuclear plenty' caused that belief to fade. More than enough power now was available to destroy all desired objectives in short order; by the late 1950s, the US air force was targeting each Soviet city the size of Hiroshima with no fewer than *three* megaton-sized weapons. Such numbers, combined with growing awareness of the effects of nuclear radiation and fallout, were persuasive. To most people they drove home the fact that, should all-out nuclear war break out, there would be neither victory nor economic and demographic recovery in the previously accepted sense of those words. Possibly there would not even a world left for humanity—including future generations—to live in.

Thereupon the number of occasions when one side or another threatened the use of nuclear weapons gradually declined, reflecting the growing sense that such threats were too dangerous for the world to tolerate. The Berlin Blockade Crisis of 1948; the Iran Crisis of 1949; the Korean War crisis of 1950 and 1953; the Taiwan Crisis of 1954; the Suez Crisis of 1956; the Quemoy Crisis of 1958; the Berlin Crises of 1958–61; the Cuban Missile Crisis of 1962; the October 1973; and the Afghanistan Crisis of 1979—all came and went without the most powerful available weapons being put to use. Some, indeed, would argue that they never even came close to being used and that much of what took place, to the extent that it did take place, was, in reality, bluff.

The growing realization of the futility of it all was also

reflected in the decline in the number of operational plans being prepared. In the USA, according to one source, there were nine between 1945 and 1949, blessed with such names as Pincher, Broiler, Bushwacker, and Dropshot. There were four between 1950 and 1957; and another four between 1960 and 1980, representing an eighty percent decline from the first period. Assuming the numbers are correct, even the Dr Strangeloves at the Pentagon seem to have given up. By the last named date the most important targets had already been surveyed many times over. Hence further development of SIOPs, or Strategic Integrated Operations Plans, became largely a question of poring over satellite photos in the hope of discovering one that had popped up since previous surveys were made.

Equally indicative of the growing international realization that nuclear weapons could well bring about the end of 'civilization as we know it' were the various agreements concluded by the superpowers with a view to limiting them and their delivery vehicles. Following some spectacular cases in which Japanese fishermen were killed by radioactive fall-out, talks aimed at prohibiting nuclear tests in the atmosphere opened in Geneva in 1958. In 1963 these led to a successful conclusion; while originally limited to the USA, USSR, and Britain, since about 1970 the ban has been observed informally even by most other nuclear powers which did not sign the original treaty, with the conspicuous exception of France. The next step was the Non-Proliferation Treaty (NPT) of 1969, which was signed by a large number of states and, together with the so-called London Regime of 1977, may actually have some good in limiting or slowing the spread of nuclear weapons to additional countries. The year 1972 saw the successful conclusion of SALT (Strategic Arms Limitation Talks), which put an upper limit on the number of intercontinental delivery vehicles maintained by each superpower, whereas 1977 witnessed the informally-observed SALT II agreement. It is true that the administration of G. W. Bush has now abrogated SALT I. However, its aim in doing so has not been to build new delivery devices but to permit the development of counters to them. In the meantime, the size of America's nuclear arsenal continued to decline until it reached

6,000 or so. Though the US National Security Doctrine now contains a reference to the 'first use' of tactical nuclear weapons against countries the USA may not like, from doctrine to practice it is a long step. Meanwhile, with each passing year the number of delivery vehicles continues to fall. Some, aging and expensive to run, are being retired without being replaced; others are converted to carry conventional munitions.

Thus, the sixty years since Hiroshima have not witnessed the most powerful weapons ever devised being used in war. On the contrary, as far as the superpowers were concerned those weapons helped create a balance of terror which, in spite of very rapid technological progress and countless international crises, proved remarkably stable and enduring. By the mid-1950s, at the latest, both superpowers were fully aware that they had nothing to gain, and everything to lose, from any attempt at annihilating each other. From that point on, whatever confrontations still took place between were increasingly limited to relatively unimportant issues in places far away from Washington DC and Moscow. It is true that competition over who would dominate these places lasted for another three and a half decades; even as it did so, though, there were growing efforts aimed at controlling and limiting the weapons that presented a danger to the continued existence of both. In the end, these efforts were more successful than anybody could have hoped even as late as 1985. As the Cold War ended and the USSR collapsed, the USA was left as the sole superpower with a nuclear arsenal far greater than any of the rest. The Warsaw Pact has disappeared. Even as it expanded into eastern Europe, NATO's main remaining function was to serve as a debating forum in which the allies wrangle over whether the should or should not conduct police action in such places as Iraq. Though other factors were also involved, the lion's part in bringing about this happy outcome was played by nuclear weapons and the balance of terror they created; rest thou in peace, post-1945 world.

The impact of nuclear proliferation

Once nuclear weapons had made the USA and USSR safe against

the kind of all-out attack that both of them had suffered in the Second World War, their effect, like inkstains, began to spread outwards. The first to feel the impact were the superpowers' close allies in NATO and the Warsaw Pact. These countries received nuclear guarantees, often bolstered by a physical presence of troops on the ground that was designed to act as a tripwire. It is true that those guarantees could never be made entirely credible; when it came to the clinch, would the USA *really* sacrifice Washington and New York in order to save Munich and Hamburg? Still, in practice nobody ever dared put them to the test, leaving the allies almost as safe against all-out attack as the superpowers themselves. Next, the demise of the Cold War made the entire issue more or less irrelevant. It created a situation where the President of France, for example, could declare that his country no longer had an enemy within a thousand miles; and where several other NATO members wondered why they still needed armed forces at all.

To the east of the Iron Curtain, countries such as East Germany, Poland, Czechoslovakia, and Hungary could have built nuclear weapons from the mid-1960s on. However, any thoughts which they may have had in this direction were smothered by the USSR, which did not favour such shows of independence on the part of its satellites. Now that the USSR is gone, apparently they still do not feel sufficiently threatened to make the effort; instead, they have contented themselves with joining NATO. Similarly in the West, virtually all 'old' NATO members (and, on the other side of the world, Japan, Australia, and New Zealand) could have built nuclear weapons from about 1960 on; again, the majority have refrained from doing so. In the case of Germany and Japan, this was due to strong domestic opposition as well as to the outcome of the Second World War that left them suspect in the eyes of their own allies. In the case of countries such as Canada, Spain, the Netherlands, and Belgium, reticence reflected the realization that nuclear weapons were a tremendously expensive undertaking which would add little if anything to their security. Still, the fact that most of these countries had everything needed to build nuclear weapons within a matter of months if not weeks is important in itself. Whatever may happen in the future, almost certainly they, too, will continue to be safe from all-out external attack even if, and when, the alliances which used to give them protection are dissolved.

Finally, two important NATO members did go ahead and built their own nuclear weapons, the first one (Britain) in 1953 and the other (France) in 1960. Both have since constructed technically advanced arsenals. Yet both found that those arsenals were completely overshadowed: first by those of the USA and then the USSR/Russia. Except in so far they afforded some doubtful protection in case the USA failed to live up to its obligations, as long as NATO confronted the Warsaw Pact the existence of the British and French nuclear arsenals only made very little difference to the overall balance between West and East. Now that the Cold War is over, those arsenals, while costing billions to maintain, probably signify even less. Whether their existence means that Britain and France are more 'secure' or more 'influential' than, say, non-nuclear states such as Germany or Japan is moot. Be this as it may, the fact is that in all the decades since 1945 not one of these potentially very powerful nations has fought a single large-scale war against any other even remotely as strong. Nor does it look as if this situation is going to change in the foreseeable future.

Nuclear developments outside the areas covered by NATO and the Warsaw Pact were much more interesting. Still, broadly speaking, they too moved in the same direction. The first developing country that, amidst much fear of impending doom, acquired nuclear weapons was Communist China. At the time its leader was Mao Zedong; a man committed to world revolution whose declarations concerning the need to destroy imperialism even at the cost of nuclear war (and the death of hundreds of millions) were perhaps the most hair-raising ever made. And yet, in practice the possession of the bomb seems to have caused Mao, let alone his more pragmatic successors, to bare their teeth less, rather than more, often. During the fifteen years from the Revolution of 1949 to the acquisition of the bomb, China was involved in no fewer than four armed conflicts, two of them large: (Korea, 1950–53), Taiwan (1954), Quemoy (1958), and India (1962). Since then there has only been one (Vietnam,

1979). Even that campaign only lasted a week or so. Picking on a small, weak country, Chinese forces penetrated to a depth of about 20 kilometres before withdrawing.

By the beginning of the twenty-first century the Chinese nuclear arsenal had become the world's third largest. Detailed information about it continues to be scarce; one reason being that, when it comes to making nuclear threats, China has acted with greater restraint than any other country. Still by now Beijing almost certainly possesses, or is capable of building, the entire range of nuclear warheads, from the strategic to the tactical. Then there is a whole assembly of different surface-to-surface missiles, including a few ICBMs capable of reaching continental USA; at least one missile-launching submarine; fighter bombers, some of them more or less state of the art; and possibly nuclear-capable artillery as well. In the face of such an arsenal another large-scale attack on China, similar to the one launched by the Japanese in 1937–45, could only be considered to be madness. Yet at the same time as large-scale interstate warfare has disappeared from east Asia, Chinese relations with most of their neighbours, including even the secessionist island of Taiwan, have become, if not cordial, at least more peaceful than ever. As of the 1990s Beijing, abandoning its previous stance, has indicated its support for the Non-Proliferation Treaty. Thus it has shown that, however different its culture may be, the nuclear facts of life are causing it to move in much the same direction as other nuclear countries already have.

To the southwest of China, India has probably been capable of building nuclear weapons from the late 1960s on. In 1974, the country launched a so-called 'peaceful nuclear explosion'. In 1985 it inaugurated a sophisticated breeder-type reactor, thus gaining unlimited access to plutonium, the basic material from which bombs are built. In 1998, perhaps to balance what was seen as a growing threat from China, it conducted not one but three nuclear tests. And yet, as in the case of China, the overall effect has been to make India less trigger happy, not more. Thus, between 1947 and 1971 there have been four wars (the Indo-Pakistani Wars of 1947–48, 1965, and 1971, and the Indo-Chinese War of 1962), since then India's largest military effort has taken place in the so-called 'Cargill War' of 1999; a time when a semi-regular, battalion-sized, infantry force coming from Pakistan advanced a few hundred metres into Indian territory and had to be expelled. Like the Chinese, the Indians now probably possess every type of nuclear weapon from the strategic to the tactical. Unlike the Chinese, they are not known to have developed ICBMs. Still some of their missiles have the range to reach every important target in Chinese territory, and others have been used to put satellites in orbit. As in every other case so far, the outcome of nuclear proliferation in South Asia has been peace. Or, at the very least, the disappearance of the kind of large-scale military operations that used to take place on the subcontinent until 1971.

Following the Indian tests, Pakistan too exploded three nuclear devices. Torn out of India's rib, Pakistan's very *raison d'être* is to present a counterweight to that country; as one of its prime ministers, Zulfikar Ali Bhutto, once put it, no dispute in the world is as ancient or as bitter as the one between Muslims and Hindus. And yet, as has just been said, in this case too the introduction of nuclear weapons has made a difference. Not only have hostilities been much reduced in size since the last full-scale war took place in 1971, but both sides have made steps, however, hesitant, towards installing some kind of mutually-acceptable nuclear regime. Thus, as far back as 1990, they signed an agreement to refrain from attacking each other's nuclear installations. Later they undertook to give advance notice of large-scale military manœuvers they might hold near the common frontier, and even as these lines were being written in spring 2004 they were engaged on the most comprehensive peace- talks in decades.

In west Asia another country widely believed to own nuclear weapons, as well as highly sophisticated delivery vehicles for putting them on target, is Israel. Unlike the rest Israel, perhaps in fear of triggering off an arms race and/or angering the USA, has neither admitted the existence of the bomb nor conducted a test when it was first assembled (probably in 1967). One could argue that, by permitting Egypt and Syria to behave *as if* their adversary did not have nuclear weapons and launch the October

1973 War, this policy of 'ambiguity' has been enormously damaging to Israel. Be this as it may, the fact remains that, since then, there have been no more wars of the same kind; even the 1982 invasion of Lebanon fell far short of its predecessors. Two of Israel's neighbors, Egypt and Jordan, are now formally at peace with it. A third, Syria, has lost so much of its military clout that another war between it and Israel seems extremely unlikely, and in fact in early 2004 President Bashir Assad was almost begging to resume talks. In view of what is taking place in the Occupied Territories nobody would call the Middle East peaceful. Still, bad as things are, they are much better than before 1973 when major hostilities used to break out every few years, leading to thousands upon thousands of dead and, at one point, raising the spectre of a World War.

Finally, elsewhere in Asia, North Korea may already have nuclear weapons whereas Iran is almost certainly doing what it can to acquire them as soon as possible. Neither of these countries is 'nice' and democratic, and neither is exactly open about the reasons behind its nuclear program. Yet, in the case of North Korea, a few nuclear bombs, assuming they really exist, have done nothing to disturb the peace of the Peninsula and may have strengthened it. In view of what happened to Saddam Hussein in 2003, a very good argument could be made that Iran's intentions are defensive; also, that Iranian possession of nuclear weapons, provided it is wisely deterred, will make the region more stable rather than less. This, of course, is guesswork. In the meantime, though, the fact that we do not yet know the consequences that ownership of nuclear weapons by these two countries may bring is no reason for ignoring the global experience of sixty years. That experience indicates that, wherever the weapons in question appear—even in small numbers, even when their delivery vehicles are primitive, and even when their owners were as unstable as Stalin is said to have been in his latter days—the outcome was peace. Or, if not peace, then at any rate stalemate.

The advent of high technology

When the first nuclear weapons were introduced it looked to all the world as if they would make the military of the countries that possessed them more powerful than ever. In fact, the opposite has happened; faced with devices that could literally blow the world apart, politicians everywhere looked at Clemenceau's dictum that war was too serious a business to be left to generals with new eyes. As far as we know, in every country that built the bomb the existing chain of command was bypassed or modified in favor of direct control by heads of state. The nuclear arsenal might be entrusted to a separate organization considered politically reliable, as in the USSR. Alternatively technical arrangements were made to ensure that the military could not fire them on their own initiative even if they wanted to. Either way, to the soldiers was left the less responsible task of playing with conventional, read second-class, weapons.

Spurred by an unlimited confidence in its power that was the product of the Second World War, a well as by competition between the superpowers, military technology grew and blossomed. The most important countries competed among themselves by building successive generations of ships, aircraft, missiles, and land fighting machines; each one larger, more powerful, and, of course, much more expensive than all its predecessors. For example, already by the mid-1950s the *Saratoga*-class aircraft carriers had grown twice as large as their biggest Second World War predecessors (from approximately 30,000 to just under 60,000 tons); and the *Nimitz*-class carriers built from the mid-1980s on were half as large again. Advanced Second World War fighter aircraft, such as late model Spitfires, Messerschmidts, and Mustangs, had a maximum speed of about 750 kilometres per hour. Less than two decades later many of their successors could fly at twice the speed of sound; some could do considerably better than that. A fighter-bomber of 1980 could carry almost as much ordnance as the heaviest bomber in 1945, and twenty years later the range to which it could do so was also the same. Finally, on land the most powerful engine installed in any fighting machine in 1945 developed around 350 horsepower. By the early 1960s the figure stood at 600, whereas in 1985 it reached 1500.

Even as existing weapons grew larger they were joined by

some that were entirely new. Among the earliest were helicopters, some of which had been tested even before World War II and which started entering the inventories around the time of the Korean War. Small and light, the first helicopters were used mainly for observation, liaison, and casualty-evacuation. As larger and better ones entered service, they were also used as flying command posts and for the transportation of troops and logistic loads. By early 1970s helicopters began to be armed with missiles, which gave them a formidable air-to-ground capability. As a result, the balance between land forces—armoured ones above all—and flying ones began to shift.

The second important technical advance that changed the face of conventional warfare consisted of guided missiles. The very first guided missiles, intended for anti-aircraft and anti-tank use, were on the drawing boards when World War II ended. By the mid-1950s some of them had entered service, but their operational impact remained limited. This, however, changed from about 1967 on. Entire families of ground-to-ground, air-to-ground, ground-to-air, sea-to-air, sea-to-sea, and air-to-sea made their appearance, improving accuracy a hundred-fold, often generating a one shot, one kill capability, and rendering warfare much more lethal than ever before. Whereas originally radar- and laser-guided missiles were very expensive, starting in the mid-1990s the introduction of GPS (Global Positioning System) made them much cheaper. Particularly in the air and at sea, and to a lesser extent on land too, they are now well on the way to replacing all but the smallest unguided (i.e. ballistic) projectiles.

Probably the third most important post-1945 development in military technology has been that of Unmanned Airborne Vehicles or UAVs. First introduced during Vietnam, and assisted by the advent of microelectronics that permitted capabilities to be improved without a corresponding growth in size and weight, they have undergone tremendous development. Both on land and at sea UAVs are now used for communication, electronic warfare, surveillance, reconnaissance, target-acquisition, damage assessment, air-defense suppression, and many similar functions. At the time of writing the first experiments are being made in equipping them with air-to-ground and air-to-air missiles. Should these experiments be crowned with success, as is likely to happen sooner or later, then clearly the days of manned aircraft will be numbered.

Coming on top of all these, the 1990s witnessed what many commentators call the Revolution in Military Affairs (RMA). The proliferation of precision-guided weapons (PGMs) apart, at the heart of the RMA are vastly improved systems of command, communication, control, intelligence (i.e. sensors of every kind, from ground radar to infra-red), and computers that serve to store, process, and display the vast amounts of data generated. Some of the systems are based on the ground, some at sea, and some in the air. Others still are carried by earth-cycling satellites. Once all the bits and pieces are in place, including a development known as 'net-centric warfare', the outcome should be vastly improved surveillance, reconnaissance, target acquisition, and damage assessment; also, much greater speed, flexibility, and lethality in orchestrating the operations of the above mentioned weapons and delivering ordnance to target.

Throughout the decade, no subject excited analysts in and out of uniform more than the RMA, with its implications and its possibilities, did. Some argued that, in the future, 'information dominance' would finally 'lift the fog of war', giving those who possessed it such a huge advantage over their enemies as to make an actual clash of arms almost unnecessary. Others questioned this, reminding us that war is a two-sided contest—in other words, that the enemy will adapt—and of what Clausewitz has to say on friction in it; the way they saw it, progress would probably be evolutionary. In the midst of this debate the 2003 war against Iraq provided an opportunity to see whether the RMA really was all that its advocates claimed. With the one reservation that, since the American elephant had already crushed the Iraqi ant twelve years previously, clearly there were limits to what could be learnt by crushing it for the second time.

Given the speed and scope of technological progress, the ability of early twenty-first century armed forces to defeat their predecessors is no more surprising than the ability, say, of Napoleonic-age armies to vanquish those of Frederick the Great. At the same time, the unfolding of the RMA should not cause us to lose sight of the fact that some of the most fundamental characteristics of conventional warfare have not changed. Perhaps the most important factor that did not change was the continued clear distinction between military power as deployed and used on land, at sea, and in the air. The range of weapons that could be launched from each of these media into the others admittedly increased; the introduction, in addition to helicopters, of hovercraft and satellites also led to some limited shifts in the boundaries between them. Still, on the whole the facts of physics prevailed. Aircraft, however, fast and powerful, have remained aircraft; ships, ships; and land vehicles, land vehicles intended for movement on land. Much as, in pre-1914 warfare, continuity was indicated by the centuries-old distinction between infantry, cavalry, and artillery, so after 1945, virtually all major armed forces retained the fundamental division into army, navy, and air force, each with its own separate organization, equipment, and missions.

Second, on land, another factor representing continuity was the dependence of post-1945 armies on motor vehicles. The logistical demands of modern war, unlike those of its predecessors, consist overwhelmingly of POL (petrol, oil, lubricants), ammunition, and spare parts; items which, being factor-manufactured, cannot be taken from the countryside but must be brought up from protected bases in the rear. Though both railways and air transport have been used for the purpose, the former are not flexible enough to follow fluid, fast-moving, operations, while the latter depends on large, secure bases well behind the front (helicopters are too expensive and too vulnerable to deliver supplies on any scale). Therefore, modern mechanized warfare is critically dependent on thousands upon thousands of motor trucks. The latter themselves can only move on a well-developed road network; during the 1991 Gulf War, the traffic was so heavy in some places that, to cross a traffic artery, it was sometimes necessary to use a helicopter. As present-day forces possess much greater firepower, and present-day engines are much more powerful, and consume much more fuel than their predecessors, in all probability this dependency will continue to grow. The results were evident in the 2003 campaign against Iraq. Fast as the American forces moved towards their objective, Baghdad, they still did no better than, say, Heinz Guderian during the early weeks of Operation Barbarossa in 1941.

Some early exponents of the RMA believed that, since it would make firepower much more accurate and much more lethal, the outcome would be to reinforce the defence. In practice, as the 2003 war against Iraq showed, this did not happen. RMA-type technology, much of it directed by means of satellites and UAVs and deployed from the air by missile-firing helicopters and strike aircraft, proved equally adaptable to the offence. As a result, much in the nature of strategy remained as it had been. In 2003, as in 1991, 1973, 1967, or, for that matter, 1939–40, in essence it consisted of gaining air superiority, preferably by launching a first strike against the enemy's air force, anti-aircraft defence, command-and-mobilization centres, and the like. Next, it was a question of striking with armoured spearheads, preferably in such a way as to outflank the enemy, penetrate into his rear, cut his communications, overrun his headquarters, and defeat his forces in detail.

Thus, in many ways, 'progress', if that is the correct term to use, was superficial. True, preparations for waging conventional war in many ways went ahead as if the Cold War was still on. However, in practice such wars as actually took place were fought between, or against, smaller and smaller opponents which, for one reason or another, had not yet acquired nuclear weapons. Though everybody talked about the RMA, in practice large parts of it were confined to the USA and Israel. The former was spending more on defence than the next ten countries combined and, as a result, opened such a vast gap in relation to everybody else that it started experiencing trouble in cooperating even with its own closest allies. The latter was spending proportionally more than twice as much on defence as the USA did. In addition it received an annual sum of over $2 billion dollars in American military aid; aid which could only allowed be used to purchase American hardware and which therefore *had* to be spent regardless of whether doing so made military sense or not. While these two raced ahead, most other developed countries kept cutting their armed forces until, by the early twenty-first century, they had been reduced to a shadow of their former selves. The situation of many others, particularly former East Block ones, was much worse still. Their old, Soviet-produced, weapons are now only fit for the junkyards. Unable to afford up to date ones, often their offensive capabilities have been reduced almost to zero.

Even the USA, in spite of spending mountains of money, in some ways was racing against itself and losing. The 1991 Gulf War was fought with weapons dating to the Reagan buildup of the 1980s, i.e. such as those which preceded the RMA; as is evident from the fact that 80–90 per cent of the ordnance used was ballistic rather than precision-guided. Since then, the US Air Force lost 36 per cent of its combat aircraft. Having seen the Advanced Tactical Aircraft project cancelled, many navy officers feel they may *never* again get a new fighter to replace their aging F-4s, F-18s, and A-6s. Nor was this the end of the matter. In 2003–4 alone two multi-billion Army projects, the Crusader gun and the Comanche helicopter, were cancelled. While the Air Force is still going ahead with its next-generation air superiority fighter, the F-22 Raptor, financial constraints are causing anticipated production schedules to be cut and there is talk of cancelling it too. In the end, its fate is likely to be similar to that of other Cold War era weapon systems, such as the B-1 and B-2 bombers. At first these aircraft were supposed to be produced in fairly large numbers. Next, progressive cuts reduced the number of operational ones so much as to turn them into white elephants; the one reason why they keep flying at all is because the Air Force refuses to admit the fact. Directed against fourth-rate, non-nuclear, countries such as Iraq or, before it, Serbia, the RMA is hardly needed. Directed against nuclear ones, it is all but useless. In this way, up to the present day, almost the sole beneficiary has been the national debt.

As the armed forces of the most powerful countries shrank, their composition changed. The wars of 1914–1945 had been the most 'total' in history, causing even countries such as Britain and the USA, which had never previously relied on general conscription, to adopt it. This, however, did not last. Beginning in the 1960s some forces started abolishing conscription. In part, this was because training short-service personnel to operate high-tech weapons and then discharging them was too wasteful. In part, it was because more and more often the military task that faced the forces in question was not home defence but campaigning in 'faraway countries of which we know nothing'. During the 1970s more and more countries moved in the same direction until, in 1996, President Jacques Chirac announced that France, the country which had originated the modern *leve en masse*, would do the same. By the beginning of the twenty-first century only a few countries still retained conscription; and even most of those were well on the way to replacing it with various forms of selective service.

By this time large-scale, conventional, wars between powerful armed forces were becoming quite rare, so much so that some commentators started talking of the 'boredom factor' affecting modern armed forces. That, plus the fact that the end of conscription transformed military service from a duty into a right, gave some women the idea that they might exercise that right as a way to 'enrich the concept of citizenship'. In the whole of history, after all, the only country that has ever *obliged* women to do military service is Israel; in the USA in 1982, a mere hint that this might happen was enough to make the Equal Rights Amendment fail. Since strength was shrinking all the time, by definition the more women entered the forces the fewer the men did so. Now women form half the population of every country. Since those populations have themselves been expanding, by the early twenty-first century almost all developed countries only required 3–5 per cent of the military manpower they had used at the peak compared to the total available. Still they were often unable to obtain enough men; which in turn caused them to turn to women and reinforced the vicious cycle whereby fewer and fewer men in any given country served.

To sum up, in the developed world since 1945, and in most of the developing ones since 1970 or 1980, the history of conventional war is one of constant, though uneven, shrinkage. True, here and there large-scale instances of it still took place. In some cases the balance of forces was so skewed that little could be learnt from them, as when the USA fought Iraq (in 2003) and, unsurprisingly, crushed it. In others, such as the Iran–Iraq War, so far behind were the belligerents in respect to modern technology that the conflict in many ways resembled not the Second World War but the First (including the use of poison gas, a weapon well-suited for stationary positions). While other factors also played a role in the process, the decisive factor was that, the more powerful a country, the more likely it was to acquire nuclear weapons and their delivery vehicles. As the armed forces of the most powerful countries shrank (in many cases to less than 10 per cent of their 1944-45 size) their composition also changed: volunteers replaced conscripts and women, men. Far from representing progress, as RMA advocates and others claim, much of this, the role of women specifically included, was best understood as degeneration. Since the basic security of developed countries is provided by nuclear weapons or the ability to build them quickly, and since cost, even in the USA, only amounted to about 4 per cent of GDP, it did not matter. The process might even have gone on indefinitely without disturbing anyone in particular. This, however, did not happen. To learn how and why, turn to the next section in this chapter.

From subconventional war to terrorism

While the armed forces of the most important countries, and, increasingly, those of many developing ones as well, talked of a revolution in military affairs and tried to implement it by buying high-tech weapons, war did not stand still. Instead of fighting each other, more and more of those forces found themselves trying to oppose others of a completely different kind. A worldwide statistical survey of the sixty years since 1945 confirms that, out of about a hundred and twenty armed conflicts, some eighty per cent were waged by, or against, entities that were not states. Some of those entities at least had a political aim of sorts. However, a growing number were private—a good example being the Abu Sayaf organization that had been infesting the Southern Philippines. They, and their opponents, could barely be distinguished from bands of criminals. Few were sufficiently large, sophisticated or well-organized to be called armies; even fewer possessed many, if any, of the modern weapon systems just described.

As many episodes (the best-known of which are the uprising against Louis XIV in the Palatinate, the Vendée uprising of 1793, and the Spanish guerrilla campaign against Napoleon) remind us, even in Europe conventional interstate war was never the only kind. Moreover, between 1600 and 1939 the Europeans themselves often fought in America, Asia, and Africa. However, what took place in those campaigns could not be compared to European warfare either in terms of size or, (unless it was a question of European forces clashing with each other) technological sophistication; very often the issues were decided in Madrid, Amsterdam, Paris, or London. By the last years of the nineteenth century, European (including, *honoris causa*, American and Japanese) military superiority had grown to the point where borders in Africa, for example, were being drawn by means of a ruler on a blank map without any reference to the local population. This, of course, also worked the other way around. From the time of the Seven Years War (1756–63) on, more and more the term 'colonial' stood for everything that was second-rate. For example, when the commanders of the German Condor Legion reported on their experiences during the Spanish Civil War they suggested that what they had encountered was 'more like colonial warfare than like a European battlefield'.

In so far as they had lost their colonies in 1918, the fact that the *Wehrmacht* was one of the first twentieth-century armies to learn that it did not have the field entirely to itself was paradoxical. As they moved into the countries of south-eastern and eastern Europe the Nazis, on Hitler's explicit orders, deliberately set out to uproot the law of war which, for three hundred years, had sought to offer protection to civilians. Those civilians, in turn, did not acquiesce in their lot but engaged in guerrilla operations against the invaders. First in Yugoslavia, Russia, Greece, and Poland, then in other countries such as Italy, France, and even peaceful Holland, Belgium, and Scandinavia, the Germans were faced by armed opposition which disrupted their rule, tied down resources, and inflicted casualties. As the number of victims shows, they were perhaps the most ruthless conquerors in history. Yet the more brutal the operations of such organizations as the SS, SD, Gestapo, and *Einsatzgruppen*, the stronger the resistance and the greater the readiness, even eagerness, of people who initially had been prepared to tolerate occupation or even assist it.

Whether, had the war lasted thirty years instead of six, Churchill's 1940 demand that Europe be 'set ablaze' from end to end could have been met and the Continent liberated even without large-scale operations can never be known; personally I think the answer is yes. As it was, the resistance in most German- (and Japanese-) occupied countries was cut short, but not before it had showed other people what could be done. The war was scarcely over when, all over colonized Asia and Africa, leaders started claiming that they, too, were subject to unlawful occupation; and that, unless the occupiers withdrew, they too would resort to armed resistance. This logic quickly led to a whole series of 'wars of national liberation' in places such as Palestine (1946–48), Indonesia (1947–49), Indo-China (1947–53, 1964–75), Malaysia (1948–60), Kenya (1953–58), Algeria (1955–62), Cyprus (1959–60), and Aden (1967–69). By 1960, the great majority of European colonies either had achieved independence or were well on their way to it. Fifteen years later, when the Portuguese finally gave up Angola and Mozambique, scarcely a single one remained.

Initially, the colonial heritage of three centuries dictated that most wars of this kind should be fought against armed forces fielded by west European countries. After 1975, though, this situation changed. The Cubans in Angola, the Soviets in Afghanistan, the Ethiopians in Eritrea, and the Israelis in Lebanon and the Occupied Territories (where, after sixteen years, all they had to show for their efforts was a decision to withdraw from Gaza), all tried their hand at counterinsurgency and failed. A similar fate overtook the Vietnamese in Cambodia, the South Africans in Namibia, the Indians in Sri Lanka, the Americans in Somalia, and the Indonesians in East Timor. Many of these wars led to so many deaths as to amount to genocide. Hence, clearly the failures were not due, as has often been claimed, to excessive scruples. To the contrary; the campaign that was arguably the mot successful of all, i.e. the British one in

Northern Ireland, was also among the most restrained and law-abiding. Some of the things the British did were not pretty. Still, they never brought in heavy weapons; or opened fire indiscriminately; or took hostages; or imposed collective punishments.

How can one explain the victories of people and organizations—call them bandits, or terrorists, or guerrillas, or freedom fighters—who, often so poor that they did not even have proper shoes, took on some of the mightiest armed forces in history and won? While circumstances differed from one theatre of war to another, at bottom the answer was always the same. Almost by definition, the more modern an army, the more advanced the military technology at its disposal, and the more specialized that technology for combatting and quickly defeating forces with similar, if less developed, equipment. That technology, though, was much less useful in fighting an enemy who did not represent a territorial state; did not have permanent bases or lines of communications; did not possess heavy weapons whose 'signature' sensors could be picked up; and, most important, could not be distinguished from the surrounding population. As far back as 1941 this rule applied the Germans trying to combat Tito's partisans. As of early 2004 it applied equally well to the Americans in Afghanistan and Iraq. The jury on these campaigns is still out; whatever the outcome, though, in both countries coping with post-occupation resistance has been considerably more difficult, and has led to considerably more casualties, than occupying them in the first place did.

Fundamentally, there are two reasons why much modern military technology is unsuitable to this kind of warfare. First, from times immemorial most of the campaigns in question took place in theatres where extensive networks of roads, supply depots, communications, etc. were unavailable. Since such facilities are vital to the operations of modern armies, however, they must be built from scratch; and, having been built, defended. As the American experience in Vietnam and the Israeli one in Southern Lebanon, for example, showed, the result can be the creation of a financial black hole as well as a situation where many of the forces, tied down to defensive missions, lose their morale and will to fight. Indeed often the majority of them hardly fire a shot. Nevertheless, feeling vulnerable at each step, they tend to collapse under their own weight.

The second reason why so much modern military technology is unsuitable for the purpose at hand is just the opposite from the first. Practically all sub-conventional conflicts and terrorism campaigns take place in extremely complicated environments. Either they are such as have been created by nature, such as mountains, forests, swamps, and the like; or else they are artificial ones made up of people, their dwellings, their roads, their vehicles, their communications, and their means of production. In such cluttered environments the electronic sensors on which modern weapons rely tend to work less well than in open spaces, which often causes the latter's range and power to translate into indiscriminateness. Take the so-called 'targeted killings' Israel has been carrying out in the Occupied Territories. First, almost unbelievably good intelligence, much of it technical and the rest human, makes it possible to trace individual terrorists as they drive in their cars. Next, in an operation that requires split-second coordination, a missile, launched from a helicopter, strikes that car even as a nearby UAV films the proceedings for the purpose of damage assessment, deriving lessons and training. Compared with Vietnam, where the Americans sometimes destroyed entire villages in order to save them, it is fair to say that no more successful strikes have been launched by any counterinsurgent, against any opponent, at any time, anywhere. Yet not only are there quite a few misses but the number of bystanders killed or injured often exceeds that of terrorists. As funerals attended by thousands of people screaming for revenge attest, on the whole the results may well have been counterproductive.

During the first forty years after 1945 virtually all these non-state conflicts, ranging from sub-conventional war to terrorism, and from wars of national liberation to ordinary crime, took place in the developing world. Since then, however, they have started spreading to developed countries as well—as the events of 9/11, when about 3,000 people in the most powerful country of all lost their lives, amply show. The results are there for all to see. Even as the Patriot Act took away some of the liberties civilized people have been taking for granted, Washington DC is being turned into a fortress; where anti-aircraft missiles used to accompany America's forces in the field, now they provide cover to the White House. From Australia to the UK, other countries are taking similar measures. For example, to defend the 2004 Olympic Games against possible terrorist acts the Greek Government is said to have spent 1.5 *billion* dollars, equal to about forty per cent of annual defence; clearly, and however much many people may regret the fact, armed conflict has indeed entered a brave new world.

Envoi

Ever since 1945, the world's most powerful fighting force has been centred on the Pentagon, Northern Virginia. As of October 2003 the man in charge, with $400 billion and enough explosive power to blow up the world many times to back him up, was Secretary of Defense Donald Rumsfeld. Having served in the same position under President Ford, Rumsfeld has long been known as an RMA enthusiast with no patience for anybody, including some of his most senior subordinates, with views different from his own. Accordingly it was interesting to see how, in a document addressed to his closest aides but leaked to the press (almost certainly as part of some bureaucratic fight), Rumsfeld chose to raise some fundamental questions about the organization that he headed. That organization, he pointed out, had been established in 1947–48 with the intent of preparing for, and if necessary waging, war against uniformed opponents broadly similar to themselves. The day when such opponents could take on the USA, however, had largely passed. As a result, were the country's Armed Forces really the most suitable instrument for combating worldwide terrorism? If not, should the task be entrusted to a new, more agile, organization? What might such an organization look like? How should it relate to other organizations responsible for America's internal security? Without any doubt, 9/11 has proven how urgent these questions have become. And yet, at the time of writing, answers to them are still, to a large extent, blowing in the wind.

Further Reading

1. The Shape of Modern War

Omer Bartov, *Hitler's Army* (Oxford, 2004)
J. F. C. Fuller, *The Conduct of War 1789–1961* (London, 1962)
Azar Gat, *The Origins of Military Thought* (Oxford, 1989)
—— *The Development of Military Thought: The Nineteenth Century* (Oxford, 1992)
Michael Howard, *War in European History* (Oxford, 1984)
Mary Kaldor, *New and Old Wars* (Stanford, 1999)
John Keegan, *A History of Warfare* (New York, 1993)
William H. McNeill, *The Pursuit of Power: Technology, Armed Force and Society since AD 1000* (Oxford, 1983)
Peter Paret (ed.), *Makers of Modern Strategy* (Princeton, 1986)
Peter Paret, *Understanding War* (Princeton, 1992)
Geoffrey Parker, *The Military Revolution: Military Innovation and the Rise of the West, 1500–1800* (Cambridge, 1988)
Hew Strachan, *European Armies and the Conduct of War* (London, 1983)
Charles Townshend, *Terrorism: A Very Short Introduction* (Oxford, 2002)

2. The Military Revolution I: The Transition to Modern Warfare

M. S. Anderson, *War and Society in Europe of the Old Regime, 1618–1789* (London, 1988)
Jeremy Black, *European Warfare, 1660–1815* (London, 1994)
John Childs, *Warfare in the Seventeenth Century* (London, 2004)
André Corvisier, *Armies and Societies in Europe, 1494–1789* (Bloomington, Ind., 1979)
Brian M. Downing, *The Military Revolution and Political Change* (Princeton, 1992)

Robert Frost, *The Northern Wars 1558–1721* (Harlow, 2000)

J. R. Hale, *War and Society in Renaissance Europe, 1450–1620* (London, 1985)

John A. Lynn, *Tools of War: Instruments, Ideas, and Institutions of Warfare, 1445–1871* (Urbana, Ill., 1990)

Geoffrey Parker, *The Military Revolution: Military Innovation and the Rise of the West, 1500–1800* (Cambridge, 1988)

—— *The Thirty Years War* (London, 1984)

Michael Roberts, 'The Military Revolution, 1560–1660', in *Essays in Swedish History* (London, 1967)

Clifford Rogers (ed.), *The Military Revolution Debate* (Boulder, Co., 1995)

Frank Tallett, *War and Society in Early Modern Europe, 1495–1715* (London, 1992)

3. The Military Revolution II: Eighteenth-Century War

Jeremy Black, *Culloden and the '45* (Stroud, 1990)

—— *War for America: The Fight for Independence 1775–1783* (Stroud, 1991)

—— (ed.), *The Cambridge Illustrated Atlas of Warfare: Renaissance to Revolution 1492–1792* (Cambridge, 1996)

Jan Glete, *Navies and Nations: Warships, Navies and State Building in Europe and America 1500–1860* (Stockholm, 1993)

Dennis Showalter, *The Wars of Frederick the Great* (Harlow, 1996)

D. J. Weber, *The Spanish Frontier in North America* (New Haven, 1992)

Russell F. Weigley, *The Age of Decisive Battles: The Quest for Decisive Warfare from Breitenfeld to Waterloo* (Bloomington, Ind., 1991)

4. The Nation in Arms I: The French Wars

Jean-Paul Bertaud, *The Army of the French Revolution: From Citizen-Soldiers to Instruments of Power* (Princeton, 1988)

T. C. W. Blanning, *The Origins of the French Revolutionary Wars* (London, 1986)

—— *The French Revolutionary Wars, 1787–1802* (London, 1996)

Michael Broers, *Europe under Napoleon* (London, 1995)

Howard G. Brown, *War, Revolution and the Bureaucratic State: Politics and Army Administration in France, 1791–99* (Oxford, 1995)

David Chandler, *The Campaigns of Napoleon* (London, 1966)

—— *Dictionary of the Napoleonic Wars* (London, 1979)

Charles J. Esdaile, *The Wars of Napoleon* (London, 1995)

Alan Forrest, *Conscripts and Deserters: The Army and French Society during the French Revolution and Empire* (New York, 1989)

—— *The Soldiers of the French Revolution* (Durham, N.C., 1990)

—— *Napoleon's Men: The Soldiers of the French Revolution and Empire* (London, 2002)

John A. Lynn, *The Bayonets of the Republic: Motivation and Tactics in the Army of Revolutionary France* (Urbana, 1984)

Peter Paret, *Clausewitz and the State* (Oxford, 1976)

Gunther E. Rothenberg, *The Art of Warfare in the Age of Napoleon* (Bloomington, Ind., 1978)

Paul W. Schroeder, *The Transformation of European Politics, 1763–1848* (Oxford, 1994)

Samuel F. Scott, *The Response of the Royal Army to the French Revolution: The Role of Development of the Line Army, 1787–1793* (Oxford, 1978)

Jean Tulard, *Napoleon: The Myth of the Saviour* (London, 1984)

5. The Nation in Arms II: The Nineteenth Century

M. Boemeke, R. Chickering, and S. Forster (eds.), *Anticipating Total War: The German and American Experience 1871–1914* (Cambridge, 1999)

Brian Bond, *War and Society in Europe, 1870–1945* (London, 1984)

R. D. Challenger, *The French Theory of the Nation in Arms, 1866–1939* (New York, 1955)

S. Forster and J. Nalder (eds.), *On the Road to Total War, 1861–1871* (Cambridge, 1997)

W. C. Fuller, *Civil-Military Conflict in Imperial Russia, 1881–1914* (Princeton, 1984)

John Gooch, *Army, State and Society in Italy, 1870–1915* (Basingstoke, 1989)

D. G. Herman, *The Arming of Europe and the Making of the First World War* (Princeton, 1996)

James Joll, *The Origins of the First World War* (London, 1984)

J. M. McPherson, *Battle Cry of Freedom: The Civil War Era* (Oxford, 1988)

Douglas Porch, *The March to the Marne: The French Army, 1971–1914* (Cambridge, 1981)

Gerhard Ritter, *The Sword and the Sceptre: The Problem of Militarism in Germany* (Coral Gables, Fl., 1970)

G. E. Rothenberg, *The Army of Franz Joseph* (West Lafayette, 1976)

E. M. Spiers, *The Army and Society, 1815–1914* (London, 1980)

David Stevenson, *Armaments and the Coming of War: Europe 1904–1914* (Oxford, 1996)

J. Whittam, *The Politics of the Italian Army* (London, 1977)

6. Imperial Wars

W. E. Allen and Paul Muratoff, *Caucasian Battlefields: A History of the Wars on the Turco-Caucasian Border 1828–1921* (Cambridge, 1953) though dated, offers a good starting-point for Russian expansion in Central Asia

Robert F. Baumann, *Russian-Soviet Unconventional Wars in the Caucasus, Central Asia, and Afghanistan* (Washington, DC, 1993)

Marie Bennigsen Broxup (ed.), *The North Caucasus Barrier: The Russian Advance towards the Muslim World* (New York, 1992) contains several interesting articles

Brian Bond (ed.), *Victorian Military Campaigns* (New York, 1967)

C. E. Callwell, *Small Wars: Their Principles and Practice* (London, 1906)

Anthony Clayton, *France, Soldiers, and Africa* (London and New York, 1988) gives a brief history of French imperialism as well as histories of French colonial regiments

Lt.-Col. A. Ditte, *Observations sur les guerres dans les colonies: organisation—éxecution: conférences faites à l'école supérieure de la guerre* (Paris, 1905)

W. J. Eccles, *France in America* (East Lansing, Mich., 1990), for French expansion in Canada

Johann Ewald, *Treatise on Partisan Warfare* (New York, 1991) offers an excellent contemporary view of the frustrations of dealing with American irregulars

Dietrich Geyer, *Russian Imperialism: The Interaction of Domestic and Foreign Policy 1860–1914* (New Haven, Conn., 1987)

A. S. Kanya-Forstner, *The Conquest of the Western Sudan: A Study in French Military Imperialism* (Cambridge, 1969) remains the best study of French military imperialism in sub-Saharan Africa

N. A. Khalfin, *Russia's Policy in Central Asia 1857–1868* (London, 1964)

Piers Mackesy, *The War for America 1775–1783* (Lincoln, Neb., 1992)

Bruce W. Menning, 'The Army and Frontier in Russia', in Carl W. Rediel (ed.), *Transformation in Russian and Soviet Military History: Proceedings of the Twelfth Military History Symposium, US Air Force Academy, October 1986* (Washington, DC, 1990)

Thomas Pakenham, *The Boer War* (London, 1979)

Douglas Porch, *The Conquest of Morocco* (New York and London, 1982)

—— *The Conquest of the Sahara* (New York and London, 1984)

—— *The French Foreign Legion* (New York and London, 1991)

Robert Utley, *Frontier Regulars: The United States Army and the Indian 1866–1891* (New York, 1973) is unbeatable

Jac Weller, *Wellington in India* (London, 1972)

7. Total War I: The Great War

Ian Beckett, *The Great War 1914–1918* (Harlow, 2001)

J. M. Bourne, *Britain and the Great War 1914–1918* (London, 1989)

Hugh Cecil and Peter H. Liddle (eds), *Facing Armageddon: The First World War Experienced* (London, 1996)

Paddy Griffith, *Battle Tactics of the Western Front* (London, 1994)

Richard Hough, *The Great War at Sea 1914–1918* (Oxford, 1983)

Alan R. Millett and Williamson Murray, *Military Effectiveness* (London and Boston, Mass., 1988). See the volume on the Great War

Robin Prior and Trevor Wilson, *Command on the Western Front* (Oxford, 1992)

David Stevenson, *Cataclysm: The First World War as Political Tragedy* (New York, 2004)

Norman Stone, *The War on the Eastern Front 1914–1917* (London, 1975)

Trevor Wilson, *The Myriad Faces of War* (Oxford, 1986)

J. M. Winter, *The Experience of World War I* (Oxford, 1988)

—— and R. M. Wall (eds), *The Upheaval of War: Family, Work and Welfare in Europe* (Cambridge, 1988)

8. Total War II: The Second World War

M. Harrison and J. Barber, *The Soviet Home Front 1941–1945* (London, 1991). The best recent survey of the Soviet war effort

H. Heer and K. Naumann (eds.), *War of Extermination: The German Military in World War II* (New York, 2000)

A. Millett and W. Murray (eds), *Military Effectiveness in World*

War II (London, 1988) surveys the elements of fighting power in every warring nation

A. S. Milward, *War, Economy and Society 1939–1945* (London, 1987). The best general survey of the home fronts

R. J. Overy, *The Air War 1939–1945* (London, 1980)

R. A. C. Parker, *Struggle for Survival* (Oxford, 1989) is the best short survey on the war

R. Rhodes, *The Making of the Atomic Bomb* (New York, 1986). Comprehensive survey of the wartime developments in nuclear weaponry

Gordon Wright, *The Ordeal of Total War* (London, 1968)—concise, stimulating, wide-ranging

9. Cold War

A. B. Adan, *On the Banks of Suez* (London, 1980)

Philip Bobbitt, Lawrence Freedman and Gregory Treverton, *US Nuclear Strategy: A Reader* (London, 1989)

Moshe Dayan, *Story of My Life* (London, 1976)

Anthony Farrar-Hockley, *The British Part in the Korean War* (London, 1990)

Lawrence Freedman, *The Evolution of Nuclear Strategy* (London, 1981)

—— and Virginia Gamba Stonehouse, *Signals of War* (London, 1990)

—— and Efraim Karsh, *The Gulf Conflict 1990–1991* (London, 1993)

Chaim Herzog, *The Arab-Israeli Wars* (London, 1982)

Alan James, *Peacekeeping in International Politics* (London, 1990)

Keith Kyle, *Suez* (London, 1991)

Robert J. Lifton and Richard Falk, *Indefensible Weapons* (New York, 1982)

Peter Lowe, *The Origins of the Korean War* (London, 1986)

Lewis MacKenzie, *Peacekeeper* (Toronto, 1993)

David Rees, *Korea: The Limited War* (London, 1964)

Bob Woodward, *The Commanders* (London, 1991)

Admiral Sandy Woodward, *One Hundred Days: The Memoirs of the Falklands Battle Group Commander* (London, 1992)

10. People's War

Ian Beckett, *Modern Insurgencies and Counter-insurgencies* (London, 2001)

John Ellis, *Armies in Revolution* (London, 1973)

Charles Esdaile, *Fighting Napoleon: Guerrillas, Bandits and Adventures in Spain, 1808–1814* (New Haven, 2004)

Geoffrey Fairbairn, *Revolutionary Guerrilla Warfare* (Harmondsworth, 1974)

Michael Fellman, *Inside War* (New York, 1989)

Martha Crenshaw Hutchinson, *Revolutionary Terrorism* (Stanford, 1978)

Walter Laqueur, *Guerrilla: A Historical and Critical Study* (London, 1977)

Peter Paret and John W. Shy, *Guerrillas in the 1960s* (Princeton, 1962)

Daniel E. Sutherland (ed.) *Guerrillas, Unionists and Violence on the Confederate Home Front* (Fayetteville, 1999)

Robert Taber, *The War of the Flea* (London, 1970)

11. Technology and War I: to 1945

B. and F. Brodie, *From Crossbow to H Bomb* (Bloomington, Ind., 1973 edn.)

T. N. Dupuy, *The Evolution of Weapons and Warfare* (New York, 1980)

J. F. C. Fuller, *Armaments and History* (New York, 1946)

J. A. Lynch (ed.), *Tools of War: Instruments, Ideas and Institutions of Warfare, 1445–1871* (Urbana, 1990)

W. H. McNeill, *The Quest for Power: War, Technology and Society from 1000 A.D.* (London, 1982)

R. L. O'Connel, *Of Arms and Men: A History of War, Weapons and Aggression* (New York, 1989)

A. R. Preston and S. F. Wise, *Men in Arms: A History of Warfare and its Interrelationship with Western Society* (New York, 1979 edn.)

Denis Showalter, *Railways and Rifles: Soldiers, Technology and the Unification of Germany* (Hamden, Conn., 1976)

Martin van Creveld, *Technology and War, from 2000 B.C. to the Present Day* (New York, 1989)

J. Wheldon, *Machine-Age Armies* (London, 1968)

12. Battle: The Experience of Modern Combat

Omar Bartov, *The Eastern Front 1941–1945: German Troops and the Barbarisation of Warfare* (London, 1985)

Charles Carlton, *Going to the Wars* (London, 1992) is about the British civil wars 1638–1641

John Ellis, *The Sharp End of War* (Newton Abbot, 1980) on the Second World War

Richard A. Gabriel, *No More Heroes: Madness and Psychiatry in War* (New York, 1987)

Roy R. Grinker and John P. Spiegel, *Men under Stress* (New York, 1963)

David Grossman, *On Killing* (London, 1995)

Victor Davis Hanson, *The Western Way of War* (London, 1989) on infantry battle in classical Greece

Richard Holmes, *Firing Line* (London, 1985; published as *Acts of War* in the US) examines men's behaviour in battle across much of history

John Keegan, *The Face of Battle* (London, 1976) remains an essential starting-point for serious study of the subject

Anthony Kellet, *Combat Motivation* (The Hague, 1982)

Hugh McManners, *The Scars of War* (London, 1994) by a Falklands veteran

S. L. A. Marshall, *Men against Fire* (New York, 1947) by the doyen of American combat analysts, probes deeply into the darker recesses of battle

Lord Moran, *The Anatomy of Courage* (London, 1966)

Ben Shephard, *A War of Nerves: Soldiers and Psychiatrists 1914–1994* (London, 2000)

Martin van Creveld, *Fighting Power* (Westport, Conn., 1982) is a masterly comparative study of German and US Army performance 1939–1945

13. Sea Warfare

George Baer, *One Hundred Years of Sea Power* (Stanford, 1994)

Ken Booth, *Navies and Foreign Policy* (London, 1977)

Julian S. Corbett, *Some Principles of Maritime Strategy*, ed. Eric Grove (Annapolis, 1988)

John B. Hattendorf (ed.), *Ubi Sumus? The State of Naval and Maritime History* (Newport, 1994)

—— and Robert S. Jordan (eds), *Maritime Strategy and the Balance of Power* (London, 1989)

—— R. J. B. Knight *et al.* (eds), *British Naval Documents 1204–1960* (London, 1993)

Richard Hill (ed.), *The Oxford Illustrated History of the Royal Navy* (Oxford, 1995)

Rolf Hobson & Tom Kristensen (eds.), *Navies in Northern Waters 1720–2000* (London, 2004)

Wayne Hughes, *Fleet Tactics* (Annapolis, 1986)

Robert S. Jordan, *Alliance Strategy and Navies* (London, 1990)

N. A. M. Rodger, *Command of the Ocean: A Naval History of Britain* (London, 2004)

Geoffrey Till, *Sea Power: A Guide for the Twenty-First Century* (London, 2003)

Frank Uhlig, *How Navies Fight* (Annapolis, 1994)

J. C. Wylie, *Military Strategy: A General Theory of Power Control*, ed. with an Introduction by John B. Hattendorf (Annapolis, 1989)

14. Air Warfare

Mark Clodfelter, *The Limits of Air Power: The American Bombing of North Vietnam* (New York, 1989). A detailed study of the failure of strategic bombing in Vietnam

R. Hallion, *Strike from the Sky: The History of Battlefield Air Attack 1911–1945* (Washington, DC, 1989). The best account of the origins and development of tactical air power

Robin Higham, *Air Power: A Concise History* (London, 1972). A general overview of the first fifty years

R. A. Mason, *Air Power: A Centennial Appraisal* (London, 1994). Challenging assessment of the nature and future of air power

J. Morrow, *The Great War in the Air: Military Aviation from 1912–1921* (Washington, DC, 1993). Comprehensive survey of the origins of air power

R. J. Overy, *The Air War 1939–1945* (London, 1980) sets air power in a wider context of economic, technical, and social issues

A. Stephens (ed.), *The War in the Air, 1914–1994* (Canberra, 1994). A stimulating set of essays on the major periods of air warfare history

15. War and the People: The Social Impact of Total War

Richard Bessel, *Germany after the First World War* (Oxford, 1993)

Brian Brivati (ed.), *What Difference Did the War Make?* (Leicester, 1993)

Paul Fussell, *The Great War and Modern Memory* (Oxford, 1975)

Charles Maier, 'The Two Post-War Eras and the Conditions for Stability in 20th-Century Western Europe', *American Historical Review* (April, 1991)

Arthur Marwick (ed.), *Total War and Social Change* (London, 1988)

Alan Milward, *War, Economy, and Society 1939–1945* (Harmondsworth, 1987)

Robert Wohl, *The Generation of 1914* (London, 1980)

16. Women and War

Rhonda Cornum (as told to Peter Copeland), *She Went to War: The Rhonda Cornum Story* (Novata, Calif., 1992)

K. Jean Cottam, 'Soviet Women in Combat in World War II: The Ground Forces and the Navy', *International Journal of Women's Studies*, xiv (1980), 345–57

Jean Bethke Elshtain, *Women and War*, 2nd edn. (Chicago, 1995)

J. R. Hale, *Artists and Warfare in the Renaissance* (New Haven, 1990)

(Mrs) F. S. Hallowes, *Mothers of Men and Militarism* (1918)

Anne Noggle, *A Dance with Death. Soviet Airwomen in World War II* (Texas A&M University Press, 1994)

Plutarch, *Moralia*, III, trans. Frank Cole Babbitt (Cambridge, 1931)

Shelley Saywell, *Women in War* (New York, 1985)

Francis Butler Simkins and James Welch Patton, *The Women of the Confederacy* (1936)

17. Against War

Geoffrey Best, *War and Law since 1945* (Oxford, 1994)

Peter Brock, *Twentieth-Century Pacifism* (New York, 1970)

Judith Brown, *Gandhi: Prisoner of Hope* (New Haven and London, 1989)

Seyom Brown, *The Causes and Prevention of War*, 2nd edn. (New York, 1994)

Martin Ceadel, *Thinking About Peace and War* (Oxford, 1987)

Mark W. Janis, *An Introduction to International Law* (Boston, Mass., 1988)

Adam Roberts and Benedict Kingsbury (eds.), *United Nations, Divided World: The UN's Roles in International Relations*, 2nd edn. (Oxford, 1993)

Jonathan Schell, *The Unconquerable World: Power, Non-violence and the Will of the People* (London, 2004)

Gene Sharp, *The Politics of Nonviolent Action* (Boston, Mass., 1973)

18. Postmodern War

D. S. Alberts and S. David, *Network-Centric Warfare: Developing and Leveraging Information Superiority* (Washington DC, 1999)

S. J. Blank *et al.*, *Conflict, Culture and History: Regional Dimensions* (Maxwell Air Force Base, Ala., 1993)

Michael Carver, *War since 1945* (London, 1986)

Marcelin Defourneaux, *Guerre des armes, Guerre des hommes* (Château Chinon, 1994)

S. J. Deitchman, *Military Power and the Advance of Technology: General Purpose Military Forces for the 1980s and Beyond* (Boulder, Col., 1983)

J. Dunnigan, *A Dirty Guide to War* (New York, 1996)

M. Kaldor, *New and Old Wars* (Stanford, 1999)

R. E. Lard and H. H. Mey (eds.), *The Revolution in Military Affairs* (Washington DC, 1999)

K. P. Magyar and C. P. Danopoulos, *Prolonged Wars: A Post-Nuclear Challenge* (Maxwell Air Force Base, Ala., 1994)

M. J. Mazarr *et al.*, *The Military Technical Revolution: A Structural Framework* (Washington, DC, 1993)

B. Owen, *Lifting the Fog of War* (New York, 2000)

T. V. Paul *et al.* (eds.), *The Absolute Weapon Revisited* (Ann Arbor, 1998)

Winn Schwartau, *Information Warfare: Chaos on the Electronic Superhighway* (New York, 1994)

A. and H. Toffler, *War and Anti-War: Survival at the Dawn of the 21st Century* (Boston, Mass., 1993)

Kosta Tsipis, *Arsenal: Understanding Weapons in the Nuclear Age* (New York, 1983)

Martin van Creveld, *The Transformation of War* (New York, 1991)

Chronology

1740–8	War of the Austrian Succession
1741 10 April	Battle of Mollwitz
1742 17 May	Battle of Chotusitz
1743 27 June	Battle of Dettingen
1745 10 May	Battle of Fontenoy
1745 4 June	Battle of Hohenfriedburg
1745–6	Jacobite Rebellion ['The Forty-five']
1746 16 April	Battle of Culloden
11 October	Battle of Raucoux
1747 2 July	Battle of Lauffeld
1756–63	Seven Years War
1757 18 June	Battle of Kolin
23 June	Battle of Plassey
5 November	Battle of Rossbach
6 December	Battle of Leuthen
1758 25 August	Battle of Zorndorf
1759 13 September	Battle of Quebec [Plains of Abraham]
1775–83	War of American Independence
1776 27 August	Battle of Long Island
1777 11 September	Battle of the Brandywine
1780 11 February–12 May	Siege of Charleston
1792–8	War of the First Coalition
1792 11 July	French Assembly Decree *La Patrie en danger*
20 September	Battle of Valmy
6 November	Battle of Jemappes
1793 August	French Convention Decree *Levée en masse*
1794 26 June	Battle of Fleurus
1796 10 May	Battle of Lodi
1797 14 January	Battle of Rivoli
October	Treaty of Campo Formio
1798–1802	War of the Second Coalition
1800 14 June	Battle of Marengo
1803–5	Second Mahratha War

1803 23 September	Battle of Assaye
1805–7	War of the Third Coalition
1805 17 October	Capitulation of Ulm
2 December	Battle of Austerlitz
1806 14 October	Battle of Jena
1807 8 February	Battle of Eylau
14 June	Battle of Friedland
1808	Prussian military reforms begin
1808–14	Peninsular War; Guerrilla warfare in Spain
1809	Franco-Austrian War
21–2 May	Battle of Aspern-Essling
5–6 July	Battle of Wagram
1812–14	Anglo-American War [War of 1812]
1812 7 September	Battle of Borodino
1813 21 June	Battle of Vitoria
26–7 August	Battle of Dresden
16–19 October	Battle of Leipzig
1815 18 June	Battle of Waterloo
1821–32	Greek War of Independence
1827 20 October	Battle of Navarino
1830–47	French conquest of Algeria
1840	Adoption of Dreyse rifle by Prussian army
1845–6	First Sikh War
1846–8	US–Mexican War
1848–9	Second Sikh War
1851	Adoption of Minié rifle by British army
1854	Crimean War
1856–60	Second Opium War
1857–8	Indian 'Mutiny'
1858–62	French invasion of Cochin China
1859	Franco-Austrian War
4 June	Battle of Magenta

24 June	Battle of Solferino
1861–5	American Civil War
1862 6–7 April	Battle of Shiloh
17 September	Battle of Antietam Creek [Sharpsburg]
1863 1–6 May	Battle of Chancellorsville
1–3 July	Battle of Gettysburg
4 July	Surrender of Vicksburg
1864 June (–April 1865)	Siege of Petersburg
August	Sherman's capture of Atlanta
September–October	Sheridan's devastation of the Shenandoah Valley
1866	Austro-Prussian [Seven Weeks] War
3 July	Battle of Königgratz [Sadowa]
20 July	Naval battle of Lissa
1868	French military reform (*Loi Niel*); adoption of Chassepot rifle
1868–74	Cardwell's reforms of British army
1870–1	Franco-German War
1870 16 August	Battle of Vionville–Mars-la-Tour
18 August	Battle of Gravelotte-St Privat
1 September	Battle of Sedan
19 September	Siege of Paris begins
27 October	Fall of Metz
2–4 December	Battle of Orleans
1871 28 January	Capitulation of Paris
1873	Ashanti War
1876–7	Sioux and Northern Cheyenne War
25 June	Battle of the Little Bighorn
25–6 November	Battle of Crazy Woman Fork
1877–8	Russo-Turkish War
1877 19 July–10 December	Siege of Plevna

1879	Zulu War
22 January	Battle of Isandhlwana
4 July	Battle of Ulundi
1880–1	Transvaal War [First South African War]
1882–95	Indochina War French invasion of Tonkin
1882 13 September	Battle of Tel-el-Kebir
1883 3 November	Battle of El Obeid
1884	Introduction of Mauser bolt-action rifle
1888	Adoption of Maxim gun by British army
1892	French conquest of Benin (Dahomey)
1895–6	Italian–Abyssinian War
1896 1 March	Battle of Adowa
1897	Introduction of French 75mm quick-firing field gun
1898 2 September	Battle of Omdurman
1899–1902	Second South African [Boer] War
28 November	Battle of the Modder River
10–11 December	Battle of Magersfontein
15 December	Battle of Colenso
1899 June–October	First Hague International Peace Conference
1900 18–27 February	Battle of Paardeberg Drift
1904–5	Russo-Japanese War
1904 25 May	Siege of Port Arthur begins
1 October	Arrival of Japanese siege artillery at Port Arthur
1905 2 January	Surrender of Port Arthur
27 May	Naval battle of Tsushima
1906	Establishment of British General Staff
1907 June–October	Second Hague International Peace Conference

1908	Formation of British Territorial Army
1912–13	First Balkan War
1913	Second Balkan War
1914–19	First World War [Great War]
1914 5–10 September	Battle of the Marne
1915 22 April–15 May	Second battle of Ypres
25 April	First landings at Gallipoli
22–6 November	Battle of Ctesiphon
7 December	Siege of Kut-al-Amara begins
1916–18	Arab revolt
1916 9 January	Final evacuation of Gallipoli
21 February–18 December	Battle of Verdun
29 April	Surrender of Townshend at Kut
31 May–1 June	Battle of Jutland
4 June–20 September	Brusilov Offensive
1 July–19 November	First battle of the Somme
1917 31 July– 12 November	Third battle of Ypres [Passchendaele]
24 October–12 November	Twelfth battle of the Isonzo [Caporetto]
31 October	Third battle of Gaza [Beersheba]
1917–22	Russian Civil War
1919–21	Anglo-Irish War
1922–3	Irish Civil War
1928 27 August	Kellogg-Briand Pact renouncing war
1930–4	Chinese 'Bandit Extermination Campaigns' against Communists
1932–4	World Disarmament Conference, Geneva
1934–5	The 'Long March'
1936–9	Spanish Civil War

1936 6 November	Siege of Madrid
1937 25 April	Bombing of Guernica
1937 7 July	'China Incident'; beginning of Sino-Japanese War
1939–45	Second World War
1941 22 June	German invasion of USSR (Operation Barbarossa)
September (–January 1943)	Siege of Leningrad
7 December	Japanese attack on US Pacific fleet at Pearl Harbor
1942 7–8 May	Battle of the Coral Sea
4–6 June	Battle of Midway
24 August	German assault on Stalingrad begins
1943 2 February	Surrender of German 6th Army at Stalingrad
5–16 July	Battle of Kursk (Operation Zitadelle)
1944 6 June	Operation 'Overlord'
1946–53	First Vietnam War
1946 22 July	IZL (Irgun) bombing of King David Hotel, Jerusalem
1948–9	First Arab–Israeli War
1950–3	Korean War
1950 15–25 September	Inchon landing
1953 20 November– 7 May 1954	Battle of Dien Bien Phu
1954–61	Algerian War of Independence
1956–75	Second Vietnam War
1956–7	Battle of Algiers
1956–8	Cuban revolutionary war
1956 29 October– 6 November	Second Arab–Israeli War
1963 5 August	Partial Nuclear Test Ban Treaty, Moscow
1963–6	Indonesian 'confrontation' with Malaysia

1967 5–10 June	Six Day War [Third Arab–Israeli War]
9–10 June	Israeli capture of Golan Heights
1968 1 July	International Nuclear Non-proliferation Treaty
1972–3	SALT (Strategic Arms Limitation) Agreement
1973 6–24 October	Fourth Arab–Israeli War
1975–84	Lebanese Civil War
1977	Second Geneva Additional Protocol
1979	SALT II (Strategic Arms Limitation) Agreement
24 December (–February 1989)	Soviet intervention in Afghanistan
1980–8	Iran–Iraq War [Gulf War]
1982 2 April	Argentine seizure of Falkland Islands
6 June–3 September	Israel–Lebanon War [Operation 'Peace for Galilee']
16–19 September	Sabra and Shatila Refugee Camp massacres
1987 October	Intifada in occupied territories, Palestine
1990–1	Kuwait War [Gulf War]
1991–2	Break up of Yugoslavia: Croat–Serb War
1992 February	UNPROFOR established in Croatia
1998	Serbian 'ethnic cleansing' in Kosovo
1999	NATO bombing of Serb forces
2000 October	New ('Al-Aqsa') intifada in occupied territories
2001 11 September	'Al Qaida' attacks on New York and Washington DC

October	US Air strikes against Afghanistan
November	US-led forces attack Taliban government in Afghanistan
2003 March–May	US-led invasion of Iraq
May	Start of Iraqi guerrilla resistance to Coalition forces

INDEX